Analyzing Social Settings

Analyzing Social Settings

A Guide to Qualitative Observation and Analysis

Fourth Edition

John Lofland
University of California, Davis

David Snow
University of California, Irvine

Leon Anderson
Ohio State University

Lyn H. Lofland
University of California, Davis

Long Grove, Illinois

For information about this book, contact:
Waveland Press, Inc.
4180 IL Route 83, Suite 101
Long Grove, IL 60047-9580
(847) 634-0081
info@waveland.com
www.waveland.com

Copyright © 2006 by John Lofland, David Snow, Leon Anderson, and Lyn H. Lofland
Reissued 2022 by Waveland Press, Inc.

10-digit ISBN 1-4786-5023-0
13-digit ISBN 978-1-4786-5023-2

All rights reserved. No part of this book may be reproduced, stored in a retrieval system, or transmitted in any form or by any means without permission in writing from the publisher.

Printed in the United States of America

7 6 5 4 3 2 1

To Judy Snow
1942–2005
The consummate non-academic observer and conversationalist.

CONTENTS IN BRIEF

List of Figures	xvii
Preface to the Fourth Edition	xix
Acknowledgments	xxi
Introduction: The Aims and Organization of This Guide	1
PART ONE GATHERING DATA	**7**
Chapter 1 Starting Where You Are	9
Chapter 2 Evaluating Data Sites	15
Chapter 3 Getting In	33
Chapter 4 Getting Along	54
Chapter 5 Logging Data	81
PART TWO FOCUSING DATA	**119**
Chapter 6 Thinking Topics	121
Chapter 7 Asking Questions	144
Chapter 8 Arousing Interest	168
PART THREE ANALYZING DATA	**193**
Chapter 9 Developing Analysis	195
Chapter 10 Writing Analysis	220
References	241
Index	273

CONTENTS

List of Figures	xvii
Preface to the Fourth Edition	xix
Acknowledgments	xxi
Introduction: The Aims and Organization of This Guide	1
I. Three Tasks: Gathering, Focusing, and Analyzing Data	1
II. Features and Aspects of Fieldstudies	2
A. Gathering Data: Researcher as Witness and Instrument	3
B. Focusing Data: Social Science Guidance	4
C. Analyzing Data: Emergence	4
III. Audiences	5
IV. Yet More Labels for Fieldstudies	5

PART ONE   GATHERING DATA   7

Chapter 1. Starting Where You Are	9
I. Personal Experience and Biography	9
II. Intellectual Curiosity	12
III. Tradition and Justification	13
Chapter 2. Evaluating Data Sites	15
I. The Overall Goal	15
II. Participant Observation and Intensive Interviewing	17
III. Detailed Assessment of Data Sites	18
A. Evaluating for Appropriateness	18
B. Evaluating for Access	21
1. Investigator Relationship to Setting	22
2. Ascriptive Categories of Researcher and Researched	23
3. Difficult Settings	25
C. Evaluating for Physical and Emotional Risks	27
D. Evaluating for Ethics	28
E. Evaluating for Personal Consequences	30
IV. A Concluding Word of Caution	32

Contents

Chapter 3.	Getting In	33
I.	Types of Settings	34
II.	The Unknown Investigator	35
	A. Public and Quasi-Public Settings	36
	B. Private and Quasi-Private Settings	37
III.	The Known Investigator	40
	A. The "Insider" Participant Researcher Role	41
	B. The "Outsider" Participant Researcher Role	41
	1. Connections	41
	2. Accounts	43
	a. Content	43
	b. Timing	45
	c. Form	45
	d. Audience/Targets	46
	3. Knowledge	46
	4. Courtesy	47
IV.	Political, Legal, and Bureaucratic Barriers	47
V.	The Question of Confidentiality	51
Chapter 4.	Getting Along	54
I.	Getting Along with Self: Emotional and Physical Challenges	54
	A. Information Overload	55
	B. Deception and the Fear of Disclosure	56
	C. Distance and Surrender	57
	1. Loathing	58
	2. Marginalization	59
	3. Sympathy	61
	4. Identification	62
	D. Physical Dangers	63
	E. Dealing with the Challenges	65
II.	Getting Along with Members: The Problems of Developing and Maintaining Field Relations	66
	A. Strategies to Facilitate the Development and Maintenance of Field Relations	67
	1. Presentational Strategies	68
	a. Nonthreatening Demeanor	68
	b. Acceptable Incompetence	69
	c. Selective Competence	70
	2. Exchange Strategies	71

	B. Strategies to Control Relational Closeness	72
	1. Preempting	73
	2. Finessing	74
	3. Declining and Withdrawing	75
III.	Getting Along While Getting Out	75
IV.	Getting Along with Claimants and Conscience: Ongoing Ethical Concerns	78
V.	Postscript: Personal Accounts of the Field Experience	79

Chapter 5. Logging Data   81

I.	Data: Fact or Fiction?	82
II.	The Logging Task	84
	A. Data Sources	85
	1. Direct Experience	85
	2. Social Action	85
	3. Talk	87
	4. Supplementary Data	88
	a. Archival Records	89
	b. Physical Traces	89
	c. Photographic Data	90
	B. Problems of Error and Bias	90
	1. Types of Error and Bias	91
	a. Reactive Effects	91
	b. Perceptual and Interpretive Distortions	91
	c. Sampling Errors	91
	2. Measures to Control Error and Bias	91
	a. Sampling Strategies	91
	b. Team Research	93
	c. Strategic Selection of Informants	93
	d. Member Checking	94
	C. The Mechanics of Logging	95
	D. Protecting Confidentiality	98
III.	Data Logging in Intensive Interviewing: Guides and Write-Ups	99
	A. Preparing the Interview Guide	99
	1. Puzzlements and Jottings	99
	2. Global Sorting and Ordering	100
	3. Section Sorting and Ordering	101
	4. Probes	102
	5. Facesheets and Fieldnotes	103

	B. Doing the Interview	104
	1. Introduction	104
	2. Flexible Format	105
	3. Ineffective Questions	105
	4. Attending, Thinking, Taking Notes, Taping	106
	5. Separate Forms	107
	C. Writing Up the Interview	107
IV.	Data Logging in Observation: Fieldnotes	108
	A. Mental Notes	109
	B. Jotted Notes	109
	C. Full Fieldnotes	110
	1. Mechanics	110
	2. Contents	112
	a. Be Concrete	112
	b. Distinguish Notationally Among Member Comments	113
	c. Record Recalled Information	113
	d. Include Analytic Ideas and Hunches	113
	e. Record Personal Impressions and Feelings	114
	f. Reminders	115
	3. Style	115
V.	Interview Write-Ups and Fieldnotes as Compulsion	116

PART TWO FOCUSING DATA 119

Chapter 6. Thinking Topics	121
I. Units and Aspects Combine into Topics	121
II. Units	122
A. Practices	123
B. Episodes	124
C. Encounters	124
D. Roles and Social Types	125
1. Roles	125
2. Social Types	126
E. Social and Personal Relationships	126
F. Groups and Cliques	127
G. Organizations	128
H. Settlements and Habitats	129
I. Subcultures and Lifestyles	131

III.	Aspects and Topics	132
	A. Cognitive Aspects or Meanings	132
	1. Ideologies (and Kindred Concepts) as Meanings	133
	2. Rules as Meanings	134
	3. Self-Concepts and Identities as Meanings	135
	B. Emotional Aspects or Feelings	136
	1. Emotion and Practices, Episodes, and Encounters	136
	2. Emotion and Roles	137
	3. Emotion and Organizations	138
	C. Hierarchical Aspects or Inequalities	139
	1. Hierarchy in Encounters	139
	2. Hierarchy in Roles and Relationships	140
	3. Hierarchy in Groups	141
IV.	Two or More Units or Aspects as Topics	141
V.	Units, Aspects, and Topics Form a Mind-Set for Coding	143

Chapter 7. Asking Questions   144

I.	What Are the Topic's Types?	145
	A. Single Types	146
	B. Multiple Types and Taxonomies	146
	C. Typologizing	148
	D. Sources and Rules of Typing and Typologizing	149
II.	What Are the Topic's Frequencies?	149
III.	What Are the Topic's Magnitudes?	151
IV.	What Are the Topic's Structures?	151
V.	What Are the Topic's Processes?	152
	A. Cycles	152
	B. Spirals	153
	C. Sequences	154
	1. Tracing Back	154
	2. Tracing Forward	155
	3. Turning Points	155
VI.	What Are the Topic's Causes?	156
	A. Requirements of Causal Explanation	157
	B. Selected Models of Causal Explanation	157
	1. Experimental Model	157
	2. Statistical Model	158
	3. Contextual Model	158

Contents

4. Case Comparative Model	158
5. Step/Process Model	158
6. Negative Case Model	158
C. Clarifying the Relationship Between Qualitative Field Research and Causal Explanation	158
VII. What Are the Topic's Consequences?	162
A. Foreground Issues in Examining Consequences	163
1. Requirements of Inferring Consequences	163
2. Consequences for Whom or for What?	163
3. Intentional and Unintentional Consequences	163
B. Examples of the Qualitative Study of Consequences	164
VIII. Where and What Is Agency?	165
A. Passivist Versus Agentic Conceptions	165
B. Agentic Questions	166

Chapter 8. Arousing Interest — 168

I. Social Science Framing	169
A. Trueness	169
1. Theoretical Candor	170
2. The Ethnographer's Path	170
3. Fieldnote and Interview Transcript Evidence	170
B. Newness	171
1. Relating to Existing Work	171
2. First Report	172
3. Unusual Setting	172
4. New Analytic Focus and Perspective	173
C. Importance	174
1. Questioning Mind-Set	174
2. Propositional Framing	175
3. Generic Concepts	177
a. Using Existing Social Science Conceptions	177
b. Discerning New Forms	178
c. Using Metaphors	179
d. Using Irony	180
4. Developed Treatment	180
a. Conceptual Elaboration	181
b. Balance	183
c. Interpenetration	184
5. Resonating Content	185

II.	Social Science Value Commitments	187
	A. Demystification	187
	B. Holistic Dispassionate Understanding	188
III.	Other Framings	189
	A. Technocratic/Social Engineering Frame	190
	B. Liberation Frame	190
	C. Muckraking Frame	191
	D. Expressive Voicing	191

PART THREE ANALYZING DATA   193

Chapter 9. Developing Analysis   195

I.	Strategy One: Social Science Framing	197
	A. Eight Forms of Propositions	197
	B. A Third Way to Contrast Propositional with Other Writing	197
	C. Number of Propositions in a Single Fieldstudy	198
II.	Strategy Two: Normalizing and Managing Anxiety	198
III.	Strategy Three: Coding	200
	A. Two Physical Methods of Coding	203
	1. Filing	203
	2. Computer Databasing	203
	B. Types of Coding Files	204
	1. Folk/Setting-Specific Files	205
	2. Analytic Files	206
	3. Methodological/Fieldwork Files	208
	C. Maintaining a Chronological Record	209
IV.	Strategy Four: Memoing	209
V.	Strategy Five: Diagramming	212
	A. Taxonomies	212
	B. Matrices and Typologies	214
	C. Concept Charts	215
	D. Flow Charts	216
VI.	Strategy Six: Thinking Flexibly	217

Chapter 10. Writing Analysis   220

I.	Preliminary Considerations	221
	A. Understanding the Social Psychological Dimensions of the Writing Process	221
	B. Plan Your Writing Time and Place	223

	II. Writing Practices	224
	A. Start Writing	224
	B. Write on Any Project Aspect, But Write	225
	C. Admit Aversion and Write Regularly Anyway	226
	D. Trust in Discovery and Surprise in Writing	228
	E. Do Not Seek Perfection or the One Right Way	229
	F. Divide and Conquer	230
	G. Draw on Standard Literary Organizing Devices	231
	H. Find Your Own Working Style	233
	I. Reread and Revise	233
	J. Seek Feedback	235
	K. Constrain Your Ego and Related Attachments	236
	L. Let It Go	237
	III. Concluding Observations	238
	A. The Fieldstudies Approach as a System of Parts	239
	B. The Similarity of All Scholarship	239
References		**241**
Index		**273**

LIST OF FIGURES

1.1	Flow Chart of the Three Tasks of Fieldstudies	2
1.1	Examples of "Starting Where You Are"	10
4.1	Gary Larson on Covert Observation	57
4.2	Summary of Factors Affecting Disengagement	77
5.1	Qualitative Data Sources, Methods, and Informational Yield	86
5.2	Types and Sources of Controls for Error and Bias in Fieldwork	92
5.3	"Blue Skies" Data Log and Filing System	97
6.1	Matrix of Studies Focusing on Topics Based on the Intersection of Units	142
7.1	Eight Basic Questions	145
7.2	Taxonomy of Material Survival Strategies Among the Homeless	147
7.3	Example of Typologizing: Grønbjerg on Environments of Nonprofit Organizations	148
8.1	Conceptual Elaboration of Ex-Psychiatric Patients' Stigma Management Strategies	182
8.2	Conceptual Elaboration of Stigma Management Strategies among the Homeless	183
9.1	Examples of Fieldnote Coding from the Charmaz Study of People with Chronic Illness	202
9.2	Forms of Taxanomic Diagrams	213
9.3	Example of a Concept Charting Diagram: Hodson on Behavioral Modes at the Workplace	216
9.4	Diagram of Homeless Careers	217

PREFACE TO THE FOURTH EDITION

Users of the third edition of this guide may find it helpful for us to summarize how this, the fourth edition, has or has not been changed. Apart from the welcome addition of two new coauthors, the major continuities and alterations are as follows.

- Although the organizational structure and chapter sequence and much of the internal organization of chapters of the previous edition have been retained, much of the book has been substantially revised. This has entailed the deletion of a good deal of older material and examples, the addition of an abundance of new examples and substantive and methodological materials drawn from more recent qualitative studies and methodological discussions, and the revision of the prose to accommodate both these new materials and the voices of the new coauthors.
- Throughout the revision process, we were mindful of the need to proceed cautiously when eliminating earlier work, not only because some of that work makes or illustrates some procedures and principles more clearly than anything that has since been written, but also because we thought it important to retain reference to earlier work in order to provide a sense of continuity between previous and subsequent generations of fieldworkers. Thus, we attempt to balance the old and the new, although the revision is skewed toward the latter.
- In addition to deleting and adding in a relatively balanced fashion, we feature a number of qualitative studies more prominently throughout the book than was the case with the previous edition. We do so in order to provide greater illustrative continuity across many of the chapters and to familiarize you more intimately with a number of relatively recent qualitative studies. Among the works drawn on in service of these considerations, four are drawn on quite extensively across a number of the chapters. These include Kathy Blee's *Inside Organized Racism: Women in the Hate Movement* (2002), Jennifer Lois's *Heroic Efforts: The Emotional Culture of Search and Rescue Volunteers* (2003), Calvin Morrill's *The Executive Way: Conflict Management in Corporations* (1995), and

David Snow and Leon Anderson's *Down on Their Luck: A Study of Homeless Street People* (1993). Importantly, for two of the studies the intensive interview is the primary data-collection procedure, whereas participation observation functions in that manner for the other two. Equally important, each of the studies focuses on strikingly different social settings populated by people who are strikingly different in a number of respects.

- The addition of some other new materials was dictated by certain technological advances and by organizational/bureaucratic innovations and/or preoccupations. Illustrative is the increasingly prominent role of computers and various software programs for qualitative analysis and the rise and institutionalization of Institutional Review Boards (IRBs) across college and university campuses. Thus, in this edition, we give greater attention to both of these matters.

ACKNOWLEDGMENTS

Numerous colleagues who have not critiqued the draft text of this edition have nonetheless had a great influence on it by means of conversations, admonitions, offhand remarks, and their field research and corresponding publications. For these diverse and diffuse forms of help and for their colleagueship, we express our deep thanks to Patricia Adler, Peter Adler, Elijah Anderson, Paul Atkinson, Howard S. Becker, Rob Benford, Joel Best, Nicole Biggart, Lodewijk Brunt, Spencer Cahill, Kathy Charmaz, Candace Clark, Dan Cress, Mitch Duneier, Robert Emerson, Gary Alan Fine, Carol Brooks Gardner, Barney Glaser, Kirsten Grønbjerg, Gary Hamilton, Ruth Horowitz, David Hummon, Albert Hunter, John Irwin, Carol Joffe, John M. Johnson, Sherryl Kleinman, Jack Katz, Michelle Lamont, Donileen Loseke, David Maines, Richard Mitchell, Calvin Morrill, Robert Prus, Charles Ragin, Gerald Suttles, Verta Taylor, Jacqueline Wiseman, and Morris Zelditch, Jr.

A manual of this sort can emerge only out of the accumulated data collection and analytic experiences of generations of naturalistic researchers. We therefore owe a special debt to all the men and women whose writings have formed the "data base" for our efforts. They are listed in the bibliography.

So, also, one best learns about something in the process of trying to explain it to other people. For us, these other people have very importantly been graduate and undergraduate students at UC, Davis, the University of Texas, the University of Arizona, UC, Irvine, and Ohio University. It is largely through our involvements in their struggles and triumphs in fieldstudies that we have formulated our conception of how to do such studies. We thank them for their patience and tenacity in dealing with successive formulations of these materials.

We are enormously indebted to Calvin Morrill, who has conducted, with David Snow, a fieldwork seminar every other year for the past 15 years at the University of Arizona and UCI. A number of the ideas and practices represented in this edition were honed and refined in those seminars.

We also are appreciative of the editorial assistance provided by Eve Howard, Jennifer Walsh, and Matt Ballantyne; and our production editor, Heidi Allgair.

INTRODUCTION

THE AIMS AND ORGANIZATION OF THIS GUIDE

This is a book of instructions on how to do a social science fieldstudy—a research genre that is also often labeled "ethnography," "qualitative research," and/or "naturalistic research." While field researchers across the social sciences may prefer one label over another, their studies are generally alike in featuring direct, qualitative observation of natural situations or settings using, mainly, the techniques of participant observation or intensive interviewing or both.

I. Three Tasks: Gathering, Focusing, and Analyzing Data

The production of high-quality social science fieldstudies is contingent upon on the successful completion of three interconnected tasks that can be thought of as the three cornerstones of this research genre. These tasks are:

- Gathering data;
- Focusing data in terms of social science concepts, questions, and issues; and
- Analyzing data and writing them up.

The order in which we list these sets of activities approximates the order in which they are performed in doing a fieldstudy. However, we must also stress that this is only a "general" order. Even though it is true that one must gather data before one can focus and analyze them, it is also true that focusing and analyzing are going on *at the same time*. It is only the linear logic of the narrative representation of the process, culminating in articles or books, that makes these cornerstone tasks appear to follow one another and to be separated in time. The reality of fieldstudies involves, instead, a complex overlapping and interweaving of the three tasks.

2   The Aims and Organization of This Guide

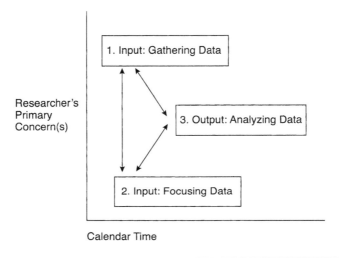

Figure I.1   Flow Chart of the Three Tasks of Fieldstudies

Keeping in mind this temporal interconnection among the tasks, we nevertheless find it helpful to think of the first two tasks—*gathering* and *focusing*—as the main, ongoing input activities. The data one is gathering provide *empirical input* and the focusing questions one is contemplating provide guiding *social science input*. The third task—*analysis*—emerges as a synthesis or *social scientific output* of the interaction between gathered and focused data. These relations are depicted schematically in Figure I.1, where gathering and focusing are shown as initial and interacting main activities that give rise to analyzing as the emergent and final activity from a social science standpoint.

The image shown in Figure I.1 is only one among several that can be helpful in conceiving relations among the tasks of gathering, focusing, and analyzing data. For example, you might find it helpful to envision their relationships in terms of the overlapping circles of a Venn diagram, wherein each of the tasks constitutes a circle that overlaps, in varying degrees, with the others (see also Miles and Huberman 1994, pp. 10–12).

II. Features and Aspects of Fieldstudies

At the abstract level of performing the tasks associated with gathering, focusing, and analyzing data, qualitative fieldstudies are not different from other methods of social research, such as surveys, content analyses, and experiments. Instead, fieldstudies differ from other methods of research only in exactly how they treat these tasks. Specifically, fieldstudies are distinctive in (1) the relation the researcher has to "the data" in gathering it, (2) the time at which data are focused, and (3) the relation of analysis to the data and the focus. Let us explain each task and provide an overview of the chapters in which we treat each.

A. Gathering Data: Researcher as Witness and Instrument

Qualitative fieldstudy differs from other research methods in that it features researchers themselves as observers and participants in the lives of the people being studied. The researcher strives to be a participant in and a witness to the lives of others. This is quite different from other kinds of research in which the investigator is not her- or himself a sustained presence in a naturally occurring situation or setting. Other researchers rely instead on documents, structured interviews, experimental simulations, and other sources that are one or more levels removed from direct observation of and participation in ongoing natural settings.

The central reason for observing and/or participating in the lives of others is that a great many aspects of social life can be seen, felt, and analytically articulated only in this manner. In subjecting him- or herself to the lives of others and living and feeling those lives along with them, the researcher becomes the primary instrument or medium through which the research is conducted. The researcher seeks to witness how those studied perceive, feel, and act in order to understand their perceptions, feelings, and behavior more fully and intimately. The epistemological foundation of fieldstudies is indeed the proposition that only through direct observation and/or participation can one get close to apprehending those studied and the character of their social worlds and lives.

The five chapters of Part One provide guidelines for achieving and managing the researcher's role as both witness and research instrument in pursuit of this up close, intimate understanding.

> **Chapter 1** Because of the central role of the researcher as both data experiencer and collector and the problematics of achieving this role, we encourage budding researchers to start where they are, using their current or past situations or interests as the springboard for research. We discuss the advantages and disadvantages of doing this and related matters in Chapter 1.
>
> **Chapter 2** Some settings are more amenable to particular research techniques than others; therefore, a process of evaluating data sites in terms of appropriateness and access is necessary. Guidelines for doing this are given in Chapter 2.
>
> **Chapter 3** Getting into a relevant site is often problematic. The mode of entry must be decided in terms of the social, political, legal, and ethical considerations discussed in Chapter 3.
>
> **Chapter 4** Once you have begun, the relationship between the research and its setting will provide a continual array of problems with which you must deal. We consider these problems of getting along in Chapter 4.
>
> **Chapter 5** The main substantive activity of the researcher is logging data. Two principal logging methods are interview write-ups and fieldnotes. Chapter 5 provides detailed instructions for doing both.

B. Focusing Data: Social Science Guidance

Although subjecting oneself as a researcher to the lives of others is indispensable in fieldstudy, that immersion must be guided by the aims and concerns of the social scientific analysis of human group life. We explain the most basic of these aims and concerns in the three chapters of Part Two.

Chapter 6 The first of these basic matters calls attention to how human group life can be viewed as different unit scales of organization and as possessing different aspects. In the analysis stage, you will select one or only a few units and aspects. Therefore, to assist you in deliberating and making these selections, we describe nine basic units of social organization in ascending order of "scale," including such familiar entities as social roles, groups, and lifestyles. In addition, we describe three frequently used generic aspects of social situations or settings: meanings, emotions, and hierarchy. Considered together, units and aspects provide possible topics of analysis.

Chapter 7 Units and aspects only provide possible objects or topics of focus. In social science analysis, one goes on to ask questions about the topics. We outline eight major classes of possible questions in Chapter 7.

Chapter 8 Topics and questions provide the formal fundamentals of social science analysis. Decisions that one makes about them anchor one as doing social science analysis. But there is yet a third, albeit more elusive, aspect of social science guidance. This is the question of performing analysis on topics and questions that will arouse interest in audiences who read your analysis. Applying and adapting generic criteria for evaluating any intellectual work, we offer suggestions in Chapter 8 on how to arouse audience interest in terms of making one's study *true*, *new*, and *important*.

Fieldstudies differ from other methods of research in that the researcher typically performs the tasks of selecting topics, decides what questions to ask, and forges interest *in the course of the research itself*. This is in sharp contrast to many "theory-driven" and "hypothesis-testing" methods of research in which the topics of observation and analysis, the questions about them, and the kinds of interest the findings might generate are all specified before one begins to gather data.

C. Analyzing Data: Emergence

In linking the process of data focusing to data gathering, fieldstudies are inherently and by design *open-ended* regarding the task of analyzing. Intellectually and operationally, analysis *emerges* from the *interaction* of gathered data (task 1) and focusing decisions (task 2).

The *purpose* of this process is to achieve analyses that (1) are attuned to aspects of human group life, (2) depict aspects of that life, and (3) provide perspectives on that life that are simply not available to or prompted by other methods of research.

As an open-ended and emergent process, it is inherently more difficult to provide surefire instructions on how to bring gathered data and focusing concerns together and into analysis. Even so, helpful procedures have been identified.

> **Chapter 9** One set of these procedures focuses on physical operations to perform on the data as aids in deciding on one's topics and questions of analysis. The most basic and central of these are the processes of coding and memo writing. We explain these and other techniques of *developing analysis* in Chapter 9.
>
> **Chapter 10** Another set of procedures pertains to representation of the analysis, and particularly to features of one's report, its elements and their ordering, and the social psychology of writing. We describe these matters and several rules of thumb pertaining to writing in Chapter 10.

III. Audiences

Although by training and practice we are sociologists, in this guide we treat fieldstudies as interdisciplinary activity and not as the special province of sociologists. Indeed, the research practices we describe are used in at least a dozen theoretical and applied disciplines with excellent effects. Aside from anthropology, political science, and history, the fieldstudy method is used in such diverse fields as administration, education, communications, criminal justice, geography, labor relations, nursing, and social work.

IV. Yet More Labels for Fieldstudies

We use the label *fieldstudies* to denote the method of research explained in this guide. But, as mentioned in the first paragraph of this introduction, not all social scientists use the same labels or concepts in the same ways. Social science often appears to be a kind of terminological jungle in which many concepts compete, and no single term has been able to command the domain before us. Often, especially in political science and occasionally in psychology, researchers simply "do it" without worrying about giving "it" a name. Anthropologists variously refer to this enterprise as *fieldwork* or *ethnography*. But as matters have developed in anthropology and other disciplines, neither fieldwork nor ethnography captures all the salient qualities of this research enterprise as it is practiced in sociology, our own discipline. And even though the fieldwork label has some currency within sociology, there are other competitors as well—such as *qualitative social research, qualitative methods, grounded theory*, and *naturalism*. (For historical discussions and/or overviews of this many-labeled tradition, see Atkinson et al. 2001, pp. 1–7; Emerson 2001, pp. 1–53; Gubrium and Holstein 1997; and Vidich and Lyman 2000.)

Among the diversity of these labels, *fieldstudies* strikes us as among the most general and encompassing; therefore, we use it as the master label for the research activities we discuss in this guide. However, we use other terms from time to time, particularly fieldwork, ethnography, naturalistic research, and the naturalistic approach. But we trust, in light of the foregoing discussion, that these minor inconsistencies will not prove confusing.

PART ONE

GATHERING DATA

Five aspects of gathering data form the initial task or phase of a fieldstudy. These are:

- the readiness to start where you are (Chapter 1),

- the preference for rich sites of direct, face-to-face engagement where intimate familiarity is acquired (Chapter 2),

- the need to deal with difficulties in gaining entrée (Chapter 3),

- the management of relations with the people in the situations or settings under study (Chapter 4), and

- the logging of data (Chapter 5).

CHAPTER 1

STARTING WHERE YOU ARE

Social researchers find themselves in an unusual relationship to the social worlds around them. They both live in these worlds and seek to develop analytic understandings that go beyond the taken-for-granted realities and perceptions within which most people experience and live their lives. More than any other kind of social inquiry, fieldwork takes advantage of researchers' personal connections to the world(s) around them, seeing those connections as avenues to potential research. What are the social worlds that you traverse in your daily life? What are the activities, issues, and ideas that you find personally engaging? The naturalistic or fieldwork approach to social research fosters a pronounced willingness, even commitment, on the part of the investigator to orient to these kinds of personal concerns. Fieldwork is time-consuming, arduous, and often emotionally draining. Starting where you are can ease your access to certain research sites and informants. It can also increase the odds that you will be able to maintain the engagement and commitment that field research requires.

Initiating successful fieldstudies requires (at least) two things: intellectual curiosity about a topic and access to settings and people from which one may collect appropriate data. Starting where you are means that you initially orient your research to aspects of your personal biography in terms of one or both of these. At times, fieldstudies may emerge from personal experiences and opportunities that provide access to social settings; at other times, they develop out of curiosity that is spurred by readings, classes, and academic conversations. Ultimately, fieldwork germinates when the researcher brings both together, engaging research settings and subjects with an intellectual and analytic agenda.

As you prepare to enter the field, then, you are well advised to reflect on where you are and what opportunities may emerge from your biography.

I. Personal Experience and Biography

A job; a physical mishap; the development, loss, or maintenance of an intimate relationship; an illness; an enjoyed activity; a living arrangement—all these and many other possible experiences may provide you with a topic you care enough about to study. These accidents or routines of current biography may give you crucial physical or psychological access (or both) to social settings. Such experiences may also spur a degree of interest or concern that can provide motivation and curiosity that, combined with access, becomes the starting point for meaningful naturalistic inquiry. Using your immediate biographic experiences as a springboard for fieldstudy constitutes what Jeffrey Riemer (1977) has called "opportunistic research."

Many social science research projects have been opportunistically based in this way. Some particularly striking examples are listed in Figure 1.1, which also demonstrates a variety of situations out of which social analyses may grow.

The interests you seek to examine through fieldwork may arise from any number of aspects of your current or past biography and life situation—ethnicity, gender, sexual preference, past identities or experiences, places of residence, family customs, class of origin, religion, and so forth. For example, Gary Alan Fine's research for *Gifted Tongues* (2001), a study of high school debate and adolescent culture, was connected to his son Todd's distinguished career as a high school debater. In a similar vein, John Irwin's interest in *The Felon* (1970), in *Prisons in Turmoil* (1980), and in *The Jail* (1985) was intimately related to his own felony conviction at the age of 21 and the five years he spent in a California state prison. And Mary Romero's study of domestic workers (*Maid in the U.S.A.*, 1992) may be said to have had its origins in the fact that as a teenager she had worked as a domestic, as had her mother, sister, relatives, and neighbors. However, in each of these cases, it was not until the researcher developed an intellectual curiosity about the topic that it could emerge as a focus of ethnographic study. Romero captures this moment of emerging curiosity in her research trajectory:

> Before beginning a teaching position at the University of Texas in El Paso, I stayed with a colleague while apartment hunting. My colleague had a live-in domestic to assist with housecleaning and cooking. Asking around, I learned that live-in maids were common in El Paso. . . . The hiring of maids from Mexico was so common that locals referred to Monday as the border patrol's day off because the agents ignored the women crossing the border to return to their employers' homes after their weekend off. The practice of hiring undocumented Mexican women as domestics, many of whom were no older than fifteen, seemed strange to me. It was this strangeness that raised the topic of domestic service as a question and made problematic what had previously been taken for granted. (1992, pp. 1–3)

It is often said among sociologists that, as sociologists, we "make problematic" in our research matters that are problematic in our lives. With the proviso that the connection between self and study may be a subtle and sophisticated one, not at all apparent to an outside observer, we would argue that there is considerable truth to this assertion. In fact, much of the best work in sociology and other social sciences—within the fieldwork tradition

Figure 1.1 Examples of "Starting Where You Are"

This person:	starting where he or she was:	developed this published social analysis:
Peter and Patricia Adler	parents of two children	*Peer Power: Preadolescent Culture and Identity* (1998)
Elijah Anderson	a resident of a mixed-class and mixed-race area of Philadelphia	*Streetwise: Race, Class, and Change in an Urban Community* (1990); *Code of the Street: Decency, Violence, and the Moral Life of the Inner City* (1999)
Judith A. DilOrio and Michael R. Nusbaumer	serving as escorts at an abortion clinic	"Securing Our Sanity: Anger Management Among Abortion Escorts" (1993)
Mitchell Duneier	walked past the sidewalk book vendors and panhandlers in Greenwich Village every day	*Sidewalk* (1999)
Rick Fantasia	working at a small iron foundry when a wildcat strike occurred	*Cultures of Solidarity: Consciousness, Action, and Contemporary American Workers* (1988)
David A. Karp	sufferer of depression	*Speaking of Sadness* (1996); *The Burden of Sympathy: How Families Cope with Mental Illness* (2001)
Diana Kendall	member of an "old name" family and symphony aficionado	*The Power of Good Deeds: Privileged Women and the Social Reproduction of the Upper Class* (2002)
Lawrence J. Ouellet	working as a truckdriver while in graduate school at Northwestern University	*Pedal to the Metal: The Work Lives of Truckers* (1996)
Frank N. Pieke	conducting dissertation fieldwork in Beijing when the 1989 Tiananmen Square student protests began	*The Ordinary and the Extraordinary: An Anthropological Study of Chinese Reform and the 1989 People's Movement in Beijing* (1996)
Clinton Sanders	human companion and owner of two Newfoundland dogs	*Understanding Dogs: Living and Working with Canine Companions* (1999)
Christopher L. Stevenson	member of a masters swimming club	"The Influence of Nonverbal Symbols on the Meaning of Motive Talk: A Case Study from Masters Swimming" (1999)
Diane Vaughan	a divorcee after 20 years of marriage	*Uncoupling: Turning Points in Intimate Relationships* (1990)

as well as within other research traditions—is probably grounded in the past and/or current biographies of its creators. That such linkages are not always, perhaps not even usually, publicly acknowledged is understandable: the traditional norms of scholarship do not require that researchers bare their souls, only their procedures.

In recent years, however, a number of fieldworkers within anthropology and sociology have bared both their souls and lives in their ethnographic texts (Ellis 1995; Ronai 1992; Rosaldo 1989). In doing so, they advocate, whether directly or indirectly, not only for starting where you are but staying there and making the personal or biographic the focus of your ethnography. Variously referred to as "autobiographical sociology" (Friedman 1990), "autoethnography" (Reed-Danahay 2001), and "telling personal stories" (Ellis and Bochner 1992), this style of fieldwork can be useful for some purposes, such as trying to understand the link between certain life experiences and associated emotional reactions, particularly of those studied. Renato Rosaldo (1989), for example, reached a clearer understanding of the emotional life and culture of the Ilongot headhunters of the Philippines, whom he had studied for years, only after the grief he experienced over the death of his wife. That grief, which he chronicles in a narrative fashion, provided the springboard for finally coming to grips with the rage associated with Ilongot grief. In this case, the researcher's own experience provided the key to understanding a parallel experience of those studied. This is quite different from analyzing and writing about one's own experiences when the purpose is only to tell a story that illuminates and gives voice to those experiences. Such stories run the risk of being read as self-indulgent and even narcissistic, or of being dismissed as sociologically uninteresting. Because of such possibilities, we strongly advise most researchers, especially beginners, to use their own experiences primarily as a point of departure and thus avoid becoming preoccupied with or fixated on where they have started.

II. Intellectual Curiosity

Not all subjects of interest to us, of course, are closely intertwined with our daily lives and personal experiences. While you should seriously consider starting research from a base in personal experience and contacts, academic interests and intellectual curiosities may also provide the impetus for engaging in a fieldstudy. Just as we find many fieldstudies that emerge from experiential opportunities, we also find that many fieldworkers formulate their initial research interests through reading and academic conversations. So, for instance, Jason Jimerson's (1996, 1999) impetus for research on welfare-maximizing norms among pickup basketball players emerged from his readings of rational choice theorists James Coleman and Robert Ellickson. Similarly, in describing his study (with several student researchers) of the social control of children in public places, Spencer Cahill

(1990) explains that "my reading made me notice aspects of my experience that had previously gone unnoticed. And, once those seen but unnoticed aspects of everyday life came into view, I decided to view and report on them" (personal communication, 2002).

The point here is that intellectual curiosity is a powerful motivator of research. Our academic interests and ideas can move us to fieldwork just as more experiential factors can. And it is often only in bringing both together that research can germinate.

III. Tradition and Justification

Fieldwork, which demands that researchers participate in the social worlds they seek to understand, has a rich history of capitalizing on investigators' biographies. Speaking of Robert Park, one of the founders of the naturalistic tradition, and his work with sociology graduate students at the University of Chicago in the 1920s and 1930s, Everett Hughes related that

> Most of these people didn't have any sociological background. . . . They didn't come in to become sociologists. They came in to learn something and Park picked up whatever it was in their experience which he could build on. . . . He took these people and he brought out of them whatever he could find there. And he brought out of them very often something that they themselves did not know was there. They might be Mennonites who were just a little unhappy . . . about wearing plain clothes . . . girls who didn't like to wear long dresses and funny little caps; . . . or children of Orthodox Jews who really didn't like to wear beards anymore (that was a time of escaping a beard, the beard was the symbol of your central Russian origin and you wanted to get it off). And he got hold of people and emancipated them from something that was inherently interesting but which they regarded as a cramp. And he turned this "cramping orthodoxy" into something that was of basic and broad human interest. And that was the case for a lot of these people. He made their pasts interesting to them, much more interesting than they ever thought they could be. (L. Lofland 1980, pp. 267–268)

Essentially, Park's genius in working with these students lay in his ability to spark their sociological imagination and to connect that imagination to their own lives. While starting where you are may cause methodological and ethical difficulties, we believe that such difficulties are a small price to pay for the very creative wellsprings of the naturalistic approach. Starting where you are provides the necessary meaningful linkages between the personal and emotional on the one hand, and the stringent intellectual operations to come on the other. Michael Schwalbe writes that his research for *Unlocking the Iron Cage: The Men's Movement, Gender Politics and American Culture* (1996a) was motivated by his desire to "study gender, identity, and emotions in a way that had bearing on my own personal growth issues"

(1996b, p. 60). Without a foundation in personal sentiment, all the rest can easily become so much ritualistic hollow cant. Julius Roth (1966) has written persuasively of the dangers of "hired hand research," of the dismal work performance of alienated labor in the scholarship business (in contrast, see Staggenborg 1988). But alienation is not limited to occasions of following someone else's agenda. If your own agenda is not personally meaningful, you may be alienated as well. Unless you are emotionally engaged in your work, the inevitable boredom, confusion, and frustration of rigorous scholarship will endanger even the completion—not to speak of the quality—of the project.

CHAPTER 2

EVALUATING DATA SITES

Having identified a group, situation, place, question, or topic that is personally interesting, you must then decide how best to pursue this interest. This requires an assessment of the most appropriate or most feasible "wheres," "hows," and "whens" of the research. We do not mean to suggest that all decisions regarding the research are, even initially, "up for grabs." As a student, for example, you may be required to write about a particular setting during a specified period; that is, the "where" and "when" of your research may be largely predetermined. Or your interests may logically imply one sort of "how" rather than another. Nonetheless, regardless of the degree of freedom you have, the process of evaluating data sites is crucial. If it is not crucial in making your own decisions, it may at least be important in terms of understanding the implications of decisions that are already made.

I. The Overall Goal

Your overall goal is to collect the *richest possible data*. By rich data, we mean a wide and diverse range of information collected over a relatively prolonged period of time in a persistent and systematic manner. Ideally, such data enable you to grasp the meanings associated with the actions of those you are studying and to understand the contexts in which those actions are embedded. Another way of putting it is that rich data enable you, to paraphrase the anthropologist Clifford Geertz (1973, p. 6), to distinguish between an eye twitch and a wink. You achieve this primarily through sustained and direct face-to-face interaction with the participants in some social location or circumstance. You wish, that is, to earn "intimate familiarity" with the sector of social life that has sparked your interest.

The naturalistic penchant for *direct* observation and apprehension of the social world reflects a certain epistemology, that is, a theory of knowledge. The central tenet of this theory is that face-to-face interaction is potentially the fullest condition for achieving intimate familiarity with the actions and orientations of other human beings. Whatever the barriers to the validity of direct knowledge of others (and they may be numerous), they are less problematic than the difficulties engendered by inference based on indirect observation and perception. (For important segments of this epistemology, see Blumer 1969, especially pp. 1–89; Schutz 1967, especially Chapter 4 and Sections C and D; Berger and Luckmann 1967, especially pp. 28–34; Znaniecki 1934; and Cooley 1926.)

Novice fieldworkers, schooled in the "bias avoidance" injunctions of experimental and survey research, often worry that if they become personally involved in their field settings they will "contaminate the data." We want to nip that worry in the bud. Later we will discuss why this concern is less troublesome than often assumed. But we do want to emphasize here that nowhere in the preceding paragraphs have we said anything about the importance of "objectivity" and, as it implies, "distance" from the object of study. Quite the contrary, we have exhorted researchers to

- collect the richest possible data,
- by achieving intimate familiarity with the setting
- through engaging in some number of behaviors relevant to the setting and in face-to-face interaction with its participants.

That is, we have counseled involvement and engagement rather than objectivity and distance—a counsel that is very much in keeping with the fieldwork tradition, at least as the tradition has developed within sociology. As we shall see in the next chapter, the dual task of raising and answering questions does call for a certain internal tension between distance and closeness in the researcher. We shall also see in Chapter 8 that a dispassionate frame of mind is particularly helpful when one is attempting to translate one's amassed data into a sophisticated and interesting analysis. But if one is to collect rich data, the tradition beckons one to "get close." So-called objectivity and distance vis-à-vis the field setting will usually result in a failure to collect much data that are worth analyzing.

As noted in the Introduction, in this guide we shall be concerned primarily with those two interrelated methods most closely associated with the naturalistic preference for direct apprehension of the behaviors, orientations, and feelings associated with the social settings and contexts that constitute the social world: participant observation and intensive interviewing. We recognize, however, that many questions, topics, settings, or situations of interest to investigators will simply not be available through these methods. There will be matters that you cannot "reach" through direct apprehension: historical settings or events, for example, or the actions of very large collective entities, such as the market, political parties, or the state. For these research problems, other texts are to be recommended (see, for example, Babbie 2003; Banks 2001; Gilbert 2001; Plummer 2001; Ragin 1987; Tashakkori and Teddlie 2003). There will also be matters whose direct apprehension requires neither participant observation nor intensive interviewing, as these terms are traditionally understood. If you are interested in the cultural products of social interaction, such as conceptions of the homeless, images of urban life, or beliefs about emotions, you might be best advised to use works of art, television broadcasts, autobiographies, transcripts of conversations or public hearings, collections of letters, magazine advertisements, or the findings from survey research as your data. Or, you may wish to focus on the moment-by-moment flow of emotional experience and have no need to do more than monitor your own subjective states (but see our caution in Chapter 1). For these sorts of research, some of what we discuss in the following pages ("getting in" and "getting along" especially) will be of little value and you will need other guides to fill in the data collection lacunae (see, for example, Bochner and Ellis 2001; Ellis and Flaherty 1992; Riessman 1993; Rodriguez and Ryave 2002; Silverman 2001; Titscher, Meyer, Wodak, and Vetter 2000). But most of the matters discussed here should apply equally well to analysts of human cultural productions and to researchers of human cultural producers.

So, with these caveats in mind, we briefly introduce the qualitative techniques of participant observation and interviewing.

II. Participant Observation and Intensive Interviewing

Participant observation refers to the process in which an investigator establishes and sustains a many-sided and situationally appropriate relationship with a human association in its natural setting for the purpose of developing a social scientific understanding of that association. This may not be the person's sole purpose for being present in the setting, but it is the primary one for conducting field research. *Intensive interviewing*, on the other hand, encompasses both ordinary conversation and listening as it occurs naturally during the course of social interaction and semi-structured interviewing involving the use of an interview guide consisting of a list of open-ended questions that direct conversation without forcing the interviewee (usually referred to as the "informant") to select preestablished responses. In either case, the goal is to elicit from the interviewee rich, detailed materials that can be used in qualitative analysis. In contrast to these two forms of intensive interviewing, which seek to discover the informant's views of a particular situation or topic or experience in or with a particular situation, "structured interviewing" (such as opinion polling) seeks to elicit choices between alternative answers to questions on a topic or situation that may not be directly relevant to the interviewee. Among other contrasts, the structured interview seeks to determine the frequency of preconceived kinds of things, while the intensive qualitative interview seeks to find out what kinds of things exist in the first place.

The literature on qualitative methodology has traditionally distinguished rather sharply between participant observation and intensive interviewing, frequently viewing the former as the preeminent method. We believe, following Sherryl Kleinman and her colleagues (1994), that this distinction is overdrawn. As numerous anthropological and sociological accounts make clear, doing participant observation in another culture, as well as one's own, involves a great deal of informant interviewing.

Classic participant observation, then, always involves the interweaving of looking and listening, of participating and asking, and some of that listening and asking may be identical to intensive interviewing. Conversely, intensive interview studies may involve repeated contact between researchers and informants (see, for example, Charmaz 1991; Klatch 1999; Morrill 1995; Williams 1989), and sometimes they may even extend over a period of years, with considerable mutual involvement in personal lives—a characteristic often considered a hallmark of participant observation. In addition, many social situations (experiencing grief over the loss of someone or something one cares deeply about, for example) may be masked in everyday interaction and thus be directly apprehensible only through intensive interviewing. Therefore, rather than being a poor substitute for participant observation, intensive interviewing is frequently the method of choice (e.g., Blee 2002; Edin and Lein 1997; Lamont 1992, 2000; Williams 1995).

In this guide, we wish to emphasize the mutuality of participant observation and intensive interviewing as the central techniques of naturalistic investigation. In what follows, we shall distinguish between them where it is necessary to do so, but most of our discussion is applicable to both. (A considerable number of general treatments of participant observation, intensive interviewing, or both are available. Among these are Atkinson, Coffey, Delamont, Lofland, and Lofland 2001; Berg 2004; Denzin and Lincoln 2000; Emerson 2001; Erlandson, Harris, Skipper, and Allen 1993; Fetterman 1998; Gubrium and Holstein 2002; Seidman 1998.)

III. Detailed Assessment of Data Sites

Assuming that you wish to gather the richest possible data using participant observation, intensive interviewing, or some combination of the two, you need to evaluate potential data sites for appropriateness, access, physical and emotional risks, ethics, and personal consequences.

A. Evaluating for Appropriateness

By appropriateness, we direct attention to the fit among your questions or interests and the settings in which and methods through which they can be best investigated. This is no small matter since the prospect of answering questions of interest can vary considerably in terms of research locations and methods. The point is that whether you begin your research expedition with a burning question, a setting of personal interest, or a proclivity to use a particular method, it is important to keep in mind that each factor will set some parameters around the others. Consequently, the fit among questions/interests, settings, and methods should be given some consideration before setting sail. While the fieldwork tradition in social science puts a premium on flexibility, it is simply a fact that some questions, research locations, topics, or methods logically necessitate other questions, locations, topics, or methods (Deutscher, Pestello, and Pestello 1993; Zelditch 1962). If you have decided to rely solely on observation of persons in public places, for example, you will not be able to collect many useful data on emotional states and processes. Or if you are interested in body management strategies in public interaction, intensive interviewing is hardly an appropriate tool, since the data you need are largely outside individual awareness. Doing research with children in a nursery school will yield little of value about day-to-day interaction of school administrators. And you are not likely to learn much about the grief experience by participant observation in a group with low rates of death or other attrition.

All of this may seem obvious, if not simpleminded. Yet, as anyone who has read any reasonable number of unpublished social science works (by professionals as well as by students) can testify, research often appears to proceed without noticeable awareness of or appreciation for the problems of appropriateness.

The circumstances of potential research projects are too diverse to yield many specific "principles" of appropriateness. We can, however, offer four general guidelines. First, using primarily participant observation is probably most fruitful when the question, topic, or situation in which you are interested is physically located somewhere, at least temporarily. If you wish, for example, to study the operation of street gangs (Horowitz 1983), to examine the interactional dynamics of inner-city youth violence (Anderson 1999), to understand the day-to-day lives of the homeless (Snow and Anderson 1993), to explore the way gender is enacted and re-created among children (Cahill 1986, 1989; Thorne 1993), or to detail culture-in-the-making in small groups (Fine 1987), observation will likely yield the richest data most efficiently.

Second, and conversely, you may be interested in what Joseph Kotarba (1980) has called "amorphous social experiences"—those aspects of everyday experience that are transinstitutional in the sense of not being embedded in or peculiar to a specific social context or setting. In that event, intensive interviewing (sometimes combined with limited observation) may be the most felicitous and possibly the only way to proceed. Examples of amorphous social experiences include living with chronic pain (Kotarba 1983), chronic illness (Charmaz 1991), depression (Karp 1996, 2001), dissolving an intimate relationship (Vaughan 1990), having an extramarital affair (Richardson 1985), and receiving and giving sympathy (Clark 1987).

Third, always consider the possible appropriateness of new or little used variants of the standard research methods. Zimmerman and Wieder (1977), for example, have reported on the field procedure of the *diary/diary-interview method*. The technique uses diaries as observational logs maintained by the person being studied; these in turn are used as a basis for intensive interviews. They recommend the technique in situations "where the problems of direct observation resist solution or where further or more extended observation strains available resources . . . [that is,] when the investigator is unable to make firsthand observations or wishes to supplement those already collected" (1977, p. 481). As another example, you might consider group or *focus group interviews* in place of or as a supplement to one-to-one interviews (For methodological discussion of focus group interviews, see Bloor, Franklin, Thomas, and Robson 2001; Greenbaum 1998; Krueger and Casey 2000; Morgan 1997). Group interviewing of whatever sort may be most productive on topics that are reasonably public and are not matters of any particular embarrassment. As well, it has the advantage of allowing people more time to reflect and to recall experiences, especially in response to other group members whose comments can trigger recollection and reflection that can result in the modification or amplification of earlier thoughts and commentary. In addition, people may not agree with one another on matters of opinion, providing instances of interchange between contrasting perspectives. William Gamson's (1992) *Talking Politics* clearly illustrates the utility of focus group interviews for getting people to discuss interactively, but not necessarily consensually, various political issues in a fashion that is less likely to surface in structured, individual interviews.

You may also wish to take advantage of today's burgeoning venues of electronic communication. In some settings, some of the participants may not be in face-to-face contact but linked instead via electronic media (e-mail, faxes, telephone and video conferences). In such cases, the achievement of intimate familiarity may require that the researcher participate in such disembodied communication networks. In his study of a computer systems firm, for example, John Workman, Jr. (1992) found it essential to monitor ongoing discussions and debates within the firm via electronic bulletin boards and to use e-mail to receive meeting notices and relevant documents, to schedule interviews, and to communicate directly with many of his informants. Since Workman's study, the use of electronic communication has expanded enormously with the proliferation of commercially established networks of game participants and mate-seekers, with nonprofit sites for discussion groups ranging from pet owners to schizophrenics, as well as organizational and informational Web sites. Just as survey researchers are adapting their methods to the Internet, qualitative researchers are exploring new ways via electronic media both to gather data on traditional research sites (as in Workman's study) and to study new, virtual research sites, as in Correll's study of a lesbian "internet café" (1995; see also L. Kendall 1998, 2002). As a simple rule of thumb we would suggest that if electronic communication is a significant part of the social interaction among those you are studying, you should plan to incorporate it in some manner in your data collection (for conducting research online, see Mann and Stewart 2001).

Fourth, you should not rule out ipso facto the appropriateness of collecting or using some quantitative data in conjunction with the data collected through participant observation and intensive interviewing. Blending or mixing different kinds of data—what has been referred to as data "triangulation" (Denzin 1989a)—has become increasingly more commonplace (see Tashakkori and Teddlie 2003). For example, Snow and Anderson (1993) supplemented their participant observation among Austin's homeless in the mid-1980s with quantitative data derived from tracking a sample of nearly 800 homeless individuals through six separate institutions within the city or the state. Among other things, these data led to a better understanding of the mental health and criminal justice experiences of the city's homeless than would have been possible through participant observation alone (Snow, Baker, Martin, and Anderson 1986; Snow, Anderson and Baker 1989; for other examples of fieldstudies collecting or using various amounts of survey, census, or other quantitative data, see Biggart 1989; Grønbjerg 1993; Morrill 1995). The use of some types of quantitative data may even be essential when conducting a "case study"— a holistic investigation of some space- and time-rooted phenomenon, such as a neighborhood, small community, organization, or social movement. (Discussion of the features, strengths, and limitations of the case study may be found in Feagin, Orum, and Sjoberg 1991; Platt 1988; Ragin and Becker 1992; Snow and Trom 2002; Yin 2003). As well, do not overlook the rich and detailed information that census data can make available to you (Myers 1992). Or, as another example, if your focus is a single moderately sized organization, a small survey of the membership may be the most efficient (and possibly the only) way to get a handle on your "cast of characters."

B. Evaluating for Access

A realistic appraisal of any proposed research necessitates our recognizing that, in combination, the nature of the research question or problem and the attributes of the investigator, the setting or situation of interest, and the people to be studied may create barriers to the acquisition of rich data. As part of your general task of evaluating data sites, then, you must be concerned with the possible existence of such barriers, with assessing their seriousness, and with considering if or how they can be negotiated. These considerations direct attention to the problem of access, which is one of the most widely discussed topics in the literature on qualitative methodology, and for good reason. Without successfully negotiating access, research comes to a screeching halt. As well, access is not simply a one-shot deal that is negotiated once and for all; rather, it is negotiated and renegotiated throughout the research and is thus an ongoing process. As such, we shall encounter it again, especially in Chapters 3 and 4. Even then, however, we shall not have exhausted the topic, for the possible combinations of investigator, setting, and participant attributes generate an almost endless litany of discrete "access situations" (For a comprehensive and practical discussion of access and various access situations, see Feldman, Bell, and Berger 2003). Our more limited and realistic goal here and in later pages is to provide you, the investigator considering your own particular access situation, with "food for thought." In the current context of data site evaluation, we shall consider three general problem areas: (1) investigator relationship to setting, (2) ascriptive categories of researcher and researched, and (3) difficult settings.

1. **Investigator Relationship to Setting**
   In an insightful and now classic essay, Fred Davis (1973) has written about two opposing orientations or stances a researcher might take toward what he or she is studying. Conceived metaphorically as the "Martian" and the "Convert," these stances capture the "dilemma of distance" encountered by all researchers. The Martian sees distance as a passageway to knowing, the Convert views it as a barrier.

   > The Martian . . . yearns to grasp the human situation with wholly fresh or, better yet, strange eyes, in a blush of wonderment as it were. In order to do this he wants to divest himself completely of the vast array of unwitting cultural assumptions, rules of thumb, modes of sensibility and—were it somehow possible—the very language, which comprises the "cognitive stuff" of our everyday worlds and beings. . . . In contrast to the Martian's desire to escape and stand wholly outside the social ontological frame of his subjects in order to see how the frame is constructed, the Convert's overriding impulse is to immerse himself ever more deeply within the frame so that the distinctive subjective currents of the group may forcibly and directly reveal themselves to him. (1973, pp. 336, 338)

   Davis's metaphorical creatures represent very real methodological preferences and debates about those preferences within the social sciences. More profoundly, however, they symbolize a tension that many researchers feel or strive to feel *within themselves*. To ask questions of, to "make problematic," to "bracket" social life requires distance (Martian). To acquire intimate familiarity with social life from the vantage point of those studied, to know, that is, the mentioned distinction between an eye twitch and a wink, requires closeness (Convert). The sensitive investigator wishes not to be one or the other but to be *both* or *either* as the research demands. This, of course, implies experiencing the contrasting tensions of surrender on the one hand and distance on the other. Experiencing these countervailing pulls is often distressing, but such discomfort can best be viewed as a "productive tension" in the sense that it is likely to contribute to more nuanced understandings and a richer and more compelling fieldstudy.

   The point for the prospective investigator assessing for access is simply this: If you are already (or will become) a member in the setting, you almost "naturally" possess (or will possess) the convert stance. You have easy access to understanding. You need, therefore, at least initially, to seek mechanisms for distancing. Conversely, if you are an outsider to the setting, a stranger to the social life under investigation, your access to questioning will be equally natural. You need, then, to seek mechanisms for reducing that distance. The moral is this: Be neither discouraged nor overconfident about your relationship to the setting. Whatever that relationship, it is simultaneously an advantage and a drawback. (For further discussion, see Adler and Adler 1987; Emerson and Pollner 2001; Monti 1992; Pollner and Emerson 1983.)

2. **Ascriptive Categories of Researcher and Researched**
Virtually all social orders place emphasis, although in varying degrees, on ascriptive categories—such as gender, age, and race or ethnicity—as important criteria for differentiating among people. The implication of this persistent "social fact" for conducting fieldwork is that it sensitizes us to the possibility that "who" the researcher is, in contrast to "who" the researched are, may throw up barriers to the acquisition of rich data. Rosalie Wax's observations, based on her several fieldstudies conducted some time ago, still cut to the heart of this problem:

> Many tribal or folk societies not only maintain a strict division of labor between the sexes and ages, but the people who fall into these different categories do not converse freely or spontaneously with each other even when they eat, sleep and live in the same dwelling. For example, a young male anthropologist might live in an Indian household and even carry on with the Indian girls and yet learn very little about what women—old or young—think, say or do.... Conversely, I, as a middle-aged woman, was never able to converse openly or informally with either the old or the young Indian men at Thrashing Buffalo. The older men, even when I knew them fairly well, would tend to deliver lectures to me; the younger men, as was proper, were always too bashful or formally respectful to say much. With the Indian matrons, on the other hand, I could talk for hours. (Wax, *Doing Fieldwork*, 1971, pp. 141. Copyright 1971 The University of Chicago Press. Reprinted with permission; see also Wax 1979)

Wax is writing about a special situation of doing research among traditional groups in rural settings, but her general point is equally applicable to doing research in contemporary metropolitan areas. If you are male and want to study a beauty parlor clique composed of middle-aged women, for example, your chances of reaching the desired "intimate familiarity" are much more limited than if you were female.

During the past several decades, numerous fieldworkers have picked up on this issue and highlighted the contexts and ways in which ascriptive categories can throw up barriers to the acquisition of rich data (see, for example, Baca Zinn 2001; Golde 1986; Olesen 2000; Reinharz 1992, Chapters 2 and 3; Skeggs 2001; Warren 2001; Warren and Hackney 2000). Zavella (1996), for example, in writing about fieldwork among Chicanas, summarizes this dilemma in a fashion that can apply to research among numerous ascriptive categories:

> ... insiders are more likely to be cognizant and accepting of complexity and internal variation, are better able to understand the nuances of language

use, will avoid being duped by informants who create cultural performances for their own purposes, and are less apt to be distrusted by those they study. Some assert that ethnic insiders often have an easier time gaining access to a community similar to their own, and that they are more sensitive to framing questions in ways that respect community sensibilities. (p. 79)

While we acknowledge the importance of being aware of the different meanings that can be associated with ascriptive researcher attributes, we also are concerned that, if viewed en masse, such sensitivities can be reified in a fashion that solidifies ascriptive differences and makes them nonnegotiable. Ascriptive identity categories are, without question, realities—albeit socially constructed ones—and therefore need to be taken into account in planning your research. But they *should not be overemphasized*. Just because you do not share certain characteristics with the persons you wish to study, you should not automatically conclude that such research is impossible or even unusually difficult. An abundance of fieldstudies resoundingly contradicts any such conclusion. Being female and Jewish, for example, did not prevent Ruth Horowitz from developing a sensitive analysis of the world of Chicano gang members (1983) nor block Sherryl Kleinman's access to ministerial students of the United Methodist Church (1984). Being adults did not deny Patricia and Peter Adler (1998), William Corsaro (1985), Gary Alan Fine (1987), Nancy Mandell (1986, 1988), or Barrie Thorne (1993) intimate access to the world of children. Nor did being a young adult prevent Jaber Gubrium (1986) or Arlie Hochschild (1973) from studying the elderly. Similarly, being white did not prevent Elliot Liebow from producing a classic ethnography of the world of African-American streetcorner men (1967), any more than being a middle-class male prevented him from entering the subjective world of homeless women (1993). And being young, white, and educated neither blocked Mitchell Duneier's access to the (mostly) elderly and (mostly) African-American working-class clientele of a South Chicago cafeteria (1992) or to poor black men who worked and lived on the sidewalks of Sixth Avenue in New York's Greenwich Village (1999), nor prevented Loic Wacquant from studying mostly African-American boxers (1998a, b). Even granting validity to internally generated critiques of the discipline of cultural anthropology (e.g., Clifford and Marcus 1986; Kuklick 1991; Lal 1996; Marcus and Fischer 1986; Rosaldo 1989; Stocking 1989), much of its rich literature remains convincing testimony to the human capacity to negotiate ascriptive, national, and cultural differences. In light of these observations, it is useful to recount Robert Emerson's (2001) conclusions regarding the insider/outsider dilemma:

The insider/outsider dichotomy highlights the relative advantages of racial/ethnic, gender and age similarities and differences. The advantages of insider fieldwork are readily apparent—more facile entrée, a higher degree of trust, easier access to the nuances of local interaction and meaning. The advantages of conducting fieldwork as an outsider are initially less apparent but can nonetheless be compelling. First, outsiders may not be held accountable to the demands for local in-group solidarity, such as appeals to ethnic loyalty, or to the restrictions of local status distinctions. Fieldworkers who are "insiders" to the local society may encounter problems on both counts.... Second, outsider fieldworkers may be able to pursue lines of inquiry and to ask questions closed off to insiders.... Third, outsider fieldwork often generates distinctive sensitivity to and methodological self-consciousness about relational processes.... In contrast, fieldwork involving a close match between the social characteristics of the fieldworker and those studied often leave relational processes implicit and unexamined. (p. 122; see also Merton 1972)

3. **Difficult Settings**
Social settings understandably vary in terms of the ease to which they can be accessed and studied. Gathering rich data through observation in open public settings can usually be accomplished with a minimum of difficulty with respect to negotiating and maintaining access (Cahill 1990; L. Lofland 1985b; Morrill, Snow, and White 2005; Nash and Nash 1994; Ortiz 1994; Robbins, Sanders, Cahill, 1991). Such is also the case with fieldwork in many quasi-public places, such as restaurants, coffee shops, bars and clubs (Allon 1979; Cavan 1966; Katovich and Reese 1987; Reid, Aman, and Bonham-Crecilius 2005; Snow, Robinson, and McCall 1991). But there are many social settings and sets of behaviors for which the negotiation and maintenance of access is much more complicated than, say, simply showing up, ordering a beer, and hanging out.

Settings that are more problematic in terms of access can vary in a multitude of ways. Some, for example, can be quite complex organizationally, involving both vertical and horizontal structures and multiple points of entrée. Certainly given the number of formal organizations (e.g., corporations, factories, hospitals, schools) that have been studied in a compelling manner via participant observation and intensive interviewing (Buroway 1979; Dalton 1959; Kanter 1977; Kunda 1992; Morrill 1995; Roy 1959/60; see Morrill and Fine, 1997, for a summary of organizational ethnography), one would be hard-pressed to claim that they are necessarily more difficult to study than other social settings or contexts. But what is certain is that access to them is more difficult to secure than it is in many other contexts. Access to some groups and organizations may also be complicated by internal conflicts and factionalization or schisms. When such is the case, association with one faction or group may not only preclude access to other groups or divisions within the setting, but may even get one labeled as an adversary. This occurred, for example, in Burke Rochford's (1985, 1994) ethnographic fieldstudy of the Hare Krishna movement in the United States. As the movement factionalized and eventually broke into antagonistic wings, some members saw Rochford as being too strongly anchored to the Los Angeles community and thus discredited him accordingly. As one member complained in assessing Rochford's scholarship on the movement:

> You grew to form a very strong identification and empathy with the fringe community. And that seriously colors a lot of work, the analysis. I know in

many cases what you are saying is party line LA fringe point of view. Admittedly you got very involved with them. . . . We feel that the way you look at the data is seriously colored by that. (1992, p. 109)

Studying up into the higher reaches of an organization or class structure can also be difficult to negotiate because "gatekeepers" often protect the occupants of these lofty strata from intrusion or disturbance and, as such, access may require working with, through, or around gatekeepers. As with research on formal organizations, an increasing number of studies—of elite surgeons (Bosk 1979), upper-class women (Kendall 2002; Ostrander 1984), business executives and corporate elite (Morrill 1995, Thomas 1994), entertainment elite (Gamson 1994), philanthropic contributors to social causes (Ostrander 1995), nuclear weapons researchers (Gusterson 1996), and national defense intellectuals (Cohn 1987)—make clear that this kind of research is doable. But access typically takes greater work and strategic enterprise than is the case in many other contexts (see, for example, Bosk 1996; Cassell 1988; Gamson 1995; Hoffman 1980; Morrill 1995; Ostrander 1993; Thomas 1995).

Additionally, some settings or behaviors may pose challenges because they are short-lived and thus provide a narrow window of research opportunity. Examples of such ephemeral activities include many behaviors that traditionally have been discussed under the rubric of "collective behavior" (Lofland 1985; McPhail 1991; Turner and Killian 1987), such as protest gatherings, celebratory crowds, and so-called panics. Such events are not always on the community calendar, and when they are, it is for a very brief time, which makes studying them difficult to coordinate with the institutional schedule of many researchers. This is not to say that collective behavior forms have been neglected. To the contrary, there are a number of fieldstudies of them (e.g., Lofland and Fink 1982; McPhail 1969; Snow, Zurcher, and Peters 1981; Wright 1978). It is to say, however, that such research is probably best done when planned with anticipation of the events in mind and using a team of researchers. The Center for Disaster Research, established in 1963 at Ohio State University and relocated to the University of Delaware in 1985, provides a prototype for such research, as it was organized to have research teams respond immediately to disasters when they occur (for a sample of associated projects, see Dynes and Tierney 1994).

Other settings may be difficult to access because of perceptions of suspicion and danger. For example, some locations may be defined by state officials as "forbidden terrain," as Cuba has been for U.S. researchers for decades (Fuller 1988). Alternatively, access may be problematic because of feelings of distrust within the setting—distrust based on fears of state action as was the case among the Aryan survivalists studied by Richard Mitchell (2002) or on fears of street-level dangers, such as those experienced by rival individuals and groups in the "cocaine culture" (Bourgois 1995, Morales 1989; Williams 1989; Williams, Dunlap, Johnson, and Hamid 1992). Even in the absence of perceived threat, some social groups, even seemingly innocuous groups like the Masons and Greek letter societies, routinely shroud themselves in secrecy and thus hamper opportunities for gaining intimate familiarity with them.

While we consider it appropriate for the prospective investigator to assess the possible difficulties inherent in the setting of interest, we do not wish to suggest that you should necessarily avoid difficult settings. The difficulty may, on closer inspection, turn out to be illusory. But even if it is real, difficulty does not necessarily equal impossibility, as the preceding citations clearly attest. And if the setting or situation is an especially significant or interesting one, even a partial study of it will be better than none at all.

C. Evaluating for Physical and Emotional Risks

In addition to the various "difficult" settings and situations that can make access a troublesome undertaking, some settings may be "difficult" in two other ways. They may confront researchers with immediate risks to their physical well-being, or they may cause emotional distress. We discuss in Chapter 4 (Section I.D) various physical dangers and risks sometimes associated with fieldwork. Here we briefly take a look at the emotional distresses sometimes associated with this approach.

There have long been urban legend-like rumors and gossip among fieldworkers about how fellow practitioners have been emotionally traumatized or overwhelmed. One "hears," for example, of a person who had established herself in a setting (say, a cancer ward), but within weeks had found it much too emotionally painful to continue, and simply withdrew. But one doesn't need to resort to legend or rumor to acquire a sense of the sometimes emotionally distressing character of fieldwork. Consider, for example, Napoleon Chagnon's first encounter with the Yanomamo Indians of Venezuela. Upon entering the village, he recounts:

> I looked up and gasped when I saw a dozen burly, naked, filthy, hideous men staring at us down the shafts of their drawn arrows! Immense wads of green tobacco were stuck between their lower teeth and lips, making them look even more hideous, and strands of dark green slime dripped or hung from their nostrils. . . . My next discovery was that there were a dozen or so vicious, underfed dogs snapping at my legs, circling me as if I were going to be their next meal. I just stood there holding my notebook, helpless and pathetic. Then the stench of the decaying vegetation and filth struck me, and I almost got sick. I was horrified. (1983, p. 10)

Although few access encounters are as dramatically shocking or traumatizing as this, in large part because most sociological fieldworkers study settings and groups in their own society, there is increasing acknowledgment and discussion of the range of emotions associated with ethnographic fieldwork. Anxiety, doubt, divided loyalties, grief, guilt, anger and disgust (even horror, in extreme cases like Chagnon's), and fear of failure in one's research are just some of the prominent emotions that scholars have discussed when reflecting on their fieldwork. Research with disadvantaged or unfortunate groups or individuals often results in emotional distress, as in Linda Dunn's (1991) sleeplessness and depression while studying battered women and Martha Copp's (Kleinman and Copp 1993) feelings of guilt over her privileged status in comparison to her informants in a sheltered workshop for the mentally and physically disabled. Yet other researchers have discussed the anxiety and distress of conflicting goals and loyalties in their research, as in Barrie Thorne's (1979) experience as both a researcher and political activist in the draft resistance movement of the 1960s. Further, as Jennifer Pierce (1995a, 1995b) has noted in her reflections on her fieldwork in a large law firm, researcher's feelings may shift over time, as did her feelings, from guilt over the possibility of betraying her male lawyer informants to resentment and anger about the exploitation of women in the firm. But while there are undoubtedly researchers who have abandoned projects because of the perceived or actual emotional toll they wrought, the foregoing examples illustrate the value of perseverance in the face of challenging emotional feelings. As with potential physical dangers, so with emotional perils: you are well advised to do your best to anticipate them and be prepared to handle them in ways that maintain your physical and emotional health. We would also emphasize that physical and emotional risks typically are no more or less prevalent in the research context than in everyday life.

D. Evaluating for Ethics

Ethical issues are an integral part of the research experience as much as they are a part of the experience of everyday life. We shall repeatedly be concerned with ethical matters in the following chapters, as they are relevant to the entire research process, from its inception through publication of the findings. Here, in the context of data site evaluation, two critical and closely related questions require the prospective investigator's serious consideration. First, should this particular group, setting, situation, or question be studied by *anyone*? Second, should this group, setting, situation, or question be studied by *me*? In asking these questions of yourself, you are assessing the potential negative *consequences* (see below) that the research or its publication might have for various parties (including yourself) and your ethical evaluation of these consequences.

Traditionally, neither question was problematic in social science. Rather, the conventional wisdom held that knowledge was always better than ignorance and that, therefore, everything that could be studied should be studied by anyone who had or could obtain access. In the last forty years, however, that conventional wisdom has come under increasing challenge.

Relative to the question of anyone doing a particular study, three kinds of challenges have been made. First, some scholars have cautioned about research on oppressed and less powerful groups because the findings might be appropriated by the more powerful to advance their interests vis-à-vis the interests and well-being of the groups studied (Sjoberg 1967a; Tunnell 1998). Second, a significant body of opinion in the social sciences holds that all, or almost all, covert research is unethical because it involves intentional deception of the observed by the observer (Allen 1997; Bulmer 1982; Erikson 1967; Warwick 1975). The American Sociological Association's *Code of Ethics* is more or less in accord with this argument, as it prohibits covert research except in those situations in which the following conditions obtain: "(1) the research involves no more than minimal risk for research participants, and (2) the research could not practicably be carried out were informed consent to be required" (1997).

And third, some feminists initially argued (sometimes only implicitly) that research in which there is an absence of equality and full sympathy between researcher and researched violates the tenets of feminist ethics (see, e.g., McNaron 1985; Oakley 1981; Stacey 1988; but see Reinharz 1993, pp. 72–75, and El-Or 1992, on the limits of intimacy with informants). A corollary line of thought recommends that feminist research be collaborative and at the service of the objectives and needs of the researched population (Cancian 1992, 1993; Taylor and Rupp 2005). However, other feminist scholars have questioned the capacity of feminist ethnography to realize these idealized principles. Diane Wolf, for instance, suggests that:

> Although feminist researchers may attempt to equalize relationships while in the field through empathic and friendly methods, these methods do not transform the researcher's positionality or locationality. The "equality" is short-lived and illusory because the researcher goes home when she is finished, reflecting her privileged ability to leave. This does not mean that attempts at more egalitarian field relationships should be abandoned but rather that they should be seen more realistically. (1996, p. 35)

Wherever you may stand with respect to these ethical challenges, you are still confronted with the question of how you should proceed. While we might wish to suggest that the decision whether or not to study a group, setting, or situation should be left to your judgment and discretion, we would be remiss to do so. Decisions regarding the ethics and legality of research involving human subjects increasingly have come under institutional scrutiny in recent years. We will discuss this issue in more detail in the next chapter, but we must note here that in order to pursue a research project you will need to demonstrate conscientious concern with institutional protocols (including completion of appropriate documents and, possibly, training) for the protection of human subjects. While all professional academic associations now have ethical guidelines that members are encouraged to follow, institutional protocols are issued by Institutional Review Boards (IRB) mandated by the federal government to ensure the protection of human subjects in scientific research. While some fieldwork— such as that conducted in "normal educational settings" and public places—may be granted exemption from IRB evaluation (upon written request), other research may require a full IRB review, including completion of "a standard protocol describing the risks and benefits of the research, as well as procedures to secure the informed consent of research 'subjects' and to safeguard confidentiality" (Emerson 2001, p. 146). As a result, you need to familiarize yourself with the federal and institutional definitions of ethical and legal research in order to assess the viability of potential fieldwork topics and settings.

E. Evaluating for Personal Consequences

A final matter warranting consideration concerns the personal consequences of one's accomplished research. Because it involves peering into an unknowable future, this kind of assessment is more a matter of guesswork than are assessments for the proximate issues of appropriateness, access, risk, or ethics. But the fact that personal consequences cannot be known with anything approximating full certainty does not mean that they cannot be considered and pondered. Imperfect forethought is better than no thought at all.

The successful completion of a research project typically occasions, for most of us most of the time, a sense of self-satisfaction. And why not? We have engaged in systematic research that has yielded a written product that is descriptively illuminating and analytically interesting (see Chapters 8 and 9). It may also provide sufficient reason for others—colleagues, the people studied, a broader readership—to respond favorably to us. Unfortunately, however, the personal consequences of a completed project are not always so positive. Three examples should give you a flavor of what we mean.

First, there is the possibility that you will experience what might be called an "ethical hangover": a persistent sense of guilt or unease over what is viewed as a betrayal of the people under study. The closer your emotional relationship to those persons, the more you can feel that both in leaving the setting and in transforming your personal understanding of it into public knowledge, you have committed a kind of treason. It is not clear whether there is any way to forestall this experience. In fact, some would argue that it is the "just desserts" of the naturalistic investigator (Davis 1961, p. 365). Just or not, it is common for fieldworkers to experience a sense of guilt or unease during their research and particular during the process of disengagement (see, for example, Heilman 1980; Stacey 1988; Thorne 1979). Such was the experience of David Snow as he began extricating himself from the Nichiren Shoshu Buddhist movement he had been studying from the vantage point of a rank-and-file convert for nearly a year and a half:

> Having been involved in little else other than Nichiren Shoshu for well over a year, it had . . . grown on me. . . . Additionally, and perhaps even more confounding, I had come to know a number of fellow participants not merely as subjects, respondents, or members of some offbeat religious

group, but as very real and personable human beings. As a consequence, I . . . felt somewhat like the con artist who does whatever is necessary in order to set up the "mark," and then, after gaining his confidence, blows the scene with the "take." On the one hand I had assumed the role of an active but controlled and skeptical participant who was treated first and foremost by the "real" members as a fellow human being and participant, and secondarily, if at all, as a sociological investigator; while, on the other hand, I was running off and using what I had learned . . . in the role of sociologist. As a consequence, not only was I enmeshed in a kind of role conflict situation, but I also found myself in a kind of ethical double bind that was a source of anxiety that rendered the disengagement . . . process more difficult than initially anticipated. (1993, pp. 20–21)

As the second example, there is the very small but nonetheless real possibility that your report will be of interest to the criminal justice system and that you may be called upon to divulge information that you withheld from the final report (the real names of participants, for example) or information that you may have acquired subsequent to the research but that you consider still covered by the confidentiality assurances (discussed just below and in later chapters) given during the research. Consider the case of Rik Scarce, a graduate student at Washington State University who, in 1993, refused to answer a grand jury's questions about participants in the animal rights movement who were the subjects of his 1990 book, *Ecowarriors: Understanding the Radical Environmental Movement* (the grand jury was investigating a 1991 raid on a Pullman, Washington research laboratory). As a consequence of his refusal, Scarce was incarcerated in the Spokane County jail for 159 days until a judge ruled that his detention had surpassed the law's intent of "coercion" and instead had become "punitive" (Monaghan 1993b). Note that Scarce's decision "not to tell" was anything but idiosyncratic. He argued that he was "bound by the American Sociological Association's code of ethics, one part of which required at the time that scholars maintain confidentiality even when this information enjoys no legal protection or privilege and legal force is applied" (Monaghan 1993a, p. A9), and the association supported this argument, filing an amicus brief on his behalf (Levine 1993). Since then, Scarce (1994) and others (Adler and Adler 2002; Leo 1995) have made a compelling case for the federal government to provide field researchers with the right to protect ethnographer's various communications with their informants.

Most well-done fieldwork reports seem to be met with praise from at least some quarters and no reaction at all from others. But there is always the possibility of a third sort of negative consequence. In addition to praise and disinterest, your written report may generate significant condemnation from your colleagues, as happened with Laud Humphreys' *Tearoom Trade* (1975) (see, for example, Warwick 1975, 1982); from the people studied, as happened in the case of Vidich and Bensman's *Small Town in Mass Society* (1968), or from both, as happened with William F. Whyte's *Street*

Corner Society several decades after its publication. (See, for example, the special issue of the *Journal of Contemporary Ethnography* edited by Adler, Adler, and Johnson, 1992, devoted to a reassessment of Whyte's classic.) Among the myriad possible charges, you may be criticized for betraying your informants, putting them at risk, writing unflattering portraits of them, not getting the story right, or getting the story right but not telling it in the right way.

In urging you to give thought to future consequences you cannot possibly predict, we risk being viewed as alarmist, as causing unnecessary and unprofitable worry. But it seems to us that this is one instance in which the following "cliche" truly deserves to be cast as "folk wisdom": To be forewarned is, at least to some degree, to be forearmed.

IV. A Concluding Word of Caution

These words of advice should not be construed as suggesting that the various problems and issues associated with site selection and its negotiation can all be resolved or determined beforehand and that you can then simply proceed without difficulty to put your research plan into practice. Nothing could be further from the truth. Naturalistic research is first and foremost *emergent*. Today's solutions may become tomorrow's problems; tomorrow's problems may provide special research opportunities the day after. "Who" you are at the beginning of the research is not necessarily the same "who" that will emerge at the end. Ethical decisions made before entering the field may prove moot; other unforeseen and perhaps unsolvable dilemmas may arise. This emergent character is what gives "being in the field" its edge, its complexity, its vigor, and, for many people, its excitement; it is also what necessitates *flexibility* on the part of the investigator.

You evaluate data sites, then, not because doing so will make your life as a researcher a bed of roses, but because doing so may help to remove a few of the thorns.

CHAPTER 3

GETTING IN

The process of deciding what is interesting to study and whether you can gain ethical access to appropriate settings may involve conversations and consultations with others, but the decisions themselves are personal. When decision is translated into action, when your intention to do research is translated into beginning that research, then you encounter the first truly social moment of naturalistic investigation: getting in and gaining the acceptance of the people being studied.

It is one thing to decide for yourself about interest, appropriateness, accessibility, and ethics; it is quite another to get all of the relevant parties to go along with your plan.

In some forms of research, the investigator has considerable power over the research "subjects." Laboratory animal research or medical research with captive human populations are extreme examples. But in naturalistic fieldstudies, the researcher does not exercise this kind of control. In this tradition, you look at and/or listen to people either because the people freely agree to it or because they do not know they are being studied. And since there is little or nothing to stop them from refusing to be interviewed, from denying an observer entrée into their lives, or from throwing out or shutting out a secret investigator who is "uncovered," getting in is of understandable concern to all potential field researchers.

The specific form of relationship a prospective investigator has or will develop with the people or setting of interest generates its own set of problems, ethical questions, and solutions regarding the process of entrée. The varieties of such relationships have been diversely formulated. Buford Junker's (1960) well-known typology of fieldwork roles—the complete observer, the participant observer, the complete participant, the observer participant—is one example. Schatzman and Strauss (1973) distinguished among watching from the outside, passive presence, limited interaction, active control, the observer as participant, and participation with hidden identity. Adler and Adler (1987) contrast what they see as the more "detached" roles of observer, observer-interactant, observer-interactant-participant, and observer-interactant-participant-investigator with the more "involved" roles of peripheral member, active member, complete member, and good-faith member. Such elaborate formulations are quite useful in some contexts, but for our purposes, a simpler set of distinctions will suffice.

We shall consider the "getting in" aspect of naturalistic research as experienced (1) by unknown investigators in both public or open settings and closed or private settings, and (2) by known investigators who are either full participants in the setting or outsiders whose research role is primary. We will conclude this chapter by discussing two additional relevant problems: legal, political, and bureaucratic barriers, and the question of confidentiality. However, before discussing these concerns, it is useful to consider more carefully a number of the ways in which settings differ in a fashion that is relevant to the investigative roles field researchers might assume.

I. Types of Settings

The relative ease or difficulty of accessing social settings is affected by a number of interacting factors. The one most often discussed concerns their placement on the previously mentioned public/private continuum. Public places are customarily thought of as spatial areas and physical structures in a community in which there is freedom of access, such as sidewalks, parks, and malls. In contrast, private places include spatial and structural domains that are off-limits to all but acknowledged inhabitants (e.g., residents and employees) and members or guests. Examples include homes, apartments, offices, and the physical locale of many clubs. Often scholars mistakenly cluster social settings or spaces at one end of the continuum without considering the extent to which there can be variability in the regulation of behavior in those settings. In some parks, for example, there is wide latitude in behavior, whereas in other parks, behavior can be more constrained. Thus, freedom of access does not necessarily imply freedom of action or the absence of behavioral constraint. Additionally, accessibility to social settings can vary in terms of the personal characteristics or attributes of the actors, whether ascribed, as with sex, age, and race, or achieved, as with education and occupation. Accordingly, some settings are inclusive in the sense that access is not contingent on specifiable personal characteristics, whereas other settings can be quite exclusive in the sense that access is contingent on certain personal attributes, be they ascribed or achieved.

Taking these three dimensions of variation into account, social settings can be usefully differentiated in terms of the restrictiveness of their accessibility. The least restrictive, and thus most open, include those "public places" in which entrée and continuing presence is not contingent on specific activities or characteristics. Somewhat more restrictive but still relatively open are those "quasi-public places" in which continuing presence is dependent upon engagement in a limited range of activities or one or more personal attributes. Restaurants, bars, coffeehouses, and public restrooms are examples. Even more restrictive and less open are what might be thought of as "quasi-private" settings in the sense that access is associated with the possession of certain credentials or attributes, such as being an employee or a recognizable member. Finally, the most restrictive and closed settings are "private places" in which access is based on actual or defacto ownership, office incumbency, or personal invitation or appointment.

These four types of social settings comprise a kind of "access ladder" that is relevant to gaining entrée in the sense that it should sensitize you to the relationship between the location of the setting you choose to study on this ladder and some of the factors you have to take into account in order to negotiate initial access to the setting. The relative importance of these factors and their negotiability can vary depending on whether you are an unknown or known investigator.

II. The Unknown Investigator

Getting in is not really a problem if you are not known as a researcher to the people you are studying. If you are a newcomer and there are no behavioral or ascriptive restrictions on entrée or if you already have a role within the setting, all you need to do is begin logging data "on the sly." What *is* problematic is the *ethical status* of covert research.

In this section, we consider three types of hidden research in relation to the different types of settings. Probably the least controversial form is research conducted in public and quasi-public places because these are the least restrictive and most open settings. Doing covert research in a quasi-private setting in which you are already a member is more questionable. The most controversial research arrangement involves the assumption of a role or an identity in a private or quasi-private setting for the secret purpose of conducting research.

Two qualifications are in order before we proceed. First, some forms of naturalistic research lend themselves more readily than others to covert research. For example, it is easier, in most instances, to conduct participant observation secretly than to engage in intensive interviewing secretly because the continued probing, unless done very deftly, is likely to arouse suspicion about one's identity and interests. While it is possible to interview "informally" without fully letting on that one is doing so (Riecken 1969; Snow, Zurcher, and Sjoberg 1982), it takes considerable skill and interactional savvy to engage secretively in full-scale intensive interviewing. Therefore, the following discussion applies only to participant observation.

Second, the types of settings that we discuss above are ideal types, conceptualized by us in this particular way for the utility they provide in thinking about entrée. While it is analytically useful to describe settings in this manner, real-world settings do not necessarily fall into such discrete categories. Whether a setting is "quasi-public" or "quasi-private," for instance, may not be all that obvious and may even change at times depending on your vantage point or role.

A. Public and Quasi-Public Settings

Public and quasi-public settings offer relatively open opportunity for observation. Both of these types of settings require situationally appropriate appearance and behaviors, but the range of behaviors accepted in public settings is particularly extensive. In a city park one must dress within an acceptable, albeit wide, range of attire and adhere to the normative expectations of public behavior (e.g., not appearing to attend too closely to the activities of others), but it is possible to aimlessly hang out without drawing attention or disapproval to oneself. Most people are allowed to be in public settings without having to engage in specific behaviors. In quasi-public settings, on the other hand, behavior is more constrained by the functions of the setting, such that participants must engage in some subset of setting-specific behavior. Aside from such constraints, participant observation in public and quasi-public places presents relatively few obstacles, thus making it relatively easy to assume the role of an unknown investigator.

Examples of field researchers assuming this role in public and quasi-public places are fairly abundant. When Lyn Lofland (1985b) observed public places (for example, waiting areas of bus depots and airports), she simply entered and sat down. When Spencer Cahill and his students (1985) studied public restrooms, their entrée "problems," aside from the obvious constraint associated with gender-specific restrooms, involved only the physical skills necessary to get through the appropriate doors. Similarly, Elijah Anderson's (1990) "access" to interclass and interracial street interaction required nothing more complex than his physical presence in the public areas of a mixed neighborhood. Likewise, there was little Allison Munch (2005) had to do other than to show up and take a seat to access a sports audience that followed an amateur men's softball team in her study of a "spectator community" in a southwest city. However, as she came to befriend and converse with a number of the regular attendees, she would sometimes indicate her research interests. But her major identity and orientation throughout the research was as a "girlfriend" of one of the players and as a member of the community. In some studies, research is conducted covertly in both public and quasi-public settings, as with Christine Horne's, Kris McIlwaine's, and Kristie Taylor's (2005) study of adult control of children in malls and retail stores, restaurants, parks, playgrounds, a zoo, an airport, bus stops, and so on. In all of these cases, as well as others, accessing and studying these settings as unknown investigators was relatively uncomplicated.

While it might be argued that such research is unethical inasmuch as it involves deceit by omission if not commission, serious ethical debate seldom lingers on this research situation. Presumably the impossibility, if not the ludicrousness, of removing the deception is one reason. As Julius Roth noted, "When we are observing a crowd welcoming a hero, it is obviously absurd to say that we should warn everybody in the crowd that a sociologist is interpreting their behavior" (1970, p. 279). The presumption that no harm can come to any of the people observed is another reason. A third, perhaps, is the frequent "ho-hum" attitude of people when they learn they are being researched, as was the case with the "spectator community" members studied by Munch when they learned of her research interests.

B. **Private and Quasi-Private Settings**

The serious ethical questioning about covert research begins when the researcher moves out of the public realm and into the private, that is, into a closed setting, access to which is not granted to just "anybody." Gary Fine has referred to this situation as "deep cover":

> In research studies in which subjects are not aware that they are under investigation, the position of the researcher is structurally equivalent to that of the undercover intelligence agent, although presumably there is a different set of motives. In that situation, the researcher may witness a wide variety of behaviors but simultaneously may find it difficult to inquire about any of these behaviors without the cover being suspect. A cover that is blown in such a situation—when subjects discover that their *new member is* actually a professional observer—may have profound implications. This uncovering discredits not only the research . . . but [also] the researcher . . . , and perhaps the entire scientific enterprise. (1980, p. 124, emphasis added)

It is precisely the "spy" quality of covert research in closed settings that raises questions about its propriety in social science. In fact, as we noted in Chapter 2, some people argue that an investigator who takes a position for the purpose of secretly researching the setting is committing the most unethical research act in the naturalistic tradition. Certainly the high value that feminists place on equality and sympathy between researcher and researched is badly and baldly compromised by the knowledge imbalance inherent in covert research (Skeggs 2001). Yet, other social scientists take a more nuanced approach, having no moral difficulties with doing covert research in public settings and relatively minor concerns about it when initiated after one already has become embedded in the setting, as when someone decides to study the line of work they have been pursuing for some time, but who are adamant that entering a setting for the purpose of secret research should not be allowed (Bulmer 1982; Erikson 1967). Julius Roth's comments, made over 30 years ago on what might be viewed as moral hair-splitting among social scientists, are still apt:

> Does the manner in which one comes to be a secret observer affect the morality of the situation? Is it moral if one gets a job in a factory to earn tuition and then takes advantage of the opportunity to carry out a sociological study, but immoral to deliberately plant oneself in the factory for the express purpose of observing one's fellow workers? If the outcome is the same—e.g., if the manner in which the observations are used is the same—I for one see no moral difference in these two situations, but I find some of my colleagues do not agree with this position. (1970, p. 279)

Wherever one stands on the ethics of covert research, it is often difficult to reach an unambiguous position without considering various overlapping ethical issues, each of which can be weighted differently by different researchers and commentators. These include the likelihood of harm, and to whom (Will covert research harm the researched?), the prospect of benefit, and to whom (Will the failure to do the research perpetuate or obfuscate an existing harm?), and the theoretical importance of a setting that can never be studied openly.

Additionally, we must admit to the view that the more adamant calls for the pristine purity of openness are just a touch naïve in several ways. First, the distinction between covert and overt research is often blurred and clouded in actual practice. In his analysis of the practice of covert participant observation, for example, Richard Hilbert (1980, p. 71) argues that there is "a mutually determining relationship between secret and open observation" in the sense that "the techniques that it takes to protect secrecy are those very techniques that are used to display public membership." Attending to and acting in accordance with setting-specific behaviors—whether in a park, at a party, or in an executive's office—are not only normal membership activity, but will be seen as such by other participants. Hilbert's point is that typically there is little discernible difference between behaviors that researchers and ethicists might label as methodologically manipulative or secretive and those that regular members engage in to sustain the setting-specific activity in the first place.

Partly because of this overlap between behaviors associated with secretive and open research, ethnographic researchers do not, despite the presumptions of the moralists, have complete control over "who" the researched will take them to be. Field researchers "may seek to present themselves in one manner or another," as Richard Mitchell has observed (1993, p. 12), "but subjects can and usually do reinterpret, transform, or sometimes altogether reject these presentations in favor of their own." They sometimes forget as well. For example, Snow and Anderson (1993) were at times surprised by the tendency for their homeless informants to treat them as homeless rather than as researchers, despite their efforts to be forthright about their identities and purposes for being in the field. This was dramatically illustrated one evening when Anderson was giving a homeless woman, whom they had known for some time and who was a key informant, a ride to an abandoned warehouse where she intended to spend the night. As she got out of the car, she asked, "Where are you guys staying tonight?" After Anderson said he was staying in his apartment and Snow was staying in his home, she replied incredulously, "Wow, you guys are living in style."

Blanket arguments against covert research also strike us as naïve and problematic in failing to recognize that there are many social settings in which entrée, and the building of rapport with setting members, needs to proceed slowly and gingerly. In some situations fieldworkers may well be able to develop viable and accepted open roles as researchers over time, but to announce one's research interests upon first entering the setting would lead to being rejected forthright. Further, sometimes one wishes to approach a setting in an exploratory manner before deciding to commit to studying it. Both of these kinds of concerns were present in Jennifer Lois's fieldstudy of a volunteer mountain search and rescue organization. In her early, exploratory forays to the group's meetings she took a low profile and did not divulge that she was taking fieldnotes and conducting proto-research, fearing that such revelations would inhibit her relations with members. Reflecting later, she observed:

> I was not entirely comfortable entering this setting covertly, although . . . it turned out to be necessary in order to establish trust with highly suspicious members. Although some may object to my use of the covert role, I believe it was an appropriate methodological tactic to aid me in gaining entrée. (2003, p. 42)

We expect that many fieldworkers have engaged in similar short-term covert participant observation and that their research would have been unnecessarily complicated, if not impossible, had they not taken this staged approach to revealing their research interests.

Given the relevance of the foregoing issues to a determination of the appropriateness and ethicality of covert research, we believe that the ethically sensitive, thoughtful, and knowledgeable investigator is the best judge of whether covert research is justified. However, the kind of research stance or position you take with respect to the setting or group studied is neither merely your decision nor a matter that you can negotiate alone with the members of the setting you plan to study. As noted in Chapter 2, you will also have to consult and acquire the approval of your college's or university's Institutional Review Board. Accordingly, we would suggest that you undertake no covert research (at least none in private and quasi-private settings) before you have acquainted yourself with the problems, debates, and dilemmas associated with such research and with local IRB protocols and mandates. As well, you should be familiar with the code of ethics (if any) of your discipline, and you should know how covert research is viewed within relevant subdisciplinary clusters. Beyond that, the following books and book chapters are recommended as useful discussions of research ethics and their intersection with the issue of covert research.

- Chapter 23 on "The Ethics of Ethnography" by Elizabeth Murphy and Robert Dingwall, in *Handbook of Ethnography* edited by Paul Atkinson, Coffey, Delamont, Lofland, and Lofland (2001).
- Chapter 3 on "Ethical Issues" by Bruce L. Berg, *Qualitative Research Methods for the Social Sciences* (Fifth Edition) (2004).
- *Walking the Tightrope: Ethical Issues for Qualitative Researchers*, edited by Will C. van den Hoonard (2002).
- Special Issue of *The American Sociologist*, Volume 26 (1995).

- *Secrecy and Fieldwork* by Richard G. Mitchell, Jr. (1993).
- *The Politics and Ethics of Fieldwork* by Maurice Punch (1986).
- *Secrets: On The Ethics of Concealment and Revelation*, especially Chapter 15 on "Intrusive Social Science Research," by Sissela Bok (1983).

III. The Known Investigator

Field researchers often assume that the major entrée problems confronting the known investigator are *strategic* rather than ethical. After all, if the researcher's identity is known, then there is nothing to camouflage, nothing to hide. As we just noted, however, such an assumption implies a rather simplistic distinction between overt and covert research. While this distinction may be useful for analytical purposes, it is essentially an artificial one. Most experienced fieldworkers understand this experientially, but few have articulated the reasons why this is so as clearly as Julius Roth, who emphasized that "*all research is secretive in some ways and to some degree—we never tell the subjects 'everything'*" (1970, p. 278, emphasis added). One reason Roth notes for the lack of candidness is that "the researcher usually does not know everything he[she] is looking for" upon initiating the study. And such initial uncertainty or ambiguity about what is interesting and worthy of attention is especially likely when the fieldworker is not a member of the setting or group in question, and is thus unfamiliar with the routines and practices that are constitutive of membership. Furthermore, it is because of this initial uncertainty about what is interesting that fieldstudies often generate serendipitous findings or conclusions. A related reason is that "some of the things [the researcher] finds of interest to study as the research goes on are things which the subjects might have objected to if they had been told about it in the beginning." Additionally, sometimes "the researcher does not want the subject's behavior influenced by . . . knowledge of what the observer is interested in" (Roth 1970, p. 279). Furthermore, there is often little point of trying to fully disclose one's range of research interests and hypotheses as they evolve because they are likely to be forgotten, as previously noted, or misunderstood or dismissed. As Roth noted in this regard:

> Even if the subjects of a study are given as precise and detailed an explanation of the purpose and procedure of the study as the investigator is able to give them, the subjects will not understand all the terms of the research in the same way that the investigator does. The terms used have different connotations to them, their experiential contexts differ, and their conceptions of the goals of the study are likely to be different. (1970, p. 279)

Finally, even when one negotiates entrée into a group or organization, the announcement and clarification of one's research identity is typically confined to interaction with key gatekeepers rather than reiterated in the course of interaction with each member in subsequent encounters.

Bearing in mind, then, that the ethical concerns engendered by covert research do not fully disappear with the decision to be a known investigator but are merely muted, let us turn to the strategic problem of entrée. This problem differs somewhat depending on where the setting falls on the public/private continuum. For reasons previously noted, gaining entrée to settings or scenes skewed toward the private end of the continuum, such as corporate offices, clubs, and exclusive, secretive groups, is much more complicated than gaining entrée into public places where there are few restrictions on access. Consequently, our discussion of the problem of entrée focuses on those contexts and settings that are more bounded and restrictive in terms of access. The problem of entrée also varies somewhat depending on whether one is already a full-fledged participant in the setting—that is, whether one is an insider or outsider.

A. The "Insider" Participant Researcher Role

The principle of "starting where you are," as we have seen, leads many naturalistic investigators to do research in their own "nests," as it were. Anyone who decides to conduct research openly, particularly in private and quasi-private places, has the task of making their intentions known, gaining cooperation from the setting participants, and, depending on the character of the setting, perhaps seeking formal permission. However, the participant researcher who is already a member or insider—what Adler and Adler (1987) call "complete membership"—has the advantage of already knowing the "cast of characters" or at least a segment of the cast. While the outside researcher must discover whom to ask or tell first, whether formal permission is required, whether a letter is necessary, and so forth, to the insider participant researcher, such knowledge is part of the badge of membership and easily (if not always successfully) put to use.

B. The "Outsider" Participant Researcher Role

The major strategic problem of getting in, then, falls to the outsider seeking admission to a setting for the purpose of observing it or securing access to individuals for the purpose of interviewing them. Researchers deal with a wide range of topics, settings, and situations, and the types of people who might stand between them and their research are necessarily much too varied for the strategies of getting through or around them to be succinctly codified. The experiences of many fieldworkers over the years, however, suggest that you are more likely to be successful in your quest for access if you enter negotiations armed with connections, accounts, knowledge, and courtesy.

1. Connections
There is a great deal of wisdom in the old saying, "It's not what you know but who you know that counts." Gaining entrée to a setting or getting permission to do an interview is not only greatly expedited if you have

"connections," but oftentimes access is well-nigh impossible without them. Two general strategies have been pursued in order to develop such facilitative connections. One is to exploit existing social ties to the setting or group of interest; the other is to identify key gatekeepers and develop ties with them. Calvin Morrill's (1995) fieldstudy of conflict management among corporate elites provides a clear illustration of the first strategy. Morrill (1995, p. 233) recounts how "a close relative," dubbed "Tag," who "was a longtime management consultant and respected member of the local business community," performed a number of critical functions in securing his access to the corporations that were the sites for the research. First, he helped Morrill identify five executives as "initial prospective informants because of their likelihood of being receptive to being interviewed." Second, Tag "'prime(d) the pump' by mentioning the project . . . to each of the five informants during routine meetings with them on other matters." And third, Tag allowed Morrill to invoke his name when necessary to facilitate gaining access.

Not all field researchers are quite so fortunate, however, as sometimes access is dependent on a whole chain of connections. In such cases, the initial contact may be at some social distance from the desired research setting but still able to link the prospective investigator to marginals who, in turn, link her or him to central actors. Such was the experience of Susan Ostrander in her study of upper-class women.

> For a period of months before beginning my project on upper-class women, a project that began as my Ph.D. dissertation, I talked with my fellow graduate students and professors about my plans. One day, a fellow graduate student told me she had worked on an electoral campaign with a woman she thought met the criteria for upper-class membership that I was intending to use. . . . I contacted this woman and told her of my interest in "learning about the role of women in some of the old and influential families in town." As is often true of first contacts, this woman was somewhat marginal to her class. . . . She nonetheless met the criteria of upper-class membership and, even more important, was known and respected by others. . . . She told me that it was important to "go in the right order. You have to start at the top." . . . She offered to call three of these [top] women for me and arrange their consent. She was successful, and I interviewed them, explaining my project by telling them that people knew a great deal about what men in families like theirs did with their lives but that very little was known about what women did. At the end of the interviews, I asked if they could refer me to other women like themselves, with similar backgrounds, and if I could use their names. They agreed and offered to call the women they mentioned to say they had spoken with me. I was in. (1993, pp. 9–10)

These examples are by no means exceptional. It seems quite typical for outside researchers to gain access to settings or persons through contacts they have already established. They cast about among their friends, acquaintances, and colleagues either for someone who is already favorably regarded by the person or persons who function as gatekeepers or for someone who can link them to such a person. This is, of course, the major principle involved in what, in interview studies, is called "snowball" or "chain-referral" sampling: a method for generating a field sample of individuals possessing the characteristics of interest by asking initial contacts if they could name a few individuals with similar characteristics who might agree to be interviewed (Berg 2004; Biernacki and Waldorf 1981; Schensul, LeCompte, Trotter, Cromley, and Singer 1999). Thus, after having been put in touch with her initial informant by a colleague, Ostrander then asked that woman to recommend others to whom she might talk, beginning the snowball or chain-referral process. In a similar vein, Morrill (1995, p. 234) employed this snowball strategy during his interviews with his initial executive informants, asking each of them if they knew of other executives who might be interested in the study. It was through these means that he was able to enlarge his sample of executives. Inasmuch as the experiences of Morrill and Ostrander are not unusual, a clear-cut directive follows: Wherever possible, you should try to use and/or build upon preexisting relations of trust to remove barriers to entrance.

The problem is that networking opportunities are not always available. Probably more often than not fieldworkers have no direct link, whether primary or secondary, to the setting or group of interest. But this is no reason for despair, as fieldworkers have long accommodated to the absence of group contacts by trying to develop ties with gatekeepers or other members who might facilitate access to other members and their activities. The classic example of this strategy is provided by William F. Whyte (1993), whose access to "Cornerville" was contingent on his development of relatively strong ties with "Doc" and "Chic," who subsequently came to function as his key informants.

2. Accounts

Part and parcel of establishing connections with those you wish to study is the account you provide for doing the research. Whether you are using the method of intensive interviewing or of participant observation, you are asking people to grant access to their lives, their activities, their minds, their emotions. They have every reason for wanting to know why they should allow such an intrusion. You should therefore plan to spend some time developing a careful explanation or account of the proposed research. Based on the experience of veteran fieldworkers, there are a number of clusters of factors that merit consideration when thinking about your entrée-level accounts. These include their content, the issue of timing, the matter of form, and their appropriate audience or targets.

a. Content

What do you need to tell your prospective hosts? How much detail should you provide? Here there are a number of interconnected "rules of thumb" suggested by a multitude of fieldstudies. First, keep your account as *brief* as possible. Most listeners are not going to be interested in the details of the researcher's "pet" enthusiasm. What they want is a brief and direct answer to the question, "Why should I let you?" and not a scholarly treatise. Should you be asked for more detail, you must certainly be prepared to supply it, but let the prospective informant ask for elaboration and clarification. Second, articulate your interests in a fashion that will be *accessible and comprehensible* to your informants. This means avoiding disciplinary jargon as well as discussion of the theoretical or methodological rationale for the study and your hypothetical hunches. Not only are your informants likely to be disinterested in this kind of detail, but your initial hunches and theoretical rationales may be proved irrelevant and even misguided as your study evolves and deepens. And even if your initial hunches are on target, their articulation runs the risk of producing what we will discuss later as a response effect. It is not surprising, then, that many researchers have found it sufficient, at least initially, to say little more than "I am writing a book on _____" or "I am interested in _____" (Horowitz 1996; Snow 1993; Williams quoted in Williams, Dunlap, Johnson, and Hamid 1992, p. 349). Third, *avoid identifying yourself in terms of labels or roles that may be alien, suspect, or accentuate status differences*, such as sociologist or criminologist. It is far better to indicate that you are a student or teacher at some nearby university. Not only are such role identities quite general and accessible to most people, but they are less likely to be seen as threatening as particular disciplinary identities. As well, they are sufficiently vague to allow for the development of more situationally appropriate roles as the research evolves. Fourth, you should be prepared to say something about *what's in it for your informants*, be they individuals, a group, or a formal organization. This involves framing the research in terms of an exchange relationship, such that both parties are beneficiaries of the research, which we will discuss in greater detail in Chapter 4 (Section II.A.2). Finally, it is advisable to make sure that your account is as *candid* as possible. If you have decided to conduct your research in a private or quasi-private setting, in which access is more problematic than in public settings, there is no point in complicating an already complicated situation by starting out with evasions or outright lies, or with promises (for example, censorship rights) you will not keep. There will be plenty of difficulties in getting along in the field despite the best of intentions and plans. Setting yourself up at the outset for later charges of deceit is simply begging unnecessary trouble. Still, it must be admitted that "fudging" one's account a bit—what Fine (1980) calls "shallow cover"—seems a fairly widespread practice (as when sociologists claim to be compiling "a recent history" rather than doing a sociological investigation). Admittedly, the above-mentioned advice to identify yourself in terms of general rather than specific roles can be construed as a kind of fudging. But it is neither a lie nor misrepresentation. Rather, such advice is congruent with the principle that it is best to begin with factual generalities about one's identities and interests, leaving the more specific aspects of identity and interest for articulation upon informant request or when and if such articulations are situationally appropriate.

b. *Timing*

At what point in the research process should you give your account? The answer seems obvious, right? You provide your account as you are trying to secure entrée. But the process is often more complex than that. First, there is the issue of whether you should divulge all of the important identifying information—who you are and what you are up to—during your initial entrée-gaining encounter, or whether the revelations should be phased or sequenced. The answer, of course, is that it depends on the context in which you are conducting your research and the extent to which it is organized hierarchically such that there are gatekeepers like secretaries who require some kind of account before granting contact with his/her administrative superiors. In such cases, it is clear that there is no one account, but that it is modified or adapted according to whom one is talking. Second, since most fieldstudies have an evolutionary character, there is likely little that can be said about specific interests and data possibilities at the project's outset, although later one may feel obligated to explain the project more fully, whether for ethical or personal interests, or both. Finally, since we have seen that informants sometimes forget what they were told earlier, we may have to retell our accounts accordingly. So just as access, particularly to private or quasi-private groups and settings, is typically negotiated and renegotiated during the course of the research, it is likely that not only will you need to reiterate your account throughout the course of the research, but you may have to modify it for different audiences and perhaps even alter or refine it as the research foci evolve and change.

c. *Form*

How should the account be communicated? Should it be delivered orally, via e-mail, or by regular mail? Again, the answer depends on the context of the research. If you are studying an informal group without a designated address or office, as with a street corner gang, high school clique, or homeless encampment, oral accounts are most appropriate. A written letter of endorsement from some institutional representative, such as a research advisor, might be useful for the purposes of verification, but there is probably little point of showcasing such institutional endorsements unless they are requested by the prospective informants. Not only might such official endorsements increase your contacts' suspicions about the research, but they may frame or color what is said or revealed if initial access is granted. Unfortunately, however, you may have little choice in how your account is communicated given the increasingly stringent mandates of the previously mentioned Institutional Review Boards. In some instances IRBs will require signed "informed consent" forms from informants, particularly for interviews, or insist that researchers read them "verbal consent scripts," which provide an overview of the study, its potential risks and benefits, and assurance of confidentiality. Apart from IRB issues, in research in private and quasi-private contexts in which there are not only addresses and offices but gatekeepers, the entrée-gaining account may not only differ as the researcher approaches different categories of participants, but it may also need to be communicated via various means. For example, Morrill's (1995, pp. 233–234) entrée-gaining interactions with secretarial gatekeepers were primarily oral, over the telephone or face-to-face, while his encounters with executives were multi-channeled, entailing introductory letters, telephone conversations, and office meetings.

d. Audience/Targets

The final set of factors that should be taken into account when formulating your account include the audience or targets. As implied above, accounts should be *appropriate to their audience:* The way the story is told (not the story itself) should be tailored to the people hearing it. What Morrill (1995) told the secretarial gatekeepers, for example, was more general and less elaborated than the accounts he presented in his initial encounters with the corporate executives whom he hoped to interview. Likewise, what Snow and Anderson (1993) revealed to their homeless informants about their research was less focused and detailed than what they told the various institutional representatives from whom they hoped to secure permission to examine their respective institutional records. Similarly, if studying young children in a school setting, what you tell the principal or director of the school and what you tell the children cannot be identical for a number of reasons, not the least important of which is the simple fact of age-related variation in language skills and information-processing abilities (on "accounting" to children, see Fine and Glassner 1979; Fine and Sandstrom 1988; Mandell 1988).

3. Knowledge

As we shall see in the next chapter, one tried-and-true strategy for getting along in the field is to adopt a "learner" or even "incompetent" role. Since you are seeking to learn, it makes sense to act accordingly; the know-it-all or expert is not likely to be "taught." Like all good things, however, this strategy can be pushed too far, and when it is, it becomes a liability. The getting-in stage of research is one point where overplaying the learner can have negative, perhaps fatal, consequences. If you are to avoid being perceived as either frivolous or stupid and dismissed as such, you should have enough knowledge about the setting or people you wish to study to appear competent to do so. How much knowledge will be enough will vary, of course. If you wish to study the "mothering" experience, it may be enough to know that the persons from whom you are requesting interviews are, in fact, females and mothers. On the other hand, the experience of a growing number of field researchers who have studied so-called "elites" in various contexts suggests the importance of conducting background research that is tantamount to acquiring a sense of "the lay of the land" (e.g., Morrill 1995; Moyser 1988; Thomas 1995). But the importance of getting the lay of the land before initiating your fieldwork full throttle holds for field research in most contexts. How much and what kinds of prior knowledge are necessary for acquiring a sense of the lay of the land will vary by whether you are an "insider" or "outsider," the scope of your research (e.g., Is it a work group or niche within an organization, or is it the entire organization?), and the extent to which what you are studying requires familiarity with the broader context in which the phenomena of interest is embedded. In focusing on the adaptive survival strategies of homeless in Austin, Texas, for example, Snow and Anderson (1993) realized that a thoroughgoing understanding of those strategies was contingent on acquiring knowledge of the various institutions and organizations that affected the routines of the homeless. Thus, early on in the research process they engaged in what can be thought of as an "ecological mapping" of the relationship between homeless hangouts or niches and the location of the relevant institutions, all of which was prefatory to the bulk of their fieldwork.

Although there is likely to be variation from one study to the next in the extent to which background information is available and accessible, you are not likely to know that until you have done a little bit of spade work. Thus, our advice is to learn what you can about the phenomena of interest and its context before pushing forward too vigorously. Having a sense of the lay of the land is likely to help you avoid some problems and increase the prospect of asking some of the right questions.

4. Courtesy

Last, since you will increase the likelihood for gaining entrée if you proceed in a courteous and respectful manner, it is useful to remember that you are acting courteously when you:

- seek interviews by writing or phoning (or both) the prospective interviewees to request their cooperation and to inquire about a convenient time and place, rather than by showing up unannounced at their homes or offices.
- inform interested parties of your research, even if you do not need their immediate cooperation and they are not going to be part of the group studied.
- take the task of getting permission from dependent or subordinate populations you wish to study (children or the hospitalized mentally retarded, for example) as seriously as the task of getting permission from their caretakers.
- help others know who you are through connections, provide them with a reasonable account of what you want to do, and demonstrate enough knowledge to suggest your competence to do it.

IV. Political, Legal, and Bureaucratic Barriers

In the preceding pages of this chapter we have discussed various stumbling blocks associated with the process of gaining entrée to a desired research site and various measures and tactics that can be employed to facilitate the process. Given the attention we have devoted to the access issue, which parallels the attention given to it more generally (see Feldman, Bell, and Berger 2003), it would be reasonable to think that it is one of the more obdurate problems confronting the field researcher. On the other hand, nearly all of the studies we have cited have successfully negotiated entrée at some level, thus suggesting that perhaps it is not such a difficult problem after all. The fact is we simply do not know what proportion of attempted fieldstudies have been derailed because of the failure to successfully negotiate entrée. Much like extinct species, these aborted studies are never heard of, in most instances, because there is no record of them. If we actually knew what percentage of attempted fieldstudies never got off the ground, we suspect that a significant proportion of that percentage failed because they were unable to surmount the challenge of access. And many of these attempted studies, we would guess, would have been foiled by various political, legal, and bureaucratic barriers. Furthermore, we believe that recent political and legal trends around the world have exacerbated the problem of "getting in," rendering some naturalistic studies exceedingly difficult, if not impossible.

There are numerous examples of various prospective research sites being declared "off limits" because of one or more of these broader contextual impediments. During the 1960s, for instance, there was a movement by political activists and some Third World leaders to prohibit field research by U.S. social scientists because they were sometimes perceived as agents of cultural, political, and/or economic imperialism. One of the best known examples of such collusion was "Project Camelot," which was a counterinsurgency project sponsored by the Department of the Army to enlist the services of social scientists to examine the preconditions of internal insurgency and to see what sorts of governmental actions might ease, worsen, or dissolve these preconditions. The project never really got off the ground as a result of adverse reactions to it in Chile, but it did raise a host of questions regarding collaborations among governments and researchers, as well as suspicions in some countries about the real interests of foreign researchers (for elaboration of the project, see Horowitz 1965 and Sjoberg 1967b).

More recently, debate has swirled around the rationale for conducting field research in and among rare, small, and vulnerable preliterate societies. The most celebrated is the previously mentioned case of the Yanamamo, the Amazon Basin, stone age Indian tribe that was supposedly unknown to most of the world until the anthropologist Napoleon Chagnon (1983) ventured upon them in the 1960s. Since then, it is claimed, little has been the same for the Yanamamo, and now they are reportedly threatened with extinction because of diseases introduced by outsiders and the incursion of commercial interests. There are also concerns about how they have been represented (Monaghan 1994). Because of such debates, and even conflict, field research among marginal and vulnerable groups, particularly in Third World countries, is looked upon with much more suspicion and concern than what was previously the case.

On other occasions national governments have prohibited research access to countries regarded as adversaries or even to the home government's own inner workings. The U.S. government's now longstanding stance with respect to Cuba, treating it as a "forbidden zone," provides a glaring example of how national policy can foreclose access (Fuller 1988; Warren and Staples 1989). And Great Britain's Official Secrets Act of 1911, making access to civil servants "very difficult," illustrates the latter (Moyser 1988, pp. 119–120).

On still other occasions, access to some kinds of research sites has been curtailed by actual or threatened defamation and libel suits by the persons or groups studied (for example, Beckford 1983; Punch 1986, Ch. 3). The chilling effect of such threats may pose yet another barrier, as social researchers question whether they can risk access in the first place.

Although the political and legal constraints of the kind noted above certainly limit the prospect of conducting field research in some settings and places, they do not constitute the pervasive, overarching constraint on field research as that posed by the evolution and diffusion of Institutional Review Boards (IRBs) across campuses in the United States. Their institutionalization can be regarded as the culmination of a trend, dating back to the 1970s, involving the increasing regulation of social research. Concern about the deceit of human subjects in medical research, as in the Tuskegee case in which black syphilis victims were intentionally misled about receiving treatment, prompted the federal government to develop a set of regulations that came to be applied far beyond the medical realm and that were designed to protect human subjects from the various physiological and psychological "harms" that might result from research on them. IRBs are the bureaucratic committees charged with administering the federal regulations at the local level, which encompasses mainly colleges and universities. Their regulatory activity includes the assessment of the risks and benefits of proposed research, the adequacy of their procedures for "subject" protection, and whether they require their subjects' informed consent.

We would guess that many field researchers agree, in principle, with the need for certain regulations to protect human subjects, but we also know that many have questioned the appropriateness of some of the initial guidelines for ethnographic field research. For example, what is the point of "informed consent" when conducting field research in public places? Because of such questions and the lobbying by social research interest groups, the federal regulations were relaxed somewhat in the case of some aspects of naturalistic field research (see Wax and Cassell 1981).

Modification and relaxation of some federal regulations has not meant that fieldstudies are exempt from initial IRB review. As of this writing, university-based fieldwork projects generally are expected to be submitted to the local IRB for initial screening. Even though the field researcher can request exemption from various regulations, such as the need for informed consent, that request is subject to IRB review and approval. If not approved, the researcher is required to submit a more elaborated protocol—one which details the risks and benefits and clarifies the steps for ensuring informed consent and informant confidentiality. Although we know that field researchers sometimes proceed with their projects without either IRB review or approval, this is rarely a choice if funding has been secured because release of funds is contingent upon IRB review and approval.

How much of a barrier do the regulations pose to naturalistic field research? It is hard to know because there is researcher variation in response to these regulations and institutional variation in their implementation. At the individual researcher level, we know firsthand that there is a lot of grumbling about the regulations and their institutional manifestations, the IRBs. However, we have yet to see an actual reckoning of the impact of the IRB process on the incidence of field research projects. While some proposed projects have been derailed, we suspect that, in most cases, IRBs are more of a nagging nuisance than an insurmountable obstacle. One of the reasons for this suspicion is that field researchers, just like the individuals they study, are quite adaptive, and therefore, as Robert Emerson has observed (2001, p. 146), "tailor their accounts of research procedures to fit the requirements of their local IRBs." At the institutional level, there is variation in the range of research that falls under the IRB umbrella. In some universities, all research—even unfunded and undergraduate research—is subjected to regulations and review; in other settings, only funded research is affected. Similarly, some IRBs interpret informed consent so literally that "covert" research in public places is eliminated as an option; other IRBs exempt such research from informed consent mechanisms on the grounds of "no risk." In the face of this complexity, the best advice we can give is to suggest that before beginning your research, you acquaint yourself both with your campus's IRB policies and with the extent to which local researchers take them seriously. In offering this cautionary advice, we do not mean to suggest that we agree with all IRB regulations and their implementation from one campus to the next. But IRBs are now significant actors in the field of actors relevant to the research enterprise across disciplines within the academy. So it would be ill-advised to ignore local IRB regulations and other relevant research codes of ethics and the extent to which they apply to your research. But even if they do apply, it is probably a good bet, as Patricia and Peter Adler (2002, p. 42) have noted, that "unanticipated situations will arise that are not covered in a research plan or proposal" and that researchers, therefore, "will always have to make situational decisions and interpretations about the ethical and safe thing to do." Because of such considerations, we agree with the Adlers (2002, p. 42), who "advocate a joint, reciprocally respectful relationship" between field researchers and the various governmental and professional oversight organizations, "more attuned to legal nuances, that looks ahead to anticipate potential problems while still respecting the fundamental bond of obligation and trust between researchers and those whom they study."

V. The Question of Confidentiality

One of the central obligations that field researchers have with respect to those they study is the guarantee of anonymity via the "assurance of confidentiality"—the promise that the real names of persons, places, and so forth either will not be used in the research report or will be substituted by pseudonyms. Field researchers subscribed to this operational principle long before the institutionalization of federal human subject protection regulations and IRBs. Indeed, the practice of assuring informant confidentiality is such a cardinal principle of naturalistic fieldwork that it has long been taken for granted within this research tradition. Of course, it is understood that confidentiality, like secrecy, is a matter of degree. In intensive interview studies, research in public and quasi-public places, or studies of fluid social groupings, individuals may be able to identify quotations from or descriptions of themselves, although it is unlikely they will be able to identify anyone else. In studies of stable communities or ongoing groups, however, pseudonyms are unlikely to prevent either interested participants or knowledgeable observers from recognizing, or at least making pretty accurate guesses about, the presumably camouflaged communities, groups, or individuals. No fieldstudy made this clearer than Arthur Vidich and Joseph Bensman's *Small Town in Mass Society: Class, Power and Religion in a Rural Community* (1968). The small town—Candor, New York—was referred to in the book as Springdale. But this pseudonym fooled few, if any, of the town's residents, who were able to identify the "who's who" in the book, even though the authors did not refer to any of the central characters by their given names. Perhaps the townspeople would not have cared much about the book had it not portrayed Springdale (Candor) as being infused by the values and ways of mass society and run by local businessmen who functioned much like big-city politicos, all in contrast to the town's projected image as an island of uncompromised democracy and small-town virtues in a sea of change. Because of this disjunction and the residents' sense that they had been duped by Vidich, who did the fieldwork, not only did the book become, according to one critic, "a source of general outrage," but Vidich was hung in effigy, and "the village's Fourth of July parade featured a float carrying an image of [Vidich] bending over a manure spreader" (Allen 1997, p. 35). Two useful guidelines are suggested by this case: the first is that the veils of disguise used to camouflage the groups or communities to which they are applied can often be seen through or lifted by those interested in doing so; and second, interest in lifting the veil is especially likely when the researcher's claims call into question, or contradict, those of the group or community studied.

Despite such occasional and critically celebrated lapses in the provision of confidentiality, its assurance remains a standard operating procedure for both known and unknown researchers. For known researchers, in fact, the guarantee of confidentiality to the people being researched is often viewed both as an essential technique for "getting in" and, once entrée has been accomplished, as a sacred trust, even in the face of imprisonment or threats of imprisonment. The previously mentioned case of Rik Scarce, who was conducting fieldwork on animal rights groups, is illustrative: He spent six months in prison for failing to turn over his subpoenaed fieldnotes and testify before a federal grand jury investigation of the "liberation" of an animal research laboratory at the university in which he was a graduate student (Scarce 1994; also see, for a similar example, Brajuha and Hallowell 1986; and Levine 1993, for the American Sociological Association's position on such cases). Because of threats posed by subpoenas and related legal entanglements not only to the provision of informant confidentiality, but to the personal and professional routines of field researchers, Richard Leo (1995), whose fieldnotes on police interrogations were subpoenaed, has joined Scarce in arguing that ethnographers should be granted federal evidentiary privilege and thus be exempted from turning over their fieldnotes or from testifying in court about what they have seen and heard. Such evidentiary privilege is very unlikely to be granted at any time in the near future, but the fact that it has become a salient issue among a growing number of field researchers underscores the importance of informant confidentiality to the field research enterprise.

Beyond the matter of protection for the people being studied, there is another consideration that argues for confidentiality as a standard practice. At their best, social researchers are neither muckrakers nor investigative reporters (although these are, of course, important societal roles). Their goal as researchers should, in our view, be neither moral judgment nor immediate reform, but understanding. The absence of names or the use of pseudonyms (if names, per se, are necessary for clarity) helps both the analyst and the reader to focus on the generalizable patterns emerging from the data and to avoid getting sidetracked into telling or hearing a "juicy" human-interest story.

In general, then, there are a number of factors that mandate the assurance of informant confidentiality as a cardinal principle of ethnographic fieldwork. As with any principle, however, there are several exceptions to this one that merit consideration. Some researchers have argued, for example, that the guarantee of confidentiality is inappropriate or unnecessary when studying publicly accountable behavior or large, powerful organizations that have the financial and political wherewithal to protect themselves (Duster, Matza, and Wellman 1979; Galliher 1980; Rainwater and Pittman 1967). Others have argued that in research with public figures, who are used to being quoted and may prefer to speak "on the record," the guarantee of confidentiality may impede rather than facilitate access to rich data (Spector 1980, pp. 103–105). As well, an increasing number of researchers believe that they have an ethical responsibility to democratize representation by giving "voice" to their informants such that they speak for and define themselves, which not only makes it well-nigh impossible to camouflage them but may, under some circumstances and with some persons, necessitate the use of their real names. Such appears to have been the case with Mitchell Duneier's (1999) main informant, Hakim, in Duneier's ethnography of 25 poor black men who worked and lived on the sidewalks of Sixth Avenue in New York's Greenwich Village. Not only was Hakim's voice resonant throughout the book, but he was featured in a number of pictures, wrote an "afterword" to the book, and was even invited to participate in a seminar with Duneier at the University of California, Santa Barbara. (For other examples of such democratic representation, see Scheper-Hughes 1992; Rubenstein 2002.) In this, and other cases of what is frequently referred to as "collaborative research," informants play a significant role in defining the foci and goals of the research, and—as exemplified in Duneier's study—they may be considered part of a research team and thus merit explicit identification and even recognition as coauthors of presentations and reports. This seems to be particularly the case in feminist participant action fieldstudies where the explicit identification of informants may involve their desire to go on record publicly regarding their experiences and feelings in hope of having some political impact, whether such potential influence is related to state politics, as in Rita Arditti's (1999) study of grandmothers who were part of the resistance against Argentine state terrorism in the late 1970s and early 1980s, or more diffuse gender politics, as in Nancy Naples' and Emily Clark's (1996) research on survivors of childhood sexual abuse. All of these examples demonstrate the basic and important point that whether or not to explicitly identify research informants should be based on the context and goals of the research.

Before promising confidentiality to your prospective informants, you might wish to consider how the foregoing "exceptions" fit with your research plans, as well as review the code of ethics of your academic discipline, your local IRB protocols, and any current federal and state statutes relative to privacy. For while these "exceptions" raise serious questions about the inevitable advisability of confidentiality in all research situations, we believe that the burden of proof that names are essential to social science field reports or to the larger scientific endeavor should be on the investigator. When in doubt, the best advice remains: disguise or obscure.

Having finally gotten access to the data, you must work at maintaining your position: You must deal, that is, with the problem of "getting along"— the topic to which we next turn our attention.

CHAPTER 4

GETTING ALONG

The Greek philosopher Heraclitus once observed that you can never step into the same river twice. Such is the case with field research, as the scenes or settings studied seldom remain static. New actors or faces often come on stage, the demeanor of those with whom we are familiar may suddenly change, and new events and problems, some mundane and others quite serious, often present themselves. As such, adjustments are continually necessary and the success of much field research is partly contingent on the willingness and ability of fieldworkers to adapt to the changes they encounter. As with most activities, however, having a game plan before entering the arena is likely to increase the prospects of achieving your objectives. Specifically, knowing a bit about what to expect, learning from the successes and failures of others, and anticipating and thus guarding against pitfalls should help make the difficulties much more manageable.

It is with this objective of making the experience of fieldwork more manageable that we proceed in this chapter. Toward that end, we divide our discussion of "getting along" into four tasks: getting along *with self*, getting along *with members*, getting along while *getting out*, and getting along *with claimants and conscience*. First, we shall be concerned with the emotional and physical challenges that investigators may encounter; second, with the problem of developing and maintaining viable field relations; third, with the problem of getting out; and fourth, with the ongoing ethical dilemmas that must be faced. Even though these four tasks are highly interrelated, we discuss them separately for the purpose of clarity.

I. Getting Along with Self: Emotional and Physical Challenges

Being a field researcher can be a stressful experience in a multitude of ways. William Shaffir and Robert Stebbins have suggested, in their introduction to *Experiencing Fieldwork*, that:

> Fieldwork must certainly rank with the more disagreeable activities that humanity has fashioned for itself. It is usually inconvenient, to say the least,

sometimes physically uncomfortable, frequently embarrassing, and, to a degree, always tense. (1991, p. 1)

Although one might quibble with the contention that fieldwork is as routinely disagreeable in the ways Shaffir and Stebbins suggest, there is little question but that it can often be physically uncomfortable, sometimes embarrassing, and usually laden with uncertainties and anxieties (see, e.g., Georges and Jones 1980; Howell 1990; Smith and Kornblum 1996; Wax 1971). Rather than trying to catalogue the full range of difficulties—probably impossible anyway—we examine four clusters of emotional and physical challenges in the belief that some forewarning may prove helpful as you go about the business of "getting along": (a) a sense of information overload, (b) deception and the fear of disclosure, (c) negotiating the pulls of distance and surrender, and (d) actual physical dangers.

A. Information Overload

Once initial access is secured, it is not uncommon to experience a sense of information overload. There is so much to see and hear, and all of it is likely to appear both phenomenally interesting and conceptually or theoretically important. This is true not only when the setting is new, unfamiliar, and perhaps strange, as when studying imported religious movements (J. Lofland 1977; Rochford 1985; Snow 1993) or homelessness (Dordick 1997; Rosenthal 1994; Wright 1997), but also even when the setting is familiar, as when studying one's own prior or current employment or avocation (Ronai and Ellis 1989; Stevenson 1999), one's experience with a disease (Karp 2001; Kotarba 1980), or the experiences of one's children (Adler and Adler 1998; Fine 2001).

A common consequence of sensory or information overload is doubt about your observational and recording capabilities, which may well make you think: "I can't get it all. There is too much going on." "I am afraid of missing something important." "This is an impossible task! How can I know what's important when I can't see or hear everything at the same time?"

Such thoughts express very real and quite common concerns. Yet, most researchers learn that the anxieties and doubts associated with this sense of overload need not be immobilizing if one keeps two considerations in mind:

- Whatever is phenomenally interesting and/or theoretically important is most likely to present itself over and over again. This is partly what sociologists have in mind when they assert that much of social life is patterned and perhaps even routinized. The practical upshot of patterns and routines for field researchers is that even if you missed them once, you are likely to see them again.
- This is so because, as we said at the outset, properly conducted fieldwork entails prolonged, sustained engagement and persistent, systematic observation (Lincoln and Guba 1985, pp. 301–305; Weick 1985, pp. 568–69), and such engagement and observation make it unlikely that you will overlook significant patterns or gloss over what is interesting and/or important.

B. Deception and the Fear of Disclosure

A second anxiety you may well experience stems from the perception that you are deceiving the people you are studying and that that deception will be revealed. This concern seems to be particularly salient among covert, unknown investigators. However, a few published reports suggest that it is experienced among known researchers as well. As noted earlier, rarely, if ever, do our accounts provide a full and detailed depiction of our interests and procedures. We have also learned that our informants frequently forget our initial claims regarding our research identities and interests. Consequently, it is not uncommon for even known researchers to fear that a direct and discomforting challenge is just around the corner.

- Did X remember that I was a researcher when she told me that? And if not, when she does remember, will she be angry or upset?
- Is this person I'm interviewing, who seems to be getting restless, about to ask me more about my research aims than I really want to tell right now?
- Is the person in charge of this group I'm studying going to notice that my research interests have shifted since I received permission to do the research, and if he does, will he still approve?

Unknown observers in public and quasi-public settings may also suffer from a nagging concern that "someone will find out." Even though the people in such settings are seldom upset when they do find out, such knowledge does not necessarily prevent the investigator from worrying. When Lyn Lofland was observing in public waiting rooms, she was always vaguely fearful that someone would challenge her continued and repeated presence. On only one occasion—in an airport—was she approached; although the official who discovered she was doing research had no objection to her remaining, she was so uncomfortable that she left almost at once and never returned.

Unknown observers in private and quasi-private settings have written little about the emotional stress of deception and the fear of disclosure. But from the reports of investigators in milder situations of deception (for example, Klatch 1987) and, more directly, from the evidence of people in nonresearch "passing" situations (spies, "closet" homosexuals, and so forth), there is good reason to presume that the fear of being unmasked—and the attendant possibilities for humiliation, embarrassment, and direct challenge like the interaction captured in the photo on the following page—may be a pressing concern.

C. Distance and Surrender

Field researchers' emotions or feelings toward their informants and the settings they study can be arrayed on a continuum ranging from extreme distance at one end to complete engulfment or surrender at the other end,

Figure 4.1 Ethnographers' ethical and practical concerns to not deceive and anger those they study leads to limited use of covert participant observation.

with feelings like loathing, marginalization, sympathy, and identification manifesting themselves between the two extremes. Although some researchers' modal feelings over the course of a study might be skewed in one direction or another, it is probably more accurate to presume that, on average, most field researchers vacillate between these extremes, thus experiencing a range of feelings. Pollner and Emerson (1983, p. 235) hit the nail on the head in this regard when they note that "on many levels, the actual conduct of field research reveals a chronic tension between the demands of involvement and withdrawal, of participation and detachment." Here we discuss emotions that mark different points on this continuum.

1. **Loathing**

   Closest to the extreme distance end of the continuum is loathing and the concomitant desire to withdraw. Few researchers have confessed to loathing the people they study or interview, however. And for good reason. After all, if your discomfort with or dislike for those you are studying is unambiguous and persistent, you are going to find it difficult to camouflage your true feelings and devote the time and energy necessary for successful data logging and analysis. Even more significantly, if your dislike of your informants and their associates is unwavering, then it is a good bet that you haven't gotten sufficiently close to them to achieve a sympathetic understanding of their beliefs, feelings, and practices. And, if that is the case, then it is likely that your final report or "telling" will be laden with "negatives" or statements of "what they are not" rather than "what they are." The anthropologist Frederick O. Gearing warned of such dangers sometime ago in *Face of the Fox* (1970).

   > Out of some unnamed array of all the kinds of men who might exist, the neighbors of the Fox [the Iowans] named one kind of man he was not. At best, then, the Fox were left undescribed, still inscrutable. But worst and most likely, they were made by that negative term inconceivable. . . . The truth value of a description which renders a people inscrutable or inconceivable is . . . zero. . . . The trouble is, of course, that such nondescriptions are so very easy, undemanding of the observer. But the way toward truth is much assisted by a simple rule of thumb: one never describes an alien people by naming what they are not. That is, whenever in a description of an alien other the words "are not" or "lack" or prefixes and suffixes like "un-" or "-less" come into mind or fall from the pen, warning bells should ring, for the chances are strong that, at that juncture, the people have been left undescribed and perhaps rendered inconceivable. (1970, p. 69)

   Because the rendering of such nondescriptions are a likely consequence of disdain for some groups and clusters of beliefs and practices, it is probably wise to avoid such groups and practices, or, at the very least, approach them with heightened self-consciousness of your biases and stereotypes. Yet, we don't want to push these caveats too strongly. After all, if preexisting dislike is used as a kind of rule of thumb for excluding some groups or settings as research possibilities, then it is unlikely that a number of field-studies of what Nigel Fielding (1993) has termed "unloved groups" would have been conducted. Certainly Kathleen Blee (2002) would not have conducted her study of women members of various racist hate movements in the United States.

   To note that initial feelings of dislike or disdain for prospective objects of research do not necessarily preclude studying the groups or settings in question does not mean that researchers are always able to bracket and control those feelings or that they don't sometimes spill over into the actual research setting. The extent to which that slippage occurs is difficult to know because researchers infrequently write about their negative feelings. There are, however, exceptions. One of the best known and most forthright confessions of loathing is found in passages from Bronislaw Malinowski's private journals, published as A *Diary in the Strict Sense of the Term* (1967). Available in print only many years after the famed anthropologist's death, the diary, kept during his research with the Trobriand Islanders (among other groups), suggests what one reviewer, Patrick Gallagher, called "a magnificent lack of rapport" (1967, p. 23):

> Even more embarrassing, he confesses to despising his subjects ("young females, blackened, with shaven heads, one of them . . . with an animal-like brutishly sensual face. I shudder at the thought of copulating with her"), to distrusting them ("They lied, concealed and irritated me. I am always in a world of lies here"), and even to abusing them ("I was enraged and punched him in the jaw once or twice"). (Gallagher 1967, p. 25)

It is not surprising that, under the circumstances, Malinowski also admits to withdrawing from contact with the "natives": "He also confesses, repeatedly, to chronic dissipation of time in reading 'trashy' novels . . . and, as frequently, to preoccupation with sexual daydreams and 'lecherous' acts" (Gallagher 1967, p. 25).

Debate continues as to whether these expressions represent Malinowski's more persistent feelings toward the peoples he studied or whether they are the honest and very human expressions of episodic rage and loathing under extraordinarily difficult field situations. Whatever the case, Malinowski's candid revelations of self stand as a strong reminder to all naturalistic researchers that entrée into a research setting does not transform an ordinary human being into a saint. Thus, you need to be prepared for the possibility that you will encounter in the field people you will loathe and to be aware of how such loathing can distort your efforts to render understandable those you are studying.

2. Marginalization

Marginalization in the context of field research appears to manifest itself in two different senses. The first, and probably most common, is the sense that you are not getting sufficiently close to your informants and their activities to understand what they are up to from their vantage point. It is the feeling that is likely to arise when you remain "an outsider" in spite of your desire and efforts to become an "insider" or at least secure access to insiders' points of view. Marginalization in this sense may be experienced by any investigator, whether unknown or known, who has had difficulty, or actually failed, in negotiating a research role or vantage point that yields the kinds of information that lead to an understanding of the informants and their activities in terms of what they are rather than what they are not. The difficulty of securing such a field research role or vantage point can result, most generally, from the failure to develop rapport and secure the trust of your informants. Rapport and trust, sociologically understood, are properties of a relationship and are evident, in the context of field relations, when informants feel reasonably comfortable in functioning as guides to the setting or group being studied, thus divulging what they know or don't know, and the corresponding confidence the fieldworker has in those informants and the information elicited from them. The failure to develop rapport or trust with some number of informants can be due to many complicating factors, including a mismatch between the social attributes (e.g., age, gender, race and ethnicity) of the fieldworker and those of the members of the group or setting studied; physical distance from one's research site, as when Angus Vail (2001) was confronted with the challenge of studying the tattoo artists and collectors he had come to know in San Francisco from the University of Connecticut where he was in graduate school; or the failure to neutralize the identities that informants may impute to you in spite of your claims to the contrary, as illustrated by a group of homeless in Austin who initially thought Snow and Anderson (1993) were "narcs" bent on arresting them, or "religious nuts" trying to save them, rather than the uncritical field researchers they claimed to be.

Marginalization, in the second sense, may occur when the fieldworker, who is not only "known" but is an "active" or "complete" member (see Adler and Adler 1987), fails to relent to the pressure, and sometimes expectation, to engage in an act indicative of greater commitment, such as giving testimony or risking arrest. Barrie Thorne (1979) experienced this sense of marginalization when members of the draft resistance movement in which she was involved and which she was studying were asked to commit themselves to an act that might result in arrest. As she recounts:

> As M. began the invitation, I felt fear in my throat. Fear, shame, guilt—both a desire to join the group that surged forward after M.'s invitation and a (stronger) reluctance since I didn't feel I could risk arrest and realized that the pressures compelling me to go forward were of a group rather than an individually thought-through kind. But that realization didn't seem to minimize the emotion. People began leaving their pews and going forward. Eventually there seemed to be only a few scattered people remaining in the pews. M. commented over the microphone, "There seem to be more up here than down there." I felt all eyes were upon me; I was sure my face was flushed; I found myself fingering my purse, almost in readiness to run up. But I didn't. . . . The group—more like a community given its size and solidarity—stood in a solid bunch, spilling out over the sides and the front of the chapel, but clearly demarcated from those of us, scattered and far from constituting a group, who remained in the pews. The spatial arrangements dramatized the gap between the committed and the uncommitted. (1979, p. 80)

While such dramatic moments highlight the difficulty of being an active or complete participant observer, marginality, in this sense, is likely to be experienced as a chronic sense of loneliness, anxiety, and perhaps even alienation. There can be a continual, often subtle, but always painful sense of separation between the observer and the observed. It is as if, daily, one were being told, "You are here and you know a lot about us, but you are not really one of us."

The sense of marginalization that can arise from the foregoing dilemmas should not be construed as automatic or naturally given, however. Many successful fieldstudies have been conducted by researchers whose ethnicity, race, gender, or age were different from those studied, as discussed in Chapter 2 (Section III.B.2). Similarly, physical distance can be successfully negotiated, as Vail (2001, p. 710) did, by arranging for "a number of brief, intensive field immersions" (to San Francisco and Oakland from Storrs, CT). Native/member identity attributions that are contrary to the field researcher's interests can also be parried, sometimes strategically, by offering resonant counter-explanations. Or they can be parried fortuitously, as when unanticipated occurrences result in member reassessment of their previous attributions. Snow and Anderson experienced such a fortuitous turning point in their research when Anderson was arrested and jailed one evening along with two homeless men. Although Snow bailed him out later that night, the arrest and jailing convinced the above mentioned group of homeless that Snow and Anderson were neither narcs nor religious proselytizers but "good guys" who could be trusted. From then on, these fellows become key informants and self-anointed "protectors," thus diluting Snow and Anderson's earlier sense of marginalization. Researchers who have experienced social pressure to engage in acts suggestive of greater commitment to the group or cause have found ways successfully to negotiate that pressure so as not to be marginalized from the group, as Rob Benford (1987) did in his research on the peace movement.

Although the above cases indicate that field researchers have successfully negotiated potentially marginalizing situations, it is probably wise to assume that the risk of such marginalization, particularly in the first sense, is a persistent one and that you should therefore be on the alert for its indicators, such as the feeling of being an outsider, of not getting the right information, and of even alienation from the group or setting being studied. Such feelings are not only likely to bias one's perspective, but their persistence may even slide over into loathing, as we suspect happened with Malinowski.

3. **Sympathy**

Just as engagement in the field can intensify or generate unanticipated feelings of disdain for your informants, or a sense of marginalization, so it sometimes also engenders feelings of intense sympathy for those studied. People everywhere experience various kinds of troubles or hardships from time to time, and it is not at all unusual for investigators to provide some forms of mundane assistance to the people they are studying, as we will discuss in the next section on getting along with members. But sometimes researchers encounter a more difficult situation of need in which the people being observed or interviewed face severe difficulties that would require a full-time commitment to alleviate. Naturalistic researchers (known or unknown) must often struggle with the personally painful question of whether to throw in the towel on doing research and give themselves over entirely to "helping" or to remain in the field as a chronicler of the difficulties, as

Carolyn Ellis (1995) did with her dying partner. In either case, it can be argued that sympathy has given way to identification.

4. **Identification**
Identification with those you are studying—or at least some subgroup or faction within the larger setting, organization, or community of interest—moves one even closer to the surrender end of the distance/surrender continuum. Such identification involves far more than sympathizing with your informants in that you come to take their accounts and narratives at face value, perhaps even internalizing their perspective. If this occurs, it is difficult, if not impossible, to step back and assess what you have heard and observed in a dispassionate, dare we say "objective," manner. Observers of qualitative field research have warned long and hard about the threat of identification via such terms as "over-rapport," "over-identifying," and "converting" (Gold 1958; McCall and Simmons 1969; Miller 1952; Schwartz and Schwartz 1955; Vidich 1955). In fact, discussions among field researchers about the danger of converting seems to be part of the lore associated with fieldwork. Yet there is little hard evidence to indicate that many, or even any, ethnographers, have ever converted. We suspect that the reason for this concern and the tendency to sometimes misread our colleagues in this regard is lodged in our failure to distinguish between sympathetic identification and overidentification. The former involves the development of a nonjudgmental understanding of the inner life and practices of our informants without actually adopting their perspective or point of view; whereas the latter entails the adoption or internalization of their point of view as one's own. The difference between the two is nicely illustrated by Kathleen Blee's previously mentioned fieldstudy of women in racist hate groups. Over time she came to acquire a sympathetic understanding of many of the women she interviewed, seeing "them in more complicated, less stereotyped ways," but without ever coming close to adopting their point of view (2002, p. 15).

Even though field researchers quite routinely withstand the pulls and pressures of converting, this does not necessarily safeguard them from presenting their findings solely from the vantage point of their informants. Of course, some field researchers advocate doing so, as reflected in fairly recent feminist writings about the importance of manifesting "deep respect," "full sympathy," and "authentic caring" in one's writings about the people studied (see Chapter 2, Section III.D). But whether or not one subscribes to such directives, the temptation to take and reflect the vantage point of your informants is especially likely when you sit down to write shortly after disengagement from the field. As Snow recounted his initial efforts to convert his fieldnotes into dissertation text,

> Each time I began to shift my notes from Nichiren Shoshu categories to sociological categories, I found myself questioning the point of it all and asking if I was doing justice to their meaning system, the way in which they organize the world, and so on. (1993, p. 20)

What Snow and many other ethnographers also found is that the passage of time usually provides the distance necessary for assessing what was going on and what was especially interesting from the standpoint of one's scholarly perspective.

Such observations return us to what we said at the beginning of this section: that polarities like distance and surrender mask the emotional complexities associated with most field research. Not only do most investigators report feelings that are mixed, shifting, ambivalent, and complex (as Sherryl Kleinman and Martha Copp's (1993) review of emotions and fieldwork makes clear), but we suspect that most also experience ongoing tension between distance and surrender. In fact, we believe such tension can be used as an indicator that one is "getting it right" from a social scientific standpoint; for its absence suggests extreme distance or extreme surrender and the perspectival and analytical biases associated with both.

D. Physical Dangers

Under the rubric of getting along with the self, we have focused so far on various emotional stresses associated with fieldwork that are rooted in the tensions between procedures, ethics, political orientations, and the norms of social science. But there is another wellspring of stress: significant physical risk. There are a number of noteworthy fieldstudies in which the threat of physical harm has been a significant feature of the research context and is associated with one or more of four different kinds of settings, groups, or subcultures. One includes zones of conflict and violence in which the risk of interpersonal and collective violence is a persistent feature of the everyday landscape. In many U.S. cities, for example, certain areas or neighborhoods are noted for high rates of crime and interpersonal violence associated with "gangs" (see, e.g., Anderson 1999; Horowitz 1983; Sanchez-Jankowski 1991; Vigil 2002). Additionally, there are many areas around the world in which intergroup violence is endemic. But if one wishes to understand the dynamics of such violence, "one must go to where violence occurs, research it at its place" (Nordstrom and Robben 1995, p. 4; example studies include Scheper-Hughes 1992, 2004; Mahmood 1996; Coy 2001; and the studies reported in Nordstrom and Robben's *Fieldwork Under Fire: Contemporary Studies of Violence and Survival*, 1995).

A second research arena for ethnography in which the threat of physical harm is quite palpable involves groups on the political and religious extremes that not only embrace the rhetoric of violence, but are prepared for and even sometimes practice it. Kathleen Blee's (2002) description of the fear she felt during the course of her previously mentioned research on women in hate groups graphically illustrates her sense of vulnerability.

> In the early stages of this research, I experienced a great deal of fear. The violent reputations of some women I wanted to interview, including the skinhead organizer whose comrades referred to her as "Ms. Icepick," did

little to dispel my concerns. As I got to know some people in the racist world, I became less afraid. . . . But in other respects, I grew more afraid as I became less naïve. For one thing, I came to realize that my white skin color would provide me little protection. Many racist activists who have faced criminal charges were turned in by other whites. . . . Moreover . . . [since] some racists see race as determined by commitment to white power politics rather than genetics, I could not assume that those I interviewed would view me either as white or nonhostile. I could not count on racial immunity from violence (2002, pp. 14–15; see also Mitchell 2002).

A third arena of danger consists of settings involving illicit activities, very often drug dealing and drug use. Regarding the dangers associated with drug dealing and smuggling she studied in a middle-class community, Patricia Adler writes:

Because of the inordinate amount of drugs they consumed, drug dealers and smugglers were particularly volatile, capable of becoming malicious toward each other or us [Adler and her partner] with little warning. They were also likely to behave erratically owing to the great risks they faced from the police and other dealers. These factors made them moody, and they vacillated between trusting us and being suspicious of us.

At various times we also had to protect our research tapes. We encountered several threats to our collection of taped interviews from people who had granted us these interviews. . . . When threatened, we became extremely frightened and shifted the tapes between different hiding places. We even ventured forth one rainy night with our tapes packed in a suitcase to meet a person who was uninvolved in the research at a secret rendezvous so that he could guard the tapes for us. (1993, pp. 22–23; see also Agar 1973, Bourgois 1995; Gould, Walker, Crane, and Lidz 1974; Williams 1989)

A final set of research sites characterized by enhanced potential risk is associated with private and commercial recreational thrill-seeking. The popularity of such activities has made them an attractive research focus, and while thrill-oriented businesses may at times exaggerate the risk, only a foolhardy ethnographer would turn a blind eye to the potential risks of studying via participant observation such activities as mountain climbing (Mitchell 1983), skydiving (Anderson 2003; Lyng and Snow 1986), high-speed motorcycling (Lyng 1998), and white-water, river running (Holyfield 1999; Holyfield and Fine 1997; Holyfield and Jonas 2003; Jonas 1999). Closely related to such thrill-seeking recreational activities are volunteer and occupational spin-offs that place their practitioners at risk, as illuminated by Jennifer Lois's (2003) fieldstudy of a mountain search and rescue unit.

The fact that we are able to refer to a number of field researchers who have dealt with the challenges of dangerous environments illustrates that ethnography in such settings is alive and well and that as long as potential threat persists in various corners of social life, some researchers are likely to put themselves in harm's way. While at times the dangers in researching a particular group or setting may be extreme enough to lead to withdrawal from the field, it is clear that some researchers seem quite willing to expose themselves to various risks.

E. Dealing with the Challenges

In the likely prospect that one or more of these emotional and physical challenges confronts you, what are you to do? As we said initially, simply knowing that such possibilities can occur may lessen their impact. But not inevitably. You may instead conclude that you should give up on the project and leave because you can't deal with the information overload you are experiencing, because your research is not worth living with deception and the fear of disclosure, because continued association with persons you find loathsome is unbearable, or because the marginalization you feel may make your continued field research seem pointless. On the other hand, you may come to feel that the needs of the people you are studying are more compelling than your other commitments. And you may even come to believe that community with the group being researched is far better than colleagueship with other researchers. But whichever end of the distance/surrender continuum you find yourself sliding toward, we encourage you, first, not to rush to disaffiliation or embracement, and second, to keep in mind that the tension you are experiencing may ultimately be an important springboard for more compelling analytic insights.

Field researchers have confronted such tensions routinely over the years, and various approaches have been advocated as offering ways to diminish the tensions or to handle them more meaningfully. Participatory action research, mentioned briefly in Chapter 2 (Section III.D), has been proposed as "a radical type of activist social research in which the people being studied, or the intended beneficiaries of the research, have substantial control over and participation in the research" (Cancian 1993, pp. 93–94; see also Stoeker and Bonacich 1992, 1993). In such studies, it has been argued, concerns of researcher exploitation and distance may be eliminated because the investigator collaborates with setting participants to find answers to questions that concern them, thus presumably researching and helping at the same time. Similarly, some feminist ethnographers have sought to reduce power imbalances between themselves and those they study by promoting ways to identify with and avoid deceiving them. While these approaches highlight ethical concerns and power imbalances, many of their practitioners (see Cancian 1993, Hammersley 1992) have come to feel that stresses and strains are unavoidable in field research. As feminist sociologist Judith Stacey has written,

> Many . . . feminist scholars share the view that ethnography is particularly appropriate to feminist research. . . . [yet my ethnographic research] placed me in situations of inauthenticity, dissimilitude and potential, perhaps inevitable betrayal, situations that I now believe are inherent in fieldwork

method. . . . The lives, loves, and tragedies that fieldwork informants share with a researcher are ultimately data, grist for the ethnographic mill, a mill that has a truly grinding power. (1988, pp. 22–23)

We believe the lesson to be drawn here is not so much that fieldwork is an imperfect methodology, but rather that engaging in fieldwork requires facing a set of tensions and working to find constructive ways to balance and manage them. And in this regard, one particular piece of advice emerges strongly from ethnographic research accounts: Keep in contact with fellow researchers and/or friends with whom these problems can be discussed, placed in context, and weighed. Indeed, one of the many important advantages of team-based field research is that it provides individual fieldworkers with colleagues who not only share an interest in the settings, individuals, and groups under study, but who are actively involved in the research. Snow and Anderson found such team field research particularly useful in their study of homelessness, with Anderson typically assuming the role of participant observer among the homeless and Snow typically assuming the role of a more detached observer, occasionally joining Anderson in the field but continuously monitoring and responding to his field activities, observations, and notes. As they write:

> Seldom was a day or evening in the field not followed by a debriefing session that included discussion of field experiences, methodological and theoretical implications, and elaborated plans for subsequent outings. Conscious and reflective enactment of these two roles enabled us to maintain involvement and detachment at one and the same time, thereby facilitating management of the [distance-surrender] dialectic characteristic of ethnographic research (Snow and Anderson 1987, p. 1344).

One of the utilities of team field research, then, is that it provides a fulcrum for balancing the countervailing tensions associated with the distance/surrender ends of the continuum of emotional involvement. Our guess is that if Malinowski and other field researchers who have succumbed to loathing had been similarly involved in team field research, they would have been less likely to experience such disdain, however periodic or continuous, for their informants because they would have had a sounding board at their disposal. A diary clearly provides an outlet for one's feelings and thoughts, but it doesn't provide a balancing perspective and voice.

II. Getting Along with Members: The Problems of Developing and Maintaining Field Relations

We have seen that the character of fieldwork can be influenced by various emotional and physical challenges to the researcher and by how they are managed. However, nothing is more important to the ongoing character of fieldwork than the number and types of field relationships developed with members of the scene or setting being studied, who function both as hosts and objects of your research. The importance of field relations to the quality of fieldwork derives from at least two factors. The first is that intimate, up-close access to the happenings, events, and routines that constitute any particular social setting is contingent upon establishing relationships with one or more members from that setting who function as "guides" to the organization and perspectives associated with those happenings, events, and routines. The second factor is that different kinds of relationships with different individuals variously situated within the setting are likely to yield different perspectives and understandings. For example, understanding of any particular school, whatever the grade level, is likely to vary depending on whether it is accessed and explored from the perspective of the students, the teachers, the administration, parents, and sometimes even the broader community.

Given the importance of field relations to what is seen and heard, we first turn to an exploration of strategies for developing and maintaining them, and then discuss strategies for controlling levels of closeness.

A. Strategies to Facilitate the Development and Maintenance of Field Relations

Although the character of field relations may be constrained by fieldwork roles (e.g., known and unknown, insider or outsider) and researcher attributes and characteristics, as discussed in Chapter 2, they are rarely determinative of the kinds of field relations that evolve. If they were, then there would be little substance to the repeated claim that fieldwork relations are continuously negotiated. This implies that the fieldworker is likely to have some elbow room or latitude for negotiating functionally viable field relationships—that is, relationships and connections that optimize what is likely to be learned. But how does the fieldworker proceed in a fashion that is most likely to yield the information sought? More concretely, what kinds of strategies do fieldworkers have at their disposal? Primary field research monographs and secondary works synthesizing these original works are filled with accounts of various strategies that have been used to facilitate relational access and informant rapport or trust (see, e.g., Adler and Adler 1987; Douglas 1976; Johnson 1975; Smith and Kornblum 1996; Wax 1971). Most of them can be regarded as variants of presentational and exchange strategies.

In considering these strategies, it is important to keep in mind that you are likely to be confronted with different relational challenges at different points in the course of your research. Early on the challenge is to develop relationships that expose you to aspects of the setting and the members' points of view so that you can acquire an empathetic understanding of that social world. This means that you want to get relatively close to the surrender end of the previously discussed emotional involvement continuum. But, as cautioned earlier, you will want to step back from time to time to gain a broader perspective on what you are learning and doing. That is, you will want to gain some distance, but without becoming marginalized or full of loathing.

Thus, throughout the course of your research, you will be confronted with the challenge of achieving both closeness and distance, but at different times. Sometimes, you will find yourself having to negotiate the centrifugal forces that may distance you too far from the events and information sources necessary for understanding the setting under study; other times, you are likely to find yourself having to counter the centripetal tendencies that sometimes pull researchers in too closely, clouding their analytic capacities, draining them emotionally, and creating unnecessary ethical or political complications. We take these centripetal and centrifugal tendencies into account in our discussion of the presentational and exchange strategies.

1. **Presentational Strategies**

   Presentational strategies involve conscious attempts to create and sustain a particular identity or definition of the situation that is congruent with one's interests (Goffman 1959). In many sectors of social life, goal achievement is partly contingent on presentational strategies. In qualitative research, based on the cumulative experience of many fieldworkers, there are several discernible methods of self-presentation that have been found to be particularly effective. These include the presentation of a nonthreatening demeanor, strategic incompetence, and selective competence.

   a. *Nonthreatening Demeanor*

   We suggested in the previous chapter that gaining entry is facilitated by proceeding in a courteous and respectful manner. Certainly this piece of folk wisdom extends to the challenge of developing and maintaining viable fieldwork relations as well. Here, however, it is not merely a matter of being courteous, but also of making sure to proceed in a fashion that does not threaten those from whom you are trying to learn or elicit some form of assistance. Thus, one of the first guidelines to keep in mind in developing viable fieldwork relationships is to be as nonthreatening as possible. We are not referring to threat in any physical sense, of course, as there is no rationale for exercising such threat within the context of research. Instead, we refer to more subtle threats, like those to the beliefs, practices, existing social arrangements, and even self-esteem, that are communicated by argument, ridicule, sarcasm, gestures of disinterest, and so forth. As Bruce Berg (2004, p. 103) writes in his discussion of what he dubs "a dramaturgical look at interviewing":

   > If you want people to openly talk about their feelings and views, you must refrain from making any negative judgments—either verbally or through visual cues. The best way to accomplish this is to accept people for who and what they are; avoid making judgment of their actions, beliefs, or life styles, even in your mind.

   Or, as Barbara Sherman Heyl (2001, p. 370) puts it succinctly: "listen well and respectfully." The argument, then, is that in most qualitative research situations, the investigator who is supportive, cordial, interested, nonargumentative, courteous, understanding, and even sympathetic will receive a good deal more information than one who acts in the opposite fashion.

This advice, however, may be considerably more difficult to put into practice than you might think. Consider how frequently in normal interaction many of us are more interested in talking than in listening, in telling than in learning, or in convincing than in understanding. Or consider the difficulty of being courteous and nonthreatening when conducting research on "unloved groups," like the racist hate groups that Kathleen Blee studied through the eyes, experiences, and voices of women members. But she was able to do so quite successfully by being open and honest about her views vis-à-vis theirs in a courteous and nonthreatening manner. "From the beginning," she tells us,

> when I asked women if I could interview them, I made it clear that I did not share the racial convictions of these groups. I explicitly said that my views were quite opposed to theirs, that they should not hope to convert me to their views, but that I would try to depict women racist activists accurately. I revealed my critical stance, but made it clear that I had no intent to portray them as crazy and did not plan to turn them over to law enforcement or mental health agencies. (Blee 2002, p. 11)

Being nonthreatening also means being sensitive and attentive to matters of appropriate grooming and dress. What is appropriate depends, of course, on the relation between the researcher as a person and the setting itself. Forty-year-old researchers observing adolescents undoubtedly make themselves and the young people appear ridiculous if they copy the latter's dress. Conversely, the casual student garb of jeans and shirt is not an appropriate costume for interviews with corporate executives, as Morrill (1995, p. 230) clearly understood when he showed up for his interviews "dressed in a . . . suit carrying nothing but a leather notebook and a small tape recorder." Yet, you want to exercise some common sense here too, especially if you present yourself as a known investigator; for there is no point of dressing down or up to such an extent that your appearance contradicts your claim to be a researcher. Thus, a guiding principle for appearance is to dress and groom in a manner that shows respect for yourself and for your hosts and is consistent with your identity claims.

b. *Acceptable Incompetence*

A naturalistic investigator, almost by definition, is one who does not understand. She or he is "ignorant" and needs to be "taught." This role of watcher and asker of questions is the quintessential *student* role. Now it happens that the idea of the ignorant student who has to be taught is a commonsensical and widespread notion. People almost everywhere feel they know and understand that role. Thus, the investigator who assumes the role of *socially acceptable incompetent* is likely to be accepted. In being viewed as relatively incompetent (although otherwise cordial and easy to get along with), the investigator easily assumes the role of one who is to be taught. Such persons *have* to be told and will not take offense at being instructed about "obvious" things or at being "lectured to." That is, such persons are in a good position to keep the flow of information coming smoothly.

There are a good many situations where the role of the acceptably incompetent would be a hindrance or danger (e.g., Crist 2001; Gurney 1985; Nordstrom and Robben 1995; Williams, Dunlap, Johnson, and Hamid 1992). But for those who are in appropriate settings and who can tolerate being what a naturalistic researcher generally is—a nonthreatening learner—the informational yield can be considerable. As a model for how this presentational strategy can be enacted successfully, you might well keep in mind how celebrated detectives, such as Agatha Christie's "Hercule Poirot" and the television character "Columbo" played by Peter Falk, would often feign ignorance and buffoonery in order to invite assistance or throw off guard those they were casually interrogating.

c. *Selective Competence*
While fieldworkers find that it is often useful to highlight their incompetence or lack of knowledge as a means of eliciting guidance and explanations from informants, the advantages of being acceptably incompetent may be limited or nullified by particular research settings, situations, questions, and relations. There are settings and situations in which it is useful instead to highlight selected personal credentials or competencies in order to be deemed more worthy of informants' time and attention or access to various kinds of data. As we have seen, businesses and government agencies, for instance, often have gatekeepers that function to guard access to personnel, settings, and agency records. In such settings, highlighting one's professional credentials may open doors that would otherwise be closed. For example, Ruth Horowitz's (1995) entrée to a welfare work program for teenage mothers was facilitated by her academic standing and the hope of some of the gatekeepers that she would serve as an evaluation researcher for the program (see also Snow, Benford, and Anderson's discussion of the "credentialed expert" role, 1986).

In other settings and with other groups, it may be beneficial to reveal a degree of insider knowledge, skill, or understanding—if you have any—in order to make informants feel comfortable and more connected with you. So, for instance, Thomas Calhoun's (Anderson and Calhoun 1992) rapport with young male street prostitutes improved, and their willingness to respond to his questions increased, when he revealed to them that he already understood some aspects of the gay "cruising" subculture. Jason Jimerson's (1996) field relations with players in his study of basketball games depended in part on his competent performance as a recreational basketball player. And Jennifer Lois (2003) found that, while she lacked competence in rescue techniques, her acceptance by members of the search and rescue organization she studied increased when she was able to demonstrate that she had the physical stamina to pursue such activities. The general point here is that while the researcher is best advised to assume a novice role and perhaps enact strategic incompetence in the field, sometimes it may be advantageous to highlight particular personal attributes that are valued in the setting.

2. **Exchange Strategies**

As we indicated in Chapter 3, the investigator is able to conduct research only because the people in the setting either consent to being observed or interviewed or don't know that research is going on. Thus, while the issue of exchange or trade-offs is a legitimate component of the naturalistic process, it is not of equal relevance to all researchers in all kinds of settings. Unknown researchers who are actual ongoing members of private or quasi-private closed settings are already contributing to their respective settings through their roles in them, thus making the issue of exchange less relevant than for known researchers in such settings who are nonmembers. But of the known researcher, setting members and prospective interviewees have every reason to ask: What do I get in return? What's the trade-off? Among fieldworkers, the most common answer has been mundane assistance of one sort or another. Sometimes the assistance has an ephemeral quality, as when observers "ratify a moral community" by "witnessing" its activity (Bosk 1985) or when interviewers provide an opportunity for their informants to talk about something they want to talk about, as was the case with many of the women Kathleen Blee interviewed. When recounting why racist women were willing to talk to her, Blee notes that

> [m]any saw an opportunity to explain their racial politics to a white outsider. . . . They were interested in me not as a potential convert, but rather as a recorder of their lives and thoughts. Their desire, at once personal and politically evangelical, was that someone outside the small racist groups to which they belong hear and record their words. (2002, p. 10–11)

More commonly, interviewers and observers provide concrete provisions or services, such as offering rides or loans, delivering messages, serving coffee, giving advice and opinions, holding illegal goods, offering physical defense, telling lies, and so on through the entire range of normal "friendly" relations typical of organized social life. For example, Ruth Horowitz (1986, p. 416) tells us, regarding the youth gang she observed, that "(w)hen one of the Lions was arrested, not only did I make a small contribution to his bail but, as the only person over 21, I signed for him. I was asked and began to contribute small sums to the group's funds for beer and wine. . . ." Likewise, Pierette Hondagneu-Sotelo (1994), during her year-and-a-half study of a Mexican immigrant barrio in San Francisco, offered assistance, albeit a greater variety, by becoming a community activist and personal helper, providing transportation, assisting immigrants in collecting paperwork and preparing their cases for legal immigrant status under new legislation, and helping them in their pursuit of employment, as well as being a sympathetic confidante for their personal and familial problems. In a similar vein, Kathy Charmaz, in her study of chronic illness, writes of attending

> several weddings as well as several memorial services of people I had interviewed. . . . I had tea with elderly women, visited elderly men; admired pictures of spouses, grandchildren, and boyfriends . . . and met family members, friends, and housemates. (1991, p. 274)

The various types of researcher assistance provided in each of the foregoing studies is not so surprising given that the populations or groups studied—Chicano gang members, Mexican immigrants, and the chronically ill and their families—all have self-evident needs. But what about groups or contexts in which the needs of the members are not so transparent as, for example, in the case of those situated in the upper reaches of the class hierarchy or occupational structure? Here too enterprising fieldworkers have found provisions or services to offer. Thus, Charles Bosk relates that he served the surgeons who allowed him to hang around by being an "extra pair of hands" and a "gofer." During the time of my fieldwork," he tells us, "I became very proficient at opening packages of bandages, retrieving charts, and fetching items from the supply room" (1996, p. 137). But what might one provide for corporate executives, who typically have access to an extensive secretarial network? Apparently not much, but Morrill did come up with two "services" he promised in exchange for his prospective informants ongoing cooperation: "public presentations consisting of general observations of their organization and . . . private exit interviews with any informant covering observations of their personal 'strengths and weaknesses'" (1995, p. 238). Even though few organizations cashed in on these offers when Morrill exited, it is reasonable to assume that such offers helped pave the way for subsequent cooperation.

Although less common, assistance may be in the form of more esoteric goods and services. For example, during his participant observation in an Italian neighborhood, William F. Whyte found himself voting four times (once in his own name, three times under assumed names) in a single local election (1993, pp. 313–317). In the context of actual field situations, you must decide for yourself where to draw the line at helping. On reflection, Whyte rejected the propriety of this highly questionable helping behavior, in part because he came to realize that you don't have to engage in all relevant behaviors "in order to be accepted by the people" studied; in part because different groups within the setting may have different standards or expectations, and in part because the field researcher must ultimately behave in accordance with his own moral standards or run the risk of "wonder(ing) what sort of person he is after all" (1993, pp. 316–317).

You must, then, draw an appropriate line as to what you will say or do in exchange for information or opportunities to secure it. You must establish limits on the kinds of exchanges. In most instances, however, you cannot forego strategic engagement in some kind of exchange. It is not only a trade-off for access, but a means for developing and maintaining viable fieldwork relations.

B. Strategies to Control Relational Closeness

As noted earlier, you are likely to be confronted with different relational challenges at various points in the course of your research. In early stages of research you will likely be focused primarily on building relationships and rapport; at other times as your fieldwork progresses, you will need to step back in order to gain a broader perspective on what you are learning and doing. Additionally, field relations require boundaries that circumscribe relational rights, responsibilities, and expectations. Those that become too intimate may impede research because the researcher comes to be defined (by others and/or oneself) almost exclusively in terms of non-research relationships and identities. While in a few cases (e.g., Lois 2003) ethnographers have managed both romantic relationships and successful research projects, most researchers seek to avoid such entanglements. Similarly, researchers tend to resist becoming complete members of the groups they study, despite the sometimes intense efforts to convert them.

While many researchers have written about the strategies they used for gaining rapport and closeness, fewer have paid sustained attention to strategies they have used to set boundaries in their relationships. Emerson and Pollner (2001) have culled from the research literature several common interactional strategies for "managing inclusive overtures," including preempting, finessing, declining, and withdrawing.

1. Preempting
Preempting involves the researcher's attempt to ward off unwanted offers of inclusion before they begin. As the old adage puts it, "An ounce of prevention is worth a pound of cure." Of course prevention requires some degree of foreknowledge regarding potential problems, which is not always possible. But where it is possible to anticipate potential problems, it may be feasible to forestall them. Three potential problems seem common enough to have been commented on by a number of ethnographers. These include the possibilities of unwanted romantic or sexual advances, of being drawn into illegal or violent behaviors, and of informant dependence on or material exploitation of the researcher.

Perhaps the most widely discussed problem in terms of managing closeness and setting limits on field relations has been women's confrontation of unwanted romantic or sexual advances. Many female researchers have at times tried to minimize sexuality in their appearance in order to avoid unwanted overtures from men, as did Gwen Dordick (1997) while doing research at a large homeless shelter in Manhattan, and as Ruth Horowitz (1986) did in her research with Chicano gang members. In addition to playing down sexual characteristics in dress, several single female ethnographers have claimed to be married or embellished upon their existing involvements. After facing unwelcome overtures from workers during her initial fieldwork at a homeless shelter, for instance, Rebecca Allahyari (2000, p. 17) writes that "To ward off [further] advances . . . when I re-entered the setting. . . . I presented my long-term committed relationship as an engagement." The intensity of advances and degree of persistence vary considerably, and in some settings may reach intolerable and/or harassing levels. When faced with such gender harassment in Manhattan's largest all-male homeless shelter, Gwendolyn Dordick recounts that she felt pushed toward more extreme preemptive measures. Each time she visited the shelter to interview homeless residents she had to wind her way through a gauntlet of shelter guards whose sexual remarks became progressively "more graphic" and their "self-professed ability to 'make [her] happy' more exaggerated." She eventually decided to try to preempt any further harassment by "com[ing] back at them aggressively":

> When one security guard suggested that I "suck" his "dick," I told him that he looked limber enough to do it better himself. When another told me that he wanted to "eat my pussy," I asked if this was because his nose was longer than his dick. This toughness earned me the respect of some of the guards as well as residents who overheard the verbal sparring. I was able to come across as neither naïve nor easily intimidated. (1997, p. 111)

A second potential problem that fieldworkers at times endeavor to preempt is being exposed to or even drawn into illicit or violent behavior. While it might be valuable to witness such activities, there are various reasons to avoid doing so, including not wishing to become accomplices in criminal activity and not wishing to have firsthand data that later could be subpoenaed. Some gang researchers, for instance, have set limits with members. Sanchez-Jankowski, for one, writes that he established a "mutual understanding . . . that I did not have to participate in any activity (including taking drugs) that was illegal" (1991, p. 13).

The third arena of relatively frequent preemptive efforts involves setting limits on the extent to which favors and assistance will be provided. So, for instance, in his research with children Gary Fine at times treated them to ice cream and took groups of them to movies, but he also took precautions to keep the children from viewing him as a source of small loans. He did this diplomatically, sometimes claiming to be out of money and at other times providing a loan, but telling children that it "was being given for one time only [so that I] subsequently had justification for refusing to loan money to that same person" (Fine and Sandstrom 1988, p. 25).

2. **Finessing**

In contrast to preempting, which involves clear negotiation of the researcher's limits, researchers also at times manage inclusive overtures by finessing the situation. It is often useful to respond to group members' requests in evasive or ambiguous ways that at least minimally satisfy their queries or expectations, but that also avoid more complete immersion than feels comfortable. In Snow and Anderson's (1993) homelessness research, Anderson often spent time on the streets with groups of homeless people who were drinking out of a group bottle of wine and who offered him the chance to participate. While he did not want to drink from the group bottle, he often accepted the bottle when it was handed to him, held it for a minute, and then passed it on as if he had taken a drink himself. At other times he made sure to have cans of beer available so that he could use an open beer as a pretense for not drinking from the group's bottle.

Proselytizing religious groups seem to have a tendency to put researchers in awkward situations that require finessing as well, as illustrated by David Van Zandt's strategy in his study of the "Children of God" to avoid discomfort he felt selling their literature. "[One]technique I used was to claim that I needed more 'Word Time' or devotional time, and request that we take a break to read" (1991, p. 14).

Finessing strategies tend to be spontaneous and highly contextualized and represent "a consummate test of the fieldworker's grasp of local culture" (Emerson and Pollner 2001, p. 251). So widely are such strategies invoked in the field that Emerson and Pollner (2001, p. 252) conclude: "evasive finessing provides one of the foundational skills of participant/observation fieldwork."

3. **Declining and Withdrawing**

Not all occasions that can lead to being drawn too close in field relations can be preempted or finessed. At times it is simply necessary or preferable to "just say no," declining to witness or participate in activities that make you uncomfortable. So, for instance, Patricia Adler writes of her ethnography of drug dealing that while for a time she accepted drug transactions occurring in her home, "we finally had to put a stop to that because we could not handle the anxiety" (1993, p. 24). As Emerson and Pollner (2001, p. 253) note, "Since declining may give offense and damage rapport, ethnographers often take care to identify indigenous methods for declining to participate in local activities." As an example they cite Terry Williams' adoption of cocaine users' reasons (e.g., "my nose is out" or "I'm coked out") for sometimes not accepting offers to use other's cocaine. Such ideal options, of course, are not always available.

In extreme cases, pressures to become more involved and to take on locally defined membership roles may even lead researchers to decide that it is time to leave the field. So, after chronically battling against being defined as sexually available to gang members, Ruth Horowitz concludes, "I was unable to negotiate a gender identity that would allow me to continue as a researcher" (1986, p. 423).

III. Getting Along While Getting Out

At some point or another all fieldwork expeditions come to an end. Either the fieldworker is so taken with the people and lifestyle observed that s/he "converts," albeit a rare occurrence as noted earlier, or, far more commonly, s/he disengages from the field and gets on with the business of fine-tuning the analysis and writing a report. But what kinds of factors prompt exit or disengagement? When should the field researcher leave the field, and what are the implications of doing so for both self and informants? Although qualitative researchers have not discussed this issue of disengagement to the same extent as they have the range of matters concerned with access, entry, and field relations, increasing attention has been devoted to the topic (Berg 2004, pp. 187–189; Gallmeier 1991; Kaplan 1991; Maines, Shaffir, and Turowetz 1980, Snow 1980; Stebbins 1991; Taylor 1991). Drawing on some of this literature, we address two broad sets of questions in this section. First, what are the set of factors that affect disengagement? And second, to whom do fieldworkers have an obligation when they exit, and how might that obligation be discharged?

Figure 4.2 provides a summary categorization of the various factors that are relevant to answering these questions. The table categorizes these factors in terms of whether they function as precipitants or impediments to disengagement and the kind of pressure, constraint, or rationale they constitute. Thus, factors compelling one to leave the field may be (a) theoretical or methodological in character, such that the scene has become so taken-for-granted that nothing seems new or interesting anymore; (b) structural, in the sense of being institutionally or organizationally based, as when one's research funds have dried up, the deadline for the term project or thesis is approaching, or one's sponsors ask them to leave— as happened to John Lofland (1977) when the local leader of an aspiring "new" religion decided that Lofland's sociological interests (which he had declared from the outset) were more sincere than his religious interests and that, despite his vague murmurings to the contrary, he was never going to convert; (c) relational or emotional, as when the fieldworker is clamoring to withdraw because of loathing, marginalization, or just sheer exhaustion; or (d) moral or ethical, as when the researcher has a contractual obligation to submit a report to the sponsor. On the other hand, the researcher may experience various countervailing pressures to stay in the field, which are listed in Figure 4.2 as impediments to disengagement. These too may be (a) theoretical or methodological, as when one feels unduly anxious about the adequacy of the data collected (what Glaser and Strauss [1967, p. 73, 227–28] call "compulsive scientism"); (b) institutionally or organizationally based, as when some groups look with disfavor upon membership withdrawal and mobilize so as to turn the straying member "back into the fold and its problem-solving practices," as Snow (1993, p. 17–21) experienced when disengaging from the Buddhist movement he had joined and studied; (c) relational or emotional, as when the researcher has come to identify strongly with the group studied or befriended a number of informants; and (d) moral or ethical, as when the researcher experiences conflicting moral or ethical obligations and a corresponding sense of guilt, as in the case of the "ethical hangovers" described earlier (Chapter 2, Section III.E).

Taken together, these various countervailing pressures and constraints suggest that getting out is likely to be more complicated relationally or interpersonally and ethically than generally presumed. However, the relational complexities of disengagement clearly are less relevant in some research situations than others. For example, if the (known or unknown) researcher has come to dislike the setting participants, or was booted out, he may be delighted simply to walk away and not look back. Similarly,

Figure 4.2 Summary of Factors Affecting Disengagement

	Pressures, Constraints and Rationalities			
	Theoretical and Methodological	Structural and Intuitional	Relational and Emotional	Moral and Ethical
Precipitants	Completion of Research Agenda or Game Plan Taken-For-Grantedness Theoretical Saturation Heightened Confidence	Exhaustion of Funds; Deadlines Expulsion Role Conflict	Marginalization Boredom Exhaustion Non-Research Ties	Obligations to Sponsor Obligations to Profession Obligations to Public
Impediments	Compulsive Scientism	Rigid Policy toward Defection Greedy Organization	Sympathy Identification Fun and Excitement	Conflicting Moral and Ethical Obligations Guilt

Revised Adaptation of David A. Snow, "The Disengagement Process: A Neglected Problem In Participant Observation Research," *Qualitative Sociology* 3: 100–122, 1979.

unknown researchers in public and quasi-public settings usually do not have to deal with the issue at all. It is less likely that they will have formed personal relationships, and, even if they have, their research locales are often of the sort in which people are expected to drift in and out. But for those investigators (known or unknown) in more stable settings who—because of close personal ties they have developed with the researched or because of future research agendas—want to maintain contact or leave open the possibility of a return, the issue is a palpable one indeed. And, as with many such issues in fieldwork, the advice implied or proffered in the literature on it (see, e.g., Carpenter, Glassner, Johnson, and Loughlin 1988; Shaffir and Stebbins 1991, Part IV) is not unlike the advice one might give or receive in everyday life. Most generally, don't burn your bridges. And, more specifically in keeping with the etiquette of departures: inform people of your plans ahead of time; explain why and where you are going; say your good-byes personally insofar as it is possible; and, if appropriate, promise to try to stay in touch.

IV. Getting Along with Claimants and Conscience: Ongoing Ethical Concerns

All of the personal and strategic problems we have discussed in this chapter are seedbeds for nagging and sometimes quite pressing ethical dilemmas and related matters of conscience. These dilemmas and concerns typically arise at the intersection of two overlapping issues or questions: To what extent are we engaging in ethically appropriate behavior as defined by our professions (e.g., American Anthropological Association, American Sociological Association), our university Institutional Review Boards, and our own personal standards? And to whom do we, as fieldworkers, have some obligation, and how do we adjudicate among these often competing obligations?

Much attention has been lavished on these concerns and questions by fieldworkers agonizing over their own behavior and relationships within a context of growing concern with research ethics and protocols, as indicated by the previously mentioned diffusion of Institutional Review Boards across university and college campuses in the United States. As you may recall, we have already discussed aspects of these issues in Chapters 2 (Section III.D) and 3 (Sections IV and V). As well, we directed you earlier to a number of key writings that address a range of issues pertaining to the intersection of ethics and qualitative research (Chapter 3, Section III.B). Thus, you are armed with a set of works and discussions that can be drawn on for guidance as you confront and navigate the issues and concerns raised above.

However, without in any way denigrating the concerns of ethicists or belittling the honestly expressed moral anguish of some researchers, we caution you not to become so preoccupied with matters of ethics and conscience that you become immobilized or find yourself unable to speak about anything other than some of the ethical quagmires and challenges associated with qualitative research. Why? Because in our view, the fieldwork situation is rarely, if ever, more difficult ethically than everyday life. And how could it be otherwise, since fieldwork is not detached from ongoing social life but is embedded in it and thus shares in the continuing ethical dilemmas of social life itself.

Given the disconcerting impossibility of doing fieldwork that is totally ethically pure, some observers might find it reasonable to conclude that the fieldwork enterprise should be abandoned. As psychologist Urie Bronfenbrenner commented more than forty years ago: "The only safe way to avoid violating principles of professional [and, we would add, personal] ethics is to refrain from doing social research altogether" (1952, p. 453). But thankfully the social science community has not come to that conclusion and qualitative research continues as a vibrant enterprise. So our recommendation is to be aware of the directives of regulatory agencies and draw on them as appropriate, as well as on your own ethical standards, but do not give up going about the business of tracking qualitatively what it is in the world that is of interest to you.

V. Postscript: Personal Accounts of the Field Experience

Throughout this chapter, we have alluded, in varying degrees of detail, to numerous accounts of researchers' field experiences, particularly as those experiences pertain to getting along with self and setting members. These necessarily abstracted and perhaps too ordered statements on "getting along" cannot really convey the full flavor of the field experience. For this, we recommend reading one or more of the following accounts, which we have ordered in terms of those that are more general in contrast to those that are setting specific:

General Overview Accounts

- Robert A. Georges and Michael O. Jones, *People Studying People: The Human Element in Fieldwork* (1980).
- John M. Johnson, *Doing Field Research* (1975).
- Hortense Powdermaker, *Stranger and Friend: The Way of an Anthropologist* (1966).
- Rosalie H. Wax, *Doing Fieldwork: Warnings and Advice* (1971).

Specific Accounts

- Kathleen Blee, "Crossing a Boundary," pp. 1–21 in *Inside Organized Racism: Women in the Hate Movement* (2002).
- Mitchell Duneier, "A Statement on Method," pp. 333–357 in *Sidewalk* (1999).

- Gary Alan Fine, "Ethnography in the Kitchen: Issues and Cases," pp. 233–253 in *Kitchens: The Culture of Restaurant Work* (1996).
- Calvin Morrill, "Anatomy of an Ethnography of Business Elites," pp. 229–255 in *The Executive Way: Conflict Management in Corporations* (1995).

Edited Volumes of Specific Accounts

- Annette Lareau and Jeffrey Shultz (eds.), *Journeys Through Ethnography: Realistic Accounts of Fieldwork* (1996).
- William B. Shaffir and Robert A. Stebbins (eds.), *Experiencing Fieldwork: An Inside View of Qualitative Research* (1991).
- Carolyn D. Smith and William Kornblum (eds.), *In the Field: Readings on the Field Research Experience* (1996).

This chapter, combined with the preceding one, may have led you to view fieldwork as "adventure." It is certainly that, as almost any veteran will testify. But it is something else as well, or it is nothing at all: It is hard, disciplined, and sometimes tedious work. What you have done thus far—getting in and getting along, and perhaps getting out—are certainly necessary aspects of the ethnographic enterprise, but they are hardly sufficient to make for a successful project. Another essential ingredient is data logging, which, if omitted, would clearly make your fieldwork little more than personal adventure. Thus, we turn to the data-logging process.

CHAPTER 5

LOGGING DATA

Data logging is a central and ongoing feature of the qualitative research process. It involves the careful recording and organization of whatever data are assembled. Fieldnotes and interview write-ups are the most basic forms of qualitative data logging, but it may also include mapping, census taking, sound recording, filming, document collection, and so forth. Further, as the research develops over time, the fieldworker must manage an ever-expanding quantity and diversity of data. In this chapter we examine the data-logging process and the management of the data set or log in a manner that will facilitate retrieval of information for analysis.

We explicitly propose the model of "logging" to emphasize similarities of social science fieldwork to the way our naturalist counterparts in biology carefully record observations on the actions and noises of the animals they research. Just as the naturalist biologist must note the minute, ordinary, and routine details of the animals under study, so the naturalistic field observer must carefully attend to the ordinary routines and conditions in which the people under study conduct their lives. Unlike many social science researchers who collect data only after having identified the relevant variables they want to record, naturalistic researchers typically immerse themselves in field settings of interest in order to discern significant foci for study. Ethnographic researchers do not so much actively "procure" specific data for recording as they seek to register the events and behaviors unfolding, or the words being spoken, before them. This does not mean that field researchers simply wait for "significant" (sociologically or otherwise) events to occur or words to be spoken and then write them down. Rather, as emphasized in the previous chapters, fieldworkers attempt to position themselves so as to facilitate observation of matters of interest, such as "how people lead their lives, how they carry out their daily rounds of activities, what they find meaningful, and how they do so" (Emerson, Fretz, and Shaw 1995, p. 2). An enormous amount of information about the settings under observation or the interview in process can be apprehended in apparently trivial happenings or utterances, and these are indispensable grist for the logging mill. Given the potential significance of seemingly insignificant ordinary details, the fieldworker must pay careful attention to consistent and meticulous documentation. Understandably, then, the naturalistic tradition views as either naïve or arrogant both the complaint of the novice investigator that he or she "didn't make any notes because nothing important happened" and the contention of professionals that he or she did not take any fieldnotes because they "get in the way. They interfere with what fieldwork is all about" (quoted in Jackson 1990, p. 18). As Rosalie Wax warned us:

> The fieldworker may also think twice about following the example of those would-be ethnographers who assert or boast that they take few fieldnotes or no notes at all. The fact is that most of the people who say that they are able to get along without taking notes do not write anything worth reading. (Wax, *Doing Fieldwork*, 1971, pp. 141. Copyright 1971 The University of Chicago Press. Reprinted with permission.)

There is, then, little if any rationale for not taking seriously the logging process. As well, it is important to understand that data logging is not merely a "memory device" that allows you to recall the extraordinarily complex range of stimuli with which you have been bombarded. While the data log certainly functions in part in this way, such an analogy misses a more fundamental point: *the logging record actually constitutes the data*. The data are not the researcher's memories which, in and of themselves, can never be subjected to systematic analysis. Rather, the data consist of whatever is logged and is thus available for careful and systematic inspection.

It is for this reason that the recording tasks are such a crucial aspect of the naturalistic analysis of social life. And it is here, perhaps more than in any other facet of the process, that the researcher requires discipline. "Getting in" and "getting along" may involve difficult ethical, personal, and professional choices; they also generate a certain excitement, especially for researchers who feel some personal attachment to the concerns of the research. In contrast, data logging is often experienced as tedious and as taking one away from the action in the field. But it will be less boring and more meaningful if you keep in mind the ultimate goal of your research, which is to use your fieldwork as the grounding for sociological analysis. When you focus on this goal, the imperative of conscientious data logging is clear; as we said above, only data that have been logged (as opposed to unrecorded memories) can be systematically accessed for rigorous analysis. The failure to engage in tenacious data logging, then, throws the entire research project into jeopardy.

We begin this chapter by briefly discussing recent challenges to the "facticity" of fieldwork data. Next we consider various types of data and provide an overview of the logging task, particularly as it pertains to intensive interviewing and to participant observation. We then consider separately the different forms the log takes in each research mode: the interview guide and write-up in intensive interviewing and fieldnotes in participant observation.

I. Data: Fact or Fiction?

While social scientists' concerns regarding the research enterprise have historically focused primarily on the issue of assessing empirical adequacy (e.g., of validity and reliability) of both quantitative and qualitative data, recent years have witnessed increased interest in the literary or rhetorical aspects of ethnography. Recognizing that there are similarities between the literary techniques used in fiction and in ethnographic writing, some contemporary social scientists have proclaimed a "crisis of representation," asserting that all ethnographic texts and the "facts" on which they are based are fictional. Norman Denzin, an articulate spokesperson for what has come to be known as the "postmodern" approach to ethnographic work, repeatedly takes on what he sees as the "dated" and epistemologically naïve viewpoint of "social realism."

> [Social realism] assumes that an obdurate social world exists and that the events, meanings, and activities in this world can be accurately recorded by a skilled interviewer-participant observer.... Consider some troubling alternatives. The ethnographers' text creates the subject; subjects exist only insofar as they are brought into our written texts.... [This] countertheory [to social realism] justifies treating each document as a separate story. *It also renders fruitless ... debates over who got the facts right.* (1992b, pp. 124–125; emphasis added)

This challenge to "social realism" in fieldwork by Denzin (1989b, 1992a, 2002; Denzin and Lincoln 2000) and others (for example, Banks and Banks 1998; Clifford and Marcus 1986; Clough 1992; Ellis and Bochner 1996), as well as the more general challenge to all human knowing posed by postmodernist philosophy, has generated considerable debate, as reflected in a host of "realist" responses (Best 1994; Charmaz 1994; Dawson and Prus 1993a, 1993b, 1994; Sanders 1994; Snow 2002; Snow and Morrill 1993, though some observers have suggested that academic patience with and interest in the debate is waning, e.g., Flaherty 2002; Manning 2002). A "how to" guide like this one is hardly an appropriate format for seriously engaging this debate, but because our views tend toward a social realist position, some response does seem in order. In Chapter 8, we shall offer a more detailed rendering of what our position entails (and how it differs from other positions) relative to the analysis of one's data. Here we want only to deal briefly with two aspects of the postmodern challenge to the notion of objectivity.

The first challenge is the charge that data are often fictional because fieldnotes filter rather than mirror what "actually" happens. We have just emphasized that researchers should register events that unfold before them, and we believe this is the appropriate mind-set to bring to the data-logging task. At the same time, we concur that all human observations of the world (whether of the social, the biological, or the physical world) are necessarily filtered. Human *perception* is always human *conception:* What we "see" is inevitably shaped by the fact that we are languaged; by our spatial, temporal, and social locations (by culture, history, status); by our occupational and various idiosyncratic concerns; and, especially relevant here, by the scholarly discipline within which our "looking" takes place. But this is the stuff of introductory philosophy and sociology courses and is hardly revolutionary material with which to blow away a generally social realist orientation to research. And to grant that researchers are selecting out only certain pieces from the raw flux of the phenomena that surround them does not say that they are creating those pieces. Filtering is not fabricating. A filtered reality is simply a filtered reality; it is not—unless we want to enter an Orwellian "Wonderland" and insist on our right to make words mean whatever we want them to mean—a fiction.

The second challenge contends that since all observation is filtered or interpreted, no ethnographic claims can be asserted as more true or accurate than other claims. Such relativism stems, we believe, from the postmodern tendency to regard fieldwork exclusively as "an interpretive act, not an observational or descriptive one" (Van Maanen 1988, p. 93). The leap from acknowledging an interpretive dimension to ethnography to viewing it as exclusively interpretative neglects other essential aspects of the fieldwork enterprise—most critically, the rigorous collection of observational and interview data. Indeed, it would be pointless to engage in fieldwork if our perceptions in the field were based solely on interpretational schemes and assumptions that we brought with us. Social realists, who have long recognized the interpretive dimension of human knowledge, reject such a solipsistic view of perception. As Herbert Blumer argued:

> One errs if he thinks that since the empirical world can exist for human beings only in terms of images or conceptions of it, therefore reality must be sought in images or conceptions independent of an empirical world.... [This] position is untenable because of the fact that the empirical world can "talk back" ... in the sense of challenging and resisting, or not bending to, our images or conceptions of it. (1969, p. 22)

Indeed, the histories of both the physical and social sciences demonstrate the necessary interplay of empirical observations and theoretical conceptualizations. Theories offer angles of vision or terminological screens for viewing certain aspects of the empirical world, but empirical data impose their own limitations by providing access to an obdurate reality within which certain ideas and concepts may be tested and refined. To view data as preordained fabrications is to fly in the face of both common sense and scientific observation. The point of entering and immersing oneself in field settings and interactions, and paying close attention to the meanings that group members attach to their actions, is to allow the world to speak back to us. Like truly dialogic conversation, conscientious fieldwork challenges our preconceptions and facilitates our attempts to test and move beyond the confines of our current understandings. And the data log, as the record of our observations, is the critical linchpin of these attempts.

II. The Logging Task

As we have indicated, the format of data logging in exclusively interview or observational studies is rather different. Nevertheless, many aspects of the logging task are pertinent to both modes. Further, fieldwork typically includes both interviews and observations, as well as other types of data. In the following discussion we consider the range of typical data sources, problems of data-related error and bias, and the mechanics of logging.

A. Data Sources

In qualitative research, the prime sources of data are the words and actions of the people you are interviewing or observing, often combined with some degree of direct experience. These are recorded mainly via written notes but also, on occasion (depending on appropriateness and resources), via photographs, films, audiotapes, or videotapes. You also may tap supplementary data sources (e.g., documents and physical traces). In Figure 5.1 we list a range of data-gathering methods and their informational yield, ranging from the richest and most full-bodied techniques to more narrow or focused strategies. While the distinctions we make are not always as clear as the table suggests (for example, intensive interviewing may involve varying degrees of observing social action), Figure 5.1 can serve as a valuable heuristic device, illustrating how the data collected in field research come from a variety of sources, each of which can provide important insights into the social world under investigation. Let us briefly examine these data sources.

1. **Direct Experience**
   When ranged along a continuum from experience-near to experience-distant research, qualitative research is an attempt to approximate the experience-near end of the spectrum, which is more likely to yield what William James (1932, pp. 11–13) called an "acquaintance with" kind of understanding rather than the more distant, abstract "knowledge about." But not all fieldwork data sources are equally close to direct experience. If we focus on the researcher, the most experience-near data come from direct personal involvement in the social world under study. Direct experience enables the researcher to enter more closely into the setting under investigation and may facilitate a deeper understanding of the context(s) of social action. While direct experience itself varies, from close personal experience with the topic or social world under study (see, e.g., Henson 1996; Humphreys 1975; Karp 1996, 2001; Pattillo-McCoy 1999) to less completely immersed experience in that world (see, e.g., Bourgois 1995; Lichterman 1996; McRoberts 2003; Rochford 1985), all forms of direct experience offer the researcher some degree of close personal exposure to the phenomenon under study. Such experience can often provide especially profound and nuanced understandings of certain aspects of the topic of study. It can also alert or sensitize the researcher to aspects of the social world that may be taken for granted or may not be particularly salient or relevant to members, especially to experienced members as compared to the researcher who is a "novice" in the setting. (For a more multifaceted discussion of the relationship between direct experience and fieldwork, see Douglas 1976, pp. 108–123.)

2. **Social Action**
   As the basic, intertwined forms of human interaction, talk and action are the fundamental sources of data for field research. While talk is accessible through a range of research methods, the capturing of social action requires *in situ* observation, although not necessarily participant observation. Social

Figure 5.1 Qualitative Data Sources, Methods, and Informational Yield

	General Qualitative Methods or Data Gathering Techniques				
Qualitative Data Sources	Participant Observation	Non-participant Observation	Informal Interviewing and Listening	Intensive Interviewing	Historical and Content Analysis	Inspection of Physical Materials
1. Direct Experience	X					
2. Social Action: what people actually do	X	X				
3. Talk: what people say	X	X	X	X		
4. Archival Records	X	X	X	X	X	X
5. Physical Traces of Social Action	X	X	X	X	X	X

*Derived from David A. Snow & Calvin Morrill's Seminar in Field & Observational Methods

action frequently includes verbal interaction, and it is important for the researcher to capture both the action and verbal aspects of situated behavior. At times, though, social action is relatively nonverbal. Nonverbal action can provide valuable data for understanding the topic of your study. So, for instance, in Melinda Milligan and April Brayfield's (2004) study of museum programs for children, the staff's use of such nonverbal actions as shining laser pointers at noisy children and spacing children's chairs far enough apart to limit their touching each other illustrated both the staff's desire to control children's behavior and the strategies they had developed for doing so. Frequently, observations of social action complement group members' talk (whether concurrent talk or talk at some distance in time from the observed action), such as when Jennifer Lee's (2002) observations of gender differences in interactions among Korean and African-American merchant-customer relations were corroborated in her interviews with merchants. But action and talk are not always consistent with each other, and it is important to document divergence as well as consistency. The degree of consistency is in fact a significant empirical question that has been a topic of longstanding analysis, and its presence or absence can yield noteworthy insights and raise analytic questions (Deutscher 1966; Deutscher, Pestello, and Pestello 1993).

3. **Talk**

The bulk of analysis in most fieldstudies is based on informants' talk—and for a good reason. Language is the key to understanding most human interactions as it is the major symbolic system for establishing meaning. There are three kinds of talk that are central to qualitative research: talk in action (that is, in the flow of activity in the setting), informal interviewing, and intensive interviewing. Each of these types of talk can capture important aspects of the social world under study.

Arguably the most valuable and least discussed type of talk is *talk in action*, by which we refer to accounts or patterns of talk formulated for a particular end in a naturally occurring situation that is part of some ongoing system of action, such as when a homeless person panhandles a passerby (as discussed in Snow and Anderson 1993). The more interested researchers are in lived experience and the management of everyday routines, the more critical to their project is the documentation of talk in action.

The talk that occurs in *intensive interviews* contrasts sharply with talk in the flow of action. First of all, interview talk, even when its focus is on action, is primarily on action that has occurred outside the immediate context of the interview—the topic of the interview is not the interview itself. But, since talk tends to be framed in response to audience, interviewees' responses to interview questions are not so much oriented to group members' meanings for action as they are oriented toward providing explanations that interviewers are likely to understand. Finally, while observation of talk in action is guided by naturally occuring events, interviews are structured by the interviewer's interests and the flow of conversation. Each type of talk can provide valuable data, and each has its own advantages. Talk in action captures meaning in its richest situated context and provides what Leroy Gould and his colleagues call "perspectives in action" (1974, pp. xxiv–xxvi), but it can only capture what is witnessed in the field. Intensive interviews, on the other hand, offer the opportunity to gain information about events beyond those the researcher has had direct access to, thus providing "perspectives of action," and also to plumb the depths of meaning of action beyond group members' talk in the field. Further, since the talk in intensive interviews can be focused by the researcher, it is possible to collect similar information from many informants.

The third type of talk, *informal interviewing*, involves asking questions *in situ*, during the course of naturally occurring activities. Such asking is certainly a normal feature of everyday life. The naturalistic investigator is simply using this fact for research purposes, although perhaps asking questions much more frequently than ordinary participants in the setting would do. Questioning of this kind is often called "casual interviewing," and it is a key part of participant observation. The observer or interviewer may also utilize a more indirect means of asking questions that David Snow, Louis Zurcher and Gideon Sjoberg have called "interviewing by comment" (1982). This is an attempt to elicit information verbally by making a statement rather than by asking a direct question. Informal interviewing sits in between intensive interviewing and talk in action. Like observation of talk in action, casual interviewing is closely linked to direct observation and tends to be connected to issues of high salience for group members. But like intensive interviewing (as opposed to observation of talk in action), it typically is directed more by the researcher.

In the quest for intimate familiarity with the social world under study, fieldworkers strive to gather verbal data (whether through intensive interviewing, informal interviewing, or observing talk in action) that provide rich understanding of the experiences and perceptions of group members. While a case can be made for the value of recording all three kinds of talk during the course of research, such an ideal must be balanced by issues of practicality and informational yield, considerations that will at times favor intensive interviewing over participant observation, and vice versa.

4. Supplementary Data

Depending on the question or questions being asked, the character of the setting, the form of research, and so on, you also may amass data through supplementary sources. Investigators frequently collect documents that are generated by the setting or that have to do with questions or topics of interest. Census taking may be useful, as may mapmaking where physical settings are pertinent. Materials on the historical aspects of a people, setting, issue, and so forth will help place the data in context. Relevant newspaper and magazine clippings may expand your understanding of the present. The proliferation of Internet sites and chat groups in recent years has produced a new and voluminous potential source of data that should be explored as well. In short, conscientious naturalistic investigators not only scan the immediate data site(s) for words and actions but also are sensitive to the possible value of a wide range of supplementary information that may come their way. Three particularly valuable kinds of supplementary data are archival records, physical traces, and photographic data.

a. *Archival Records*

Archival records include a range of written materials, from private documents (such as diaries, letters, and personal photographs) to public and commercial records (such as court transcripts, real estate listings, and newspaper articles). Both private and public documents, which constitute an important category of "unobtrusive measures" (Webb, Campbell, Schwartz, Sechrest, and Grove 1981; see also Plummer 2001), can be sources of rich data. W. I. Thomas and Florian Znaniecki (1927) pioneered the sociological use of private documents in their compelling analysis of immigrants' letters to chart the experience of Polish immigrants to the United States in the early 1900s. More recently, numerous scholars have engaged in extensive content analysis of newspaper articles. Cynthia Bogard's (2003) study of the social construction of homelessness as a national social problem, for example, draws heavily upon newspaper articles on homelessness from the late 1970s to the mid-1980s in the *Washington Post* and the *New York Times*. Organizations from soup kitchens to multinational corporations produce volumes of public and private records that may shed light on a variety of relevant issues. Further, many public archives, such as U.S. Census Reports (available on the Internet at www.census.gov) and the Uniform Crime Reports (available at www.fbi.gov/ucr) contain local/regional and nationally aggregated statistical and demographic data that may be valuable for comparative purposes. Indeed, the range of potential archival records is enormous, including visual and audio materials in addition to written documents. Such documents can significantly enrich fieldstudies, although they have considerable potential for error and bias—a matter we will discuss below.

b. *Physical Traces*

Just as the naturalist biologist relies upon physical signs of activity to track the activities of other animals, the naturalist fieldworker may find it useful to observe and document the physical traces of human doings. Such traces, which comprise another type of "unobtrusive measures" (Webb, Campbell, Schwartz, Sechrest, and Grove 1981), include both erosion and accretion measures. Erosion is exemplified by the wear on the materials or paths on which people walk, such as tiles, carpets, sidewalks, and trails, or on the material items they use, such as chairs and couches, clothes, books, and car tires. Accretion of human traces, such as cigarette butts, fingerprints, and lipstick, may also provide equally interesting and compelling insights, as was the case when Snow and Anderson (1993) found a high density of makeshift homeless encampments in the areas surrounding Austin's two main day labor exchanges. The documentation of physical traces in the fieldworker's data set can be quite valuable, but their meaning and representativeness must be evaluated in the context of other relevant observations.

c. *Photographic Data*

Since Douglas Harper's (1982) photographic oral history of a railroad tramp in the early 1980s, the use of photography in fieldstudies has become an increasingly popular methodological technique for documenting and analyzing other social worlds and lives. The emphasis here is not so much on the discovery and analysis of informant photographs, as with family and wedding albums (see Walker and Moulton 1989), but with the use of the camera to capture the faces, activities, and routines of those studied. Such photographic data is sometimes used as a supplement to more traditional ethnographic fieldwork, as in Mitchell Duneier's *Sidewalk* (1999), and other times as the basis for elaborating a visual narrative, as in Harper's evolving work, including his account of the uses and misuses of technology through the experiences of a backwoods mechanic (1987) and his portrait of change and decline in a dairy farm community (2001). This latter stream of work that features the camera as its primary research tool is reflected in the journal *Visual Studies* (previously titled *Visual Sociology*) and methodical accounts of such research (Harper 2000, 2003; Margolis 1990; Pink 2001; Schwartz 1989). This research approach both overlaps with and is distinctive from the fieldwork elaborated in this guide.

B. Problems of Error and Bias

We indicated in Chapter 2 that naturalistic investigation, with its preferences for direct apprehension of the social world, has somewhat fewer problems with validity than do research traditions that rely on indirect observation and perception. Nonetheless, the naturalistic researcher must critically assess the truth and meaning of every piece of information collected. By truth, we mean the degree to which the data provide an accurate, factual depiction of the observed events and behaviors, both verbal and nonverbal. We realize that there is likely to be some variation in the extent to which ethnographic descriptions get at the truth—or facts of the matter—with some providing more careful and accurate depictions than others. It is also the case that even the most careful and accurate of fieldstudies are unlikely to capture fully the social world portrayed. Thus, when we speak of truth, we have in mind "close approximations" of the empirical world (see Snow 2002, p. 499; Snow and Morrill 1993, p. 10) rather than descriptive exactitude. The closer the approximation, the more truthful, and presumably compelling, the ethnographic account. Meaning, on the other hand, refers to the contextualized understanding of "the facts." Given that factual observations may be more or less accurate, depending on a variety of factors, and that there may also be variation in the meaning of events and happenings among your informants, it is critical that you rigorously assess the accuracy of the observations that you log as data by considering the various threats to the accuracy of those data and what measures might be taken to reduce or control those threats.

1. **Types of Error and Bias**
   The threats to the accuracy of your data, and thus your final report, can be thought of as types of error and bias. In general there are three kinds of contaminating error and bias, each of which can be traced to particular roles and role relationships, observer status characteristics, and the observer's interpretive frame of reference. The three types include:

   a. *Reactive Effects*
   Reactive effects are invalidating effects that result from the influence of the observer's presence or behavior on the phenomenon under study. They are the contaminating effects of the observer's research role, personal characteristics, and/or perspective on the observed, with the consequence that researchers may not be observing the very thing they hoped to observe and that they may, in fact, believe that they are observing.

   b. *Perceptual and Interpretative Distortions*
   These distortions include errors that emanate from the research role and/or the observer's personal characteristics and perspective independent of the information observed.

   c. *Sampling Errors*
   These errors encompass the various limitations on the investigator's ability to observe a reasonable sampling of relevant aspects of or variations in the phenomenon being observed because of the biasing effects of the observer's research role, personal characteristics, or theoretical perspective.

   The cross-classification of each of these types of threat with their various underlying sources yields a variety of more concrete types of error and bias, each of which can contaminate your data, distort your findings, and render your final report less truthful and compelling than it might have been in the absence of such error or bias. These various concrete errors and biases are summarized, along with the controls discussed below, in Figure 5.2.

2. **Measures to Control Error and Bias**
   Given these various contaminating threats to your data and findings, the question arises as to what might be done to control them. There are, of course, no one or two magic panaceas. However, there are a number of measures that can be employed to neutralize or limit the likelihood of these contaminating/distorting effects by addressing their general sources.

   a. *Sampling Strategies*
   The sampling associated with qualitative fieldwork is usually purposeful (sometimes called judgmental sampling) rather than random or probability-based. Whereas random sampling is most appropriate when the research aim is enumerative generalization—that is, from the sample to some larger population for which the parameters are known in advance, purposeful sampling is appropriate when the population parameters are not known and/or when you want to learn about select cases or variation across a set of

Figure 5.2 Types and Sources of Controls for Error and Bias in Fieldwork

General Source of Error or Bias	Reactive Effects	Perceptual and Interpretive Distortions	Primary Sampling Errors	Controls
Role and Role Relations	• observer may be seen as an outsider, a spy, an intimate, etc.	• overidentification or under-identification • distance or surrender • too much or not enough rapport	• barrier to other roles and role relationships	• maximum variation sampling • team approach • prior ethnography • use of "deep" informant • triangulation
Personal Characteristics of Observer	• sex, age, education, race, ethnicity people under study, etc.	• mood, prejudices, beliefs about topic or	• avoidance of certain situations and people	• team approach • triangulation
Interpretive Frame of Reference	• passing on to informants one's own views, feelings, etc.	• structuring attention—seeing only those things that are consistent with one's assumptions and propositions	• avoidance or neglect or certain occasions, people, or places	• sampling extreme and typical cases • team approach • member checks • external audit

*Derived from David A. Snow & Calvin Morrill's Seminar in Field & Observational Methods

cases. Of the various kinds of purposive sampling (see Erlandson, Harris, Skipper, and Allen 1993; Patton 1990), several are particularly helpful for reducing error and bias. For example, *maximum variation sampling*, which is a Darwinesque strategy in which the aim is to discover the diversity or range of the phenomena of interest, provides a useful antidote to error and bias that emanate from singular research roles or role relationships by pushing the researcher to consider ways of looking beyond the most convenient contexts or those to which his role grants him primary access. *Sampling extreme or deviant* cases—that is, cases that are outliers or unusual in comparison to what appears to be the more typical cases, helps to guard against the bias that may be associated with both the researcher's role or interpretive/ theoretical perspective. Similarly, what Glaser and Strauss call *theoretical sampling* (1967, pp. 45–77) reduces the prospect of premature theorization and conclusion by encouraging the researcher to look to other situations, groups, or subgroups to see if the emerging understandings hold or apply.

b. *Team Research*

In contrast to the traditional "lone ranger" approach to fieldwork, in which a single researcher does the entire project, team field research involves the "triangulation," or coordination and integration of two or more researchers so as to increase access to different voices, multiple perspectives, and various relevant situations and encounters, thereby helping to guard against the biases associated with a single role and set of role relationships, the personal characteristics of the researcher, and his or her preferred interpretive point of view. Simply put, team field research allows for the adoption of multiple roles and positions relevant to the context studied, thus increasing the prospect of discerning greater variety in behavior and perspective than is likely when the research is conducted by a single fieldworker.

c. *Strategic Selection of Informants*

A third strategy for reducing the prospect of error and bias, particularly those that emanate from the limitations of most research vantage points and/or roles and role relationships, is to select informants who are themselves positioned differently within the group or setting studied, and who might therefore provide access to different kinds of information. Morris Zelditch's (1962) distinction among three uses of informants—as surrogate census takers, observer's observers, and representative respondents—reminds us of the informational utility of considering the different ways in which prospective informants might function as sources of information depending on how they are situated within the context of interest. Some may have access to events or places not accessible to the single researcher, as with the surrogate census taker and observer's observer; others may function as bridges or conduits to other possible informants, and still others may function as ideal-typical or representative members of a group insofar as it is possible to establish that there are such modal members. Although some groups or settings may have representative members, close investigation is likely to reveal different types of members—such as novices or rookies, converts, apostates or heretics—for which representative types or cases might be discerned.

d. **Member Checking**

Member checking, or validation as it is sometimes called, involves the solicitation of group or setting members' assessment of the researcher's hypotheses, findings, or analyses (Bloor, Frankland, Thomas, and Robson 2001, pp. 387–394; Erlandson, Harris, Skipper, and Allen 1993, pp. 142–143; Rochford 1992). Insofar as this strategy is feasible, it can provide an additional check on observational and interpretative errors. However, this strategy must be used with caution for a variety of reasons, including the likelihood that group members will neither approach nor assess the material presented with the theoretical concerns and issues that are likely to have animated the research.

As the foregoing discussion emphasizes, it is critical to question the accuracy of your data and to take actions that will facilitate their veracity, but it is equally important to understand the context in which the "facts" occur: the situations in which behaviors are enacted, accounts are given, and documents are created. The facts of social life are *socially embedded artifacts*, and the researcher's understanding of the data requires that they be accurately placed within the subjective and intersubjective contexts that make them meaningful. One of the great advantages of participant observation is that it enables the researcher to contextualize observations since they are witnessed in close proximity to informants' experiences. And sensitive intensive interviewing, while at times quite distant from the social action being discussed, still encourages the interviewee to elaborate the situational concerns that frame, for them, the meaning of their experience. Field researchers frequently find that the "facts" take on significantly different meanings when placed in different social contexts. So, for instance, survey researchers and psychiatric clinicians have documented high rates of symptoms of clinical depression among the homeless. Such symptoms have included subjective feelings of irritability, excessive worry, insomnia, loss of weight, and heavy alcohol and drug use. But as Snow, Baker, Martin, and Anderson (1986) have argued, while such "symptoms" may legitimately be viewed as indicators of mental illness among more affluent and domiciled populations, for the homeless they may more reasonably reflect problems of living in severely deprived material circumstances. The facts of high rates of unkempt appearance and demoralization among the homeless are indisputable, but the meaning of those facts may be dramatically different when the behaviors and subjective states of informants are placed in context.

A similar need for contextualization exists in relation to verbal statements and exchanges. It is extremely important for field researchers accurately to capture verbal data, but it is also important to avoid the mistake of evaluating verbal statements solely in terms of their accurate representation of some external reality. The bare "facts" of verbal interaction—the statements made by interviewees and the exchanges observed among conversational participants, for instance—must be evaluated in the context of the conversation. So, for instance, the identity talk among the homeless often involves fanciful embellishments or fabrications regarding past actions. Nonetheless, these verbal avowals of identity are highly meaningful attempts to create a sense of personal worth in social interaction with street peers.

Finally in this regard, field researchers must likewise assess archival materials, whatever their source, in order to place them in the most appropriate interpretive frame of reference. Organizational records are situated accomplishments and the more you understand about their creation, the deeper your understanding of the "facts" (for a geminal treatment of this issue see Garfinkel, 1969).

C. The Mechanics of Logging

Throughout the research process, the fieldworker is involved in amassing the various kinds of data that we have discussed and, as the research progresses, an ever-expanding quantity and diversity of these data must be managed. Further, these data must be stored in a way that facilitates access of information for ongoing and future analysis. In this section we offer some advice and examples regarding the mechanics of data logging in order to help researchers effectively handle what at times can feel like overwhelming mountains of information.

We can begin by considering five basic requirements for effective data management with the goals of facilitating qualitative data analysis.

1. You must be able to log or record data promptly.
2. Data must be available for duplication.
3. Data must be available for coding.
4. Coded categories must be easily accessible for examination and analysis, including tabulations of specific kinds of activities, characteristics, etc.
5. Since coding categories tend to emerge and be revised over time, data must be accessible for revised coding.

There is no uniform system used by fieldworkers to log their data. Any system that enables you to accomplish the activities listed above will suffice. But some *system* is necessary.

One common system is to maintain computer files that include all of your fieldnote entries, interviews, and various other data documents that are relatively easily stored in electronic files (e.g., digital photos and audio files), while maintaining hard copy files of those data (e.g., organization newsletters and magazines) that are not easily stored electronically. (Be sure to keep updated hard copies, external mobile drives or CDs of all data stored on your computer. We cannot emphasize the importance of backup copies too strongly!) These data files are then available for coding and recoding as your analysis takes shape. For organizational clarity and ease of access, hard copy files should mirror the organization of the project's computer files, when possible. Access to your data will be facilitated by keeping updated tables of contents for both hard copy files and computer files. An example of such a system, based on Leon Anderson's ongoing skydiving research, is provided in Figure 5.3.

In the near decade that has passed since the last edition of this book, computer technologies have continued to expand. The video and audio capacities of computers have improved, and today it is possible to conduct interviews on digital recorders and to log the audio interview transcripts directly onto computers. Music, photos, and video are now all easily stored and accessed on computers, and extensive amounts of data, ranging from organizational records to personal documents, are available on the Internet. The proliferation of and improvements in computers has facilitated both the logging of data and their use in presentations and reports. Indeed, it is almost unthinkable today for social science researchers to do research without computers. But, while the ubiquity of the personal computer has simplified both the initial recording of the log and its duplication, the computer and its associated software have added new and complex levels of decision making to the research process.

A considerable number of software programs for the manipulation and analysis of qualitative data are currently available. They become especially relevant, of course, in a later research stage than the one we are discussing here. But, because using them for analytic purposes may require special formatting of the log and may even require using them to log, you should decide whether to use one and, if so, which one, before transcribing a single interview or writing up a single fieldnote entry. As we discuss in Chapter 9, we have as yet no solid demonstration of the merits of using these programs for analytic purposes, but there seems little doubt of their value for data storage and retrieval purposes. General discussions of the uses of computers in qualitative work and comprehensive overviews of appropriate and available programs and applications are now readily available (Dohan and Sanchez-Jankowski 1998; Fielding 2001; Kelle 1995; and Weitzman 2000). You should review one or more of these texts to acquaint yourself with the many data manipulation possibilities inherent in normal word-processing programs (for example, word counts, multiple filings of entries, movements of copies of entries in and out of established files, and so forth) as well as to help you decide whether the more specialized analytic programs might work for you.

Our advice at this juncture is to consider moving beyond your current level of computer skills but not too much beyond. In the early stages of learning qualitative research, you will face sufficient challenges in collecting, logging, and analyzing your data without compounding the difficulty of the task by adding to it the burden of learning higher levels of computer literacy. As Dohan and Sanchez-Jankowski emphasize, "The hard work in coding data is intellectual, not mechanical. Computer assistance does not relieve the ethnographer of the need to spend many hours devising, revising, and applying an

Figure 5.3 "Blue Skies" Data Log and Filing System

I. Data Organization in Computer Files and Hard Copy

  Fieldnotes
  Interviews
    Jumpers
      General
        One-time Jumpers
        Student Jumpers
        Experienced Jumpers
      Handicapped Group Members
        Pieces of Eight (amputee skydiving group)
        Silent Free Fallers (deaf skydiving group)
        Wheelchair Club (paraplegic and motor-impaired skydiving group)
      Nontraditional Group Members
        Skydivers over Sixty
        Pink Mafia (women's skydiving group)
    Dropzone Owners
    Skydiving Coaches & Organizers
  www (Internet) Data (printed pages)
    Dropzone.com Materials
      Safety Discussion Forum
      Personal/Social Forum
      Women's Forum
      Disability Forum
      Events and Gatherings Forum
    Handicapped Skydiving Groups Web Site Materials
      Pieces of Eight (amputee skydiver group)
      Silent Free Fallers (deaf skydiver group)
    POPS (Parachutists Over Phorty) Web Site
    Drop Zone Web Pages (data on 50 U.S. dropzones)
    U.S. Parachutist Association Web Page
      State and Federal Regulations
      Injury and Fatality Reports

II. Hard Copy Only Data

  Skydiving Magazines
    Parachutist Magazine
    Skydiving Magazine
  DZ Documents
    Injury Waiver Forms
    Miscellaneous Brochures

III. DVD or VHS Copy Only

  Skydiving Videos
    Instructional Videos
    Entertainment Videos
    Event Videos

indexing system that is reliable and valid" (1998, p. 482). Since the intellectual/analytic skills are tantamount, if you are on a tight time schedule (e.g., taking a methods course where you are expected to complete a small study by the end of the term), you would be wise to rely on the word-processing and organizational capacities of your computer and the "cut and paste" school of data manipulation and analysis that we shall describe in Chapter 9. However, if you are already familiar and comfortable with a variety of software programs and have a sufficiently long time period within which to work on your field-study, then by all means be open to using an analytic program.

D. Protecting Confidentiality

In most naturalistic investigations, the question of providing confidentiality to the people studied (discussed in Chapter 3, Section V) does not usually arise until the write-up stage (see Chapter 10). That is, it is ordinarily only when the fruits of your research have been transformed into analysis that you become concerned to disguise identities and locations (if disguise is what you intend). However, some types of sensitive research push this concern with confidentiality backward in time, starting at the point of data logging. If you are studying people engaged in illegal or politically suspect activity, for example, or people involved in activities kept secret from their associates, or well-known figures who are speaking openly only with the assurance that it is "off the record," you may want to take considerable precaution with the data log itself. Carol Warren's handling of her research log on "closeted" gay men is exemplary:

> Tape recorded interviews were stored without identifying tags (although voices could be identified), and were erased after transcription and use. Field notes were kept in unlocked storage; however, pseudonyms were used throughout the recording of field notes, and a master list of names matched to pseudonyms [kept in locked storage] was discarded following the write-up of the material. (1977, p. 96)

Warren's cautions a quarter century ago were prompted solely by a personal concern for the people she was studying. Current researchers, on the other hand, are guided by the requirements imposed by Institutional Review Boards (which may, among other things, demand the use of pseudonyms throughout the data-logging process) and the "consciences" of their professional associations. The American Sociological Association's *Code of Ethics*, for example, states that, "Sociologists [should] take reasonable precautions to protect the confidentiality rights of research participants" [ASA *Code of Ethics*, 1997, 11.01(a)]. The ASA code goes on to say, "Confidential information provided by research participants . . . or others is treated as such by sociologists *even if there is no legal protection or privilege to do so*" ([ASA *Code of Ethics*, 1997, 11.01(b)], emphasis added). Given such an injunction, sociologists should understand confidentiality practices in data logging as strategies not only for protecting the people they study but also for protecting themselves.

III. Data Logging in Intensive Interviewing: Guides and Write-Ups

As we have seen, the data-logging tasks in intensive interviewing and participant observation are similar in many ways. But there are also several important differences. Therefore, we will now consider each mode of data logging separately.

In intensive interviewing, you initially log the data via an instrument known as an "interview guide." We thus discuss the preparation of such a guide, then go on to the matter of doing the interview with the guide, and finally consider the production of the actual log: the writing up of the interview.

A. Preparing the Interview Guide

The interview guide is considerably less formal or structured than the questionnaire or interview schedule used in survey research or opinion polling, but the care with which it is created is no less crucial. Its production requires serious thought.

1. Puzzlements and Jottings

Logging data by means of intensive interviewing with interview guides reasonably begins with you, the prospective investigator, taking some place, class of persons, experience, event, or abstract topic as problematic or as a source of puzzlement. If you take this puzzlement seriously and decide to pursue it as a topic of investigation, and if you judge that interviewing is the most appropriate procedure (see Chapter 2), you then sit down in a quiet place and ask yourself, "Just what about this thing is puzzling to me?" Without worrying about coherence, begin to jot down questions about these puzzling matters and, at various times over several days or weeks, continue to do so. Questions may occur at odd moments—while you are taking a shower, listening to conversations, driving, opening mail—so you should keep a small notebook handy at all times. In this phase, it is also useful to mention the topic to friends, acquaintances, and associates; they may suggest additional questions or stimulate new dimensions of puzzlement. Jot these down as well.

What are you doing at this stage? You are "teasing out" and recording those things defined as puzzling in the context of your own and your associates' understandings, whether based on personal experience and biography or intellectual curiosity (see Chapter 1). You are preparing to use what you have come to define as puzzling as a point of departure for interviewing. If your evolving puzzlements are not already stimulated in part by issues and questions in the social sciences, then you should spend some time locating and reading books and articles on the particular, concrete matter of concern. In reading, you can discover what others who have written about and studied this matter found puzzling and what kinds of questions they ask and note the kinds of answers they have offered.

2. Global Sorting and Ordering

As these puzzlements accumulate, it is likely that you have also been thinking about the kinds of general clusters or topics into which these various puzzlements fall. You should also have recorded ideas on the overall structure or organization of the puzzlements, because eventually you must give these puzzlements or questions a global or comprehensive design. If they have been written on separate pieces of paper or on a computer, you can thus begin to sort them into separate piles or clusters. Several sortings and resortings may be necessary in order to establish the number of clusters—or, more abstractly, topics—that seem best to arrange your accumulated concerns. Whatever the several topics, it is not necessary to strive for any kind of sophisticated social scientific sense in formulating them. Indeed, it is preferable for the topics to be quite straightforward and commonsensical, the better to communicate with the people to be interviewed.

The following is an example of global organization, drawn from Lyn Lofland's (1982, 1985a) research on loss and connection. Note that it is clear, straightforward, and arranged in a semi-chronological order that is likely to be easily understood by informants.

1. Who is lost?
2. When?
3. Tell me about the relationship prior to "loss": dyadic career.
4. Tell me about the loss itself.
5. Prior loss experience.
6. Immediate response to the loss: emotional, physical, behavioral.
7. Development/changes through time regarding feelings and actions.
8. Looking at the relationship from the current perspective.

A second example of global organization is drawn from Calvin Morrill's (1995) study of conflict management among corporate executives. This guide moves from general issues regarding the corporation for which the interviewees work and their place in it to questions that are more directed toward eliciting information regarding conflict and conflict management. Morrill developed the guide over the course of early interviews with executives and structured it so that the questions could be asked in a single interview or over multiple interviews.

1. Type, Size, and Nature of Business
2. R[espondent]'s Responsibilities and Routines
3. Philosophy(ies) Regarding Executive Practices in the Corporation
4. Extent and Nature of Social Contacts and Communication in Business
5. Changes in the Business over Time
6. Characteristics and Evaluation of Effective Executives
7. R's Personal Background and Future Goals

8. Kinds of Conflicts in the Business
9. R's Experiences and Strategies in Managing Conflict
10. Consequences of Conflicts for the Business
11. Presence and Practice of a (formal or informal) Code of Ethics (1995, pp. 245–248)

As the above examples suggest, it is useful when constructing your global design to try to adopt the perspective of the people you will be interviewing and to think about what will make sense to them. If some topics are of a sensitive character or potentially embarrassing to them or to you, it is often better to address these toward the end of the interview. The hope is that by treating the less sensitive material first, you will build trust and rapport during the course of the interview itself, making it easier subsequently to deal with more tension-laden topics. Sometimes it is wise to begin with relatively neutral "facesheet items" (see Section II.A.5 below) as an innocuous way of getting into the question-and-answer process.

3. **Section Sorting and Ordering**
Once you have tentatively established an overall design for the guide, assuming it does not constitute the entire guide, you can turn to particular piles of puzzlements within the overall design and begin to plan a reasonably logical ordering of concerns and questions. For example, global section 6 of Lyn Lofland's interview guide on loss and connection (dealing with immediate responses) contains the following questions:

1. What exactly did you do in the first days or week following the loss? Different from normal?
2. What exactly did you feel in the first days or week following the loss? Different from normal?
3. How did others act toward you? How did you feel about their actions?
4. Did the loss seem appropriate, timely, untimely, meaningless, meaningful?
5. Did the loss in any sense seem to free you? How?
6. [If appropriate,] did you attend the funeral or other services?

Similarly, in keeping with the principle of building some rapport before addressing sensitive topics, Morrill decided to ask questions that "more naturally led into information on trouble cases" (1995, p. 247) either in the later part of single interviews or in follow-up interviews. In this latter section of the interview guide, he arranged a set of questions that directly explored relevant issues:

1. How do you survive long enough in this company to get to the top?
2. What kind of executive do you respect?
3. How do you enforce a decision down the line (i.e., to a subordinate)?

4. How much latitude do you feel you have in the decisions you make? What kinds of procedures do you have to follow?
5. Have you experienced a situation in which a top executive subordinate wasn't performing up to your expectations?
6. What kinds of problems arise between people you supervise? (1995, p. 247)

4. **Probes**

In interview guides, the emphasis is on obtaining narratives or accounts in the person's own terms. You want the character and contour of such accounts to be set by your informants. You might have a general idea of the kinds of things that will comprise the account, but still be interested in what they provide on their own and the terms in which they do it. As the informants speak, you should be attentive to what is mentioned and also to what is *not mentioned* but which you feel might be important. If something has been mentioned about which you want to know more, you can ask, "You mentioned _____. Could you tell me more about that?" For things not mentioned, you might ask, "Did _____ happen?" or "Was _____ a consideration?"

Such questions are called probes. In interview guides, a series of probes are often connected to a specific question in order to remind the interviewer to probe for items that might not be mentioned spontaneously. In exploring her informant's "relational careers," Lyn Lofland's guide for her study (1982) contains a reminder to probe for the following:

- How did the relationship develop?
- What sorts of things done together?
- What sorts of things talked about together?
- Intensity of time together in a typical week/year.
- Changes in intensity through time.
- Emotional tone.
- Changes in emotional tone.
- Importance placed by you on the relationship.
- Changes in importance.

And Calvin Morrill included the probes below to encourage executives to provide detailed responses to his interview question, "Have you experienced a situation in which a top executive subordinate wasn't performing up to your expectations?"

- How did you handle that situation?
- What would you consider the proper way to handle such a situation?
- Do you have any formal procedures for these kinds of situations? (1995, p. 247)

In providing these examples, we do not mean to suggest that every question must be outfitted with one or more prepared probes. It may happen that you do not, at a given time, have much idea of what to probe for. Many on-the-spot probes are likely to be used spontaneously in order to amplify or clarify an account. And many kinds of questions may not require probes (although they can doubtless be invented for any question).

5. **Facesheets and Fieldnotes**

    For purposes of identification, bookkeeping, and generally keeping track of the interviews and social characteristics of interviewees, interview guides commonly devote a page or so to gross factual data. Such a page is often the first sheet of the guide and is therefore called the facesheet. Items typically appearing on the facesheet include such things as a very general statement of the purpose of the interview, the interviewee's name (or a code number, if the topic is a sensitive one and names keyed to code numbers are to be kept in a separate place), date and time of the interview, location/place of the interview, relevant social characteristics (e.g., age, sex, education, ethnicity, religion, place of birth, occupation), and assurances of confidentiality and a brief statement of potential risks, if any (see below).

    Beyond information of this sort, additional social items will probably be cast according to the purposes of the interview and will therefore vary a good deal from one study to another. Even though the facesheet is typically the first sheet, facesheet questions are not necessarily the first questions you ask. Depending on the topic, the degree of trust, and so forth, it may sometimes be preferable to go directly into the interview itself after giving the introduction. In that case, the facesheet questions are sometimes treated almost like a formal afterthought, a minor duty that you have to perform in interviewing. In addition, interviewers often find it useful to append a post-interview comment sheet to the guide. This is not material that is shared with the informant. Rather, it is simply a space for you to jot down fieldnotes on the interview itself after you and the informant have parted. You may include a description of the setting (if it is new to you) and the informant (beyond that noted on the facesheet), the emotional tone of the interview, any particular difficulties (methodological or personal) that were encountered, your own feelings during and about the experience, insights and reflections, and so on. The jotted notes on such sheets are later incorporated (perhaps in expanded form) into the interview write-up and become a portion of the data log. Remember also that intensive interviewing may involve you in relationships with your informants that transcend the interview encounter or encounters. If that is the case, fieldnotes recording extra interview observations and conversations may be appropriate; you can add such notes to the relevant interview write-ups so that they become part of the data log.

    Finally, academic researchers today are frequently required by Institutional Review Boards to obtain signed informed consent forms from those they interview prior to conducting interviews. In fact, many review boards require that a copy of the informed consent form accompany the application for IRB approval. The informed consent document is typically required to contain a brief explanation of the research, some assessment of potential risks and benefits, and a statement of if and how the interviews will be kept confidential. Many review boards provide boilerplate for some portions of the consent form. In composing such forms it is important to keep them as brief as possible and also to frame them in a non-alarmist and noncontroversial manner. There is little to be gained by trying to be overly specific and complex in regard to these issues in your communications with interviewees, especially in the early stages of research.

B. Doing the Interview

We have already discussed much about the social relational aspects of interviewing (Chapter 4). Here we shall deal with the more technical matters of introduction, format, leading questions, interviewer activity during the interview, and the use of separate guides.

1. Introduction

Recall from Chapter 3 (Section III.B.2) that the "getting in" phase of intensive interviewing requires an "account"—an introduction, as it were, to the potential informant. This account provides an overview of the content of the interview and its connection to the larger project, the probable length of time required, promises of confidentiality if appropriate, and so forth. At the time of actually conducting the interview, you should repeat much of this material and, if called for, provide additional information. The goal at both stages is to acquaint the person honestly and clearly with what you are asking her or him to do. The list of self-instructions Fred Davis developed in his guide for interviewing handicapped people (1960) more than 40 years ago still provides a stellar example of proper introductory material:

- Explain the purpose and nature of the study to the respondent, telling how or through whom he came to be selected.
- Give assurance that he will remain anonymous in any written reports growing out of the study and that his responses will be treated in strictest confidence.
- Indicate that he may find some of the questions farfetched, silly, or difficult to answer, the reason being that questions that are appropriate for one person are not always appropriate for another. Since there are no right or wrong answers, he is not to worry about these and do as best he can with them. We are only interested in his opinions and personal experiences.
- He is to feel perfectly free to interrupt, ask clarification of the interviewer, criticize a line of questioning, etc.
- Interviewer will tell respondent something about himself—his background, training, and interest in the area of inquiry.
- Interviewer is to ask permission to tape record the interview, explaining why he wishes to do this.

In addition, as we mentioned above, many universities require that you gain "informed consent" at the start of an initial interview with an individual. If that is a requirement at your university, then you should blend your general introductory remarks to the interview with any material that your IRB mandates. Doing so will usually lead to a smoother flowing introduction than treating the two matters separately. You will also probably want to vary the style and order of coverage according to the dictates of the circumstances.

2. **Flexible Format**
As you can see from the wording and layout of the interview guide examples provided above, a guide is *not* a tightly structured set of questions to be asked verbatim as written, accompanied by an associated range of preworded likely answers. Rather, *it is a list of things to be sure to ask about when talking to the person being interviewed.* For this reason, the interview instrument is called a *guide* rather than a schedule or questionnaire. You want interviewees to speak freely in their own terms about a set of concerns you bring to the interaction, plus whatever else they might introduce. Thus, interviews might more accurately be termed *guided conversations.*

It happens that people vary a good deal as to how freely they speak or how chatty they are. When you encounter less verbal interviewees, it is likely that you will go through the interview guide in the order that you have set up the questions. The interviewee may provide little in response to each question, thus pushing you on to the next question.

Fortunately, however, many people are quite talkative. In response to a given question they will raise all manner of leads and puzzlements that may merit pursuit, either at that point or reasonably soon thereafter. (Ideally, you should pursue such a lead at a moment when it is also of concern to the interviewee.) Also, in the course of talking about things the interviewee cares about, he or she may inadvertently answer some of the questions in other parts of the guide. The interview guide in such cases provides a checklist, a kind of inventory of things you want to talk about during the interview. You can check them off as they are accomplished. Further, in cases where you conduct multiple interviews with the same individual, the interview guide can help you keep track of the new and old questions that remain to be explored.

3. **Ineffective Questions**
In developing and asking questions, it is important to be cautious about asking questions that are likely to produce either (or both) self-fulfilling or superficial responses. Self-fulfilling answers are perhaps most likely to occur when the phrasing of your questions communicates what you believe to be a preferable response. Questions so posed are known as *leading questions.* Thus, instead of starting off with "Don't you think that ... ?", begin with something like "What do you think about ... ?" Instead of "Is it not likely

that . . . ?", use something like "How likely would you say it is that . . . ?" Superficial responses on the other hand, tend to be produced by *closed questions*, that is, queries that do not encourage the interviewee to provide rich details in their answers. As Kathy Charmaz has noted, leading questions and closed questions can be largely averted if you consider in advance the kinds of data they are likely to elicit:

> Any competent interviewer shapes questions to obtain rich material and simultaneously avoids imposing preconceived concepts on it. Keeping questions open ended helps enormously. . . . Consider the difference between these interview questions:
>
>> Tell me what a "good day" is like for you.
>>
>> Do you feel better about yourself on a "good" day?
>
> The first leaves the response open to the experiences and categories of the participant. . . . The second closes down the discussion and relegates the answer to a yes or no. This question assumes both the definitional frame and that participant and interviewer share it. (2002, pp. 681–682)

Two basic rules follow: First, study your interview questions. Second, make sure they are neither leading nor closed.

4. **Attending, Thinking, Taking Notes, Taping**

   In our view, it is imperative, insofar as possible, that you tape-record the interview itself. Since there is no strict order of questioning and since probing is an important part of the process, you must be alert to what the informant is saying. If you have to write everything down at the same time, you are unlikely to be able to give him or her adequate attention. You must be thinking about probing for further explication or clarification of what is now being said, formulating probes that link current talk with what has already been said, thinking ahead to asking a new question that has now arisen and was not accounted for in the guide (plus making a note so you will not forget the question), and attending to the informant in a manner that communicates to her or him that you are indeed listening. All of this is hard enough in itself. Add to that the problem of writing it down and you can see that the process of note taking in the interview decreases your interviewing capacity. Therefore, if conceivably possible, *tape-record.* Then you can interview. (In group interviews, or their variant, focus group interviews, taping with adequate equipment becomes even more crucial; see Krueger and Casey 2000, Morgan 1997. For an excellent summary of strategies for ensuring high-quality tape recording, see Poland, 2002, p. 638.)

   But there are dangers in tape recording, too. Some people have found themselves not listening to the interviewee because they assume they have it all down on tape. The best way to fight against this tendency is to take sparse notes—key sentences, key words, key names, and the like—in the course of the interview and to keep close account of what has already been talked about and what remains to be talked about. This is note taking in its best sense: for the purpose of staying on top of what is going on in the interview. You take notes on what has already gone on and on what has come up that you should ask about before the interview is over. (You also have a basis for reconstructing the interview should the interviewer's worst nightmare occur: the tape recording fails!)

5. **Separate Forms**
   Because the interview guide provides a checklist and a memory device (a place for taking small notes during the interview), it is wise to use a fresh copy of the guide for each interview. For most researchers, located in settings where reproduction is easy and inexpensive, this should not prove burdensome. The advantage is that the annotated guide for each separate interview becomes a recording and memory device at the time of writing up the interview and during full analysis. For jotting purposes, too, you should be careful not to cram the questions and probes together on a page, but rather space them out, leaving ample room for notes.

C. Writing Up the Interview

Having completed the interview, the tape is transcribed and you then study the transcript and begin to analyze it. However, three strong cautions should be given about such transcriptions:

1. You should make every effort to transcribe all the interviews yourself rather than turning the task over to a "hired hand." It is in the process of transcribing that you truly "hear" what the person has said, and, as such, this is a period in which analytic insights are most likely to occur.

2. If you must turn over the transcription task to another, then plan to review the transcript while listening to the tape so as to correct the errors that are likely to occur when the transcribing is done by a person who was not present for the interview. (See Poland 2002, p. 631 for examples and discussion of transcription error.)

3. Do not let the transcriptions not done by you pile up without studying them as they become available. You should spend, at minimum, as much time immediately studying and analyzing the interview material as you spent in the interview itself.

Ideas for analysis should be set down in the form of memos. Possible requests for a reinterview of the same person on particular topics should be considered. As we will explain in Chapter 9, you should perform "coding" and "memoing"—the heart of the process of developing analysis—as you go along, rather than after all the interviews are done. (See Chapter 9 for the rationale behind these admonitions and for explanations of the specific procedures involved.)

It is not a mandated convention to transcribe every word, exclamation, or pause in the interview. Assuming that you are doing the transcripts yourself, there may be entire answers or descriptions given by the interviewee that you will feel need only to be summarized or recorded as having occurred. If you later want to have a verbatim version of a particular part of the interview, you can easily locate and transcribe it. However, interviewees' responses that are particularly deep, insightful, and/or detailed, and that may be especially valuable for analytic development, should certainly be transcribed in their entirety.

The written record of the interview, then, is an amalgam of the following:

- summaries and notes of what the informant said generally at some point,
- verbatim transcription of responses that seem important at the point of the write-up,
- fieldnotes of relevant extra-interview encounters with the informant,
- personal emotional experiences,
- methodological difficulties or successes, and
- ideas—tentative pieces of analysis (matters discussed as *codes* and *memos* in Chapter 9).

One other point: In the course of writing up the interview, new questions and puzzlements are likely to occur. These should be recorded and later considered for incorporation into future interviews as questions or probes. If there are a great many new questions, you should consider reinterviews.

Interviews of this kind tend to produce a rather large amount of rich material. Before long, you have assembled a significant data log that you need somehow to manage. Indeed, the management problem is such that researchers who conduct studies utilizing qualitative interviewing tend to employ rather few interviews. While a few studies may be based on a hundred or more interviews (see Edin and Lein 1997; Lamont 2000; Morrill 1995; Vaughan, 1990), it is our impression that most are based on considerably less than a hundred interviews (see Blee 2002; Hondagneu-Sotelo 2001; Liebow 1993; Smith 1990). Such numbers seem quite reasonable given the objective of depth over breadth and the material management problem.

IV. Data Logging in Observation: Fieldnotes

What the write-up is to intensive interviewing, fieldnotes are to participant observation: the crucial data log out of which the analysis will emerge. For better or worse, the human mind tends to forget much that has occurred and to do so rather quickly. Thus, it is of utmost importance that you write down what you have observed as soon as possible after you have observed it. While different styles of fieldwork vary in their emphasis on the importance of the daily logging of fieldnotes (see Emerson, Fretz, and Shaw 1995, pp. 17–19), our approach is solidly in what Emerson et al. refer to as the "participating-to-write style" (p. 18). Aside from getting along in the setting, the fundamental concrete task of the observer is taking fieldnotes. From our vantage point, if you are not doing so, you might as well not be in the setting. Observers in many public settings are often able to take notes on the spot because of limited interactional obligations, and they may do so continuously during their entire time in the field. They will need later to transform their handwritten scrawls into typed copy, certainly, but the recording process itself is relatively unproblematic for them. For the majority of naturalistic investigators, however, the process involves a more complex sequence involving the making of mental notes, jotted notes, and then full fieldnotes (Roger Sanjek's similar rendering of the process also includes a threefold sequence: scratch notes, fieldnotes proper, and fieldnote record [1990b, pp. 95–103]. See also Bernard, 1994, Ch. 9, and Emerson, Fretz, and Shaw 1995).

A. Mental Notes

Let us assume you are meeting with people or attending an event. The first step in taking fieldnotes is to evoke your journalistic sense of what constitutes a descriptive report. From reading newspapers, magazines, and the like, you are already familiar with the character of "sheer reportage." It concerns such matters as who and how many were there, the physical character of the place, who said what to whom, who moved about in what way, and a general characterization of an order of events.

The initial task in the process of writing fieldnotes is to orient your consciousness to the task of remembering such items. This act of directing your mind to remember things at a later point may be called making mental notes. You are preparing yourself to be able later to put down on paper what you are now seeing.

B. Jotted Notes

If you are writing actual fieldnotes only at the end of a period of observation or at the end of a day (a relatively typical practice), you may find it useful to preserve these mental notes as more than traces filed away in the brain. Such traces have a very high rate of decay. One way to preserve them provisionally is with jotted notes. Jotted notes consist of all the little phrases, quotes, key words, and the like that you put down during the observation and at inconspicuous moments. They have the function of jogging your memory at the time of writing fieldnotes. Many fieldworkers carry small, pocket-sized tablets or notebooks precisely for the purpose of jotting down notes. However, any surface will do: the cover of a book, a napkin, the back of a pamphlet, and so forth.

As mentioned above, whether you are a known or an unknown observer, the general rule of thumb is, "Don't jot conspicuously." Of course, you may also be doing interviewing in the field while observing. In that case, you should take notes of the kind described for intensive interviewing. Indeed, the interviewees will expect you to take some kind of notes to indicate that you are indeed seriously interviewing them! And there may be other occasions when someone expects you to write something down on the spot. There also may be occasions when note taking in the setting is not only appropriate for you but also for all the other participants (see, e.g., Clark-Miller and Murdock 2005). But in ordinary day-to-day observation it seems wisest not to flaunt the fact that you are recording. If you are a known observer, the observed are already well aware of being observed. You need not increase any existing anxieties by continuously and openly writing down what you see and hear. Rather, jot notes at moments of withdrawal and when shielded.

If you are spending a relatively short time (e.g., a few hours) in the field, you may feel confident in your ability to recall your observations after leaving the field, as did Snow and Anderson (1993) in shorter fieldwork stints with the homeless. But in such cases it is critically important to jot down reminders of key events, talk, or impressions immediately after you leave the field.

Whatever your technique for jotting notes (and it may vary from situation to situation), fieldworkers have found the following principles (several adapted from Emerson, Fretz, and Shaw 1995, pp. 31–35) useful:

1. Jot down details of what you sense are important components of observed scenes or interactions.

2. Jot down concrete sensory details about action and talk, paying special attention to those you could easily forget.

3. Use jottings to signal general impressions and feelings you have, even if you are unsure of their significance at the moment.

4. When field observations bring back memories of previous events, jot the memories down—identified as such—in your jotted notes.

5. Avoid confusing evaluative assertions with descriptive jottings.

6. Never write your jotted notes on both sides of anything!

C. Full Fieldnotes

At the end of the day (or of a shorter observation period), you should cloister yourself for the purpose of making full fieldnotes. All those mental notes and jottings are not fieldnotes until you have converted them to a running log of observations.

1. Mechanics

Before we discuss the typical contents of fieldnotes, some "mechanical" aspects need to be described. As a general rule, *write promptly*. Full fieldnotes should be written no later than the morning after an observation day. If you observed only in the morning, then write them up that afternoon. If you observed only in the afternoon, do the notes that evening. The underlying rule is to minimize the time period between observation and writing. As Emerson, Fretz, and Shaw note, writing "*immediately* after leaving the setting produces fresher, more detailed recollections that harness the ethnographer's involvement with and excitement about the day's events" (1995, p. 40).'

Psychologists have found that forgetting is very slight in the first few hours after a learning experience but accelerates geometrically as time passes. To wait a day or more is to forget a massive amount of material. Happily, it has also been found that memory decays very little during sleep. That is, forgetting has more to do with the acquisition of new experience than with the sheer passage of time. Therefore, it is reasonably safe to sleep on a day's or evening's observations and to write them up the first thing the next morning, thus avoiding the necessity of staying up half the night. But if you wait for days, you are likely to remember only the barest outlines of the observation period. And even if you can remember more than the barest outlines, the chances are excellent that what will be erased from memory are those small but constitutively significant phenomena that are omnipresent in social life but which are easily glossed over due to their mundane or transitory nature. Long delays between observation and fieldnote entry increases the likelihood that your notes will contain, for example, no information on your own fleeting emotions, much less the expressed fleeting emotions of others. Nor, as another example, are your notes likely to contain much description of small gestures, facial expressions, body movements—those important ephemera that we so easily forget.

As we have previously emphasized, writing fieldnotes takes *personal discipline* and *time*. It is all too easy to put it off for a day or so, especially since actually writing the notes may take as long or longer than the observation. Indeed, as a rule of thumb you should plan to spend at least as much time writing as you spent observing. This, of course, is not invariant. Some observers spend considerably less time on notes and are still able to perform good analysis. Many others have been known to spend considerably more than equal time in writing up their notes. How much time you personally spend depends, too, on the demands of the setting you are observing, the stage of your research, and the proportion of your total time being devoted to the study.

But one point is inescapable. All the energy and enthusiasm generated by actually being out and about mucking around in some setting must be matched by cloistered rigor in writing down what has taken place. Indeed, the optimal amount of time to spend in the field should be calibrated to the ethnographer's ability to complete robust fieldnotes on her observations. As Emerson, Fretz, and Shaw observe:

> Limiting time in the field ... lessens the likelihood that the fieldworker will forget what happened or become overwhelmed by the prospect of hours of composing fieldnotes. For beginning ethnographers, we recommend, when possible, leaving the field after three to four hours in order to begin writing fieldnotes. (1995, p. 40)

A cautionary tale in this regard is provided from Snow and Anderson's (1993) research with the homeless. During an intense winter storm, Anderson spent several days and nights without a break on the streets and in shelters with homeless informants, observing their routines and responses in the face of the extreme circumstances. By the time he left the field he had accumulated over a dozen pages of jotted notes that required almost a complete week of focused labor to expand into full fieldnotes.

Such experiences underscore the importance of finding a block of time and a place to record your observations shortly after they were made. A shortcut some field researchers take is to tape or digitally record their observations. This can be a useful strategy if you have access to such equipment, but it should not be misconstrued as a substitute for elaborating your fieldnotes. Certainly there are a number of advantages to "talking into the tape": most of us can speak faster than we can write, and recording instruments allow us to log observations while engaging in such routine daily tasks as driving or walking. Unfortunately, for every advantage, there always seems to be an equal disadvantage. In this instance, the problem is that, as with interviews, recordings on tape are not directly available for analysis. To be useful, they have to be transcribed. And as we discussed above, transcription is a tedious, time-consuming process. It will probably take you longer to transcribe your dictated full fieldnotes than it would have taken to record them in written form in the first place. The temptation will be great to put the job off until "later" when you "will feel more like doing it." Some researchers have reported starting out by dictating their notes but having to give up the practice because "later" simply never came. If you are extremely disciplined and compulsive about your work, you may find the tape recorder a faithful assistant. But if you have even the slightest tendency toward procrastination, stick to your keyboard.

2. **Contents**

Of what do fieldnotes consist? Basically, they are a more or less chronological log of what is happening to and in the setting and to and in the observer. More specifically, the types of material described below typically and properly appear in fieldnotes. For the most part, fieldnotes are a running description of settings, events, people, things heard and overheard, and interactions among and with people, including conversations. Each new physical setting, person, interactional episode, and event observed merits a description. You should also record changes in what you are observing. Since you are likely to encounter many of the same settings, people, and other phenomena again and again, you need not repeat such descriptions, but only augment them as changes occur. In the early stages of fieldwork, researchers should cast a wide net in order to capture a broad array of incidents and interactions. Later fieldwork observations may become more refined as the researcher's interests become more developed and focused.

In addition to these temporal concerns, we think the writing of fieldnotes and their content should be guided by the following considerations:

a. **Be Concrete**
Rather than summarizing or employing abstract adjectives and adverbs, attempt to be behavioristic and concrete. Attempt to stay at the lowest possible level of inference. This means conscientiously trying to *avoid* "glossing

over" what you are observing by describing it in terms of such general adjectives as pretty, ugly, funny, depressed, untidy, or well-dressed. Instead, you want to describe the graphic details on which such attributions might be based. As well, avoid, as much as possible, employing the participants' descriptive and interpretive terms as your own. If Person A thought Person B was happy, joyous, depressed, or whatever, report this as an imputation of Person A. Try to capture Person B's raw behavior, leaving aside for that moment any final judgment as to B's actual state of mind or the "true meaning" of his or her behavior. The participants' beliefs as to the "true meaning" of objects, events, and people are thus recorded as being just that—beliefs. Also, since the notes will be chronologically arranged, you should keep records of the approximate times at which various events, including comments and conversations, occur.

b. *Distinguish Notationally Among Member Comments*
Novelist and social observer Truman Capote claimed to be able to recall verbatim several hours of conversation. Such an ability is strikingly unusual. More typically, people recall some things word for word and many other things only in general. Whether you are giving a verbatim account should be indicated in your fieldnotes. In order to do so, you need to *adopt some notational system that enables you to distinguish among member comments in terms of how exactly they are recalled.* For example, in their study of a mental hospital, Anselm Strauss and his colleagues used quotation marks to signify exact recall, apostrophes to indicate verbal material of which they were less certain, and no markings when they could recall the substance but not the wording of what was said (Strauss, Schatzman, Bucher, Erlich, and Sabshin 1964, p. 29). Others have suggested alternative notational systems (Emerson, Fretz, and Shaw 1995, pp. 74–79), but the precise system is less significant than just having one.

c. *Record Recalled Information*
As observation periods mount up, you may find yourself recalling—often at odd moments—items of information you have not previously entered into the fieldnotes. An occurrence you previously saw as insignificant or simply forgot now presents itself as meriting record. Summoning it up as best you can, enter the item's date, content, the context, and so forth into the current day's notes.

d. *Include Analytic Ideas and Hunches*
As you compile your fieldnotes you should resist any urge to impose an overall coherence to your entries and observations. Your goal in writing fieldnotes should be simply to get detailed descriptive accounts on the page. Field observations and recollections occur in "real time" and reflect the episodic and disjointed nature of lived experience. They typically contain "bits and pieces of incidents, beginnings and ends of narratives, accounts of chance meetings and rare occurrences, and details of a wide range of unconnected matters" (Emerson, Fretz, and Shaw 2001, p. 353).

The coherent framing of portions or all of such material is a task for a later stage in the research process (discussed in the last section of this book). Further, as we note above, your fieldnote descriptions should be concrete and behavioristic, capturing action, character, and context, while minimizing explicit theorizing and interpretation.

However, your fieldnotes should also provide a running record of your early analytic musings and proto-conceptions regarding what you are observing. If you are working at it at all, analytic ideas and inferences will begin to occur to you; for example, how things are patterned in the setting, how present occurrences are examples of some sociological or other concept, or how things "really seem to work around here." Some of these ideas may seem obvious and trivial; some may seem farfetched and wild; and many may seem in between. *Put all of them into the fieldnotes.* The only proviso is to be sure to mark them as *analytic ideas or inferences.* A good way to do this is to enclose them in brackets or to relegate all such conceptual and theoretical musings to a separate section of the fieldnotes.

When you eventually withdraw from the setting and concentrate on your analysis, you should thus have more than raw field material. The period of concerted analysis is greatly facilitated if during the fieldwork itself you are also logging conceptual material, creating a foundation of possible lines of analysis and interpretation. Such material may range from minute pieces of analysis to broad ideas about the master theme or themes of the study. In Chapter 9, we will discuss these aspects of fieldnotes more fully as the processes of *coding* and *memoing.* It is quite likely that you will have more of these codes and memos on analytic directions in your notes than you will ever include in the final report. But, by building a foundation of tentative pieces of directions for analysis, your final analytic work should be much less trying, as it should be largely a matter of selecting from and working out analytic themes that already exist.

e. *Record Personal Impressions and Feelings*
In addition to providing a record of the setting, people, events and transactions observed and of analytic ideas, fieldnotes are used for recording *your impressions and feelings.* You have personal opinions of people, emotional responses to being an observer and to the setting itself. As noted in earlier chapters, you can feel discouraged, joyous, rejected, loved, and so forth. To provide some degree of distance, you should also record whatever aspects of your emotional life are involved in the setting. If you feel embarrassed, put down, looked upon with particular favor, or if you fall in love, hate someone, have an affair, or whatever, this private diary should keep track of such facts. This can serve at least three important functions. First, in being (at least privately) honest with yourself about your feelings toward objects, events, and people, you may find that some of the participants also feel quite similar things and that your private emotional response was more widespread, thus providing a clue for analysis. In feeling, for instance, that some person in the setting is getting unjustly treated by a turn of events,

and getting privately angry over it, you may also discover later that many other people privately felt the same way. And a fact of this kind may lead down important analytic trails. Second, your emotional experience, even if not shared by others in the setting, may still suggest important analytic leads. For example, repeated experiences of anxiety or disquiet when talking with informants may simply mean that you are finding the fieldworker role a difficult one. But it may indicate that the worldview of the people you are studying is far more distant from your own than you have yet appreciated. Third, you will periodically review your fieldnotes, and during analysis you will work with them intensively. A concurrent record of your emotional state at various past times can later, away from the setting and in a cooler frame of mind, allow you to scrutinize your notes for obvious biases. You become more able to give the benefit of the doubt in cases where you were perhaps too involved or uninvolved in some incident. This running record of your opinions, impressions, emotions, and the like, should, of course, be labeled as such in the notes through some notational scheme and/or by lumping them together in a separate section of the notes. (For a detailed discussion of the "use and abuse" of emotions in fieldwork, see Kleinman and Copp 1993.)

f. Reminders

Any given day's observations are likely to be incomplete. An account of an incident may lack an adequate description of a given person's behavior or conscious intentions. The incident may only be sketchily known. A well-described incident may lead you to look for further occurrences of events of that kind. In other words, a given day's notes raise a series of observational questions and call for notes for further information. It is reasonable to make these notes as you are writing up your full fieldnotes. You can then review and assemble them as reminders of unobtrusive questions to ask particular people or of things to look for. In fact, you might designate the final section of the day's fieldnotes for a list of reminders about what to do and/or look for during the next outing.

3. Style

The final aspect of fieldnotes of concern here involves what might be thought of as stylistic issues. One such issue concerns the matter of length: How long and full should the notes be? How many pages should notes run for a given observation period? It happens that observers differ enormously in the detail and length of the fieldnotes they keep. Some seem to be frustrated novelists and have been known to write 40 or more single-spaced pages on a three-hour period of observation. Other observers might write only a few pages. Here there are no set rules. Settings differ enormously, as do observers' verbal compulsions. The kinds of phenomena to which observers are sensitive may vary quite widely as well. At minimum, though, you ought to write up at least a couple of single-spaced typed pages for every hour of observation. It is quite likely that you will want to write much more.

Given our earlier discussions of confidentiality, and the fact that fieldnotes are confidential documents that are typically shared with only a small circle of others (e.g., teacher, mentor, team members), there is no reason to be overly conscientious about matters of grammar, punctuation, and narrative flow. It is far more important to focus your energy on elaborating the details of what you observed or heard. As well, there is no reason to be particularly guarded about your feelings regarding your informants, observations, and fieldwork experience. However, it is important, as noted earlier, not to confuse your feelings with your observations and therefore to have some mechanism for distinguishing them.

Taken together, these caveats remind us that the objective in writing fieldnotes is to get information down as efficiently, correctly, and honestly as possible. It is also important to keep in mind that while your full fieldnotes in toto are not likely to be public documents, some portions of your fieldnotes will inevitably find their way into your future reports, since they provide the evidentiary basis for the claims and analysis that you will make. Awareness of this should lead you to approach fieldnote writing differently from the way you would approach writing in a personal diary, where the writing need not provide background knowledge. Given the future broader audience for portions of your fieldnotes, for instance, you should write them with an eye toward rich detail and relative completeness, at least when you are documenting an event that is highly significant to those in the field setting—and thus quite likely to be excerpted from your fieldnotes in future reports.

We have perhaps made fieldnotes sound intimate and revealing and therefore fascinating reading. To a degree they are. But the overwhelming portion consists of running descriptions that often are mundane, uneventful, and even dull. Indeed, if they were otherwise, people would simply publish their fieldnotes. Rather, fieldnotes are elaborated and largely unanalyzed descriptions that will serve as the basis for subsequent analysis. Therefore, do not assume that the fieldwork venture, and writing fieldnotes in particular, will be an exciting affair. Patience and persistence are required here as with many endeavors in social life. Still, fieldnote writing can be punctuated by periods of elation and joy over the events observed, the fact that you have captured some aspect of them on paper, and even over the occurrence of insights and ideas about what you have observed.

V. Interview Write-Ups and Fieldnotes as Compulsion

If all of the above advice about writing up interviews and keeping detailed fieldnotes sounds unbearably tedious, take heart. Once you have established a regimen of transcribing and note taking relative to interviews and of jotting regularly and then making disciplined, full notes relative to observation, these tasks can come to have a demand and a logic of their own. You can come to feel that unless something your informant said is not only on the tape but also transcribed or summarized, or that unless something you observed appears in your full notes, you are in peril of losing the words or the actions. That is, you can come to experience a compulsion to write up everything lest it be lost forever. Upon reaching that level of felt responsibility for logging data, you are fully engaged in fieldwork.

The preceding chapters describe only the first part of the story of doing naturalistic research. The whole point of starting where you are, of getting in and getting along, and, most especially, of logging data, is the performance of social science analysis. We now turn to that challenge.

PART TWO

FOCUSING DATA

While gathering data in the ways described in Part One, the researcher also begins a second major line of activity, that of focusing those data. By "focusing," we mean that the investigator begins to envision:

- possible topics on which to concentrate,

- questions to ask about those topics, and

- treatment of them that will arouse interest.

Discussed in Chapters 6, 7, and 8, respectively, each is a form of consciousness that, when applied to data, begins to turn those raw materials into a work of social science. We say "begins" because a third activity—that of analysis (described in Part Three)—is also necessary.

Prior to analysis, though, the researcher needs to understand the nature of social science topics, questions, and interests, which we cover in the following three chapters.

CHAPTER 6

THINKING TOPICS

In order to endow the things we perceive with meaning, we normally ignore their uniqueness and regard them as typical members of a particular class of objects (a relative, a present), acts (an apology, a crime), or events (a game, a conference). After all, "If each of the many things in the world were taken as distinct, unique, a thing in itself unrelated to any other thing, perception of the world would disintegrate into complete meaninglessness" (Simpson, 1961, p. 2). Indeed, things become meaningful only when placed in some category. A clinical symptom, for instance, is quite meaningless until we find some diagnostic niche (a cold, allergic reaction) within which to situate and thus make sense of it. (Zerubavel, 1991, p. 5)

And so it is in the social sciences. In order to make sense of the things we observe, we classify them as instances of some category of meaning, typically preestablished in terms of theory, prior research, or some indigenous folk system of classification. The title concept of this guide to qualitative observation and analysis—"social settings"—constitutes one such categorical domain. But taken alone it is too broad and abstract to be of much help in focusing the questions we might ask about what we have observed. For purposes of more focused inquiry and understanding, then, we need more refined ideas about social settings, ideas relating to their units of social organizational scale and to their substantive aspects. When combined, units and aspects form the topics for analysis that ultimately enable us to make social scientific sense of our observations.

I. Units and Aspects Combine into Topics

All social settings arise at the intersection of one or more *actors* engaging in one or more *activities* (behaviors) at a particular *time* in a specific *place*. These four coordinates provide a point of departure for categorizing and conceptualizing our data, but we can do even better by considering the extent to which these dimensions vary in terms of organizational scale, that is, in terms of magnitude, period, or size. Thus, the four basic dimensions of scale are (1) the number of actors (people, collectivities, groups) involved, (2) the various activities or behaviors engaged in or displayed,

121

(3) the period of time involved or on which we focus, and (4) the physical size of the space or territory the setting occupies. Variation in one or more of these four dimensions yields different *units* of organizational scale. At a lower level on these four dimensions, the analyst might, for example, focus on a unit involving only two people engaging in one focal behavior (a conversation) over a period of only a few seconds in the physical space of only a few square feet. Even more microscopically, one might focus on the tiny "speech acts" of a single person. At much higher levels of social organizational scale, the unit might contain thousands of people considered in the perspective of decades as they interact over many square miles. Prototypical units at this scale include the urban neighborhood, the small city, and the rural town.

By *aspects* of social settings we mean forms of their social content or substance, irrespective of their scale. Below, we address three broad aspects on which researchers frequently focus: cognitions, emotions, and hierarchy.

As mentioned, specific units and aspects taken together provide guiding *topics* in the task of focusing data. After more fully explaining what we mean by units, we will show how they combine with aspects to form topics.

Before proceeding, it is important to keep in mind that the units and aspects we are about to elaborate are embedded in the broader holistic entity termed *society* and that they can be studied in terms of the various institutional domains constitutive of society (e.g., family, economy, polity, religion, education, medicine) and the various issues and tensions associated with the functioning of these institutions with respect to social class, race and ethnicity, gender, and age (what is typically discussed under the rubric of stratification and inequality). What we outline in this chapter (and in every other chapter, for that matter) is a tool kit of focusing ideas that can be brought to bear on any social thing in any of the institutional domains and with respect to any issue of organization and stratification. We feel it is important to stress this point to forestall the possible concern that we have not addressed one or another substantive matter that is of key interest to particular people. Our answer to this concern is that any substantive social matter can be analyzed insightfully when guided by the focusing concepts explained in this chapter (and combined with the guidance provided in other chapters).

II. Units

Although there are some commonly employed units of social settings, there is no definitive and agreed-upon set of them. Therefore, what we present here as units is a set of categories one can see in fieldwork reports rather than a definitive depiction of the units of social science. The practical meaning of this for you as a researcher is that you should feel free to adapt and innovate in thinking about the scale or scales of social organization at which you are going to focus your analysis (or analyses).

The units are arranged roughly from the microscopic to the macroscopic in terms of increasing numbers of actors, activities, duration, and space. Put differently, the scale of social organization is increasing as we move from unit to unit. It is important to recognize, therefore, that each new unit introduced contains units discussed prior to it rather than being separate from them.

A. Practices

Among the smallest units of a social setting are social or cultural practices—the recurrent categories of talk or action on which the observer focuses as having analytic significance. Because they are recurring and often regularized features of everyday life, most practices are regarded by those who engage in them as rather routine and unremarkable. Examples include getting dressed in the morning, driving to work or school, exercising, doing homework and studying, praying, setting the table, eating dinner, and so on. Sometimes these practices are interrupted or called into question by self or others because we have done them wrong or in a way that others find objectionable or noteworthy, and we therefore are required to account for our action (Scott and Lyman 1968). Such accounting behavior, along with similar practices used to justify one's discrepant actions or align them with cultural beliefs or individual or collective identity (see Sykes and Matza's "techniques of neutralization" [1957] and Stokes and Hewitt's "aligning actions" [1976]) constitute one set of practices that has been widely studied by field researchers. Examples include assessment of the accounts 25 convicted murderers provided for their crimes (Ray and Simons 1987); analysis of the accounts students manufacture in order to justify "frittering" away time rather than studying (Bernstein 1978), missing class (Kalab 1987), and cheating in school even though they know it is wrong (McCabe 1992); tracking how members of a "natural food cooperative" engaged in an aligning action, called "discounting," that enabled them to preserve their collective identity in spite of pursuing contradictory activity (Pestello 1991); and eliciting accounts from 62 U.S. Army generals regarding the reasons for their successful careers (Dowd 2000). Of course, not all accounting behavior is retrospective. It can also be triggered by the anticipation of future conduct being called into question, as Elizabeth Murphy (2004) found in her study of how mothers sometimes "account, in advance, for the possibility that they may eventually feed their babies in ways they consider suboptimal" (p. 129). Such studies of accounting practices are interesting not only for what they reveal about the character of the practice in a specific setting, but also in terms of the trans-situational character and structure of accounting practices in general.

The range of practices on which fieldworkers might focus is almost limitless, as illustrated by studies of how students who do well on their exams express their joy without shaming or humiliating those students who did poorly (Albas and Albas 1988); of how women "cool out" men in singles bars and nightclubs (Snow, Robinson, and McCall 1991); of boundary work in nursing homes for the elderly (Åkerström 2002); of ideological work among rural, hippie communards (Berger 1981), Hare Krishna devotees (Rochford 1985), and gay and ex-gay Christian men (Wolkomir 2001); of identity talk among peace movement activists (Hunt and Benford 1994); and of how workers try to "make out" (Burawoy 1979) or try to control the structure of their work through various compliance and resistance practices (Hodson 1991).

B. Episodes

In contrast to practices, episodes are more remarkable and dramatic to the participants and therefore to the analyst as well, for the simple reason that they are not fully anticipated and/or do not occur so routinely or regularly. Divorce, sudden epidemics of disease and illness, criminal victimization, crime sprees or waves, social and natural disasters, and crowd disorders such as riots and so-called panics, are all examples of episodes. Indeed, a significant portion of several sociological specialties are devoted to the analysis of episodes as, for example, in the study of deviance, crime, disasters, crowd behavior, and social movements.

Episodes can differ in the number of people and activities involved, as well as in terms of the span of time and territory they cover. Episodes of crowd behavior, whether of protest or celebration, can vary in all these ways (McPhail 1991). Some crowds associated with collective behavior are single events that occur once in order to protest a particular political decision or celebrate a sports victory or championship. On other occasions the event may recur over an extended period of time, as was the case with a series of victory celebrations recurring over a five-week period at the University of Texas in 1977 when students converged on Saturday evenings to celebrate collectively their football team's unexpected victories and rise in the national rankings (Snow, Zurcher, and Peters 1981), a repeated gathering of religious pilgrims to view what was perceived as an apparition of the Virgin Mary during the 1990s on a farm in Georgia (Davis and Boles 2003), and a series of protest crowds that mobilized in three communities in the greater Los Angeles area over a six-week period in opposition to the invasion of Iraq (Corrigall-Brown and Oselin 2003). And on still other occasions, multiple instances of a collective action event, such as riots, may occur across cities and over an extended period of time, constituting a wave or cycle of collective action (see Traugott, 1995, for conceptual clarification). And this spatial and temporal diffusion of episodes of collective action is particularly relevant to understanding the dynamics of social movements (Tarrow 1998) and revolution (Goodwin 2001).

C. Encounters

An encounter is a tiny social system formed when two or more persons are in one another's immediate physical presence and strive to maintain a single (ordinarily spoken) focus of mutual involvement. They differ from the units discussed above (and from some that follow) in that they tend to be bounded social systems maintained by the relations among the people who are present. Perhaps the prototypical example is the cocktail party or college mixer in which attendees are clustered in numerous encounters, with the life span of each lasting only as long as the people remain together. Typically, this is not for very long. In fact, most encounters have a similar life span, enduring only a few minutes, although some may last a few hours. Copresence in public restrooms (Cahill et al. 1985), sidewalk verbal exchanges (Anderson 1990; Duneier and Molotch 1999), requests for minor aid in public settings (Gardner 1986, 1995), solicitation of donations via begging and panhandling (Lankenau 1999; Snow and Anderson 1993), and the commercial transaction between customer and vendor or salesperson (Lee 2002; Prus 1989) are all common illustrations of encounters. Regarding the latter, Robert Prus's *Making Sales* (1989) details ethnographically the set of vendor practices involved in a sales encounter, such as presenting products, generating trust, neutralizing resistance, obtaining commitments, and so on. Perhaps even more prosaic are committee meetings, job interviews, and class and seminar meetings in school settings and work places.

D. Roles and Social Types

A common orientational tendency for humans as they go about their daily routines is to categorize the array of actors encountered in terms of culturally based repertoires of social roles and/or social types. While scholars sometimes quibble over the character of social roles and types, the fact of the matter is that interactants typically act toward each other as if the other is an incumbent of a particular role or impute identities to them that are consistent with the image of a particular role or social type. Thus we consider each briefly.

1. Roles

In their clearest form, roles are constituted by clusters of behaviors associated with a particular position in a relational network or matrix. Take the position of quarterback on a football team, for example. We recognize and know the quarterback apart from the center or fullback primarily in terms of the cluster of behaviors s/he enacts during the course of the game. The same is true for the role of mother, father, student, or professor. No single behavior makes for a professor; rather, the professor role is comprised by a set of behaviors that cohere in relation to other relevant roles—such as students, teaching assistants, administrators, and research subjects—that can be thought of as the professor's "role set." Interactionally, then, a role functions as a kind of orientational device that we use to situate and make sense of the behaviors of others with whom we are interacting or observing and that we use to organize our own behavior in relation to theirs.

There is an abundance of qualitative research that focuses on different formal and informal roles and the processes through which they are negotiated, enacted, and/or exited. Examples include the myriad studies of "doing gender" (Copes and Hochstetler 2003; De Welde 2003; Leyser 2003; Murphy 2003; Wesely 2003). Studies of the Navy disbursing officer (Turner 1947), the cocktail waitress (Spradley and Mann 1975), the college athlete (Adler and Adler 1991), the various conflicts experienced by sorority "hashers" (Zurcher 1983), and the process of role exit, as in the case of becoming an ex-priest or -nun (Ebaugh 1988), are among the many fieldstudies focusing on roles that are more or less formal. And field research on more informal and ephemeral roles include studies of volunteers in disaster work crews (Zurcher 1983), participants in a friendly poker game (Zurcher 1983), and the process through which patrons of karaoke bars become regular performers (Drew 2001).

2. **Social Types**
Social types overlap with the concept of social roles, yet are distinctive from them and thus provide another category for "coding" people. More concretely, social types are constructs that fall somewhere between individual, idiosyncratic behavior and formal or informal role behavior, thereby allowing conceptually for a "finer discrimination than the formal . . . structure recognizes" (Klapp 1958, p. 674). Well-known examples include the "underdog," the "bully," the "wise guy" or "smart ass," and the "Uncle Tom." Social types identified and found analytically useful during the course of qualitative research include "the convert" (Snow and Machalek 1983), "the old head" in traditional black communities (Anderson 1990), and "the public character" among book vendors on the streets of Greenwich Village (Duneier 1999). In these and other cases, a number of factors are identified as indicators of the social type in question.

E. **Social and Personal Relationships**

Two parties who interact with some interdependence and who view themselves as "connected" to one another, however briefly, form a social relationship. Such pairings vary in myriad ways: the character of the prevalent emotions, the degree and source(s) of interdependence, the amount of trust, the parties' relative amounts of power, what each knows about the other, the degree to which the relationship is anchored to place, and whether it is temporally fleeting or more enduring. Research on social relationships has tended to focus on those that occur among intimates, such as among family members and close friends, and those that occur in formal organizations and work settings. Well-known examples of the former include Elijah Anderson's (1976) study of the black men who hung out at Jelly's, Mitch Duneier's (1992) ethnography of the five black men who met almost daily at "Slim's table," and William F. Whyte's (1993) classic study of the relationships and activities of the Italian street-corner group he called "the Nortons." However, more recent research has revealed that personal social relationships may not only thrive in public and quasi-public places (Anderson 1990, 1999; Duneier 1999; L. Lofland 1998; Morrill, Snow, and White 2005), but that these relationships may sometimes be quite fleeting or ephemeral and yet manifest most of the corporeal and emotional markers of intense, intimate personal relations more typically associated with the private realm. The strip club lap dance is an example of such highly charged, but temporally compressed, personal relationships in the public/quasi-public realm (Massey and Hope 2005).

F. Groups and Cliques

A few people who interact with some regularity over an extended period of time, who conceive of themselves as a social entity (a "we"), and who have some criteria or understanding for determining membership, form a social group. Organized leisure-time groups, informal leisure and work groups that arise in bureaucratic contexts, gangs, cliques, and families are prime examples. Since the research on these and other group forms is abundant (e.g., Anderson 1976; Duneier 1992; Horowitz 1983; Suttles 1968; Whyte 1993), we focus here, for illustrative purposes, on cliques.

Cliques are basically an organizationally embedded informal circle or network of friends or colleagues whose members regard themselves as mutually interconnected in some fashion or another. Much like weeds, cliques tend to grow in all variety of organizational contexts, but take somewhat different forms depending on the characteristics of the context.

Thus, in observing executives in several commercial and industrial firms, Melville Dalton (1959, pp. 57–65) not only found the existence of cliques, but also noticed that the webs of informal ties among them assumed different forms depending on their relation to the formal structure of the encompassing organization. He identified three basic forms: "vertical cliques," which were usually found "in a single department . . . between a top officer and some of his subordinates;" "horizontal cliques," which "cut across more than one department and embrace(ed) formal equals"; and a "random clique," which drew its members from across divisions.

At the opposite end of the age structure are the cliques that flower among children and adolescents. In their ethnography of preadolescent culture and identity among the youth they studied in their community over an eight-year period, Patricia and Peter Adler found that cliques were a "dominant feature of the children's lives" (Adler and Adler 1998, p. 56). Although the composition and character of the cliques varied somewhat depending on school size and demographics, grade level, and classroom organization, they found that "[f]or every age level, within each gender group, and in every school with a population of over eighty students, not only were there cliques," but they were typically stratified into four main groupings.

> At the high end was the popular clique, comprising the exclusive crowd. Below them were the wannabes, the group of people who hung around the popular clique hoping for inclusion. Next was the middle group, composed

of smaller, independent friendship circles. At the bottom were the social isolates, which found playmates only occasionally, spending most of the time by themselves. (1998, p. 75)

Not surprisingly, such clique structures tend to reproduce themselves at the adolescent and high school level, as August Hollingshead (1975) found many years ago in his fieldstudy of Elmtown's youth, who were distributed among three cliques: the elite, the good kids, and the grubby gang. Cliques also surface among college students. In his ethnographic study of student life at Rutger's University in the late 1970s and 1980s, for example, Michael Moffatt (1989) found that cliques formed among some of the students in the dormitory in which he lived for awhile (see pp. 95–103). So wherever some numbers of individuals who share similar characteristics are aggregated, it is a good bet that you are likely to find the formation of cliques or some other informal grouping, such as gangs. One of the reasons for the formation of such informal groupings is that they facilitate the adaptation of people to their circumstances, especially when there is too little structure or perhaps too much, as often seems to be the case within the context of large-scale bureaucratic organizations, like high schools, colleges, factories, prisons, and mental asylums.

G. Organizations

Large organizations, according to Charles Perrow, are "the most important feature of our social landscape," at least in the United States and other large-scale modern societies (Perrow 2002, p. 1). Inasmuch as such organizations are conceived as consciously formed collectivities with formal goals that are pursued in a more or less articulately planned fashion, it is difficult to disagree with Perrow's contention. After all, there are few aspects of one's daily life that are not affected by formal organizations. Consider your morning daily routine, for example. You go to work or school, both of which are formally organized contexts; you probably travel by car or public transportation, both of which are the material extension of large-scale corporate or governmental organizations; and at midday you take a lunch break, often and maybe even routinely frequenting fast-food restaurants, which are typically local franchises of large corporate organizations, such as McDonald's, Burger King, and Taco Bell. Because of such considerations, it is not surprising that the study of organizations is a major area of inquiry in the social sciences and that qualitative field research has contributed significantly to this field.

Some major topics scholars of organizations examine include the circumstances of their formation, how they recruit and control members, the ways in which members adapt to organizational constraints and control, the types and causes of the goal-pursuit strategies they adopt, and the causes of their growth, change, or demise. Gideon Kunda's (1992) ethnographic study of the engineering division of an American high-tech corporation sheds light on the first two of these topical concerns: managerial control and member adaptation. Kunda found a dialectic between managerial efforts to control the "Techies" who worked in the firm by imposing the corporate culture and the ways in which the Techies experienced this culture. Rather than becoming more committed to it over time, the Techies ironically became more cynical about the firm's strategies and structures. Interestingly, Kunda's findings parallel those Erving Goffman (1961a) found in a strikingly different organization: a mental asylum. There, Goffman found, inmates would often engage in various informal "secondary adjustments" that could be construed as member attempts to develop or maintain a self that was separate from the one the institution attempted to impose. Other kinds of member adaptations have been noted in other kinds of organizational contexts. Still among the best known is Donald Roy's (1959/60) ethnography of how fellow factory workers dealt with their extraordinarily monotonous jobs. Employed in such a job (one that involved stamping leather or plastic parts all day), Roy observed that his work group took a break almost every hour, which served to punctuate the monotony, and that these breaks corresponded with different times throughout the day. The various temporal breaks included: "peach time" (group sharing of a peach), "banana time," "window time," "lunchtime," "picking-up time" (someone coming for their latest output), occasional talk, "fish time," and "Coke time."

Other organizational dynamics and issues examined via qualitative field research include Nicole Biggart's (1989) ethnographic study of direct selling organizations, such as Mary Kay Cosmetics and Shaklee, and the ways in which they sometimes strategically obscure "the economic in the social" by emphasizing respectively "skin care" and "good health" (pp. 116–117); Vicki Smith's (1990) observational study of the experiences of middle-level managers confronted with organizational restructuring in a large California bank; Gary Alan Fine's (1996) ethnography of the organization and culture of restaurant work; and Calvin Morrill's (1995) study of the causes and management of conflict among executives in American corporate suites. (See Morrill and Fine [1997] for a detailed overview of ethnographic contributions to organizational sociology.)

H. Settlements and Habitats

Complexly interrelated sets of practices, encounters, roles, groups, and organizations, existing within a socially defined territory and performing a range of life-sustaining functions can be thought of as settlements of one kind or another. Very large settlements—cities of many thousands or even millions—are considerably beyond the grasp of the naturalistic researcher. But the study of smaller settlements—villages, towns, ghettos, neighborhoods, and blocks—is richly represented in naturalist fieldstudy literature. The classic anthropological study, for example, is a descriptive account of an entire "simpler" society, typically premodern and quite small or of some feature of the society that is used as the key to understanding the totality, as illustrated by Edward Evans-Pritchard's (1937) fieldstudy of witchcraft and oracles among the Azande; Margaret Mead's (1928) examination of sex and temperament among the Samoans; Napoleon Chagnon's (1983) focus on violent rituals among the Yanomamo tropical forest Indians on the border between Venezuela and Brazil; and Clifford Geertz's (1973) study of "cockfighting" among the Balinese. Thus, the traditional analytic unit for much work in anthropology has been the settlement or the activities and practices that are regarded as the embodiment of its character and organization. The same is true for much sociological ethnography, with a number of such studies also regarded as fieldwork classics. Four of these, interestingly enough, focus on Italian (or mixed-Italian) neighborhoods in large cities: William E. Whyte's *Street Corner Society: The Social Structure of an Italian Slum* (1993) in Boston's North End; Herbert Gans's *The Urban Villagers: Group and Class in the Life of Italian-Americans* (1962) in Boston's West End; Gerald Suttles's *The Social Order of the Slum: Ethnicity and Territory in the Inner City* (1968) in Chicago; and Jonathan Rieder's *Canarsie: The Jews and Italians of Brooklyn Against Liberalism* (1985) in New York.

Much recent work within anthropology and sociology continues to follow this traditional focus on some kind of settlement. Exemplars include Mercer Sullivan's (1989) comparative ethnography of street crime and legitimate employment among youth in three Brooklyn neighborhoods; Elijah Anderson's (1990) fieldstudy of relational encounters among residents who differ in terms of race and class in two adjacent neighborhoods in Philadelphia and his follow-up study of the "code of streets" as it operated primarily in inner-city ghetto areas in the same city (1999); Nancy Scheper-Hughes's (1992) study of the violent character of everyday life in a Brazilian community; Michael Bell's (1994) ethnography of village life in a rural hamlet in the environs southwest of London; Mary Pattillo-McCoy's (1999) study of a black middle-class neighborhood; and Katherine Newman's (1999) study of the working poor in two New York inner-city neighborhoods.

Overlapping with the concept of settlements is what Mitch Duneier (1999) calls "a sustaining habitat." Among the questions that intrigued him as he did his field research that culminated in *Sidewalk* was why did poor black men, most of whom were unhoused, come to congregate in and around Sixth Avenue in New York's Greenwich Village (pp. 123 and 143). His answer was that this area became a sustaining habitat for these folks because of the confluence of a number of contributing factors: "a density of pedestrians" and businesses, "the availability of cheap or free food," "an abundance of public places to sleep with relative impunity," "many people who are sympathetic to unhoused people and are willing to give money and food to them," and trash cans that contain "high-quality magazines" and other salable items (pp. 144–153). The analytic utility of Duneier's observations is that the link between places and clusters of activities and orientations is largely a function of the conjunction of elements necessary to sustain those activities. In other words, different places—be they intersections, a block or two, a neighborhood, or a larger community—have different "carrying capacities" and thus come to be associated or paired with some lifestyles or subcultures rather than others.

As in most naturalistic research, the study of settlements or habitats is normally conducted by a lone investigator. (See, in addition to the studies cited above, Baumgartner 1988; Ellis 1986; Gans 1967; Horowitz 1983; Kornblum 1974; McRoberts 2003; Venkatesh 2000.) As long as the unit is not too large—that is, no larger than a contained neighborhood or a small town—this has proved a satisfactory arrangement. However, the study of larger settlements—medium-sized towns or small cities—requires the use of research teams, sometimes of considerable size. Robert Lynd and Helen Lynd's pioneer study of Muncie, Indiana (1929), for example, was made possible by a research team composed of the authors, two additional investigators, and a staff secretary; and the restudy performed by Caplow, Bahr, Chadwick, and Williamson (1982) was even more elaborate. The data for Arthur Vidich and Joseph Bensman's study of a rural community in upstate New York (1968) was produced by a larger project, the "Cornell Studies in Social Growth," which involved a substantial research team. And W. Lloyd Warner's famed study of Newburyport, Massachusetts—known as the "Yankee City" study—was the work of a number of other major investigators and a host of students, mostly undergraduates, from Harvard and Radcliffe. (For a summary of these Yankee City studies, as well as of other community studies prior to the 1960s, see Stein 1964.)

I. Subcultures and Lifestyles

The last unit of social organization to which we draw your attention is variously conceptualized by social scientists as subcultures (Fine and Kleinman 1979) and lifestyles (Zablocki and Kanter 1976). Although there are fine-tuned distinctions among them, we lump them together here because they connote a mixture of behavioral, normative, and cognitive elements that together characterize the way of life or orientation of a set of similarly situated individuals and that distinguishes them from other groups or aggregations within or across other social units. As well, whether the researcher thinks in terms of subcultures or lifestyles, they all constitute patterns of accommodation and/or resistance to social forces and changes confronting the individuals that comprise them, as Paul Willis (1977) demonstrated with respect to the British working-class youth he studied, Talmadge Wright (1997) argued in relation to the homeless activists and movements he observed in San Jose and Chicago, Leila Rupp and Verta Taylor (2003) observed in their multifaceted study of drag queens in Key West, and as researchers of gangs have found repeatedly (Horowitz 1983; Sarchez-Jankowski 1991; Vigil 2002).

When thinking in terms of subcultures or lifestyles, it is important to keep in mind that the patterns of adjustment or accommodation that define them can originate in response to various cultural, status, and economic factors. Thus, in writing about the bases for different lifestyles, Benjamin Zablocki and Rosabeth Kanter (1976) distinguished among lifestyles in terms of those dominated by a person's location in an economic system and those that are not. They divided economically dominated lifestyles, in turn, into three types: (1) property-dominated, as in the "elite ranks of the upper class"; (2) occupation-dominated, as in those occupational pursuits that virtually absorb their practitioners; and (3) poverty-dominated, as in American urban ghettos. Due in part to the greater ease of access to those situated at the bottom end of the socioeconomic structure, it is not surprising that the third type appears to have been studied most often ethnographically. Just consider, for example, the numerous naturalistic field-studies of one or more aspects of the current wave of homelessness in the United States (e.g., Dordick 1997; Liebow 1993; Rosenthal 1994; Snow and Anderson 1993; Wagner 1993; Wright 1997). These and other studies reveal that even when a lifestyle or subculture grows out of particular economic circumstances, it very often evolves to encompass realms of life other than just the material.

Not all subcultures or lifestyles are so elaborated, nor are all of them anchored in members' economic circumstances. Instead, they may be riveted to a particular activity, as with nudity (Douglas and Rasmussen 1977), tattooing (Sanders 1989; Vail 2001), and "hanging-out" (Harrison and Morgan 2005); to a particular sexual orientation, as with lesbians and gays (Krieger 1983); or to an anti-system value orientation, as with neo-counterculturalists (Epstein 1991), survivalists (Mitchell 2002), and teenage satanists (Lowney 1995).

III. Aspects and Topics

Few researchers attempt to capture the full sociological substance of the unit or units on which they are focused. Rather, as we have noted above, they zero in on one or more "pieces" of that substance. We refer to these "pieces" as aspects and to the combinations of unit(s) and aspect(s) as topics. To enumerate all aspects of all the units that qualitative researchers have written about would necessitate many volumes. But since our goal is to be illustrative rather than exhaustive, we limit ourselves to a small sample of studies concerned only with cognitive, emotional, or hierarchical aspects of one or another unit.

A. Cognitive Aspects or Meanings

Inasmuch as humans act toward things partly on the basis of the meaning those things have for them (Blumer 1969), one of the most fundamental aspects of any unit is a cognitive one (whether embedded in or imputed to the unit). Broadly conceived, meanings are the linguistic categories that define the objects to which we are oriented and thus constitute our reality and influence our action toward those objects. It is because of this ineluctable link between meaning, orientation, and action that naturalistic field researchers emphasize the importance of accessing and understanding the meaning systems of those studied (Denzin 1989b; Emerson 2001; Geertz 1973). There are, of course, a good number of frequently used words or phrases that are analogous to or overlap with meanings, such as interpretations, definitions of the situation, typifications, ideology, beliefs, norms, frames, worldviews, perspectives, and stereotypes. While there are nuanced differences among some of these concepts, all of these terms direct attention to the socially constructed character of our social worlds and the objects that constitute them. Consequently, for the purposes of simplification and illustration, we use meanings here as an umbrella concept for considering the cognitive dimensions or aspects of the various units of social organization.

1. **Ideologies (and Kindred Concepts) as Meanings**
   Meanings vary in terms of the range of situations to which they apply. At the broader level are packages of meaning that are life-encompassing in that they can be of relevance to virtually any topic that might be discussed. Such packages are variously called ideologies, worldviews, weltanschauungs, or philosophies. While meanings of this sort may be of relevance in an analysis of smaller-level units, such as practices or encounters, they are usually treated as aspects of units at the level of groups or above. Thus, in studies of groups or organizations, for example, a significant section of the research report is often devoted to "ideology" (e.g., Kunda 1992; Smith 1990; Snow 1993).

   Analyses of the ideologies or worldviews of groups and organizations often center on the question of how participants bring the scheme into play in defining or repairing some problematic topic or issue. Bennett Berger has referred to this as "ideological work." One of the conundrums Berger encountered in his study of rural communards in upstate California in the 1970s was the disjunction between some of their ideological beliefs and some of their behaviors, as when their child-raising practices contradicted basic tenets of their communal ideology. In order to get a conceptual handle on the remedial discourse the communards engaged in so as to "maintain some semblance of consistency, coherence, and continuity" between their beliefs and actions, Berger (1981, p. 22) coined the concept of "ideological work." In examining change and adaptation within the Hare Krishna movement in the United States in the later half of the 1970s, Burke Rochford (1985, p. 192) similarly found the movement was confronted with a number of contradictions "between its professed beliefs and day-to-day practices of its members" that it attempted to repair through engagement in various forms of ideological work specific to the movement. Both the Berger and Rochford studies indicated that ideological work is likely to be called forth when beliefs and member behavior contradict each other. But other research has shown that such ideological work may also be necessary when beliefs and events in the world are discordant. For example, in John Lofland's (1977) study of a religious group with a "world-saving" ideology, members believed that they were destined to make thousands of new converts, worked hard to achieve that goal, but failed to do so in the early stages of its career. How then, Lofland asks, did the group reconcile this chronic gap between aim and actuality? His answer is that it drew upon its ideology to fashion three basic explanations for its repeated failures.

- First, the American group was an offshoot of the Korean founding body, which had gone for years without success before beginning to make large numbers of converts. They would remind themselves that they were perhaps only following "the Korean pattern."
- Second, they would apply their general "principle of restitution," which held that God and Satan alternated in their influence. Current failure was due to Satan's dominant influence, which would later be counter-balanced by God's good influence on prospects in the making of converts.
- Third, members believed that God would deliberately withhold his help from them in order to see how well they could do on their own. Current failure was testing for strength. (1977, pp. 244–245)

2. **Rules as Meanings**
Rules (or norms) constitute another broad category of meanings. They differ from other meanings mainly in the degree of positive moral preference attached to them and in the clarity of their formulation, with some being legally or bureaucratically codified. Specific units may be analyzed, then, in terms of the kinds of rules that are operative, if any, and the extent to which participants use them to guide their conduct. Sometimes rules are so fully codified and articulated by the participants that the analyst has little to do beyond writing them down. Other times rules are uncodified and informal but still widely understood, as Elijah Anderson found in his study of interpersonal violence among inner-city youths. According to Anderson's observations, interpersonal violence, as well as other interpersonal public behavior, is governed by the operation of a set of informal rules he dubbed a "code of the street."

> The rules prescribe both proper comportment and the proper way to respond if challenged. They regulate the use of violence and so supply a rationale for allowing those who are inclined to aggression to precipitate violent encounters in an approved way. (Anderson, 1999, p. 33)

And on other occasions, the rules are both uncodified and largely unarticulated, leaving the analyst with the task of discerning them from the regularities of actors' behavior. In Lyn Lofland's study of stranger encounters, for example, she outlined six principles or rules that people seemed to be using to maintain their privacy and social distance during these encounters.

- First Principle: Minimize Expressivity. Keep one's facial expression impassive . . . .
- Second Principle: Minimize Body Contact. Keep oneself to oneself . . . .

- Third Principle: Look Before You Sit. Keep oneself apart . . . .
- Fourth Principle: Minimize Eye Contact. Keep one's eyes to oneself . . . .
- Fifth Principle: When in Doubt, Flee. Keep oneself protected . . . .
- Sixth Principle: When in Doubt, Disattend. Keep oneself aloof . . . . (1985b, pp. 153–155)

3. **Self-Concepts and Identities as Meanings**

How one views oneself as a kind of person (one's self-concept) is among the most important meanings associated with one's life. Indeed, our self-concepts and identities are not only reflections of how we are situated in relation to others, both vertically and horizontally, but they are the central orientational devices with which we navigate and negotiate our everyday lives. This is one of the central themes of Erving Goffman's (1959) *The Presentation of Self in Everyday Life*, and it has been accented repeatedly in numerous naturalistic fieldstudies of the self in all kinds of social contexts, as illustrated by Norman Denzin's (1987a, 1987b) analysis of "the alcoholic self" as he came to understand it over the course of a five-year study of active and recovering alcoholics within the context of Alcoholics Anonymous; Patricia and Peter Adler's (1991) multiyear study of the "glorified self" of big-time college athletes within the context of the university in which they were employed at the time; Rebecca Allahyari's (2000) analysis of "moral selving" among volunteers to two charities aiding the homeless; and Kathleen Blee's (2002) interview-based examination of "the racist self" among women in right-wing extremist movements. These and other such studies suggest that the self and self-concept are relevant aspects of most units of social organization when approaching them from the standpoint of the actor.

The same also holds for the overlapping concept of identity. Inasmuch as interaction with others is contingent on the reciprocal establishment of identities, it is arguable that identities are relevant to most social situations and contexts. Of the various perspectives on identity (e.g., dispositional, structural, constructionist), one of the most influential within sociology focuses on the link between roles and identity. It argues that the names we use to refer to ourselves and others depend in large part on the roles we play or are perceived as playing. Identities exist, it is claimed, only "insofar as the person is a participant in structured role relationships," and they are "limited only by the number of structured role relationships one is involved in" (Stryker 1980, p. 60). Hence, if you are like most people, you are likely to have a good number of identities, but not all of them are of equal importance to you or others. Moreover, the relative salience of any particular identity is likely to vary with whomever you are interacting with at the moment. When engaged in practices or encounters with your peers, for example, your role identity as a son or daughter is likely to be of much less importance than your peer group-based identity.

Examining various issues relating to role identities has been a focus of much qualitative research, particularly that inspired by the symbolic interactionist perspective in sociology. Much of this research has focused on how individuals who are the incumbents of stigmatizing social roles resist the identities associated with those roles by asserting contrary or alternative identities. One of the significant themes of Erving Goffman's *Asylums* (1961a), for example, was the ongoing adaptation of inmates to the "mortified self" or identity implied by the inmate role. Other studies have followed this line of inquiry, including examination of the identity work practices among the homeless (Snow and Anderson 1987), identity construction among gay men with AIDS (Sandstrom 1990), the construction of alternative personal identities among residents of chronic care facilities (Paterniti 2000), the management of gay identities in combat units of the Israeli Army (Kaplan and Ben-Ari 2000), and the transformation of various "spoiled identities" in different contexts (Oselin 2004; Ponticelli 1999).

B. Emotional Aspects or Feelings

To separate cognitive and emotional aspects of units—to separate meanings from feelings—is, of course, to distort the experienced world (Forgas 2000). As we will see in the examples below, cognitions are an integral part of feelings just as emotions are an integral part of meanings. But we separate them here for two reasons: it simplifies our expository task, and it is consistent both with the recent (re)discovery among social scientists of the centrality of emotion to human social life and with the corresponding growth in the volume of published research on the topic (see, e.g., Stets 2003).

1. Emotion and Practices, Episodes, and Encounters

Insofar as you are interested in the emotional aspects of social life, a good place to begin your observations is with the more microscopic units of analysis, since it is in these contexts that the actual conduct of behavior is enacted and emotions are routinely displayed. After all, the aim of accounting practices is to normalize interaction and stave off the prospect of embarrassment (see Section II.A in this chapter), the substance of many encounters ranges from the management of emotion display (Hochschild 1983) to angry recriminations (Denzin 1984) and jealous tirades (Ellis and Weinstein 1986), and the content of some episodes includes varied emotional displays, ranging from panicky flight (Johnson 1988) to ecstatic revelry (Lofland 1985, Ch. 2) to violent outbursts (McPhail 1994).

At the level of practices, Candace Clark's (1987) study of the exchange of sympathy in everyday life provides an enumeration of normatively prescribed and routinely performed verbal conventions that help maintain a reasonable flow of sympathy between and among persons. These conventions include: (1) using genuine and serious situations and events as the justification for claiming sympathy; (2) claiming sympathy at reasonable and legitimate intervals; (3) actually making the claim to sympathy when the justification is real and the interval is within the acceptable levels; and

(4) repaying the gift of sympathy with gratitude, deference, esteem, or sympathy itself (summarized from Clark 1987).

At the level of episodes and encounters, Jack Katz (1999) has conducted a field-based examination of the conditions that conjoin to make motorists "pissed-off"—what is journalistically called "road rage"—on the streets of Los Angeles. The emotionally heated but fleeting, and thus episodic, encounters between passing drivers results, he argues, from

> a distinctive process of interactive interpretation (e.g., the imputation of "dumbness" to the offending driver), a specific experience of metamorphosis (e.g., the bodily or corporeal experience of anger), and a focused narrative project (e.g., "flipping off" the "dumb" offending driver) are the individually necessary and jointly sufficient conditions for becoming pissed off when driving. (1999, p. 24)

And in a combined focus on practices, episodes, and encounters, Jennifer Lois (2003, pp. 85–113) provides a field-based analysis of search and rescue workers' strategies for managing their emotions in crisis encounters. She elaborates four stages of emotion management in rescue operations, including emotion practices in (1) preparatory anticipation, (2) performing rescues, (3) release of feelings following rescue completion, and (4) redefining of feelings after emotional release. At each stage, rescuers devise practices for handling the particular challenges that confront them. In performing "on the edge" in dangerous rescue operations, for instance, rescuers frequently experience an "adrenaline rush" with concomitant emotions of fear and urgency that threaten clear thinking and rational action. They responded in such fateful encounters by learning (1) to use signs of adrenaline rush as situational cues to mobilize their defenses against potential loss of control, (2) to prioritize their actions, narrow their focus, and follow a clear sequence of steps to achieve the rescue, and (3) to depersonalize and detach from victims during critical parts of the rescue operation. In many respects, these and other practices constitute part of what might be thought of as the "subculture" of search and rescue workers.

2. **Emotion and Roles**

    Many roles generate emotional problems or experiences that are unique to or uniquely configured in them. Erving Goffman (1961b) highlighted this point in his seminal essay on "role distance," wherein he discussed how some occupational roles, such as the surgeon, require the incumbent to resort to various devices in order to distance themselves from their patients and the implications of their task so that they don't become too emotionally involved and thus ineffective. Other qualitative researchers have similarly observed related kinds of emotional problems or challenges associated with various roles. Allen Smith and Sherryl Kleinman report, for example, that in their encounters with the human body, medical students "often experience a variety of uncomfortable feelings including embarrassment, disgust, and arousal" (1989, p. 58) that formal training, per se, does little to alleviate. The authors were interested in how students managed these "uncomfortable" and "inappropriate feelings," and their analysis thus focused on identifying the various strategies the students used for coping with, if not eliminating, the problems. In his participant observation study of the professional socialization of mortuary science students, Spencer Cahill (1999) similarly found not only different emotional responses among the students to work associated with the role of funeral director, but that these different responses were key in distinguishing the successful from the unsuccessful students, thus showing that roles may vary in terms of the kinds of affect or emotion required to perform them.

For some other roles, the key is not so much what one actually feels but whether the role incumbent is able to control and/or display feelings in a fashion that is consistent with his or her objective. This is what Arlie Hochschild (1983) calls "emotion work," and is illustrated by Tiffani Chin's (2000) field examination of the ways in which parents manage their emotions so as to affect their sixth grade children's chances of getting into the best private high school possible. When this emotion work is done within the context of paid labor, such dramaturgical control of feelings constitutes what Hochschild dubbed "emotional labor" (1983). In a nutshell, it encompasses the management of emotion in accordance with organizational "feeling rules," as Hochschild observed the Delta flight attendants she studied do repeatedly and routinely.

3. **Emotion and Organizations**

The importance of Hochschild's research and the conceptual scheme she developed for the study of organizations is twofold: it emphasizes that the control and display of emotion may be important dimensions of many jobs, thus linking emotion and labor; and, because an increasing proportion of paid work is embedded within various kinds of organizations in the modern world, it links emotion and organization. Since establishing these connections, Hochschild's work, particularly the concepts of emotion work and emotion labor, have been drawn on by a growing number of qualitative scholars studying the place of emotion in different kinds of organizations. Thus, studies have been conducted on how therapeutic discourse constitutes professional feelings among staff in a residential psychiatric facility in Israel (Yanay and Shahar 1998), on how commercial adventure enterprises, such as river rafting companies, help to manufacture the very emotional experiences their novice consumers desire (Holyfield 1999), and on how the emotions generated within some support groups are used as resources to sustain commitment to the group (Wolkomir 2001). Recent research has also rediscovered the relevance of emotion to the study of social movements and the organizations that sponsor their protest activities (see, e.g., the selections in Goodwin, Jasper, and Polletta 2001).

That emotion would figure significantly in the functioning of therapeutic and adventure groups and organizations, as well as in the operation of social movement organizations, is not so surprising. But there is an increasing volume of research that indicates its relevance to understanding organizations more generally, including large-scale corporate organizations (Fineman 1993; Van Maanen and Kunda 1989). Especially illustrative are Nicole Biggart's (1989) study of two direct selling organizations, Mary Kay Cosmetics and Shaklee, and Jennifer Pierce's (1995a) study of gender within the context of law firms. In Biggart's study, both organizations were identified as "charismatic" capitalist enterprises in which the emotions of "awe" and "loyalty" bind employees to their employers. By "teasing out" and listing the ways in which these emotion-suffused enterprises differ from the traditional rationalist bureaucracy, Biggart is able to see them as a distinct "type" of organization (See Table 4, p. 130 of her book for comparison of contrasting features.). In Pierce's research, significant attention is focused on the emotional aspect of work in contemporary law firms and the ways in which normative expectations of emotion work among law firm employees is stratified according to both gender and official organizational hierarchy. Gender-based "emotional double-binds," she argues, reproduce the gendered structural features of law firms as sex-segregated workplaces (1995a, p. 183).

C. Hierarchical Aspects or Inequalities

Given the pervasive and frequently problematic character of hierarchy and stratification in social life, it is hardly surprising that a concern with inequality is a prominent feature in sociological research. This is as true among fieldworkers focusing on the more micro levels as it is among macro-oriented analysts focusing on economic and political "systems." Here we can only draw upon a few examples from the abundant literature in this area to illustrate how fieldworkers have incorporated attention to hierarchical aspects of social life in their analysis of various units, particularly encounters, relationships, and groups.

1. Hierarchy in Encounters

The encounter is certainly one of the most micro-level units one can study. Yet oddly enough, it is also a location that allows one to observe both the *operation of macro systems of inequality* (based on class, race, or sex, for example) in the lives of human actors and the *creation and re-creation of those systems* by individual human actors. Analyses of encounters reveal, for example, that stratification arrangements may be communicated and enacted through diverse practices, some of which can be quite stylized and ritualized as Elijah Anderson found in his dissection of the elements of the "street etiquette" practiced in encounters between individuals separated by both class and race. Such encounter-embedded stylized practices include (1) ballet-like sequences for street passing, (2) the use of dogs as walking companions, (3) rituals guiding the carrying of cash, and, as illustrated in the following passage, (4) elaborate eye- and face-work.

Many people, particularly those who see themselves as more economically privileged than others in the community, are careful not to let their eyes stray, in order to avoid an uncomfortable situation. As they walk down the street, they pretend not to see other pedestrians, or they look right at them without speaking, a behavior many blacks find offensive. (1990, p. 220)

2. Hierarchy in Roles and Relationships

The relationships between unequals are fertile ground for understanding hierarchy, and modern workplaces offer rich settings for such observations. Oftentimes the research focus is on the relationship between two or more roles within the workplace or setting. The character of the hierarchical relationship between service workers and their customers, for example, has been a frequent topic of field research, with the interactional dominance of customers commonly highlighted. As we have noted, many fieldstudies over the past two decades have focused on the emotional labor required of employees in commercial settings. A substantial number of these studies, including Arlie Hochschild's (1983) geminal study of airline attendants and collections agents and Robin Leidner's (1993) research on insurance salespeople and fast-food chain workers, have focused considerable analytic attention on how service businesses demand that workers engage in deferential emotional labor toward their customers. Interestingly, Drue Johnston and Norris Johnson's (1988) research on the Beverly Hills Supper Club Fire in Southgate, Kentucky, found that this same pattern of deference and demeanor holds in disaster episodes.

The server role was extended to serve customers in a very different fashion—to help them exit the building and escape the danger.... Most of the employees had no training or experience in coping with disaster; they nevertheless seemed to accept the new responsibilities toward their customers as part of the job. The patrons, too, seemed to accept the employees' extended roles by following their directions. (1988, p. 49)

Some studies examining worker/customer role relationships also analyze the strategies that service workers use to cope with the demeaning aspects of their relationships with customers, as clearly demonstrated in Greta Paules' (1991) fieldstudy of "power and resistance" among restaurant waitresses. Studies of professionals and their clients, in contrast, often depict a situation in which the relational "edge" is reversed. In their study of how medical students in residency manage time pressures, for instance, William Yoels and Jeffrey Clair (1994) describe various strategies that residents use to control the length of their interactions with patients, such as examining medical records prior to entering the room or (alternatively) reading their charts while patients are talking, avoiding eye contact, and interrupting patients who try to discuss psychosocial aspects of their illnesses. In addition to providing medical residents with some control of their time, such techniques also express and reinforce residents' dominance in physician-patient relationships.

3. **Hierarchy in Groups**
   Members of groups generally rank one another and possess different degrees of influence over one another. Collectively considered, these personal differences in power, influence, and centrality form a group hierarchy or system of status inequality. There may be struggles over placement in the hierarchy, over the hierarchy itself, or between two or more hierarchies in the same setting; nonetheless, a ranking system tends to exist, even if it is fluid and changing. In their aforementioned study of preadolescent peer cliques, for instance, Patricia and Peter Adler devote considerable effort to explicating common patterns of clique structure, including two primary patterns of leadership:

   > The most powerful and pivotal role in the clique was the leader's. Cliques usually took the single-leader mode, with one person serving as the most forceful member of the group, dominating over the others. The leader had the power to set the clique boundaries, include or exclude potential members, raise or lower people in favor, and set the collective trends and opinions. . . . A second form that cliques less commonly took involved two leaders [who] . . . could operate in tandem, as friends, or more often independently, often with an element of competition. (1998, p. 77)

   Fieldworkers, of course, have also observed status hierarchies and analyzed status dynamics in a wide range of adult groups, from William F. Whyte's (1993) analysis of stratification among the "Nortons" street corner group in Boston in the late 1930s to Jennifer Lois's (2003) examination of status hierarchy among volunteers in a search and rescue group in the mountains of Colorado.

IV. Two or More Units or Aspects as Topics

The dominant imagery of the foregoing description of units and aspects combined into topics is that of one unit combined with one aspect. This is fine as a way to start and can work well as the guiding image of a study if it fits satisfactorily with the data at hand and with one's more specific substantive concerns. But this is also only one image or formula. Possible additional images or generic formulae include conjoint or simultaneous focus on (1) one aspect of two or more interacting units at the same scale of social organization, as in Lois's (2003) research on the subculture of search and rescue workers and their various emotion management practices, Katz's (1999) research on emotion in various episodes and encounters, and Johnston and Johnson's (1988) examination of the hierarchical role relationship between servers and customers in a disaster episode; on (2) one aspect of two or more interacting units at different scales of social organization, as in Snow and Anderson's (1993) study of homeless street life in Austin, Texas, and Duneier's (1999) ethnography of sidewalk vendors in

Figure 6.1 Matrix of Studies Focusing on Topics based on the Intersection of Units and Aspects.

	ASPECTS		
UNITS	Cognitive	Emotional	Hierarchical
Practices	Snow and Anderson 1993	Lois 2003	Hodson 1991
Episodes	Davis and Boles 2003	Katz 1999	Johnston and Johnson 1988
Encounters	L. Lofland 1985b	Katz 1999	E. Anderson 1990 and 1999
Roles/Social Types	Duneier 1999	Cahill 1999	Johnston and Johnson 1988
Relationships	Blee 2002	Hochschild 1983	Yoels and Clair 1994
Groups	J. Lofland 1977	Blee 2002	Adler and Adler 1998
Organizations	Kunda 1992	Pierce 1995a	Pierce 1995a
Settlements and Habitats	Duneier 1999	Scheper-Hughes 1992	Newman 1999
Subcultures and Lifestyles	Snow and Anderson 1993	Lois 2003	Wright 1997

New York's Greenwich Village; and on (3) two or more aspects of units at the same scale or at different scales of unit organization, as with Pierce's (1995) examination of how gender comes into play both emotionally and hierarchically in law firms, and Blee's (2002) study of women and gender relations within racist hate groups. These examples, as well as others, are plotted on Figure 6.1, which constitutes a matrix of previously discussed studies that focus on topics derived from the intersection of one or more units or aspects. The suggestion, then, is that one can conceive of social reality as "units" and "aspects" of units and also as fields of interactive relations between or among two or more units and aspects.

V. Units, Aspects, and Topics Form a Mind-Set for Coding

The ideas of units and aspects and their intersection yielding topics should be thought of as providing a scheme for helping you to make analytic sense of the data you are logging. Specifically, units and aspects forming topics make up the mind-set you bring to the activity of coding your data, a major activity you carry on in developing analysis, which we discuss in Chapter 9.

Bringing such an analytic scheme to your data is to be distinguished from mechanically applying specific units and aspects to the data. We emphatically urge the former rather than the latter. While you want to be mindful of units and aspects, you want to remain flexible about exactly what units/aspects/topics you will pursue in coding and in evolving analyses. This chapter should provide you a general orientation to the kinds of things to consider when coding data, not a preformed template of things for which to code. But you should also feel free to use any specific units, aspects, or topics described above if they help in coding your data. You should also be open to drawing on units, aspects, and topics we do not mention in this chapter.

Units and aspects combined into topics provide the first of the three analytic lines along which you want to focus your data. The second line of focusing is to ask questions about those topics, the task to which we now turn.

CHAPTER 7

ASKING QUESTIONS

Achieving an elaborated understanding of units and aspects—topics, as treated in the last chapter—is partly contingent on the questions asked about them. Although any particular topic might invite an array of questions, there are at least eight basic questions social analysts commonly pose about the social topics they investigate. These and their relations to each other are presented in a schematic overview in Figure 7.1. To assist in grasping all eight as we discuss them in this chapter, think of the middle six in Figure 7.1 (numbers 2 through 7) as forming three sets of two questions each as follows:

- Questions 2 and 3, **Frequencies and Magnitudes**, ask how often we observe something and its strength or size.
- Questions 4 and 5, **Structures and Processes**, ask how, in detail, something is organized (structured) and how it evolves or operates over time (processes).
- Questions 6 and 7, **Causes and Consequences**, ask what factors account for the occurrence or development of something (causes) and what effects something has (consequences).

These six questions generally are preceded by the question of what the "something" is in the first place—that is, Question 1, the question of its **type or types**, calling for a depiction of its defining features. As well, the six middle questions often imply some kind of strategic action and thus suggest an eighth question, that of **human agency**, which brackets the foregoing seven and asks how people strategize their actions in and toward situations and settings.

We have spatially arranged the elements of Figure 7.1 to highlight how the foregoing questions are commonly coupled and also how they are different from one another. Thus:

- Questions 1, 2, and 3 (types, frequencies, and magnitudes) are shown external to the box that represents the topic under study in order to display them as matters we observe from the outside.
- Questions 4 and 5 (structures and processes) are shown inside the box symbolizing the topic in order to indicate that structures and processes are internal

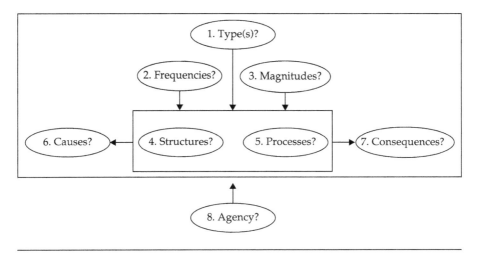

Figure 7.1 Eight Basic Questions

properties of the object of study. (Also, the phrase "structure and process" is a common social science coupling.)

- Questions 6 and 7 (causes and consequences) are shown to the left and right of the box, symbolizing the topic in order physically to represent causes as coming *before* the topic of study in time and in order physically to represent consequences as coming *after* the object of study in time. (The phrase "causes and consequences" is also a common coupling in social science language.)
- Question 8 is shown outside the large box around the first seven questions in order to represent it as an entirely different kind of question, that of active human agency.

We hope that referring back to Figure 7.1 and the overview given here will assist you in understanding the eight questions that we will now discuss in some detail.

I. What Are the Topic's Types?

One of the most important but often unappreciated moments in social science analysis is the act of posing and answering the question, "What is this thing or cluster of things I see before me?" Such a broad categorization question typically invites a somewhat more delimited question: "What is this an instance of?" "What type of some previously identified unit or aspect is it?" Or, more concretely, "What specific *type* of encounter, group, organization, emotion, or hierarchy is it?"

A. Single Types

Many important advances in social analysis are simply insightful depictions of a single type of practice, relationship, meaning, hierarchy, or other unit or aspect. Consider, for example, Erving Goffman's (1961a) isolation of the concept of the "total institution." He developed this organizational type after considering the features of the particular organization he was studying (a mental hospital) and how these features were similar to those of other organizations not traditionally associated with asylums, such as monasteries, boarding schools, prisons, and the like. By asking himself what were the *general* features of that hospital and other similar organizations, he developed the idea of the "total institution."

> When we review the different institutions in our Western society, we find some that are encompassing to a degree discontinuously greater than the ones next in line. Their encompassing or total character is symbolized by the barrier to social intercourse with the outside and to departure that is often built right into the physical plant, such as locked doors, high walls, barbed wire, cliffs, water, forest, or moors. These establishments I am calling *total institutions*. . . . A basic social arrangement in modern society is that the individual tends to sleep, play, and work in different places, with different coparticipants under different authorities, and without an overall rational plan. The central feature of total institutions can be described as breakdown of the barriers ordinarily separating these spheres of life. (Goffman 1961a, pp. 4–6)

B. Multiple Types and Taxonomies

This logic is readily extended to conceiving numerous types that are variations of some more general cultural entity or type. Such multiple "typing" is especially likely when observing more than one concrete setting and there is interesting variance among the units encountered across the settings. Looking back through Chapter 6, we see as a salient feature of a number of the works cited the elaboration of multiple types, including:

- types of accounts students develop to justify frittering away time, missing class, and cheating (Bernstein 1978; Kalab 1987; McCabe 1992) (Section II.A);
- types of cliques in schools (Adler and Adler 1998) (Section II.F.1);
- types of medical student role strategies (Smith and Kleinman 1989) (Section III.B.2); and
- types of organizations (Biggart 1989) (Section III.B.3).

Often the identification of types leads to the development of a *taxonomy*, which is basically an elaborated list of all types of a meaningful cultural category or phenomenon within a particular sociocultural context. Development of a taxonomy begins with a cultural or theoretical category, such as students, and then enumerates the members of that category according to a question of interest, such as "What kinds or types of students are there?" The above mentioned studies of various student accounts provides a point of departure for answering that question by suggesting that some students are "fritterers," some are "skippers," and some are "cheaters," but it is not clear that these are either mutually exclusive types or exhaustive, two considerations we turn to below. More fully developed taxonomies can be found in the research of David Snow and his colleagues on homelessness in various cities and with respect to various substantive issues. For example, they have developed, for both descriptive and analytic purposes, taxonomies of resources mobilized by homeless social movement organizations (Cress and Snow, 1996, pp. 1094–1096), outcomes sought by homeless social movement organizations (Cress and Snow, 2000, pp. 1066–1068), and the material survival strategies of the homeless. The later taxonomy, which is reproduced in Figure 7.2 for illustrative purposes, is an ethnographically elaborated answer to the question, "How do the homeless survive materially on the streets?"

Figure 7.2 Taxonomy of Material Survival Strategies Among the Homeless

1. **Institutionalized Assistance**
   1A. Institutionalized Labor (Working for Street Agencies)
   1B. Income Supplements
      1B.1. Public Assistance
      1B.2. Assistance from Family and Friends

2. **Wage Labor**
   2A. Regular Work
   2B. Day Labor

3. **Shadow Work**
   3A. Selling/Peddling/Vending (Informal Sales Work)
      3A.1. Selling Junk and Discarded Items
      3A.2. Selling Illegal Goods and Services
         3A.2a. Selling Drugs
         3A.2b. Prostitution
      3A.3. Selling Plasma
   3B. Soliciting Public Donations
      3B.1. Panhandling
      3B.2. Performing in Public
   3C. Scavenging
      3C.1. Scavenging for Food
      3C.2. Scavenging for Salable Goods
      3C.3. Scavenging for Money
   3D. Theft

Derived from Snow and Anderson 1993, Chapters 4 and 5.

C. Typologizing

On occasion, the topics under study seem to possess some complex but systematic interrelation. In such a case, you can often discover what that interrelation is by specifying a small number of relevant variables whose *conjoint* variations accurately incorporate the patterns you have already discerned (and point out others you have not yet fully contemplated). This process of charting the possibilities that result from the conjunction of two or more variables is variously called substructing (Miles and Huberman 1994, p. 184), dimensionalizing (Strauss and Corbin, 1990, pp. 69–72), and *typologizing*, which is our preference.

For example, in examining the diverse environments in which American nonprofit organizations operate, Kirsten Grønbjerg (1993) found that the complexity of the diversity of their environments was fruitfully reducible to and articulated by a conjunction between just two underlying and dichotomized variables. As Figure 7.3 shows, these variables are the degree to which a nonprofit's environment is dominated by private sector providers of the same kind of service (treated as yes or no) and the degree to which the public sector is dependent on a nonprofit organization for the service it provides (also treated as yes or no). Thus "substructed" or "typologized," the myriad of variations in the environments of nonprofits is simplified into the four basic patterns shown in Figure 7.3—the patterns of cooperation, accommodation, competition, and symbiosis.

Typologizing thus helps to make an analysis more systematically coherent, and, by showing the logical possibilities, it can sometimes call attention to existing but unnoticed patterns or to the empirical absence of a logically possible pattern (thus raising the question of why it is absent).

We must caution, however, that typology construction can easily become a sterile exercise. Unless performed within the context of full and extensive knowledge of and sensitivity to the actual setting, it will reveal

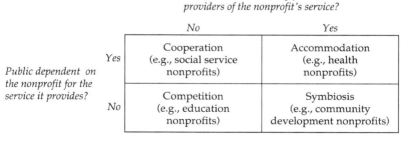

Figure 7.3 Example of Typologizing: Grønbjerg on Environments of Nonprofit Organizations. (Adapted from Grønbjerg 1993, p. 20, Table 1.1.)

little or nothing. Arbitrary box building is not a substitute for a close feel for the actual circumstances.

D. Sources and Rules of Typing and Typologizing

It is often assumed that the types identified, the taxonomies elaborated, and the typologies constructed during the course of fieldwork are fully grounded in the sense that they are based solely on what we see or on what our informants tell us. But this is not always the case, as some types and typologies are derived primarily from existing theoretical categories or concepts, and some are a blend of theoretical and folk categories. Thus, there are at least three generic sets of types and typologies based on their respective sources: folk-elicited or folk, theoretical or abstracted, and mixed. Of those listed above, the types of student accounts, school cliques, and medical student role strategies are essentially folk-based, whereas the typology of lifestyles is more abstracted or theorized, and the types of organizations and taxonomy of survival strategies are essentially mixed. One is not necessarily better than the other. Rather, their respective categoric and analytic utility depends largely on what you want to know and the questions you ask.

Whatever the basis of the types, taxonomies, or typology, however, there are, as suggested earlier, two basic procedural rules or guidelines you should try to follow:

- First, you should choose the content of the classification or type in such a way that you can place each case into only one category thereof. This is called *the rule of mutual exclusiveness*.
- Second, the categories you devise should make it possible to classify all (or almost all) of the relevant cases. This is called *the rule of exhaustiveness*.

If many of your cases fit into more than one of your taxonomic or typological categories, then it should be fairly obvious that your categories are misconceptualized or inappropriate. As well, if a good number of your cases do not fit into the taxonomy or typology, it is evident that there is a mismatch between your empirical materials and your conception of what is going on or what you have seen. Such caveats and concerns do not mean that sometimes there may be some cases that defy taxonomic or typological categorization. But such residual cases should be few in number and explicable in terms of your ethnographic understanding of the setting or context in which they are embedded.

II. What Are the Topic's Frequencies?

It is often useful and important to count how frequently something occurs and to summarize the frequency tabulations in terms of simple descriptive statistics like percentages and measures of central tendency, such as means (averages), medians (the number dividing the frequency distribution in half, with half of the frequencies falling below and half above the median) and modes (the most frequently occurring number). There are, of course, quite elaborate procedures for counting or estimating the occurrence of phenomena and for summarizing and analyzing the frequencies and their correlates statistically. But these procedures, which are codified under such rubrics as "descriptive and inferential statistics" and "survey research," are outside the scope of this manual. There are, however, a number of general methods texts that provide an introduction to these procedures and the issues to which they speak (see, for example, Babbie 2003; Schutt 2004; Singleton and Straits 1999).

The issue of more complex forms of counting and statistical analysis notwithstanding, we want to emphasize that there are many important counts that can and should be done, both of and across units and aspects, in fieldstudies. They can range, of course, from relatively simple counts, such as the number of times a group meets over a six-month period or the average number of people at group functions, to somewhat more complicated counting activities, such as:

- the number and percentage of different types of homeless who engage in different kinds of identity talk (Snow and Anderson 1993, pp. 213–228);
- the frequency in which executives in different types of corporations engage in different kinds of conflict management actions (Morrill 1995, see Tables 4.1, 5.1, and 6.1, pp. 107, 158, and 194 respectively);
- the number of different kinds of collective actions (e.g., collective vocalizations and collective locomotion) and the frequency of their occurrence in crowd gatherings (McPhail 1991, pp. 149–190);
- variation in the frequency and percentage of income-generating strategies, average expenses, and measures of hardship among welfare-reliant and wage-reliant mothers (Edin and Lein 1997, see Tables 4-7 to 4-9, pp. 110, 111, and 113 respectively); and
- the frequency and percentage of different strategies parents use to control their children in different kinds of public places (Horne, McIlwaine, Taylor 2005).

Whatever the nature of counting activity, whether simple or complex, some fieldworkers appear to eschew it out of methodological or ideological obstinacy. But doing so can be empirically and analytically foolhardy, for there are a number of good reasons for resorting to counting:

- to get a sense of the frequency with which various topics of interest are represented in a large batch of data;
- to acquire a firm indication of the extent to which various events or behaviors are actually represented within emerging topical categories;
- to verify a hunch or hypothesis in more than a cursory manner; and
- to keep you analytically honest, protecting against bias (see Miles and Huberman 1994, p. 252 for discussion of some of these).

III. What Are the Topic's Magnitudes?

The question of frequencies refers to occasions of something occurring, whereas the question of magnitude refers to the strength, intensity, or size of instances of an occurrence. As with the determination of frequencies, determining magnitude is a quantitative question that, in more sophisticated forms, involves complicated measurement procedures that we do not treat in this guide. The same works referred to above, however, provide introduction to measurement issues and procedures. Nonetheless, one should not shy away from thinking about and establishing magnitudes should this question loom as central in one's data and analysis.

IV. What Are the Topic's Structures?

The idea of structure, considered from a social scientific standpoint, directs attention to the way in which focal units, aspects, or topics are organized. The existence of most, and perhaps all, of the focal units we discussed in the previous chapter imply the existence of some underlying structure or organization. And there can even be an underlying structure to our cognitive orientations and our feelings. Structure, then, is a pervasive, although not always directly visible, feature of most of what we observe in human social life.

In sociology, the idea of structure manifests itself primarily in the concept of social structure, which is certainly one—and some would argue perhaps the most important—of the discipline's cornerstone concepts. It is variously referenced as patterns of interaction and interdependence, relational connections, webs of association, or networks of social ties among individuals, groups, communities, or nations that produce some measure of order and routine. More succinctly, it can be thought of as arrangements of people, groups, communities, and/or nations in relation to each other in a fashion that gives social life a measure of predictability and order. Given this general conceptualization of social structure and its centrality to understanding significant aspects of social life, it is hardly surprising that much fieldwork has sought to elaborate the character and functions of social structures underlying or associated with the topics studied. To acquire a sense of the flavor of such structural elaborations in published fieldstudies, you might look over one or more of the following concrete examples:

- William F. Whyte's analysis of the relationship between "social structure and social mobility" and "the social structure of racketeering" in *Street Corner Society* (1993);
- Gerald Suttles' elaboration of "ordered segmentation" and "institutional arrangements" in *The Social Order of the Slum* (1968);
- Patricia Adler's discussion of "the social organization of drug world relationships" in *Wheeling and Dealing* (1993); and
- Gary Alan Fine's examination of "the kitchen as a place and space" and "the organization and aesthetics of culinary life" in *Kitchens* (1996).

There are many other examples of fieldstudies focusing in part on the underlying structure of the topics of investigation, but the foregoing should suffice in providing you with both a working appreciation of the character of such studies and the importance of grasping the relationship between structure and the topics observed. Thus, in most of the studies you might pursue, you will certainly want to consider asking questions about the relevant structures.

V. What Are the Topic's Processes?

Equally important as structure to understanding most phenomena you are interested in is the idea or concept of *process*. It is partly for that reason that we have coupled structure and process in Figure 7.1. In many respects, they are flip sides of the same analytic coin, although they are not always weighted equally from the vantage point of different theoretical perspectives. Some perspectives, such as classical Marxism and structural-functionalism, emphasize the primacy of structure, whereas other perspectives, like symbolic interactionism and social constructionism, accent process. Like structure, process does not lend itself to simple definition or conceptualization, but it commonly conveys a sense of development, emergence, progression, or evolution, thus suggesting "a series of actions, changes, or functions" that result in a particular outcome. Implied in this common dictionary conceptualization are four related concepts that are helpful in thinking about processes: stages, steps, periods, and phases.

- A *stage* is "a period or step in a process, activity, or development" or "one of several periods whose beginning and end are usually marked by some important change of structure" in "development and growth."
- A *step* is "a stage in a gradual, regular, or orderly process."
- A *period* is a "time often of indefinite length but of distinctive or specified character" or "a division of time in which something is completed and ready to commence and go on in the same order."
- A *phase* is a "stage or interval in a development or cycle: a particular appearance or stage of a regularly recurring cycle of changes."

For the purposes of this guide, these four terms are synonyms. We have listed and defined each in order to clarify the idea of processes by highlighting the variety of words with which you can describe their elements.

Another way of getting a handle on the idea of process is considering three basic forms of process that researchers often seek to observe and analyze: cycles, spirals, and sequences.

A. Cycles

A cycle is a "recurrent sequence of events which occur in such order that the last precedes the recurrence of the first in a new series." Since the dawn of humankind, much of social life has been explicitly organized in terms of cycles, based first upon astronomical and climatological changes, such as the setting and rising of the sun and seasonal changes, and then on the calendarization of both these naturally occurring changes and significant markers or moments in the history of a people, such as Christmas and the corresponding "holiday season" in the Christian world. And even our sentiments (e.g., feelings, orientation) toward various groups and social issues or problems tend to be calendarized in that they wax and wane in a cyclical fashion (Bunis, Yancik, and Snow 1996).

In addition to standard calendar-based cycles, there are revolving regularities of a less planned, recognized, and scheduled nature. The occurrence of social protest and social movements exhibits such ebb and flow. Sidney Tarrow (1998) coined the concept of "cycles of protest" or "contention" to capture and problematize analytically the cyclical character of such phenomena. It is not just the clustering of protest and movement activity that varies across time, but cycles of activity can also occur within movements. Thus, in analyzing several years in the history of a small, "end-of-the-world" religion, John Lofland (1977) observed that the group went through four cycles of collective hope and despair over the problem of making converts. The group was committed to the goal of making many thousands of converts. In stark contrast to this goal was the fact that the group could interest, much less convert, very few people. Each of the four observed cycles of hope and despair over three years had the following characteristics:

- Some event occurred, or some plan was devised, that provided a collective sense of hope that many converts would soon be made.
- Action was organized around the event or plan.
- This action eventually failed, in the group's own estimation.
- The failure led to a collective sense of despair of ever attaining the goal.
- The group then came full circle back to a new event or plan (adapted from Lofland 1977).

B. Spirals

Some processes do not show the degree of relative stability seen in the more institutionalized cycles. Instead, they display a spiral pattern, a "continuously spreading and accelerating increase or decrease." One of the more familiar forms of this phenomenon is seen in the tension or conflict between social units that are hostile to one another, as in the case of conflict between nation-states, tribes, neighborhoods, and aggregations of individuals who have collectively mobilized against some institutional authority. Such tensions and conflicts can also arise within formal organizations, as Calvin Morrill (1995) documented and analyzed in his previously mentioned study of conflict and conflict management among executives within corporations. When antagonisms and conflicts break out among actors, whatever the collective unit, they are often analyzed in terms of a spiral of *escalation* or *de-escalation*. Max Heirich provides a graphic illustration of a spiral of escalating conflict in his study of the Berkeley free speech movement in the early 1960s, appropriately titled *The Spiral of Conflict* (1971).

The idea of spiraling processes has also been found analytically useful in understanding how individuals sometimes end up in a particular state or situation. Edwin Lemert's (1962) analysis of the process by which a person is labeled and hospitalized as "paranoid" rests basically on the notion of spiraling interaction such that each new step is triggered by the previous one. In their analysis of why and how it is that some individuals became homeless, David Snow and Leon Anderson similarly invoke the logic of a spiraling process, albeit downward:

> Whatever the predominant pathway to the street in any given city, . . . we suspect that in all cities they are the product of interaction among structural and biographic factors that takes the form of a downward spiral in which one factor triggers or exacerbates another until the traveler has fallen onto the streets. (1993, p. 171)

C. Sequences

The most common and probably broadest rendering of process is as a time-ordered series of steps, events, or elements that constitutes what is called a sequence. Sequences can vary in a number of ways (see Abbott 1995, pp. 94–96), including whether they are recurrent or nonrecurrent. Cycles can be thought of as a variant of sequences in that they typically recur, as in the case of economic cycles and cycles of protest, while spirals may be either recurrent or nonrecurrent. Sequence analysis is conducted across the social sciences through a variety of methods and can thus take different forms (see Abbott 1995, for a review). In qualitative research, sequence analysis has been conducted in at least three ways: by tracing back from a common starting point, by tracing forward after a particular event, and/or by trying to identify key turning points.

1. Tracing Back

Perhaps the most common starting point is an outcome. For example, a person has embezzled money, used a certain drug, or converted to an unfamiliar religion; a crowd has rioted; an organization has disbanded; a community has adopted a growth-limit law. All of these occurrences can be seen as outcomes that can and have triggered sequence analyses entailing the identification of steps or events that led to the outcome in question. Such analyses typically begin with the researcher asking, "How did this build up?" or "How did it happen?" and then traces back through the histories of various cases of that outcome. Your aim, inductively, is to scrutinize relevant cases in order to glean a process or processes from them. In a trace-back analysis, the researcher attempts to discern any typical stages through which the actors or action pass in a process that culminates (or does not culminate) in a particular outcome.

Jennifer Lois provides a concrete example of this mode of sequential analysis in her previously mentioned participant observation study of socialization to a volunteer search and rescue group in the western United States. Her focal question was not why some individuals join the group, but how they become full-fledged or core members. Her analysis reveals that volunteers learn to conform to the group norms associated with consciousness, resources, and commitment through a two-stage process involving, first, a "change in status from new to peripheral member" and, then, "from peripheral to core member" (2003, p. 132).

2. **Tracing Forward**
Alternatively, you may be concerned with what happens *after* a decisive event, as in, for example, veterans returning from wars, people being told they are dying, newlyweds adapting to marriage, or communities being hit by a disaster and faced with problems of recovery. An example is Bradley J. Fisher's analysis of the three phases of "career descent" among the institutionalized elderly confronting their own declining levels of health and physical ability (1987). The three phases included resistance to staff evaluation, which constituted the cognitive dissonance phase; acceptance and tarnished self-image, the cognitive consonance phase; and revised opinion and adjustment, called the enhanced self-image phase.

3. **Turning Points**
A third starting point is to consider "turning points," those "short, consequential shifts that redirect a process" (Abbot 2001, p. 258), thus affecting some kind of substantial change in the course of the phenomenon being observed. Although the concept of turning point can be of relevance to understanding macroscopic processes, such as shifts in political alignments, business cycles, and even the direction of history (Abbott 2001), it has been used by qualitative fieldworkers, particularly those influenced by aspects of symbolic interactionism, to get a conceptual handle on significant biographic or personal change. Extending Everett Hughes' (1971) linkage of turning points with important changes in careers, either moral or occupational, Anslem Strauss, for example, found the concept—which he basically defined as "critical incidents that occur to force a person to recognize that 'I am not the same as I was, as I used to be'"—to be central to his analysis of identity transformations (1962, p. 67). Similarly, Norman Denzin, using the language of "epiphanies," directs attention to those "interactional moments that leave marks on people's lives . . . creating transformational experiences" that leave them "never again quite the same" (1989b, p. 15). Such transformational experiences, or turning points, are a fundamental element of John Lofland and Rodney Stark's conversion model (1965), which was derived from Lofland's fieldstudy of the early American converts to the group that eventually became known as the Unification Church. In the context of the movement studied, they note that "all preconverts . . . had come to a moment," at or about the time of their initial encounter with the

group, "when old lines of action were complete, had failed or been disrupted, or were about to be so, and when they faced an opportunity (or necessity), and the possibility of the burden, of doing something different with their lives" (Lofland and Stark 1965, p. 870). To illustrate, they provide examples from the lives of a number of their informants, including Miss Lee, whose "academic career had been disrupted by long illness from which she recovered upon meeting" the movement's leader (1965, p. 870).

Questions have been raised not about the existence of turning points but about the ease with which they can be identified (see, e.g., Snow and Phillips' [1980] critique of Lofland and Stark's use of the concept, as well as Lofland's [1978] concern about the concept in relation to conversion). Nonetheless, it is a concept that has considerable currency in some areas of social science, such as the study of the life course (see, e.g., Gotlib and Wheaton 1997; Sampson and Laub 1993), in large part because it provides a handle for accessing and thinking about social processes and changes in the direction or course of individuals, groups, organizations, and even nation-states.

Whatever the form of qualitative process analysis you pursue—be it the analysis of cycles, spirals, or sequences or some step within a sequence—its descriptive and analytic power resides in the details it enables you to note and connect as individuals move through or negotiate daily life or dramatic changes in their life course, as collective events unfold, or as groups and organizations evolve and change. No other technique enables you to observe and note up close the details of how things happen, proceed, and change as they are occurring in the course of daily life.

VI. What Are the Topic's Causes?

It is commonplace for many laypersons and some social scientists to assume that it is relatively easy to establish the causes of something. Such is not the case, however, as the longstanding debate, anchored in the writing of the philosopher David Hume ([1739]1978), about the possibility of establishing the causes of social phenomena testifies. This debate notwithstanding, the social sciences have generally been enamored of the idea of social causation, and many of its practitioners have proceeded "as if" it is possible to identify the causes of most social phenomena. Indeed, it is arguable that the most frequently asked question in social science is: "What are the causes of Y?" or "Are the observed changes in Y due to observed changes in X?" or, more colloquially, "Is the wiggle in Y due to the waggle in X?"

Here we do not want to get into the various philosophical and statistical arguments about the possibility or impossibility of establishing social causation, as these are matters about which philosophers and logicians of science are much more conversant. Rather, we will merely identify a number of models of social causation that appear in one form or another in the social science literature and then discuss which, if any, of these models is compatible with qualitative field research. It is first necessary, however, to consider the requirements for causal explanation.

A. Requirements of Causal Explanation

In order to say with any reasonable degree of confidence that "A causes B," it is generally agreed that at least four conditions must be operative:

- First, there must be *variation in the "dependent variable."* For whatever you want to find the causes of, you must have instances of its occurrence and nonoccurrence, or its presence and absence, or some indication of variation in its magnitude. That is, you must begin with variation in the dependent variable. This is what we have referred to above, in question 3, as the determination of magnitudes—the size, intensity, or scale of something.

- Second, there must be *variation in the "independent variable."* You must consider the measured variation in the dependent variable conjointly with some other measured variation that you provisionally think causes it in some sense. This presumed or hypothesized variable is typically referred to as the independent variable.

- Third, the *variables should be ordered temporally*, such that the presumed cause precedes the effect in time. In other words, you should be able to establish that the presumed independent variable temporally preceded the dependent variable.

- Fourth, you have to deal with *the problem of spuriousness*. You must be able to show that the covariation between the independent and dependent variable is not due to the influence of a third variable, commonly referred to as an intervening variable. This is the classic problem of "correlation not proving causation." Some other unknown factor, or some known but unmeasured factor, may be the cause or among the causes.

B. Selected Models of Causal Explanation

With these four requisite conditions for establishing some level of causation as backdrop, we list below a number of ways in which causality and causal explanations are discussed and explored empirically in the social sciences, without presuming that they are either exhaustive or accepted by most social scientists. These models, and perhaps others as well, are variants of either probabilistic or determinative approaches to causal explanation, which are generally considered the two generic models of causality (Sobel 1993). They are arranged here on a continuum from the most probabilistic to the most determinative.

1. *Experimental Model*: Causation assessed on the basis of measured differences in a dependent variable (Y) associated with the presence/absence, or varying degrees of presence, of the independent variable (X), among a

matched random assignment of research subjects in a tightly controlled setting (see Campbell and Stanley 1963; Sobel 1993).

2. *Statistical Model*: Causal relationships assessed on the basis of statistical evaluation of correlation and temporal priority among a random sample of subjects, with emphasis on avoiding or controlling for potential spurious associations (see Blalock 1979; Sobel 1993).

3. *Contextual Model*: Specification of the contextual factors contributing to the occurrence of the phenomenon of interest by providing, metaphorically, nurturant soil for the phenomenon to grow. The specified conditions are not determinative, but increase the probability of the occurrence or appearance of the phenomenon (see Ragin 1987; Skocpol 1984).

4. *Case Comparative Model*: Identification of the configurations of present or absent conditions that account for the occurrence or nonoccurrence of specified states or outcomes. The aim is to identify the necessary and sufficient conditions that account for the phenomena of interest (see Ragin 1987, 2000).

5. *Step/Process Model*: Specification of a causal process based on the identification of the steps associated with experiencing or realizing a particular state or condition. This is sometimes referred to as the "value-added" model in that each step in the process narrows the range of alternatives and thus increases the prospect of moving to the next step (see Meyer and Conrad 1957; Smelser 1962).

6. *Negative Case Model*: The specification of causation through the systematic search for negative cases or instances, and revision of the causal explanation until it accounts for all known cases (see Becker 1998, pp. 194–212; Katz 2001).

C. Clarifying the Relationship Between Qualitative Field Research and Causal Explanation

Can qualitative field research contribute to specifying the causal factors or dynamics leading to the occurrence of a phenomenon of interest? Can field research as discussed herein help to understand the conditions that account for variation in whatever is being explored? The answer is conditional in that it depends on the purpose of the study and which of the above causal models are being employed. Regarding the first condition, most qualitative fieldstudies are not well suited for divining definitive answers to causal questions for the simple reason that they are oriented to identifying and elaborating "how" things get done or happen rather than specifying "why" they occurred. It is arguable, of course, that the "whys" are often embedded in the "hows," but relatively few ethnographic fieldstudies attempt to ferret out the character of that relationship. Additionally, few fieldstudies satisfy the sampling conditions associated with the experimental and statistical models, either in terms of the representativeness or size of the sample. Therefore, rarely can a fieldstudy pursue the kinds of causal explanation linked to these two models. Since these are the two dominant models of causal explanation in the social sciences, it is not surprising that qualitative field research is generally thought to be of little, if any, analytic utility when it comes to causal explanation. And clearly this is the case for most qualitative research, which typically pursues questions other than causal ones and/or topics for which matters of measurement and statistical enumeration are of little, if any, relevance. As Erving Goffman noted in describing his fieldwork in a mental hospital:

> Desiring to obtain ethnographic detail regarding selected aspects of patient social life, I did not employ usual kinds of measurements and controls. I assumed that the role and time required to gather statistical evidence for a few statements would preclude my gathering data on the tissue and fabric of patient life. (1961a, p. x)

Yet, qualitative fieldstudies often report findings in a way that suggests a causal connection, as illustrated by the following observations:

- Class consciousness, rather than being a characteristic that individual workers must possess in order to engage in collective action, actually arises during the course of such action (Fantasia 1988).
- Patterns of conflict management among corporate executives vary primarily in terms of different organizational normative orders (Morrill 1995).
- The propensity to engage in street violence and/or the way in which potentially violent confrontations are handled varies with whether the interactant comes from "decent" or "street" families (Anderson 1999).
- Having a "racist self" and harboring racist beliefs often follow, rather than precede, association with racist hate groups (Blee 2002).

Such observations clearly imply a causal connection, even if the language of causality is not always used, inasmuch as it is argued that the event, state, or condition in question owes its occurrence, at least in part, to the prior occurrence of some other event, state, or condition. Thus, in each instance there is implied or actual variation in both the focal topics or dependent variables (e.g., class consciousness, patterns of conflict management, street violence, and racist beliefs) and the causal or independent variables (e.g., collective action, different organizational normative orders, family type, socialization into hate groups) as well as implied or established temporal priority. What is left open-ended is the matter of spuriousness—that is, whether there are factors or conditions other than the one accented that might be equally or more influential. However, the above observations and the studies on which they are based do not rule out the possibility that other unspecified conditions or variables are at work. Rather, they merely assert the importance of a condition, context, or set of conditions that appear to be nurturant of or conducive to the occurrence of the phenomenon in question. In other words, such studies identify and elaborate one or more *necessary conditions* for the occurrence of the focal phenomenon, but without specifying the set of conditions that are either theoretically or empirically sufficient for explaining its occurrence. And, in doing so, they are providing a kind of causal account that is consistent with the *contextual model* identified above. To illustrate further, consider Diane Vaughan's (2003) report for the Columbia Accident Investigation Board regarding the causes of the *Columbia* and *Challenger* spaceship disasters. Her basic argument, which is summarized in the phrase "history as cause," is that a series of interacting decisions and events established the conditions for the occurrence of both disasters. This analysis, she writes,

> shows how previous political, budgetary, and policy decisions by leaders at the White House, Congress, and NASA . . . impacted the Space Shuttle Program's structure, culture, and safety system . . . , and how these in turn resulted in flawed decision-making . . . for both accidents. The explanation is about system effects: how actions taken in one layer of NASA's organizational system impact other layers. History is not just a backdrop or a scene-setter. History is a cause. History set the *Columbia* and *Challenger* accidents in motion. (Vaughan, 2003, p. 195)

Again, the possibility of other contributing factors is not ruled out, but the confluence of the program's structure, culture, and safety system provides the contextual conditions that allowed for the "flawed decision-making" that facilitated the occurrence of the accidents. Such explanations are more probabilistic than determinative in that some set of conditions or context is posited as increasing the odds of certain events occurring but without asserting definitively if and when these events will occur. As in the case of most statistical analyses, there remains unexplained variance. In other words, the accounting of all of the factors that might explain the phenomenon of interest is incomplete. And, as a consequence, relatively cautious language often permeates qualitative reports, as reflected in such phrases as: "It seems to be the case that . . . ." or "It appears that . . . ." But some qualitative research offers less probabilistic and more determinative statements regarding the relationships among the phenomena observed, as is the case with works associated with the latter three causal models listed above.

The first of these three more determinative models is the *case comparative method*, as embodied in the technique of "qualitative comparative analysis" (QCA) devised and elaborated by Charles Ragin (1987, 2000). Based on the logic of Boolean algebra, this technique facilitates identification of the necessary and sufficient conditions underlying the occurrence of one or more events when comparing a relatively small number of cases. Unlike the quantitative approaches, which generalize the influence of individual variables across a number of cases and have additive and linear assumptions about the influence of variables, QCA is conjunctural in its logic, examining the various ways in which specified factors interact and combine to yield a particular result or outcome. This increases the prospect of discerning diversity and identifying different pathways that lead to an outcome of interest. Dan Cress and David Snow's (1996, 2000) comparative ethnographic study of homeless social movement mobilization among fifteen homeless social movement organizations (SMOs) in eight U.S. cities illustrates the application of QCA. In one analysis seeking to explain variation in the organizational viability (measured in terms of temporal survival, meeting frequency, and the capacity to conduct collective action campaigns) of the fifteen SMOs, they found that differences in viability were best accounted for by the number and combination of resources secured and the presence of a benefactor (organization that provided 50 percent or more of the resources). Based on these findings derived via the use of QCA, Cress and Snow concluded that "sustained, effective protest for the poor requires strong (viable) organizations predicated on the mobilization of essential resources" secured from "nonconstituency-based facilitative organizations" (1996, p. 1107). Thus, for this study, as well as other prospective comparative ethnographies, QCA provides a set of procedures for comparing a small number of cases in terms of the multiple and conjunctural causes of the events or outcomes in question.

The second way in which qualitative field researchers have sometimes approached the matter of causality in a determinative fashion is by following the logic of the *step/process or value-added model*. As suggested above, the model is akin, analogically, to the assembly line production process in which each stage shapes further the character of the product, such that there is a progressive narrowing of the range of possible outcomes. Each stage or step is thus viewed as a necessary but insufficient condition for the occurrence of the behavior or event in question, but taken together they constitute the sufficient conditions. Illustrative is John Lofland and Rodney Stark's (1965) previously mentioned conversion model, which posits that "total conversion," involving both behavioral and verbal commitment, is the result of the accumulation of seven "necessary and constellationally-sufficient conditions" (p. 874). The first three factors in the model are regarded as "predisposing" in that they exist prior to contact with the group and function to render the individual susceptible to conversion. The remaining four factors are classified as situational contingencies in that they lead to recruitment and conversion to one group rather than another. In the absence of these situational factors, conversion will not occur, no matter how predisposed the individual. Accordingly, conversion is conceptualized as a value-added process in which the addition of each new condition or contingency increases the probability that conversion will occur.

The final and most determinative causal model employed in some qualitative work is variously referred to as the *negative case analysis* and/or *analytic induction*. The objective is to establish a definitive relationship between the phenomenon to be explained and the explanatory or causal factors by progressively redefining the relationship between them through the careful inspection of cases, involving the search for negative cases.

Jack Katz, who employed this logic in his field investigation of when and why legal assistance staff lawyers burn out (1982), succinctly articulates the procedures:

> When encountering a "negative case"—evidence contradicting the current explanation—the researcher must transform it into a confirming case by revising the definition of either the explaining or explained phenomenon. The researcher is enjoined to seek negative cases and the resulting opportunity to modify the explanation. There is no methodological value in piling up data of a sort already determined to be consistent with the theory. (Katz 2001, p. 331)

This model of causal analysis, which was initially articulated by Thomas and Znaniecki (1934), was employed in a number of studies of types of "deviance" in the late 1940s and early 1950s—Lindesmith on opiate addiction (1947), Becker on marijuana use (1953), and Cressey on embezzlement (1953)—and then seemed to fall out of favor as the result of a number of critical discussions of the procedure (e.g., Turner 1953). But it has been dusted off and resuscitated somewhat in Katz's analysis of laughter in a funhouse (1999) and Michael Flaherty's examination of the experience of the passing of time (1999).

To note these different models that qualitative researchers have used to think about and assess causal connections and relationships is not to suggest that there is agreement about the utility of these models or that the findings of the illustrative studies have been accepted without critique. Nor do we mean to suggest that these models are prominently featured in the work of most qualitative fieldstudies. To the contrary, as suggested earlier, most qualitative, ethnographic fieldstudies do not seek directly to establish causal connections or explore causal questions. But generalized disinterest in doing so does not mean that causal explanation is beyond the grasp or outside the logic of qualitative research. Certainly the above examples provide counterpoints to that sometimes taken-for-granted assumption as well as models for thinking about the causal relationships among the events, practices, and behaviors observed.

VII. What Are the Topic's Consequences?

Among the eight questions, many social science projects address three: descriptive elaboration of the phenomena observed, specification of the causes that underlie their occurrence and variation, and identification of their consequences. Having addressed the first two of these, we turn to the matter of consequences. Of course, the question of consequences overlaps with the matter of causes in that consequences can be seen as the second half of the causal question. That is, we now view the dependent variable as an independent variable and attempt to look at its dependent variable consequences.

A. Foreground Issues in Examining Consequences

Before looking at some examples of qualitative studies exploring the consequences of the topics of interest, it is necessary to clarify a number of issues.

1. Requirements of Inferring Consequences

Because the question of consequences can be construed as the question of causes "pushed forward," the four standard requirements of causal inference (Section VI.A above) also apply here—that is, you should have discernible variation in your dependent variable, and so on. As we have noted, these conditions are not pertinent to the aims of much qualitative research and generally hard to satisfy in most qualitative fieldstudies. However, as we have just shown, there are both models of qualitative causal analysis and examples of the application of those models. So pursuing causal questions is not completely foreign to qualitative researchers. Such is also the case when it comes to assessing the consequences of topics of interest.

2. Consequences for Whom or for What?

When considering the consequences of a particular line of action, social practice, social arrangement, or organizational form, it is important to be explicit about who or what is impacted. For whom, or for what, is the topic in question consequential, and in what ways? How did this practice or initiative affect group A in comparison to group B? For example, did the initiative (the demolition of low-income housing) advance the interests of group B (developers) in contrast to group A (low-income residents)?

Consideration of such questions during the course of your field research and advanced analysis (Chapter 9) forces you to ask more focused and penetrating questions that are likely to sharpen your analysis. And, in doing so, you are less likely to reach premature conclusions about the character of the consequences of a particular practice or line of action.

The importance of raising such questions can be traced at least to the now fairly long-standing critique of the theoretical perspective called "functionalism," which presumed that the persistence of a social practice, line of action, or institution contributed to the maintenance of some larger system or whole. While that presumption may certainly be empirically correct in one sense, it can also be terribly misleading inasmuch as it directs attention away from the ways in which the practice or action in question may negatively affect some people, groups, or systems. Thus, for both analytical and political purposes, it is important that you are aware of the possible range of consequences of the phenomenon you are investigating.

3. Intentional and Unintentional Consequences

It is also important to be alert to the possibility that the consequences of the phenomenon you are examining may be intended or unintended. In other words, they may be the result of purposive, strategic organization and/or action, or they may be unintended in the sense that they were not planned, strategized, or pursued in a goal-directed fashion. A classic example of such unintended consequences is provided by Robert Merton's well-known argument that corrupt political machines in American cities functioned to provide alternative routes of social mobility for talented persons in disadvantaged ethnic minorities. Political machines thereby contributed to the urban political and social stability by diffusing potential alienation among members of some ethnic groups (1968, pp. 126–136). As a further example of unintended consequences, consider the concept of "iatrogenesis," which essentially means diseases or maladies of medical origin. Hence, the frequently mouthed ironic aphorism: "If you want to get sick, go to the hospital." This "iatrogenic principle," as Louis Schneider once noted, "is a very far-reaching one" that extends well beyond medical contexts (1975, pp. 4–14). And, not surprisingly, its operation has been featured, although not in that language, in various ethnographic texts, ranging from Clifford Shaw's *The Jack-Roller* (1930) to Erving Goffman's *Asylums* (1961a) to Stefan Timmermans' *Sudden Death and the Myth of CPR* (1999).

The point of highlighting these works, then, is to make you mindful of the unintentional consequences of some social practices and processes. While field researchers have generally attended more closely to intentional consequences and associated strategic action, as we will see shortly, unintended consequences are not only worthy of investigation in their own right, but they often reveal aspects about social life that illuminate it in ways we had not previously considered.

B. Examples of the Qualitative Study of Consequences

With the foregoing issues in mind, let us consider a few examples of the qualitative study of consequences. We noted above that, when exploring a topic's consequences, what was previously the dependent variable frequently becomes an independent variable. Such was the case in Cress' and Snow's previously mentioned study of homeless social movement organizations in eight cities. Recall that in the initial analysis, the objective was to account for variation in the organizational viability of fifteen homeless SMOs (1996). In a subsequent examination of the factors that account for difference in the outcomes or consequences of the mobilization activities of these SMOs, organizational viability was one of four sets of independent variables hypothesized to affect outcome attainment. The other independent variables included the use of disruptive tactics, political mediation, and the character of each SMO's framing efforts. Regarding the relative influence of these variables, as determined via their use of the procedures of QCA, Cress and Snow conclude:

> Our findings identify the importance of organizational viability and framing activities for obtaining targeted outcomes by homeless SMOs. When these conditions are present and occur in conjunction with political mediation, the particulars of which affect the types of tactics that are associated with successful outcome attainment, we found that the homeless SMOs are likely to have their greatest impact. (2000, p. 1101)

Another example of field research that addresses the topic of consequences is provided by Ruth Horowitz's (1995) study of a year-long GED and job-training program for teenage black mothers. Horowitz's field observations revealed that two different groups of program staff approached their interactions with the program's students in distinctively different ways. One group of staff members adopted a hierarchical approach. These staff, whom she terms "arbiters," embraced a role of professional expertise and viewed themselves as distinctively different from the program's clients, whose behavior they sought to control. The other group of staff members, whom she refers to as "mediators," identified themselves primarily not as professionals, but as mothers and older women, thus emphasizing their current and future similarities to the young women in the program. Horowitz argues that these different approaches produced significantly different consequences in terms of the messages they provided the young women about who they were and who they could become. The arbiters subjected the teen mothers to a dependent and degrading experience with the consequence that they discouraged independence and personal decision-making. On the other hand, the mediators' interactions and discussions with the program clients conveyed a sense of respect and community and, as a consequence, provided the teen mothers with a role model for and encouragement to pursue a degree of personal empowerment.

Just as in the case of asking and pursuing causal questions, these two studies demonstrate that qualitative fieldwork can also contribute to understanding the consequences of a particular topic, whether it encompasses certain behaviors, practices, or lines of argumentation.

VIII. Where and What Is Agency?

We have discussed seven questions that the analyst asks about social *topics*, be these *units*, *aspects*, or some combination of them. All of these questions, with perhaps the exception of those focusing on processes, may be seen as variations on a single canon: that most human action, whether individual or collective, is determined by forces beyond the awareness or control of the actors themselves. Here we will elaborate this canon and contrast it with a more agentic approach to the analysis of social life, which also raises a different set of questions.

A. Passivist Versus Agentic Conceptions

The view of human action suggested by nearly all of the seven foregoing questions can be thought of as a *passivist* conception. From this vantage point, humans appear to be much like passive automatons, responding programmatically to internal codes and dispositions or magnetically to the pulls and structures of external forces. In this approach, as Herbert Blumer has observed, humans are treated as more or less neutral media through which social forces operate and out of which social forms and organizations are composed (1969). Types, frequencies and magnitudes, structures, and causes and consequences all have their own reality in which humans appear as incidental features or ciphers in the workings of social organizational units and their aspects.

The problem with this conception is not that it is wrong but that it is incomplete. Social structure and organization do have their own reality. But there is another reality and corresponding set of questions we need to consider in order to attain a more well-rounded and balanced understanding of human behavior. This alternative reality is suggested by what can be called the *agentic* conception of human social behavior. It views humans as creative and probing creatures who are coping, dealing, designating, dodging, maneuvering, scheming, striving, struggling, and so forth—that is, as creatures who are actively engaged in and attempting to negotiate their social settings. From this vantage point, as Blumer (1969) emphasized, social actors take into account the structural and cultural constraints that impinge on the situations in which they find themselves in the course of developing their respective lines of action. The focus, then, is on how people construct, negotiate, and manage their actions in various situations.

B. Agentic Questions

Once you grasp this more agentic image of social actors, be they individuals or collectivities, you are confronted with "how" questions that we suggested earlier (Section VI.C) animate much qualitative field research: "How do things get done?" "How do people go about doing what they are doing?" "How do individuals go about the business of pursuing their interests?" When asking such "how" questions, you are essentially focusing on the strategies actors use to do whatever it is they are trying to accomplish. Thus, from an agentic standpoint, you focus your inquiry and analysis by asking "What are the strategies that the actors are using or employing?"

In asking and pursuing questions about strategy, there are actually three questions that you will want to explore: (1) What is the situation, scene, or task? (2) Is it an habituated, taken-for-granted, routinized situation or task, or is it a problematic one in the sense that action has been called into question, thwarted, or derailed? (3) What are the strategies being employed in dealing with the situation? It is no doubt easier to discern strategic talk and action in relation to problematic situations because the actors are more likely to be conscious of what they are trying to do, or actually doing, than is the case with routinized behavior. So it is probably best initially for you to track questions of strategy in the context of more problematic situations. Numerous studies we summarized in the preceding chapter illustrate this tack, with the following sampling being illustrative:

- Section II.A, on practices: Accounting practices of individuals when in situations in which their behavior is called into question (e.g., Dowd 2000; Kalab 1987; McCabe 1992).

- Section III.A.1, on ideologies and meanings: Engagement in "ideological work" when group members are confronted with a disjunction between their ideological beliefs or professions and their behaviors or practices (e.g., Berger 1981; Lofland 1977; Rochford 1985).
- Section III.A.3, on self-concepts and identities: Identity work engaged in by individuals in various situations in order to repair or transform role-specific or imputed "spoiled identities" (e.g., Paterniti 2000; Ponticelli 1999; Sandstrom 1990).

These examples highlight the character of strategic, agentic action in relatively microscopic situations, but such strategic action is prevalent in more large-scale situations and contexts as well, as also illustrated by studies mentioned in the previous chapter:

- Section II.B, on episodes: Collective, strategic expression of feeling and/or grievance in episodes of collective celebration and/or protest (e.g., Corrigall-Brown and Oselin 2003; Davis and Boles 2003; and Snow, Zurcher, and Peters 1981).
- Section II.G on organizations: The fairly widespread "secondary adjustments" of rank and file members of total institutions (mental asylums) and work organizations (factories) to the humiliation and/or monotony experienced (e.g., Goffman 1961; Hodson 1991; Roy 1959/60).
- Section III.B.3, emotion and organizations: How commercial organizations strategically manufacture, obscure, or stratify the emotional aspects of their enterprises (e.g., Biggart 1989; Holyfield 1999; Pierce 1995a).

We tend to lose appreciation of the fact that structures and organizations are constructions because of the peculiar human propensity for *objectivation,* as Berger and Luckmann termed it (1967, pp. 60ff). Humans themselves devise strategic social arrangements but then lose sight of that fact over time because the "structure" presents itself as an "object" (thus the term *objectivation*). Focusing on agency or strategy is one way to "de-objectify" social arrangements (and, as we will explain further in the next chapter, demystify them). In de-objectivation we come to realize that no social arrangement simply "is." Rather, arrangements are incessantly constituted and reconstituted, and this can be seen by focusing on how members or actors go about the business of doing what they do, thus decomposing social arrangements into their strategic components. By pursuing actor's strategies, then, the agentic vantage point injects life into the social by bringing agency back into both the descriptive portrait and analysis of the phenomena observed.

Topics (described in Chapter 6) and questions (discussed in this chapter) provide two of the three major lines along which one focuses one's data. To these we need now to add a third consideration, that of arousing audience interest in the particular topics and questions you select for analysis. We address this third matter in the next chapter.

CHAPTER 8

AROUSING INTEREST

Asking a question (Chapter 7) about a social science topic (Chapter 6) achieves two of the three ways in which researchers seek to focus their data. The third way of focusing data addresses the question of what makes a fieldstudy report interesting to a social science audience. Readers of reports respond to them with varying levels of enthusiasm. They hail some as of major importance, regard others as trivial, and perhaps view most somewhere in between. It must be recognized, of course, that readers sometimes disagree among themselves on the degree to which a report is interesting. Nonetheless, there does seem to be a reasonable amount of agreement on features that make a report more interesting and whose absence makes them less so. Several scholars have provided insightful observations about the qualities that contribute to compelling qualitative reports. Drawing upon their work and our own observations, in this chapter we discuss three vital characteristics of compelling social science fieldstudies. Formulated as questions that readers ask about reports, they are:

1. Is the report *true* in the sense of its observations or assertions being empirically compelling and procedurally trustworthy?
2. Is the report *new* in the sense that it does not simply repeat observations that have already been made or answer questions about topics in reports that have already been published?
3. Is the report *important* in one or another of several senses we explain below?

We want in this chapter to suggest procedures and strategies that maximize the likelihood that social science readers will respond to your report as true, new, and important. Taking the three together, positive responses to each question form an overall assessment that your report is interesting and useful in that it advances empirical, conceptual, or theoretical understanding of some aspect of or topic about the social world. We discuss trueness, newness, and importance as understood within a *social science framing* of collecting, ordering, and interpreting data. We will first elaborate what we are calling "social science framing" and then discuss a number of alternative framings that have currency among different networks of scholars. Against the background of our explication of social science framing, we will suggest that while alternatively framed reports may have humanistic or other merit, they are not "social scientific" in the sense we develop in this chapter.

I. Social Science Framing

The concepts of trueness, newness, and importance are quite abstract and their exact meanings therefore vary as a function of the contexts in which they are given specific application. Such is the case here. The meanings of trueness, newness, and importance we elaborate are specific to the collection and analysis of qualitative social science data in the fieldstudy genre.

A. Trueness

The notion of truth can quickly lead to intense philosophical debate. As Jack Douglas has noted, there are various kinds of abstract truth, such as religious truth, aesthetic truth, and philosophical truth, as well as the "massive realm of everyday life truth" (1976, p. 5). In speaking of truth within a social science framing of qualitative research, we are referring to truth as understood within what Martyn Hammersly and others have referred to as a "subtle realist" tradition wherein the idea of accessible "independent, knowable phenomena" is retained from "naive realism," but without presuming that the reality depicted is an exact or perfect representation in the sense of being completely correspondent to the one examined (Hammersly 1992, pp. 50–52; see also Flaherty 2002; Hammersly and Atkinson 1995; Snow 2002). From this vantage point, getting at the truth means "securing a close *approximation* of the empirical world" (Snow and Morrill 1993, p. 10) that is procedurally "trustworthy" (Erlandson, Harris, Skipper, and Allen 1993).

The empirical accuracy or trueness of a report is produced through the systematic data collection strategies described in previous chapters of this guide—particularly in efforts to avoid error and bias in observations (Chapter 5, Section II.B) and in estimating frequencies and magnitudes (Chapter 7, Sections II and III) and making assertions of causes and consequences (Chapter 7, Sections VI and VII, respectively).

In the end, readers have only the report of your research and they are therefore especially attentive to how its particulars do or do not give them confidence that the factual materials asserted are accurate. We agree with Roger Sanjek's (1990a) argument that readers of field reports look, specifically, for three kinds of validating discussions and practices that he calls "canons of ethnographic validity." Methodologically careful researchers are, therefore, well advised to provide discussions and practices that implement these canons in their reports and to have previously engaged in the activities that give rise to them. Borrowing Sanjek's captions, with slight modifications, these criteria are as follows.

1. **Theoretical Candor**
   The facts asserted and that are now subject to a trueness assessment are organized and analyzed in some substantive fashion. The reader's faith in the accuracy of the empirical details is enhanced if the researcher provides a truthful explanation of how he or she came to employ the particular form of analysis that organizes the facts. Unavoidably, only some facts from among a vast number of other available facts are actually reported, and this reporting is structured by one's analytic or theoretical apparatus. "Candid exposition of when and why" such schemes were developed "enhances ethnographic validity" (Sanjek 1990a, p. 396).

2. **The Ethnographer's Path**
   The criterion of "theoretical candor" reports one's view of the sources of one's analysis. An account of the ethnographer's path, in contrast, reports with whom one interacted, in what sequence, and how. In some studies, this is a "description of the path connecting the ethnographer and informants" (Sanjek 1990a, p. 400). More broadly, the ethnographer's path consists not only of the people with whom one interacts, but also the other avenues of information gathering, including the range of data discussed in Chapter 5, Section II.A. A report should contain an account of both the practical and theoretical considerations that led the researcher to gather data from these specific sources. Faith in the truth of a fieldstudy report is enhanced to the degree that the author has made a candid and compelling case for the relevance of the data-collection path.

3. **Fieldnote and Interview Transcript Evidence**
   The third canon of ethnographic validity goes beyond the preceding one by reporting (1) the procedures for processing and analyzing the data and (2) the practices of presenting data in the report. Regarding procedures, how one recorded data and worked with them should be described along with the processes of developing analysis. The credibility of a fieldstudy is strongest when the reader is provided with a clear description of systematic and theoretically warranted processes of data collection and analysis. Further, sufficient amounts of the empirical materials should be presented to enable the reader to both understand and judge the theoretical and empirical claims made in the report. Fieldnote and interview transcript evidence additionally lends credibility to a report by providing testimony of the researcher's participation in the world under study—what Clifford Geertz (1988) has referred to as the compelling "I-witnessing" or "being there" rhetoric of ethnographic accounts.

   These three kinds of discussions and practices do not absolutely ensure that readers will assess one's report as true or empirically compelling. However, they do provide a mind-set with which to approach the data and that serves to heighten your concern with empirical trueness. Fully executed and reported, these practices at least move one well along the road to fulfilling the evaluative standard of trueness and therefore toward being of interest to an audience. (Additional aspects of these three canons are addressed in Altheide and Johnson 1994; Coffey and Atkinson 1996; Erlandson, Harris, Skipper, and Allen 1993; Lincoln and Guba 1985.)

The theme running through these three practices is that of exercising and exhibiting *methodological concern and caution* in one's treatment of data throughout the report. As Murphy and Dingwall note, researchers have a "double responsibility" in enabling readers to assess their claims to truth:

> First, they have a responsibility for rigorous and self-critical conduct, analysis, and interpretation of the research. . . . Second, they have a responsibility to present the readers of research with sufficient information to allow the latter to decide whether their proposed findings are adequately supported. (2003, p. 174)

Attention to the foregoing concerns and other issues raised in this chapter provide a means for meeting these responsibilities.

B. Newness

When exploring the possibility of studying a particular situation, group, or topic, it is commonplace to hear students lament, "It has already been studied, so what's the point?" Such a reaction is based in part on the reasonable desire not to waste resources assembling facts that are already well established or repeating ideas that are already developed and widely known. But it also is often founded in the failure to realize that there are various dimensions to newness and different strategies for developing or accenting newness, a number of which we elaborate.

1. Relating to Existing Work

An obvious and rather easy first strategy in assessing the possibilities for originality in your research is to use library resources to discover the degree to which your field setting, group, or topic has already been studied. Even if it has, you should not despair, as ethnographers have engaged in what Michael Burawoy (2003) calls the "focused revisit": returning to the site of previous studies to conduct new research. Examples include Burawoy's revisit (1979) to a factory initially studied by Donald Roy (1959/1960), Derek Freeman's (1983) visit to Samoa to reassess Margaret Mead's classic work (1928), and the journalist Marianne Boelen's (1992) revisit to the neighborhood William F. Whyte immortalized in *Street Corner Society* (1993). Just as each of these revisits found something interesting to say about the previously studied settings, you are likely to do so as well, in large part because things change for a variety of reasons elaborated by Burawoy (2003; see also, Adler, Adler, and Johnson 1992; Holmes).

Likewise, you can check on concepts, analyses, and theories you are thinking of using or developing. As with settings and groups, you may see that your approach differs in some way that becomes a form of newness.

Beyond direct library checking, one highly efficient strategy of checking on existing work is to identify specific people who have done work that is similar to what you propose. Face-to-face, telephone, mail, or electronic contact with as many such people as is practical is very much in order and, indeed, makes your project much more interesting and informed than using library sources alone.

There is also a wide range of ways in which newness can be pursued within the context of already well-established analyses. In his penetrating work on the "that's interesting" response to research (as contrasted with the "that's obvious" and "that's absurd" responses), Murray Davis notes a variety of ways in which newness can be crafted, including articulating:

- What seems to be an . . . unstructured phenomenon is in reality a . . . structured phenomenon [and vice versa].

- What seem to be assorted heterogeneous phenomena are in reality composed of a single element [and vice versa].

- What seems a stable and unchanging phenomenon is in reality an unstable and changing phenomenon [and vice versa].

- What seem to be similar (nearly identical) phenomena are in reality opposite phenomena [and vice versa]. (Davis 1971, pp. 313–325)

2. **First Report**

    Current societies are continually modifying existing social formations and practices or churning up new ones. Such changes not only stimulate interest among social science audiences, but they provide a major rationale for conducting qualitative research. Indeed, as Jack Katz (1997) has observed in his discussion of the warrants typically used by qualitative researchers to justify their studies, most of the early Chicago School fieldwork focused on examining new social realities and new forms of social problems. Recent examples of such new social formations include "junk bond" markets explored by Mitchel Abolafia (1996), online chat communities like the "BlueSky" MUD (Multi-User Domain) studied by Lori Kendall (1998), and the senior citizen and handicapped skydiving groups reported by Leon Anderson (2003).

3. **Unusual Setting**

    Social situations and settings differ in the degree to which they are socially defined as strange, ideologically or behaviorally exotic, prurient, violent, and so on. Such unusual settings also tend not to be well or often documented. Further, participants in such settings or situations are often perceived as beyond the pale of popular understanding. "Thus," writes Jack Katz:

    > a close and unprecedented description of any practice or population that is either, on one hand, especially low, despised, or fascinated with troublemaking or, on the other, especially elite, dripping with respectability, or charismatically inspired, should make a fair bid for attention. (1997, p. 392)

Some researchers, we might note, have been able to use the strategies of the first report and the unusual setting at the same time. For example, in the early 1970s, Laud Humphreys (1975) did the first sustained observation of homosexual encounters in public toilets—a report that aroused a great deal of interest in terms of its empirical disclosures and, as previously discussed, the ethics of its methodological procedures.

4. New Analytic Focus and Perspective
No fieldstudy is likely to examine satisfactorily all of the sociologically significant dimensions of a given social world. As we discussed in Chapter 7, fieldwork involves focusing on and asking questions about selected topics regarding a setting or group. Therefore, new reports of previously explored settings may make original contributions by virtue of focusing on topics, or units or aspects of those topics, that have not been the subject of earlier analysis.

A report may also be perceived as new and noteworthy when the author presents a novel conceptual or theoretical focus. This can be achieved in at least three ways: through theoretical discovery, extension, or refinement. The most widely discussed has been theoretical discovery or the development of taxonomies and mini-concepts from fieldstudy research—as exemplified in "grounded theory" practices discussed by Barney Glaser and Anselm Strauss (1967) and Kathy Charmaz and Richard Mitchell (Charmaz 2001; Charmaz and Mitchell 2001), among others. But theoretical newness can be achieved through "theoretical extension" as well. Here the author's claim to newness involves extending preexisting theoretical or conceptual formulations to groups or settings other than those in which they were first developed or intended to be used. Examples include Cal Morrill's (1995) extension of the concept of "reciprocal aggression," a term that had been developed and applied by anthropologists to conflict management in a variety of horticultural and preliterate societies, to conflict management among corporate executives in U.S. businesses. Similarly, Scott Hunt and Robert Benford (1994) extended Snow and Anderson's (1987) concept of "identity work," which was originally focused on identity construction among homeless individuals, by applying it to organizational identity work within social movement organizations.

Alternatively, an original contribution can be achieved through "theoretical refinement" or the modification of existing theoretical perspectives through the close inspection of a particular theoretical proposition or concept with new field data. This can occur in conjunction with or independent of extension. Michael Burawoy's "extended case method" (1998; Burawoy et al. 1991) constitutes an example of refinement via extension, as illustrated by his revisit and re-elaboration of his earlier work in Zambia (1972). Refinement independent of extension, on the other hand, is illustrated by Spencer Cahill's (1999) ethnographic study of the professional socialization of mortuary science students, wherein he refines theorizing and research on secondary socialization through the introduction of the concept of emotional capital. (For a more detailed treatment of theoretical discovery, extension, and refinement, see Snow, Morrill, and Anderson 2003.)

C. Importance

The issues of truth and newness are vital components in arousing interest among social science readers. But accuracy of representation (trueness) and original contribution are primarily threshold tests for attracting readers' attention. However much a report may need to have these qualities, it is not of any special interest simply by virtue of them. It also needs to be of some importance, which constitutes the third critical quality of research reports.

The interest-arousing dimension of "importance" is broader, more vague, and more difficult to assess than are the dimensions of trueness and newness, and its assessment is more contentious even among social science audiences. Nonetheless, it is possible to point to a number of framing practices that, if used, tend to prompt the response "that's important." In our assessment, there are five of these. The more of them used in a report, the more likely social scientists evaluating it are to deem it important. Not all social scientists think that all five need be present in a single report, and few reports strongly exhibit all five simultaneously. Even so, the five form a package, so to speak, of desirable framing features and provide a set of evaluative standards relating to importance.

1. Questioning Mind-Set

The hard-won and continually precarious hallmark of the modern mind-set that is applied in social science framing is the assiduous application of the proposition that *there is no final word* (Rauch 1993). Instead, *all* representations of reality of whatever kind must always be taken as tentative claims requiring searching examination. Indeed, this questioning or skeptical mind-set represents a fundamental difference between everyday common sense approaches to "reality" and a scientific approach. As Alfred Schutz (1962) has observed, in everyday life we navigate our way largely through the *suspension of doubt*—basing our actions on the way things seem to be. A scientific approach, on the other hand, entails the *suspension of belief*—an open and active questioning of received knowledge and taken-for-granted assumptions. In historical perspective, the unremitting application of *questioning* or *skepticism* is likely a key cultural element in the rise and advance of market economies, political democracies, and liberal science, including social science.

In all these areas, questioning in the form of unceasing skeptical investigation has been, to one or another degree, institutionalized. The opposite mind-set of *absolutism* also continually asserts itself and seeks to hold one or another representation of reality beyond questioning or skeptical inquiry. In the absolutist view, there is a final word on claimed reality, and these claims must be accepted on the basis of authoritative proclamations or moral imperatives that are viewed as beyond question. The scientific counterview is that every claim and perception must be open to scrutiny. The central assertion of the questioning mind-set is therefore: "Do not block the way of inquiry" (Charles Sanders Peirce, frontispiece epigraph to Rauch 1993, p. vii).

The difference between the scientific and absolutist approaches lies in the mandate that those who embrace the scientific mind-set must willingly and openly subject their ideas and preconceptions to critical examination. It is imperative for social scientists to display this self-critical ethos and to demonstrate their willingness to question themselves and their ideas. Although the questioning mind-set is not easily codified as an exact set of operations one performs on one's data and in one's analysis, several of the methodological strategies that we have discussed represent systematic ways to submit your perceptions and theoretical conceptualizations to potential empirical disconfirmation. The range of measures to control error and bias that are described in Chapter 5, Section II.B.2, especially purposeful sampling techniques, team research, and member checking procedures, all represent systematic efforts to acquire new and potentially disconfirming data. By describing these procedures in your report, you can provide readers with evidence of a rigorous and questioning mind-set.

This critical approach pertains as well to how researchers treat the realities asserted by the people they are studying. In absolutist treatments, these realities are assumed to be either true or false, either good or bad, but neither the judgments nor the realities being judged are themselves topics of examination. In contrast, the questioning mind-set "brackets" the realities of the people studied as proper topics of inquiry. The question is not simply how empirically accurate the group members' claims are but, also, the role that those claims play in the world under study.

Finally, the questioning mind-set is also revealed in exercising caution in one's ultimate research claims. The judicious acknowledgment of limits to generalizability and an assessment of the conditions under which one's claims are likely to hold (called "scope conditions" by some methodologists) are far more compelling to social science audiences than less painstaking claims. In the end, the credibility of research reports, and thus the degree to which they will be deemed important, is fundamentally dependent on demonstrating rigorous and self-critical data collection, analysis, and interpretation of the findings.

2. **Propositional Framing**

The second framing practice that contributes to a positive assessment of importance is much more concretely operational in character than the questioning mind-set. The purpose of asking questions (Chapter 7) about topics (Chapter 6) is to develop social science answers. These answers may be thought of as propositions about social situations or settings. Such propositions form the thesis or theses around which your data are made meaningful. They are conclusions you have reached through the analysis of your data and may involve stating a hypothesis, formulating a concept or typology, or providing a general interpretation.

The eight questions explained in Chapter 7 provide eight basic forms of propositions that are answers to the eight questions. Stated abstractly, these are:

1. Type: X exists (or X-1, X-2, X-3, X-n exist).
2. Frequencies: X occurs in Y units in places 1, 2, 3, n over Z periods of time.
3. Magnitudes: X is of Y size, strength, or intensity.
4. Structures: X is structured in terms of 1, 2, 3, n.
5. Processes: X exhibits a process with the phases or cycles of 1, 2, 3, n.
6. Causes: X is caused by factors 1, 2, 3, n.
7. Consequences: X has consequences 1, 2, 3, n.
8. Agency: In X, people use strategies and tactics 1, 2, 3, n.

Article-length reports are commonly organized in terms of only one of these eight propositional forms, with one or two others perhaps receiving secondary attention. Even book-length reports may be organized in terms of only one, although books are more likely to feature two, three, or even four (but rarely all) of them.

Let us try to sharpen this depiction of propositional answers to questions about topics by showing how it is a specialized application of a more general distinction. In the broader domain of writing per se a distinction is commonly drawn between "subject writing" that describes a topic or area and "idea writing" that propounds a thesis or makes an assertion.

> Some people use the word idea to mean something like "topic" or "subject," phrases that indicate an area of potential interest, such as "economics" or "a cure for cancer".... These phrases might be said to be "broad" or "narrow" subjects, but they are not yet ideas because they do not say anything about economics, or a cancer cure.... The noun economics is not an idea.... "Economics is bull" is an idea.... The difference between noun phrases that are not ideas and statements that are ideas lies in the predication: Ideas are sentences; they complete a thought by connecting a verb to the noun phrase. Saying something about a subject requires making some kind of connection between it and something else. (Gage 1987, pp. 48–49; emphasis in the original)

In parallel, social science propositions are idea writing rather than subject writing. Propositions are assertions about topics—interpretational framings of factual observations. Notice that each of the eight propositions given above makes portions of the data you have collected meaningful by framing them in a perspective bigger than their sheer phenomenological existence. They are transformed into ideas. No longer singular observations, they are interpreted as examples of types, frequencies, processes, structures, strategies, and so on. Propositions, then, are the ideas that provide broader implications or a context of meaning for your data. Social science audiences expect more than a listing of undigested facts. For a report to be interesting, authors must develop ideas or propositions that establish broader implications, an interpretation, or a context of meaning for their data.

3. Generic Concepts

The propositional framing sought in social science research is, moreover, generic rather than localized or historically particular. Generic propositions speak not only to local meanings and actions, but have some broader, more general significance. Rather than primarily reporting the chronological activities observed in a situation or setting and organizing the report in chronological or purely descriptive terms, a generic framing seeks to specify abstract propositions of which the local or historical particulars are instances. In other words, the local and particular are categorized upward, as illustrated by the following examples drawn from studies summarized in previous chapters:

- The limited peer relationships that children develop in specific activities or locations as instances of *compartmentalized friendships* (Adler and Adler 1998).

- Corporate executives pursuing grievances against each other in a moralistic "tit for tat" manner as examples of *reciprocal conflict management* (Morrill 1995).

- The body language and movement practices that occur in public encounters between persons of different racial and class groupings framed as instances of *street etiquette* (Anderson 1990).

In each of these studies, the analysts have used their rich qualitative data "as a base for formulating concepts that transcend the particular settings in which the data were gathered" (Prus 1996, p. 141). The goal is to translate the specific materials under study into instances of more widely relevant and basic social types, processes, or whatever (Prus 1987, 1994; Zerubavel 1980). In its "upward categorization,"generic framing finds fundamental human themes and concerns in obscure and sometimes seemingly trivial social doings. The situation under study is lifted out of its historically unique details and placed among the array of matters of interest to broad audiences. In one sense, generic framing is an effort to see the universe in a grain of sand.

There are at least four "tricks of the trade," so to speak, that social scientists sometimes use to stimulate their imaginations when they seek to advance generic conceptualizations. The first two (*using existing social science conceptions* and *discerning new forms*) involve relatively straightforward strategies for developing analysis. The other two "tricks of the trade" (the *use of metaphor* and the *utilization of irony*) involve a more literary turn of imagination. We discuss each briefly.

a. *Using Existing Social Science Conceptions*

One obvious possibility in generic conceptualization is to incorporate already existing generic social science concepts into your analysis, perhaps refining them in the process as discussed in Section I.B.4. The corpus of social science literature is an invaluable resource for qualitative researchers, providing an extensive array of theories and concepts that social scientists have found useful over time in analyzing groups and social settings. In settings that have previously been studied, certain kinds of theoretical conceptualizations or propositions are likely to have already been developed or applied to the settings' members and their activities. While it is possible to develop your analysis without being familiar with previous social science work in the area, you are at a serious disadvantage if you do so and thus run the risk of rediscovering what is already quite well understood. Further, if your audience is largely a social science audience, you will be expected to demonstrate a significant degree of knowledge and understanding of the empirical findings and theoretical analyses of those who have come before you. Acknowledging their work and relating your own research to theirs (in both positive and critical ways) is an important means for demonstrating your commitment to building generic framings that move beyond historic local particulars of individual cases.

In your efforts to develop or apply generic concepts, you may also find it useful to consider the possibility of extending concepts from other settings to the setting you are studying (as discussed in Section I.B.4 above).

b. Discerning New Forms

A second rather modest but nonetheless important and creative device in generic propositional framing is to discern new variations on established types of social units or aspects and on answers to the eight questions described in the previous chapter. *New variations or forms* tend, in practice, to be answers to Questions 1 and 4: "What type is it?" and "What is its structure?" Erving Goffman's notion of the "total institution" (discussed in Chapter 7, Section I.A), for example, was a new form at one time. But "new form" answers can also be associated with the other questions, as the following previously discussed examples illustrate:

- Question 5: "What Are the Topic's Processes?" Identifying the stages through which volunteers to a search and rescue group move from being peripheral members to full-fledged or core members (Lois 2003).

- Question 6: "What Are the Topic's Causes?" Having a "racist self" and harboring racist beliefs are most often preceded by association with racist hate groups (Blee 2002).

- Question 7: "What Are the Topic's Consequences?" Program managers of welfare programs may diminish the opportunity for agency and encourage dependency while espousing values of self-sufficiency and independence (Horowitz 1996).

- Question 8: "What Is Human Agency?" Residents in chronic care institutions construct (real and imaginary) personal narratives as a means to assert positive personal identities and to manipulate their interactions with institutional caregivers (Paterniti 2000).

As mentioned previously, the churnings of the modern world are constantly throwing up new and significant variations on all sorts of things. This newness extends to generic propositions regarding new social types, structures, processes, and the like. Persons seeking to articulate experience in this way ought, therefore, to make discoveries along these lines. Furthermore, new generic propositional articulations of new social patterns perform a quite valuable public service, as we will discuss below. However, as with the use of existing social science concepts, the creative discernment of new forms requires familiarity with existing social science analyses. Without some knowledge of previous social science work, you simply cannot know if a kind of socialization, family type, or organizational process is in fact new.

c. *Using Metaphors*

In the effort to move your analysis from the local particulars to broader generic categorizations, you may also find it useful to utilize one or both of two common literary techniques. The first is the creative application of metaphors. Dictionaries commonly define the word *metaphor* as "a figure of speech in which one kind of object or phrase literally denoting one kind of object or idea is used in place of another to suggest a likeness or analogy between them (as in, the ship plows the sea)." More broadly, metaphor involves "seeing something from the viewpoint of something else" (Brown 1977, p. 78). In social science framing, the simplest formula is "X as Y," as in Murray Melbin's creative analysis of *Night as Frontier* (1987), a study in which features of the literal concept of "frontier" are applied to "the night." Melbin argues that "time, like space, can be occupied and is treated so by humans. . . . Nighttime social life in urban areas resembles social life in former land frontiers" (Melbin 1987, p. 3). One of the most creative social scientists of the twentieth century, Erving Goffman, frequently employed metaphors in creating generic propositional framings, as in viewing:

- the problem of failure in social life in terms of the classic confidence game in which everyone is a mark, operator, or cooler (Goffman 1962).
- contact among strangers as a theatrical situation of "performers" and "impression management" (Goffman 1959).
- mental patients as having careers (Goffman 1961a).
- psychiatry as an instance of the "tinkering trades" or as a mere service occupation subject to the same venal tendencies (Goffman 1961a).

The point of metaphor is not simply and mechanically to translate one realm into another, but rather to "provide a new way to understand that which we already know [and to reconstitute] . . . new domains of perception" (Brown 1977, p. 98). As a guide, then, the device of metaphor counsels a playful turn of mind, as when the Catholic Church is referred to as the General Motors of religion, heart surgeons are said to run a boutique practice, and Hilton Hotels are called factories for sleep (Brown 1977). Metaphors thus facilitate broad generic conceptualizations because they move you away from local particulars toward more abstract patterns, focusing your attention on previously unseen similarities among ostensibly dissimilar phenomena. Metaphors also provide a way to sharpen your analysis by teasing out unexpected insights. In sharpening insight, and thus spurring audience interest, the use of metaphor is similar to irony, the final technique we discuss for developing generic propositions.

d. Using Irony

The term *irony* is ordinarily defined as "a state of affairs or events that is the reverse of what was or was to be expected: a result opposite to and as if in mockery of the appropriate result." One applies it as a social science frame by being attentive to causes, consequences, and other aspects of social topics that are paradoxical, unintended, or unrecognized by participants.

Irony is often used with regard to questions of function or consequence (Chapter 7, Section VII). In such cases, one looks beyond the recognized and intended (or manifest) functions to the unrecognized and unintended (or latent) functions. Robert Merton, a champion practitioner of sociological irony, claimed that "it is precisely at the point where the research attention of sociologists has shifted from the plane of manifest to the plane of latent functions that they have made their distinctive and major contribution" (1968, p. 120). Merton himself provided many powerful examples of this precept (see Stinchcombe's assessment, 1975), but others have found analytic utility in its application as well. Indeed, what is known as the "functionalist perspective" is suffused with irony. Historically, functionalists (and others using functionalist arguments) have propounded a variety of ironic latent functions of "social problems." Kingsley Davis has argued, for instance, that "increased prostitution may reduce the sexual irregularities of respectable women" (quoted in Schneider 1975, p. 325). And Herbert Gans (1972) has chronicled a range of functions or benefits that poverty provides for those who are not poor. But non-functionalist qualitative researchers have also employed irony in order to accent or highlight their findings, as reflected, for example, by Nicole Biggart's (1989) study of "charismatic capitalists," John Lofland's (1993) labeling of the peace activists he studied as "polite protestors," and Calvin Morrill's (1995) finding that the same kinds of vengeance rituals that anthropologists have found among tribal societies are also operative in corporate boardrooms.

As these examples demonstrate, the use of irony as both an analytic and literary tool in qualitative research brings to light associations that are typically not seen and, in doing so, underscores the importance of the inquiry and report.

4. Developed Treatment

If two people independently research and publish reports that are substantially identical and do so at the same time, the report that is the more thoroughly developed, both empirically and conceptually, is understandably more likely to be regarded as important. The classic case of this in the history of science is the relation between the work of Charles Darwin and Alfred Russell Wallace, both of whom independently formulated the theory of evolution. Indeed, Wallace might have published before Darwin except for a British gentlemanly agreement in which their respective formulations were made public simultaneously. But, nonetheless, it is Darwin, rather than Wallace, who is commonly credited with the theory. This is because Darwin, not Wallace, performed the exhaustive research, developed the theory in detail, and published several elaborate reports. Wallace's report was true and new, as far as he had gone, but he did not develop the theory in detail nor base his formulation on much data. Darwin, in contrast, spent decades developing diverse forms of data and elaborating the theory in terms of them. As a result, Darwin's work had a much more solid evidential base and thus was more compelling than Wallace's sketchily formulated speculations. Therefore, Darwin, rather than Wallace, is usually credited with the invention of the theory of evolution.

The situation is the same in social science. Indeed, publications that display all of the other framing practices relating to importance (and are also true and new) are not scarce. That is, writings of a questioning mind-set that are framed with generic propositions and are resonant (discussed below) are not hard to come by. But, in the absence of empirical and conceptual development, serious social scientists regard these writings as merely skillful exercises in speculation. This begs, of course, the question of what constitutes a "developed" treatment? While standards of this are not exact or entirely agreed upon regarding qualitative fieldstudies, we find that many social scientists assess development along three dimensions: (1) degree of conceptual elaboration, (2) balance between conceptual elaboration and data presentation, and (3) interpenetration of conceptual elaboration and data presentation.

a. Conceptual Elaboration
The dimension of conceptual elaboration refers to the number of major conceptual or analytic divisions and subdivisions that form the main body of the report. In grounded theory language, this dimension is referred to as conceptual density, specificity, and interlinkage or integration (Strauss and Corbin 1990, pp. 109, 121, 253–254). The central concern is that the researcher should provide evidence of having given detailed thought to the one or more propositions used to structure and analyze the data. The prime evidence of such detailed thought is a conceptual scheme of some reasonable complexity that works in tandem with the other two dimensions of development that we will describe in a moment.

Because particular studies and their data vary so much, it is difficult to specify precise numbers of concepts—of major divisions and subdivisions of one's report—that one ought to elaborate. We can, however, offer a general rule of thumb based on our observations of journal articles over the years. They suggest that successful article-length reports frequently have on the order of two to five major elements elaborating a proposition and a similar number of subdivisions within some or all of the elements. Two examples (summarized in Figures 8.1 and 8.2) from the literature on stigma management can serve to illustrate this. The basic proposition of both articles is very similar: in a context of social stigmatization, members of the group under study (the mentally ill in Nancy Herman's article and the homeless in Anderson, Snow, and Cress's article) engage in stigma management strategies to reduce the personal impact of stigmatization and to influence their relations with others. This proposition is elaborated through the descriptive analysis of various types of stigma management strategies.

These examples demonstrate effective conceptual elaboration in article-length reports and sensitize us to the possibilities of conceptual under-elaboration and overelaboration. In article-length reports, under-elaboration occurs when there is an absence of any organizing proposition or when only one or a few concepts are used without their elaboration. Overelaboration, on the other hand, is seen in article-length reports where the conceptual

Figure 8.1 Conceptual Elaboration of Ex-Psychiatric Patients' Stigma Management Strategies

Type of Stigma Management	Subtype	Description (examples given in text)
Selective Concealment		Concealing illness from selected others
Therapeutic Disclosure		Disclosing illness as a way of handling personal feelings about it
Preventive Disclosure		Disclosure to prevent being inadvertently exposed
	With Medical Disclaimers	Framing in medical terms to reduce "personal responsibility"
	With Coaching	Role playing with a "coach" prior to disclosure
	Educational	Disclosure in an effort to "educate" others
	Normalization	Disclosure combined with efforts to normalize interpersonal relations
Political Activism		Participation in activist groups that challenge stereotypes of mental illness and conventional standards of normalcy

Derived from Nancy J. Herman. 1993. "Return to Sender: Reintegrative Stigma-management Strategies of Ex-psychiatric Patients." *Journal of Contemporary Ethnography* 22: 295–330.

Figure 8.2 Conceptual Elaboration of Stigma Management Strategies among the Homeless

Type of Stigma Management	Subtype	Description (examples given in text)
In-Group Strategies		Strategies engaged in with other homeless individuals
	Substance Use	Use of alcohol and drugs as a way to relieve stresses associated with stigmatization
	"Hanging Out"	Whiling away time with street friends with no goal-oriented expectations
	Identity Work	Assertions of positive personal identities in contrast to homeless status
Out-Group Strategies		Strategies used in interactions with domiciled individuals
	Passing	Endeavoring to pass as a non-homeless person
	Covering	Minimizing others' attention to homeless status by focusing attention on other attributes
	Individual Defiance	Aggressive individual challenging of status affronts
	Collective Action	Participation in activist groups that challenge stereotypes of the homeless and advocate for policies to reduce homelessness

Derived from Leon Anderson, David A. Snow, and Daniel Cress. 1994. "Negotiating the Public Realm: Stigma Management and Collective Action among the Homeless," pp. 121–143 in *The Community of the Streets*, edited by Spencer E. Cahill and Lyn Lofland. Greenwich, CT: JAI Press.

scheme consists of dozens of concepts and distinctions, giving the impression that the researcher has become more interested in the scheme than in the data the scheme is supposed to help us understand.

b. *Balance*

The possibilities of under-conceptual and overelaboration lead into the second dimension of developed treatment: the degree of balance between a conceptual scheme and the presentation of data. Extremely overelaborated conceptual schemes squeeze out, so to speak, the opportunity to present data. This may be termed the error of *analytic excess*. An author making this error has become so engrossed in the logic of abstract analysis that he or she fails to report very much of the rich, concrete reality to which the analysis purportedly refers. The reader may learn a great deal about the author's mind, but very little, concretely, about what is going on in the setting. There is too little description of the many events that occurred, and the participants are almost never quoted.

The error of *descriptive excess*, in contrast, involves providing too much description relative to analysis. The author has become so engrossed in rendering the concrete details of a setting that he or she loses connection with analytic concepts and ideas that could help to order, explain, or summarize the details. Such reports resemble simple histories or journalistic descriptions. Reports that suffer from either analytic or descriptive excess are unlikely to attract wide interest among social science audiences since they fail to achieve the integration of data and interpretation that helps to make qualitative articles compelling. A balance of field evidence and analysis enables the reader to both grasp the author's generic conceptualizations and be convinced of their value in making sense of a slice of the social world under study.

As with the dimension of elaboration, there are no precise rules regarding balance, only order-of-magnitude guidelines. The one we suggest is that somewhat more than half the pages of an article-length report should consist of qualitative data: accounts of episodes, incidents, events, exchanges, remarks, happenings, conversations, actions, and so forth. Somewhat less than half should be analysis: the major proposition or propositions, abstract categorizing and discussion of the meaning, application, and implications of the data, and so on.

c. *Interpenetration*

The dimensions of conceptual elaboration and balance come together to achieve thorough development in the third dimension, that of the interpenetration of data and analysis. As a concrete feature of reports, interpenetration refers to the continuing and intimate alternation of data and analysis as text. Specifically, analytic passages do not go on very long without reporting empirical materials, and vice versa. This alternation makes the relation between the data and analysis more evident and conveys ways in which they form a whole.

An example of this alternation is provided by the section of Nancy Herman's article that analyzes how former mental patients may seek to normalize the perceptions others have of them. The section begins with a relatively long paragraph that explains the concept of "normalization" (with reference to Fred Davis as originator of the term and several other authors who have used the concept). Herman then moves into a discussion of efforts at normalization among former mental patients, leading to an exemplary quote from one of her informants. She writes:

> Ex-patients whose stigma could be considered 'discreditable,' that is, not readily or visibly apparent to others, would discuss such information for

preventive reasons, thereby rendering them 'discredited in the eyes of others.' They would then attempt to negotiate with normals for preferred images . . . and nondeviant conceptions of self and for definitions of mental illness as less stigmatizing. Discussing his use of this technique, "Weird Old" Larry, a 59-year-old ex-patient, stated,

> The third time I got out [of the hospital], I tried to fit right in. I told some of my buddies and a couple of others about my sickness. It was easier to get it out in the open. But what I tried to show 'em was that I could do the same things they could, some of them even better. I beat them at pool, at darts . . . I was holding down two jobs—one at the gas station and [the other] at K-Mart. I tried to show them I was normal. . . . The key to success is being up front and making them believe you're just as normal as them. . . . You can really change how they see and treat you. (Herman 1993, p. 317–18)

This section of the article then moves back to analysis, then again to an illustrative quote, with the entire section consisting of three informant quotes integrated with five analytic paragraphs that refine the concept of normalization as it was observed by Herman during her study.

This mode of appearance in the text of the report is based on the analytic process of the grounded induction or theory generation, which we will discuss in the next two chapters. In this way, interpenetration is not merely an appearance in the report, it is the logical consequence of a thorough working through of the data in analytic terms.

Low degrees of (or the absence of) interpenetration may be thought of as data and analysis segregation. Such segregation is seen, for example, in reports where the researcher devotes the first and last sections to an elaborate conceptual scheme. The middle parts consist of low-level, commonsensical descriptions that the author does not relate to the conceptual scheme reported in the first and last sections. That is, the analysis seems tacked onto the data at each end of the report rather than evolved from the data or used to analyze them. Because the two are not in intimate interplay throughout the report, the relation between the data and analysis is unknown. This failure to interpenetrate data and analysis in the report often signals, in fact, that the researcher has done little, if any, analysis.

These three textual practices of elaboration, balance, and interpenetration form a discipline of guiding constraints that result in a developed treatment, as exemplified by the studies highlighted in Figures 8.1 and 8.2. These practices stimulate—even if they do not absolutely ensure—a conscientiousness and thoroughness of work that prompt audiences to take one seriously—that is, to see one's report as important and, therefore, as interesting.

5. **Resonating Content**
The interest with which social science reports are met depends to a significant degree on the framing practices that we have discussed so far. But the reception of social science reports is also influenced by the degree to which

the report is felt to resonate with broader human experience and fundamental human concerns. Within the vision of social science per se that is summarized in the foregoing framing practices, social scientists are drawn to topics and conceptual substance that address fundamental existential concerns and to problems that confront everyone else (and they display, at times, the same proclivity to fad and fashion in addressing these that we see in everyone else).

The frail humanity that social scientists share with everyone else means that the specific content or substance of one's developed, generic propositions will be assessed in terms of their felt relation to one or another common and deep human theme. We label this the dimension of "resonance," the degree to which the content reverberates with and evokes existential concerns. In the formulation of Snow and Benford (1988, p. 207), audiences ask, "[Does it] strike a responsive chord? Does it inform understanding of events and experiences within [our] world?"

There are, however, a large number of issues and topics that resonate at any given time with a range of audiences. How is one to select from among them? As a moral and ethical choice, rather than a research or logical decision, we cannot presume to say what you should choose. We confine ourselves, instead, to suggesting some of the factors one might take into account in making decisions about resonance.

In our view, the first and most important factor ought to be: Does the topic and analysis in your report resonate with you? Do you feel (and we mean feel rather than believe or perceive) that the contents of your report are saying what you want it to say about something you deeply feel to be important? If you do not feel a resonance with the content, it is unlikely that you will be able to produce a report that resonates with your audience. But if you answer the above questions affirmatively, you at least have a personal baseline resonance from which to proceed. While this may not be enough to guarantee resonance with a broader audience, at least you will have the satisfaction of believing in what you have done. Moreover, the fad and fashion nature of popularly resonant topics may mean that your audience has yet to arrive and that you are a pioneer of newly resonant substance.

A second factor to consider is the current resonance status of the content. At any given time in academic and popular culture, some concerns are much more high-profile than others. While we do not want to encourage mindlessly jumping onto some current resonance bandwagon, it is clearly useful to be sufficiently mindful of and conversant in contemporary intellectual and popular issues to be able to engage high-profile issues when it is appropriate.

Third, while, as we have suggested, there is considerable fad and fashion in resonant topics, there is no monolithic uniformity. Different issues may resonate deeply with various subgroups of social scientists. Further, while resonance may ebb and flow to a degree, there are many human concerns that are enduringly resonant and seldom fade entirely from view. The struggle of individuals and groups for human dignity in the face of adversity, for instance, has maintained such an enduring resonance over time even though it has been more widely resonant at some times than at others.

Because of (1) the great number and variety of resonant topics, (2) the fad and fashion manner in which given topics are "hot" or "cold," and (3) the wide variety in potential resonance among people, many social scientists tend to be quite hesitant about (and ambivalent in) using resonance—at least consciously—in assessing the importance of a report. Given this hesitance, we advise you to be sure to pay sufficient attention to the other four framing practices (as well as to the trueness and newness of your report). In doing so, you are more likely to present your findings and analysis in a compelling and convincing manner. In short, resonance is far from completely under your control. Make sure you control the things you can. And then at least you can feel confident that you have produced a solid piece of research, one that is worthy of resonance, should the time be right.

II. Social Science Value Commitments

In the foregoing, we have elaborated the three general criteria commonly employed in evaluating qualitative fieldstudy reports. The generic criteria of trueness, newness, and importance therefore have the somewhat specialized meanings that we have just given. Our suggestion in applying these three criteria is that the more each is met, the greater will be the interest aroused among social science audiences. Further, we would argue that the framing practices that we have described provide a distinctive social science contribution to the broader society. These practices are grounded in value commitments that we believe make the approach we have delineated particularly important in contemporary society. Several interrelated values undergird this approach. Two of these values are the *questioning mind-set* and the *search for generic understanding* that we discussed earlier in this chapter. Two other critical values include a commitment to the *demystification of social arrangements* and *dedication to holistic dispassionate understanding*. In this section of the chapter, we briefly clarify these values and reflect on how they combine to provide a vital angle of vision for understanding social life and addressing social issues. We then contrast this approach with popular alternative framings that have challenged it in recent years.

A. Demystification

In complexly differentiated societies, ordinary people playing out their ordinary lives are enmeshed in devising and enacting ideas and activities that are responsive to their immediate needs. Immersed in such action, they rarely have the time or resources to assemble information on the multiple facets of their situations, to reflect on their meaning, to envision larger contexts in which they might variously be interpreted, or to contemplate feasible and conceivable alternatives to their situations. Additionally, the alliances, accommodations, ruses, mutings, euphemizations, and other necessary avoidances of ordinary life may lead people to miss seeing many aspects of their situations and to develop legitimizing and accommodating meanings for what they do see (see Douglas 1976).

Phrased in yet other terms, the human tendency to objectify social reality pushes from consciousness the wider appreciation that the objectified reality is only one among many possibilities. Consistent with the questioning mind-set, social science stimulates this recognition by rendering any "existing world . . . an object of scrutiny, not acceptance . . . . [It is only] one among many possibilities" (Gusfield 1981, p. 192). Peter Berger has labeled this penchant for questioning, or getting behind and deconstructing objectified realities, as the "debunking motif" in sociological consciousness. It is a:

> built-in procedure for looking for levels of reality other than those given in the official interpretations of society, [a mandate to] look beyond the immediately given and publicly approved interpretations . . . [in order to] observe the machinery that went into the construction of the scene. . . . The [social analyst thus] "looks behind" the facades of social structure. (Berger 1979, pp. 9–10)

As a consequence, questioning social science "presents a world that is political rather than a world of technical necessity. If choice is possible, if new and alternative modes of acting are possible and imaginable, then the existent situation hides the conflicts and alternatives that can be imagined" (Gusfield 1981, p. 193). Social science of a questioning bent is thus a way in which "to penetrate the veil of the apolitical. . . . It makes us aware of the sheer difficulty of avoiding choice between alternatives, of having to engage in the world of politics and moralities, [of having] to take a stand without the benefits of a clear and commanding social vision" (Gusfield 1981, p. 195).

These social science aims are, of course, moral aims, the aims of widening peoples' perceptions of their situations and of enlarging their perceptions of social arrangements. Such enlargements hopefully open the way to humane social change. And, as will become obvious, these aims and practices are very different from the *selective* demystifications preferred in other approaches.

B. Holistic Dispassionate Understanding

The several value themes we have now described imply value-committed views of (1) the *time frame* in which to think of social science as an activity, (2) the *social frame* in which to think of its pertinence, and (3) the *emotional frame* of mind in which to do research.

1. Temporally, research is valued as a complex activity of successive and unending revisions carried out over an extended period of time. This is to be distinguished from framings we will describe below in which specific

research efforts are conceived and valued as tactics in battle skirmishes or isolated virtuoso or prima donna performances.

2. Socially, social science in general and fieldstudies in particular are distinctive, disciplined forms of human inquiry and knowing that are addressed to important and long-term human concerns and values. Even though the *proximate* audience for and evaluators of research must be other social scientists, the *larger* audiences are all humans who care about the topic of study. In this, social science parallels other science. The proximate audience of cancer research, for example, must be competent, evaluating cancer researchers, but the larger audience is everyone and anyone who cares about cancer.

3. Emotionally, researchers often care very much about their research and the issues it may raise, but, consonant with the way in which their work is framed temporally and socially, they try also to be reasonably *dispassionate*—that is, balanced and judicious in their research and analysis. While some advocates of deep and abiding emotional engagement might characterize such dispassion as emotionally distanced and uncaring, such a stance bears no resemblance to the attitude we are recommending, which simply involves an attempt to grasp the larger picture and to examine and reexamine all data and concepts patiently and carefully. Of course, this is difficult to accomplish if you succumb to what we referred to earlier as the polarities of distance or surrender and the biases associated with each (see Chapter 4, Section I.C), hence, the analytic utility of adopting a balanced and dispassionate orientation to the social worlds and materials studied.

III. Other Framings

There are, and have long been, alternative approaches to the kind of social science framing that we have presented. As one might expect, recent challenges to social science framing and values differ considerably among themselves and vary in terms of which of the value commitments of social science they reject. Even so, they tend to be alike in desiring to use social science work to further the interests of one or another social category, a political or religious view advocating for such a categorization, or some combination of category and point of view. For these challenges, the question of "social science for what or whom?" is answered by advocacy for a particular grouping rather than in terms of the broader values of inquiry, knowledge, demystification, and the like that we have enumerated.

In so serving a particular grouping, the range of appropriate topics of inquiry and what to say about those topics is restricted, as is the application of the questioning mind-set. Within these restrictions, an important task—if not the master frame—becomes that of performing, by means of research, a technical or moral evaluation that serves specialized interests. Activist partisans, rather than social scientists and more general audiences, are therefore conceived as the targets for the arousal of interest.

As an abstract master template of sorts, this evaluative frame is applied in varied specific formulations. We briefly explore four main patterns of application: social engineering, liberation, muckraking, and expressive voicing.

A. Technocratic/Social Engineering Frame

Politically and socially mainstream researchers and audiences who view research as information with which to improve or control a social setting or situation in the short-term future are probably the largest group using an evaluative frame. Often in this pattern, the aims, assumptions, and perspectives of authorities responsible for a social setting are taken as the aims, assumptions, and perspectives of the researcher. For this reason, this pattern is sometimes referred to as technocratic or social engineering, meaning that the researcher is the specialized and expert investigator of questions posed by authorities, and the answers developed by researchers serve those authorities. Considerations of relative technical efficacy and efficiency figure centrally. The rubrics "applied sociology," "clinical sociology," "policy research," and "evaluation research" are sometimes employed to distinguish this pattern and its audiences. Sometimes, also, the contrast between social science and social engineering is expressed as the difference between the sociology *of* something and sociology in something, as in the well-articulated difference between "the sociology *of* medicine" and "sociology in medicine" (also see Hammersley 1992, Chapter 7; Shils 1961).

B. Liberation Frame

Although the political substance and relations to authorities differ, liberation audiences and researchers are like social engineers in taking on and striving to further the aims, assumptions, and perspectives of another grouping. In this case, however, the researchers adopt the vantage point of a disadvantaged or otherwise mistreated set of persons and seek, by means of the research, to champion it. Paralleling the mainstream improver's aim to be helpful to authorities, radical liberationists seek to be useful to selected oppressed groups. The explicit goals of such research include enabling members of marginalized groups to individually and collectively challenge the social arrangements that are perceived as oppressing them. In one variant on this pattern, researchers are enjoined not to report anything on an oppressed grouping that might be of use to oppressors in maintaining their domination. Other terms sometimes denoting liberation audiences include "liberation sociology," "participatory action research," and "critical sociology" (see also Hammersley 1992, Chapter 6; Shils 1961). Viewed from the vantage point of earlier discussions, the problem with this framing is that it skews the research too far toward the "surrender" end of the distance/surrender continuum (see Chapter 4, Section I.C).

C. Muckraking Frame

The two audiences and their researchers just described feel positively about the groupings they are researching or serving and seek to frame their reports in ways that are helpful to them. An obvious alternative approach—the flip side to the liberation frame—is to identify a grouping as especially reprehensible and to frame one's research in ways that attempt to undermine the group's ability to engage in exploitative practices. Rather than conceal facts that might be used against members of a category, one seeks explicitly to uncover such facts—usually in the service of an oppressed group. While a number of fieldworkers have conducted muckraking studies—Tim Diamond's (1992) critique of nursing home care and Nancy Scheper-Hughes's (2000, 2004) research on the global trade in body organs, for example—the intimate relations and contextualized understandings that develop in fieldwork tend to limit the extent of purely negative exposés. Thus, it is probably arguable that liberation fieldwork is more likely than muckraking fieldwork to be imbalanced analytically. But when the latter does occur, it is likely to be skewed too far toward the "distance" end of the continuum and thus be equally biased and imbalanced.

D. Expressive Voicing

During the past several decades, with rise of "postmodernism(s)" (for the connection to ethnography, see Gubrium and Holstein 1997, Chapter 5; Spencer 2001; and Chapter 5.I), the topic of "voice" has come to prominence among some fieldworkers who have criticized the traditional authorial voice in qualitative research reports. These critics believe that the impersonal, reportorial writing in traditional realist ethnography exhibits a "voice from nowhere" that obscures the authorial privilege taken by the author in the research and reporting processes. Three primary alternatives to third-person realist ethnography have been proposed. In the first, researchers are advised to make themselves more visible in their reports. Some have argued that the researcher should be "front and center" in the report, especially in revealing their personal responses to the people studied, their researcher roles, and even their view of life and existence in general (e.g., Behar 1996; Lockford 2004; Rabinow 1977). Second and more commonly, some scholars have suggested that the voices to be expressed should be those of the people being studied, presented in as direct a manner as possible without the potential distorting clutter of the researcher's opinions and interpretations. Working within this vein, researchers function in a participatory, collaborative fashion, helping those with whom they work to articulate their stories and experiences (e.g., Behar 1993; Kemmis and McTaggart 2000; Taylor and Rupp 2005). The third proposed alternative is to write "evocative *autoethnography*" that focuses on describing one's own personal—and particularly, emotional—experiences (e.g., Ellis 1995; 1997; Reed-Danahay 1997; Ronai 1992).

While the criticism of traditional ethnographic voice has had some positive influence in qualitative research (e.g., an increased concern with attending to and documenting one's emotional reactions in the field, as noted in Chapter 5 IV.C.2), each of the suggested remedies described here tends to deflect the researcher from the analytic goals that are regarded as the raison d'etre for conducting fieldstudies within the social scientific frame. In the first case, the researcher's experiences—often in the form of extended "confessional tales" (Van Maanen 1988)—tend to take preeminence over the activities of those being studied. In the second case, the analytic responsibilities attendant upon social science research have been jettisoned in favor of reporting what presumptively "voiceless" populations believe and wish to communicate about their condition. This is the fieldworker as "stenographer," to paraphrase Snow and Morrill's (1993) critique of this position, or the researcher as "ethnograph," to use Clinton Sanders's (1994) terminology. Finally, the third approach confines the researcher to subjective self-observation at the expense of engaging with and learning from broader social observation and shares more affinity with the writing of autobiographical essayists than that of social science researchers.

As laudable as the foregoing framings may be in terms of some values, their practitioners do not engage in a number of social science practices or subscribe to many of the social science values that we have elaborated. Most significantly, each of these approaches fails to sustain an open and broad-based questioning mind-set and tends to lead to conspicuously imbalanced and/or biased reports. Suspension of belief is narrowed in pursuit of advocacy of a particular kind of institutional liberation or allegiance to a somewhat different authority (e.g., the "inviolability of subjective experience"). While there is an overlap between social science audiences and audiences for whom these frames make a study particularly important, these framings themselves stray beyond qualitative social science research as we have framed it in this chapter.

In conclusion, what does all we have covered in this chapter say about arousing the interests of audiences? We think it says two things. First, if you want to catch the attention of social scientists you want to strive for trueness, newness, and importance following the meanings of these terms that we have elaborated. But, second, just as cancer researchers direct their work to one another for evaluation but also to wider audiences, social scientists also have larger and wider values and audiences. You therefore want to shape your work for both social scientists and wider audiences.

PART THREE

ANALYZING DATA

The tasks of gathering data (Part One) and focusing them (Part Two) come together in the third task of analyzing them. In pursuing this task, the fieldworker concentrates on:

- developing analysis guided by the considerations we describe in Chapter 9, and

- writing analysis assisted by suggestions offered in Chapter 10.

CHAPTER 9

DEVELOPING ANALYSIS

Analysis involves a kind of transformative process in which the raw data are turned into "findings" or "results." Reference to this transformative process is made, either directly or indirectly, in most conceptual discussions of qualitative analysis. For example, Harry Wolcott claims that this transformation process involves, "at a rudimentary level," sorting "data bits into broad categories," or, more abstractly, following "systematic procedures . . . in order to identify essential features and relationships consonant with the" descriptive materials (1994, pp. 23–24). Similarly, Robert Emerson says analysis involves "moving beyond more or less descriptive characteristics of those . . . studied to offer explanations of observed phenomena, or to propose even more elaborate conceptual framings of these matters" (2001, p. 282).

Implied by these conceptual statements as well as others are four defining features of the process:

(1) The results or findings arise through an analysis process that is *skewed in the direction of induction* rather than deduction. Deductive analysis begins with theoretically derived hypotheses and then proceeds to test (confirm or falsify) them via data that were assembled in accord with the orienting theoretical perspective. Inductive analysis, on the other hand, is data-based in that the analysis is driven by the data themselves. Thus, when empirical or theoretical observations emerge inductively, they are often said to be "grounded" in the sense of emerging from the ground up rather than being called forth by prior theoretical constructs. This "grounded" metaphor should be used cautiously, however. As noted in Chapter 8 (Section I.B.4), much, and perhaps most, qualitative fieldwork findings of some theoretical or conceptual significance are not so much novel discoveries as they are "extensions" or "refinements" of existing work (see Snow, Morrill, and Anderson 2003). Prior familiarity with other potentially relevant bodies of work, theoretical or empirical, is obviously a necessary condition for developing extensions and refinements, but actually making those connections should be triggered by one's empirical observations.

(2) Because of the inductive character of qualitative analysis, it follows that the *researchers are the central agents in the analysis process*. Whether the research

is conducted by a single researcher or by a team, the primary analytic agents are the researchers themselves. It is not a process that can be farmed out to independent analysts nor, as we have noted and will note again, to computers and various software programs.

(3) Because of both the inductive and agent-driven character of qualitative analysis, it is a *highly interactive process* between the researcher and the data. Just as qualitative fieldwork typically entails researcher immersion in a setting, so analysis of the accumulated data requires the researcher to immerse her- or himself in that data.

(4) Given the inductive, agent-driven, and highly interactive character of qualitative analysis, it follows that the process is *labor-intensive and time-consuming.* "Making it all come together," as Paul Atkinson has put it, is something that "has to be worked at" (quoted in Strauss and Corbin 1990, p. 117). In other words, analysis should be pursued in a persistent and methodical fashion rather than in a haphazard, seat-of-the-pants manner.

Given these characteristic features of qualitative fieldwork analysis and its importance to the production of interesting fieldwork reports, you might think that there would be widespread understanding among fieldworkers as to how it should be done. Such is not the case, however. Rarely will you find fieldworkers elaborating in their reports how they did their analysis or arrived at their conclusions. As Margaret LeCompte and Jean Schensul have observed:

> Many ethnographers describe their analysis in somewhat mystical terms, suggesting that the themes and patterns emerge from the data as they read their fieldnotes over and over again, somewhat as hikers emerge from the mist on a foggy beach. Unfortunately, *how* these themes and patterns emerge, and what *causes* them to emerge, is left unclear. (1999, pp. 45–46, emphasis in original)

Nor has there been an extensive textual tradition of providing step-by-step procedures for doing analysis. This is not to say, however, that no published instruction has existed—Glaser and Strauss's *The Discovery of Grounded Theory* (1967), the first edition of this volume (1971), and Spradley's *Participant Observation* (1980) are early "guidebooks." But even these plus two additional editions of *Analyzing Social Settings* (1984, 1995) and works by Strauss and Corbin (1990), Miles and Huberman (1994), Wolcott (1994), Coffey and Atkinson (1996), and LeCompte and Schensul (1999) have not managed to squash the widespread presumption that interesting qualitative fieldwork analysis is the result of what Paul Atkinson has cynically dubbed "romantic inspiration" (1990, p. 117).

In what follows, we draw upon this extant textual tradition to propose a number of strategies for "working at" analysis in a reasonably systematic and methodical manner. We do not claim that these strategies are the only ones meriting consideration, that all are used by every analyst, or that any one will work for every analyst every time. But we do believe that their use can be of significant help in making your research report interesting and well received.

I. Strategy One: Social Science Framing

The matters we described in previous chapters come forward and inform analysis. Most particularly, this "bringing forward" can and should take the form of conceiving your goal as that of providing a social science framing of your data. As detailed in the previous chapter, this general approach seeks to develop an analysis that is empirically compelling, sheds new empirical and/or theoretical light on the topic, and is important (Chapter 8, Section I). Relative to the third of these three—importance—the goal is to formulate generic propositions that sum up and provide order in major portions of your data.

As described in the previous chapter, a generic proposition is an answer to a question (as discussed in Chapter 7) posed about a topic (as described in Chapter 6). And, as we also indicated in the last chapter, there are other ways to phrase the quest for generic propositions, so do not feel you need to think in terms of this phrasing alone. Other phrasings we mentioned before can work as well, such as forming a hypothesis, developing a thesis, formulating a concept, addressing a problem, and providing a general interpretation.

A. Eight Forms of Propositions

To underscore the relevance to analysis of the matters described in the previous part of this guide, we refer you back to the articulation of the eight different propositional forms in Chapter 8 (Section I.A). Chapters 6 and 7 are replete with summaries of examples of all of these eight basic types of propositions. Scanning through those chapters as you are also thinking about your data in propositional terms can help you to discern how you can use one or more of these forms of basic propositions to organize your data.

B. A Third Way to Contrast Propositional with Other Writing

In the previous chapter, we contrasted generic propositional framing or "idea" writing with "subject" writing and with "historically particular" writing (Chapter 8, Sections I.C.2 and 3). There are variations on these two alternative forms of writing, as well as other genres of writing that can be contrasted to the analytic, propositional form. There is no need to review here these various alternative forms of writing with the exception of one: the "ordinary term paper." We mention it not only because it is the primary mode of written representation among undergraduate students, but also because it is strikingly different than the propositional framing that we have advocated. The undergraduate term paper is of the review-summary genre that is typically modeled on encyclopedia or other reference book articles, the sources from which much of the information in these papers is often taken. In contrast, the objective of the fieldwork report—at least from our vantage point—is an analytic one, entailing the development of empirically based propositional answers to varied questions about social life and organization (see Cuba, 1988, and J. Lofland, 1995, for further elaboration). Thus, these two forms of framing and writing have little in common. Accordingly, our advice is straightforward: Put aside notions of ordinary term papers when beginning your data analysis and proceed, instead, to think and write as an analytic, qualitative fieldworker.

C. Number of Propositions in a Single Fieldstudy

There is of course the question of how many propositions one ought to develop in a field project. The weaseling but accurate answer is: It depends. Among other factors, it depends on: (1) how long one is in the field and how much data one collects, (2) the stage of the project we are talking about, and (3) the number and scale of reports one plans and completes.

Brief projects, especially those done by students, quite reasonably result in but one report that centerpieces only one major proposition, with brief and subsidiary attention given to others. However, given the inductive character of qualitative fieldwork analysis, even quite small-scale projects can generate, in undeveloped form, a great many possible propositions early on in the research process. These numerous propositional possibilities are derived from one's fieldnotes or interview transcriptions during the course of the coding and memoing operations which we will discuss shortly. In this fashion, the single proposition or small number of propositions that help to shape your analysis result from a process of winnowing out many other possible, central propositions.

Longer-term projects that collect more data and that are projected to result in several reports or a book tend to develop several (but commonly less than a half dozen) major propositions, and even books typically follow the model of the single report in tending to treat only one major proposition in a single chapter.

II. Strategy Two: Normalizing and Managing Anxiety

As noted in the opening paragraphs of this chapter, formulating potential major propositions from your data is essentially an *inductive* activity that is contingent on your persistent and methodical interaction with the data. You get *from* data, topics, and questions, on the one side, *to* answers or propositions, on the other, through intensive immersion in the data, allowing your data to interact with your disciplinary and substantive intuition and sensibilities as these latter are informed by your knowledge of topics and questions. Initially these topics and questions function as guides rather than determinants of your analysis, as you begin with an open-ended and open-minded desire to understand the social situation or setting on its own terms. Doing so, however, almost guarantees that you are likely to feel some anxiety and perhaps even frustration, for you are ultimately confronted with the challenge of finding some social science significance or order in your materials. This can appear to be a daunting and even impossible task at first blush, not only because of some of the ethical and emotional issues discussed in Chapters 2 (see Section III.E) and 4 (see Section I.C) but also because of what is likely to appear to be a chaotic and rapidly expanding body of materials to comb through and analyze. But *fear not!* Feelings of anxiety and difficulty in the face of open-ended tasks are commonplace. Moreover, there are a number of considerations and/or strategies that are helpful in managing these quite normal feelings and fears. Let us point out five of these here and deal with others as they arise in the rest of this chapter.

- The first anxiety-management principle is *to recognize* and accept *the fact that analyzing qualitative field data is neither a mechanical nor easy task*, and therefore it is likely to generate anxiety. Recognition of this fact should serve to normalize it and provide you with a sense of comfort that you are like most everyone else when faced with the challenge of making sense of data.

- A second way of coping with and managing this naturally occurring anxiety is *to get started on analysis early in the data-collection phase of your project*. That is, begin thinking analytically and examining your data accordingly shortly after you have entered the field rather than waiting until your fieldnotes are fully developed and completed (see Chapter 5, Section IV.C). As Miles and Huberman have emphasized, data analysis—which they define broadly to include data reduction, data display, and conclusion drawing and verification—"occurs continuously throughout the life of any qualitatively oriented project" (1994, p. 10). Qualitative analysis is not, then, something that you begin in earnest after you leave the field; rather, it should occur coterminously with your data collection. It will consume more time and attention as your fieldwork project evolves, of course, but it overlaps considerably with data collection. And this temporal overlap should dilute your anxiety because it means that your analytic work will be stretched out over time with the result that you should know a good deal about the character and analytic possibilities contained within your data well before you actually leave the field.

- A third anxiety-management principle is to *work* just as *persistently and methodically* at the task of analyzing your data as you did at collecting it, and with an eye toward shaping your analysis in the propositional form outlined above.

- A fourth anxiety-reducing principle to keep in mind is that the sheer accumulation of information ensures that you will, at minimum, be able to say *something*, even if that something is not as analytic as you might like and is not known to you at the moment.

- A fifth way of diffusing whatever anxiety you might experience is to *get together with other students in your class or seminar or cohort* who are similarly engaged in a qualitative fieldwork project. The formation of such a work group, whether constituted formally or informally, is likely to function much like a "support group" in the sense of helping you work through some of the analysis-related problems and issues with which you are confronted, thereby reducing your associated anxieties and increasing your confidence in your project.

Keeping in mind and/or pursuing these five anxiety-management principles should enhance your confidence that you will inductively generate an analytic statement along the lines of a propositional answer to one or more questions regarding one or more topics in the social situation or setting you are studying. Also, the not infrequent sense of satisfaction and exhilaration that comes from working through and over your data in a fashion that yields an analytic advance—whether in the form of discovery, extension, or refinement—should provide further incentive for proceeding with the analytic task in a persistent and methodical manner. Very much like the satisfaction felt in solving any other puzzle, finding one or more propositions in the chaos of "mere data" can be an enormously positive scholarly experience.

III. Strategy Three: Coding

Qualitative field analysis essentially begins with the activities of "coding" and "memoing." They constitute much of what it means to "work at analysis." Although coding and memoing are typically conjoint activities, we discuss them separately here for the ease of presentation, and we begin with coding since it is the initial and more basic activity.

The essence of coding is the process of sorting your data into various categories that organize it and render it meaningful from the vantage point of one or more frameworks or sets of ideas. It is the "process of defining what the data are all about" (Charmaz, 2001, p. 340) by "relating (those) data to our ideas about" them (Coffey and Atkinson, 1996, p. 27), whether those ideas emerge from the ground up or are extensions or refinements of existing theoretical frameworks (see also LeCompte and Schensul, 1999, pp. 45–47).

The words for these organizing ideas applied to the items or chunks of data in your fieldnotes or other materials, or to the answers of the questions asked about those strips of data, constitute *codes*. They are conceptualized variously as the "names or symbols used to stand for a group of similar terms, ideas, or phenomena" that you notice in your data (LeCompte and Schensul, 1999, p. 55); "tags or labels for assigning units of meaning to . . . information compiled" during your study (Miles and Huberman, 1994, p. 56); or, more abstractly, the labels we use to classify items of information as pertinent to a topic, question, answer, or whatever.

Whether conceptualized simply or abstractly, coding essentially occurs via two overlapping sorting and categorizing processes called *initial coding* and *focused coding* (Charmaz 2001; Strauss and Corbin 1990). Initial coding, also referred to as "open" coding (Strauss and Corbin, 1990, pp. 61–74), is where the rubber hits the road, so to speak, as you begin to condense and organize your data into categories that make sense in terms of your relevant interests, commitments, literatures, and/or perspectives. Initial coding begins by inspecting your interview transcriptions or fieldnotes line by line and asking of each discrete item and/or chunk of information—be it an event, behavior, or place—such general open-ended questions as the following:

- What is this? What does it represent (Strauss and Corbin 1990, p. 63)?
- What is this an example of (Cuba 1988, p. 35)?
- What is going on? What are people doing? What is the person saying? What do these actions and events take for granted? How do the structure and context serve to support, maintain, impede, or change these actions and statements (Charmaz 2001, p. 142)?

Examples of initial coding in response to such questions are provided in the left half of Figure 9.1, which is drawn from Kathy Charmaz's study of people with a chronic illness (1991). One of the characteristic features of initial coding is that the codes are generally quite *numerous* and *varied*. Here, for example, Charmaz suggests eleven different, albeit overlapping codes, to capture and categorize what's going on in the four sentences.

Focused coding, on the other hand, is "less open-ended and more directed than line-by-line coding" and "is considerably more selective and more conceptual" as well (Charmaz, 2001, p. 344). It builds on initial coding in three ways: by usually beginning after the former is well under way and has accumulated; by using a selected number of the expanding or more analytically interesting initial codes to knit together larger chunks of data; and by using these expanding materials as the basis for asking more focused and analytic questions, such as the following:

- Of what *topic*, unit, or aspect is this an instance?
- What *question* about a topic does this item of data suggest?
- What sort of an *answer* to a question about a topic does this item of data suggest (i.e., what proposition is suggested)?

Once you begin focused coding, then, you have already decided that some number of your earlier codes are appropriate for categorizing your data more thoroughly and for further analytic elaboration. And, while in the process of elaborating a selected number of initial codes, you are simultaneously winnowing out less descriptively and analytically useful ones. Furthermore, some of these elaborated codes may begin to assume the status of overarching ideas or propositions that will occupy a prominent place in the analysis. The right half of Figure 9.1 provides examples of two such selected and focused codes—"avoiding disclosure" and "assessing potential losses and risks of disclosure"—in the Charmaz study.

Figure 9.1 Examples of Fieldnote Coding from the Charmaz Study of People with Chronic Illness

Line-by-line coding	Fieldnotes	Focused coding
shifting symptoms, having inconsistent days *interpreting images of self given by others* *avoiding disclosure*	If you have lupus, I mean one day it's my liver; one day it's my joints; one day it's my head, and it's like people really think you're a hypochondriac if you keep complaining about different ailments. . . . It's like you don't want to say anything because people are going to start thinking, you know, "God, don't go near her, all she is—is complaining about this." And I think that's why I never say anything because I feel like everything I have is related one way or another to the lupus but most of the people don't know I have lupus, and even those that do are not going to believe that ten different ailments are the same thing. And I don't want anybody saying, you know, [that] they don't want to come around me because I complain.	*avoiding disclosure*
predicting rejection *keeping others unaware* *seeing symptoms as connected* *having others unaware* *anticipating disbelief* *controlling others' views* *avoiding stigma*		
assessing potential losses and risks of disclosing		*assessing potential losses and risks of disclosing*

Adapted from Charmaz 2001, pp. 343, 344.

Whatever the scale or size of a field project, the researcher is likely to devise dozens or even hundreds of codes that organize the flow of reality captured in the fieldnotes into categories or domains that are related to one another in terms of one framework or another. And, in doing so, codes also are "efficient data-labeling and data-retrieval devices . . . (that) empower and speed up analysis" (Miles and Huberman, 1994, p. 65). Thus, without some coding scheme, systematic qualitative data analysis is well nigh impossible.

A. Two Physical Methods of Coding

The cognitive act of assigning a code is the first step in disaggregating your data, but the act is not complete until you have performed a second step: physically placing the coded data in the same place as other data that you have coded the same way. There are two major ways in which you can do this: filing and computerized databasing.

1. Filing

Prior to the widespread availability of personal computers beginning in the late 1980s, coding frequently took the specific physical form of filing. The researcher established an expanding set of file folders with code names on the tabs and physically placed either the item of data itself or a note that referenced its location in another file folder. Before photocopying was easily available and cheap, some fieldworkers typed their fieldnotes with carbon paper, wrote the codes in the margins of the copies of the notes, and cut them up with scissors. They then placed the resulting slips of paper in corresponding file folders. After the advent of cheap and easily available photocopying, some fieldworkers simply made as many copies as they had codes on each fieldnote page and filed entire pages. Such physical operations created one or more file drawers of file folders containing coded data.

2. Computer Databasing

As noted in Chapter 5, the growing availability of relevant computer hardware and software has made it possible for researchers to perform these same basic coding and filing operations much more quickly and efficiently than in the past. The logic of coding is the same, but there is the added advantage of instantaneous filing in one or more files, thus eliminating the labor-intensive acts of physically copying, cutting up, and placing by hand items of data in different file folders. Additionally, computer databasing enables you to search through your data and to retrieve, recode, refile, and enumerate coded items and relate them to one another in a much more consistent and rapid fashion than was formerly possible. Because of advantages that computers offer for data input, categorization, and consolidation, we think that all fieldstudy investigators should give serious consideration to exploring the analytic utility for their projects of both the ordinary word-processing programs that contain impressive coding and filing capabilities (e.g., Word and WordPerfect) and several of the qualitative data analysis programs now available (e.g., ATLAS, Ethnograph, HyperResearch, NUD*IST, Nvivo). Not only are there a good number of such software programs that can be compared in terms of different criteria, but there are now a growing number of descriptions and assessments of these programs as well as of computer-aided analysis more generally. We recommend a number of these for your consultation:

- Coffey, Amanda, and Paul Atkinson, "Complementary Strategies of Computer-Aided Analysis." Chapter 7 in *Making Sense of Qualitative Data* (1996).
- Dohan, Daniel, and Martin Sanchez-Jankowski, "Using Computers to Analyze Ethnographic Field Data: Theoretical and Practical Considerations," *Annual Review of Sociology* (1998).
- Fielding, Nigel, and Raymond M. Lee, *Computer Assisted Qualitative Research* (1998) [Or, see Nigel Fielding's "Computer Applications in Qualitative Research." Chapter 31 in *Handbook of Ethnography*, edited by Paul Atkinson, Coffey, Delamont, Lofland, and Lofland (2001)].
- Weitsman, Eban A., "Software and Qualitative Research." Chapter 30 in *Handbook of Qualitative Research*, edited by N. Denzin and Y. Lincoln (2000).

Although we encourage you to explore the relevance of one or more of the available software programs for coding and organizing your data, we caution you again, as we did in Chapter 5 (Section II.C), not to presume that computer databasing and qualitative software programs are shortcuts or magical keys to developing compelling and important analyses. At best, they expedite and expand data organization, storage, and retrieval possibilities, but they cannot do the hard work of data analysis, which requires certain intellectual and creative skills that, to date, only the analyst can bring to the enterprise. All of the above recommended works recognize and emphasize this distinction. As Coffey and Atkinson conclude in their discussion of computer-assisted qualitative data analysis (CAQDAS), "none of the computer programs will perform automatic data analysis. They all depend on researchers defining for themselves what analytic issues are to be explored, what ideas are important, and what modes of representation are most appropriate" (1996, p. 187).

The conclusion suggested by such observations and assessments strikes us as straightforward: Be exploratory and definitely use the computer and perhaps one of the software programs to organize and store your data, but do not assume that either will automatically code or analyze those data in an interesting and compelling fashion.

B. Types of Coding Files

Issues of file folder versus computer databasing aside, you are confronted with the decision of developing a number of basic filing categories in which to code and sort your data. Based on our experiences and discussions with other fieldworkers, we recommend the development and maintenance of three broad sets of generic files: (1) folk or setting-specific files; (2) analytic files; and (3) methodological or fieldwork files.

1. **Folk/Setting-Specific Files**
   Although you want to develop your analysis along the lines of the social science framing mentioned earlier in the chapter and elaborated in the previous chapter, the various situations and behaviors that are the object of your research are complex entities that require considerable time and attention in order to understand them in their own mundane terms. Thus, rather than begin by transforming local or site-specific categories into more abstract, analytic ones, you should initially establish sets of coding files that are faithful to and capture the central elements of the setting in the language and category schemes of those who populate and negotiate the setting on an everyday basis. In other words, initially establish folk or setting-specific files. These files are extremely important because they not only contain the materials for whatever descriptive accounts you eventually develop, but they also constitute the empirical base for demonstrating that "you were there" and directly observed or experienced what you are trying to get a handle on analytically.

   Earlier (Chapter 6, Section I), we noted that all social settings are constituted by one or more *actors* (individuals, groups, organizations, etc.) engaging in one or more *activities or behaviors* in a specific *place or locale* at a particular *time*. Accordingly, you can begin by unpacking and coding your data in terms of these generic coordinates. More concretely, establish:

   - a set of files for the array of actors you encounter, with a separate file for each actor;
   - a set of files for the activities and/or events in which they are participating, with a separate file for each; and
   - a set of files for the places or spaces in which these actors and their actions are situated.

   What about time? Usually you will not need a separate set of files for keeping track of the times in which actors appear, activities or events occur, or they both come together at a particular place, unless temporality is the focus of your analysis, as with Michael Flaherty's (1999) examination of how passing time is experienced phenomenologically. However, you will want to be methodical about recording the date and time for each file observation—that is, for example, the date and time in which actor X was encountered or observed or when a particular event occurred or activity was observed. Doing so will enable you to examine processual questions and issues more carefully and systematically should that become a topical focus or question as your analysis develops.

   As well, you should either indicate in your file the activity in which actor X was engaged and the place/locale of the encounter or cross-file your observation on actor X by simultaneously placing it in a particular activity or event file and in a file for a specific locale or place. Such cross-filing or multiple coding, along with the above mentioned temporal notation, will enable you to establish the connections between actors, activities, place, and time in an organized and systematic fashion.

Initially, you should develop coding files for every actor you encounter, every major setting-relevant activity and/or event, and the range of places in which the actors have been encountered and the activities/events observed, and cross-file for each as indicated above. This may seem like a rather daunting task, but there is no way of knowing in advance which actors, activities, or places may emerge as most significant, as indicated by the number of entries or slices of data contained in the file or by the file's eventual analytic relevance. To be sure, not all of the actors, activities, or places will prove equally salient descriptively or analytically, but it would be descriptively and analytically premature to presume to know that in advance of coding. For example, in their coding and analysis of the data that eventually culminated in *Down on Their Luck*, Snow and Anderson (1993) established a set of files titled "focal settings," which included separate files on twenty-five different places (e.g., nonprofit street agencies, commercial establishments, parks, city agencies, street corners), which the homeless variously frequented. As the analysis progressed, it became increasingly clear that some settings were much more fundamental than others to the daily lives and routines of homeless, as well as more salient analytically, but the establishment of such patterns was based on the "fatness" of the files resulting from the coding process rather than from some a priori hunch or bias.

Getting and keeping a handle on local life and its organization at this mundane or street level is greatly assisted, then, if you develop, maintain, and review data coded and organized as suggested above. Additionally, the development of these folk or setting-specific files can assist in the rapid location of base, descriptive information otherwise buried in the chronological notes or obscurely labeled in the analytic codes. And these folk or setting-specific coding files are likely to stimulate or refine analytic coding by pointing to patterns not anticipated or fully congruent with existing theoretical/analytic schemes or codes.

2. **Analytic Files**
In establishing analytic files, you ask of your slices, units, or chunks of field observations questions of the kind elaborated in Chapter 7 and that can be further transformed into the propositional format spelled out in Chapter 8 (Section I.C.2) and discussed again earlier in this chapter (Section I.A). Here, rather than asking what kind of folk activity or event is this, or where did it occur, you ask analytic "focusing" questions of the kind indicated at the beginning of this section. There is no one way to ask such questions, of course, as they can range from the general and more abstract to the more concrete and focused.

Examples of more general and abstract analytic questions include:

- What kind of sociological topic, unit, or aspect is this event or activity?
- Is it illustrative of a particular analytic type or kind of process?
- To which of the formal kinds of propositions is it most relevant?

Examples of more concrete and focused questions include:

- Does it say something about the actor's self or identity?
- Is it strategic action and, if so, what kind?
- What was the consequence of this line of action or account for the actor(s)?

Whatever analytic questions are asked, the point is that you are now thinking about and playing with your data in terms of social science framing and therefore various social scientific concepts, processes, and perspectives. Accordingly, the development of these analytic files will depend in large part on the focused coding discussed earlier and your "memoing" practices, which we will discuss shortly.

Just as there is no one form for asking analytic questions, so there is no one set of established guidelines for engaging in analytic coding and establishing and developing analytic files. However, the following guidelines can be discerned in the published projects and methodological reports of many fieldworkers, including our own:

- *Adopt an Emergent and Experimental Posture*: While coding for folk or setting-specific files is a fact-keeping and housekeeping enterprise, analytic coding is more emergent, venturesome, and experimental (although the coder is also prepared to classify items of information in fairly obvious terms). This is especially true in the early stages of a project when the fieldworker is not yet particularly concerned about the eventual viability of a file code or whether it will ultimately make any kind of sense. The aim, instead, is to generate as many separate codes and files as one is prompted or inspired to during the course of inspecting the data. The task of reckoning with these emergent and venturesome analytic impulses comes later, during the period of final analysis.

- *Engage in Regular Coding*: The requirements of interviewing and observation, as well as other facets of life, affect the frequency with which fieldworkers can engage in coding and filing. Whatever the interval, the field wisdom, as noted earlier, is to start coding quite early in the research process and to engage in it as regularly as possible. Miles and Huberman go so far as to assert that you should "always code the previous set of field notes before the next trip to the site. Always—no matter how good the excuses for not doing it" (1994, p. 65). We think this is a bit extreme given the practicalities of life, but the spirit of their directive is well taken.

- *Engage in Extensive and Pervasive Coding*: Since coding is an emergent, open-ended, and time consuming activity, questions are often asked about how extensively and pervasively it should be conducted. More concretely, how many codes should one generate overall, and how many should one apply to, say, a single page of fieldnotes or interview transcriptions? There is no magical or pat answer to such questions, as it all depends on the richness of the data, the regularity of the coding, and the creative capacities and insights of the field coders as they engage and interact with the data. In general, however, you are well-advised to code as extensively and pervasively as possible. In practical terms, this means reading line by line, sentence by sentence. Doing so does not guarantee creative analytic insights, but not doing so does decrease the likelihood of generating such insights and ultimately developing an excellent analysis.

- *Engage in Multiple Coding of Single Items*: Here the process of multiple coding or cross-filing initiated with the establishment of folk files is accelerated in the sense that you should code any given item, unit, or chunk of field data in as many files or code categories as seems appropriate. (This is exemplified in Charmaz's coding shown in Figure 9.1.)

- *Treat Folk Coding and Analytic Coding as Overlapping Tasks*: Although there is no set pattern among fieldworkers regarding the temporal relationship between folk or setting-specific coding and analytic coding, the recommended relationship is much the same as that applied to previously discussed relationships between data collection and data analysis: approach them as overlapping rather than as mutually exclusive tasks. While folk coding will certainly be dominant in the initial stages of the coding process, creative, analytic flashes and insights may materialize at any moment when inspecting the data. But it is also the case that the further you are into the coding process, the more frequent the development of analytic codes and files. So it is reasonable to expect analytic coding to evolve over time and then expand as the more setting-specific, mundane coding progresses and then begins to decline.

- *Category Saturation and Subdivision*: Instances of some codes occur with such frequency and regularity that one develops a file with an enormous number of included data points or items of information, often far more than seems needed or is manageable. Analysts proceed in one of two directions in this circumstance. On the one hand, you can inspect the instances in the code file more closely for how they vary among themselves in ways that make for more fine-grained analysis. That is, you can elaborate the code itself to identify subdivisions. On the other hand, such close inspection may lead to the conclusion that no further inspection is required or that what might be done is not important enough to do. In these events, you may assess the category as "saturated" and cease coding for it.

3. **Methodological/Fieldwork Files**

    Most of your field data will be coded into the folk and analytic files, but not all of your materials will be of descriptive or conceptual or theoretical analytic relevance. Instead, some of it is likely to bear directly on your fieldwork procedures—that is, on the data-gathering challenges, issues, and feelings discussed in Chapters 2 through 4 in Part I. And this is especially the case if you attentively recorded your research experiences, impressions, and feelings as suggested in Chapter 5 (Section IV.C.2). It is for the coding, sorting, and analysis of such materials, then, that you will want to establish sets of methodological or fieldwork files. These files can serve a number of important functions. Most obviously, they will greatly assist in writing this part of your report. (For examples, see the specific accounts of fieldwork experience provided at the end of Chapter 4). Additionally, these files are likely to provide you with materials relevant to our discussion of "trueness" in Chapter 8 and thus provide another basis for enhancing the credibility of your final report, as we will discuss further in Chapter 10. And finally, these files may contain materials that provide the basis for reports or papers on aspects of the process of fieldwork itself (see, e.g., Adams 1998; Ellis 1995; Horowitz 1986; Rochford 1994; Salzinger 2004; Scheper-Hughes 2004).

C. Maintaining a Chronological Record

Splitting the materials into folk or setting-specific, analytic, and fieldwork files helps immeasurably in organizing your data and developing an analysis. In fact, we would argue that odds of developing a compelling analysis are miniscule in the absence of the development of such files. But these files can also obscure the temporal evolution of your field data and notes, as well as the context in which they are embedded. When you scrutinize a particular piece of filed material, for example, the question can arise: What else was happening at the time, or what else was the person saying, that seemed irrelevant then but now seems important? You want, that is, to be able to look back at the more general context, and, to do this easily, you need an intact chronological record of the past. You should therefore keep a full set of your materials in the order in which you originally collected them.

A chronological set of materials is also useful for locating information that is not readily available in one or another of the files. And it is useful simply for reading and reviewing from beginning to end as a stimulus to thinking about larger patterns and larger units of analysis (as outlined in Chapter 6).

IV. Strategy Four: Memoing

In the course of coding, whether initial or focused, it is extremely important to get in the habit of writing down your ideas about your various coding categories and their interconnections, and even about your procedures and fieldwork experiences. These written-out notes about such ideas and experiences are called *memos* (Charmaz 2001; Glaser 1978; Miles and Huberman 1994; Strauss and Corbin 1990). Writing these memos (memoing) constitutes "the intermediate step between coding and the first draft of your completed analysis" (Charmaz, 2001, p. 347) and is thus fundamental to making sense of your data. As Charmaz has observed, "many qualitative researchers who do not write memos become lost in mountains of data and cannot make sense of them" (2001, p. 347).

Although most discussions of memoing accent its analytic and theoretical utility for the development of "grounded theory" (Charmaz 2001; Glaser and Strauss 1967; Strauss and Corbin 1990), we believe it is equally relevant to theoretical extension and refinement as discussed in Chapter 8 (Section I.B.4). As suggested above, memoing can also be useful for clarifying basic codes and revisiting and fine-tuning methodological issues and procedures. Miles and Huberman note in this regard that while "memos are primarily conceptual in intent" they can also be useful for thinking about, clarifying, and improving upon "any aspect of the study—personal, methodological, and substantive" (1994, p. 72). This more expansive view of memoing is in accord with Strauss and Corbin (1990), who suggest three kinds of memos: code memos, theoretical memos, and operational or methodological memos.

1. *Code memos* are notes that elaborate and clarify the codes and the assumptions underlying them. The objective of writing them is to make sure that the codes are descriptive and/or conceptually appropriate and as unambiguous and non-repetitive as possible. In many respects, elaborating and clarifying your codes is akin to what quantitative researchers do when they seek to operationalize clearly their dependent and independent or causal variables.

2. *Theoretical memos*, to paraphrase Barney Glaser, are the "theorizing write-ups" of your ideas about your codes and their relationships as they strike you while coding. They exhaust, at the moment in which you write them, your "momentary ideation" based on the data inspected and coded, with perhaps a little conceptual elaboration (1978, pp. 83–84). As you continue to code and analyze your data, however, you may very well write new memos that build on the earlier ones and lead to a clearer and more elaborated conceptual or theoretical understanding of the phenomenon in question. Thus, theoretical memoing is a procedure that not only continues throughout the entire coding process, but may even continue once the coding is completed as you develop your analysis further by revisiting and refining earlier theoretical memos. Although the slices and chunks of fieldnotes that stimulate theoretical memos may be coded into both the folk and analytic files, it is likely that theoretical memos will be generated most frequently in tandem with the focused coding of analytic files.

3. *Operational/procedural memos* consist of the notes you write to yourself and team members, if any, regarding the whole gamut of procedural challenges, issues, and strategies associated with gathering data, as explored in Part I, including plans to do something about emergent challenges and issues. These memos may take the form of directions to modify one or more procedures, such as securing a wider range

of informants; leads to follow up on, such as exploring the prospect of accessing alternative data points or sources; or reflections on how your fieldwork procedures and experiences inform some general methodological issue or practice, such as gaining access, styles of interviewing, or disengagement. Just as theoretical memos are most likely to spring from the intersection of focused coding and analytic files, so the methodological files are likely to be the primary source of inspiration for operational/procedural memos.

Whatever the basic genre of memo being written, you need not fret about its length. What Glaser had to say about the length of theoretical memos applies to all fieldwork memos: they "can be a sentence, a paragraph, or a few pages" so long as they "exhaust" your thinking about the issue or topic at the moment (1978, p. 84). However, you do need to be relatively compulsive about memo-writing and realize that it will become a larger feature of your work as your analysis develops, even as the range of topics with which they deal becomes narrower (i.e., codes become more focused). The reason for this recommended compulsiveness is because of the salience of memoing to developing a compelling analysis. As Miles and Huberman note in this regard, memos "are one of the most useful and powerful sense-making tools at hand." (1994, p. 72)

We have just provided an overview of "coding" and "memoing," and suggested that they are critical and ongoing steps in the process of developing analysis. However, we want to reintroduce two caveats noted earlier about these two strategies along with the other ones discussed in the preceding pages. The first is that we do not presume that coding and memoing, as we have unpacked them, are the only steps or means to developing compelling analyses. The problem is that field researchers too rarely elaborate how they get from their data, topics, and questions to their findings and conclusions. The result is a kind of "black box," or a variant form of what J. Lofland termed "analytic interruptus" (1970), between the data-gathering and writing phases of the fieldwork enterprise that contributes to the sense that qualitative analysis is often the result of a mystical process or romantic inspiration. Of course, there are a few exceptions to this tendency, particularly in relation to the use of computer programs for qualitative analysis. One such example is Thomas J. Richards and Lyn Richards's "data-theory bootstrapping" approach (1994), which is linked to the computer qualitative analysis program called NUD*IST. But even here, inspection of their operations indicates that they are, generically, much the same as coding and memoing. So while coding and memoing may not be the only critical practices in developing analysis, we would contend that they are necessary steps in the analytic process. And second, we want to reemphasize that while the articulation and application of coding and memoing are associated closely with the "grounded theory" approach to developing analysis, they are of broader relevance and utility, being fundamental as well to what we previously discussed as theoretical extension and refinement.

V. Strategy Five: Diagramming

Generically, a diagram is a succinct visual representation of one or more relationships among parts of something, as in the classic genealogical family tree. Within the social science context, diagrams have been defined as "visual representations of relationships between concepts" (Strauss and Corbin 1990, p. 197) or as "data displays" that present information visually and systematically in the form of various "types of matrices, graphs, charts, and networks" (Miles and Huberman 1994, pp. 11, 91). However conceptualized, the distinguishing feature of diagrams or data displays is that they concisely order or represent the relationship among two or more elements or aspects of a setting that have been determined to be descriptively or theoretically relevant to its operation or functioning.

In thinking about diagramming, it is useful to keep in mind that the word diagram is both a noun and a verb—that is, it is both an object or a product of analysis and, when diagramming, an activity within the analytic process. As Miles and Huberman have emphasized, the creation and use of displays (diagrams) is not separate from analysis, it is *part* of analysis. Designing a display—deciding on the rows and columns of a matrix for qualitative data and deciding which data, in which form, should be entered in the cells—is an analytic activity (1994, p. 11).

Because we are elaborating the development of analysis in this chapter, we focus on diagramming as an activity and, therefore, strategy of analysis. We find that many fieldworkers, including ourselves, have developed diagrams not only as useful supplements to extended textual passages, but also as alternative forms of visual representation. Here we examine briefly four forms of diagramming—taxonomies, matrices and typologies, concept charts, and flow charts—and refer you to Miles and Huberman's *Qualitative Data Analysis* (1994) for a much more comprehensive discussion of diagramming and the range of diagrams or data displays you may want to consider.

A. Taxonomies

We noted earlier in the guide that one of the basic functions of qualitative fieldwork is to describe the characteristics of the phenomena or topic observed and the forms it displays. To do the latter is to provide answers to a number of the focal questions raised in Chapter 7, as well as implied by the eight forms of propositions, such as: What are the topic's types? What are the stages, steps, or sequences in a process? What are the set of factors that interact to cause topic X? Or, what are the strategies/tactics for doing a particular task or realizing a particular end? Although the answers to these questions are most often expressed via written text, they can also be elaborated diagrammatically as a taxonomy. As suggested in Chapter 7 (Section I.B), a taxonomy essentially is a diagrammatic display of all of the forms of the folk or theoretic category being studied. It shows what is presumably a thorough listing of all of the terms that are variants of the focal category or topic and how they are

Strategy Five: Diagramming 213

connected. To illustrate, we refer you back to Figure 7.2, which provides, in outline form, a taxonomic elaboration of an answer to the question of how the homeless survive materially on the streets. There we see three core types of material survival strategies, with each having two or more subtypes. There are, of course, forms other than the outline one for representing taxonomies diagrammatically. These include the tree or network form and the box diagram, both of which are shown, along with the outline form, in Figure 9.2.

1. Outline Diagram

                  Focal Topic/Phenomenon

       A.
            1.
                  a.
                  b.
            2.
            3.
       B.
       C.
       D.
            1.
            2.
            3.

2. Tree/Network Diagram

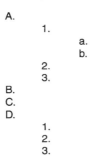

3. Box Diagram

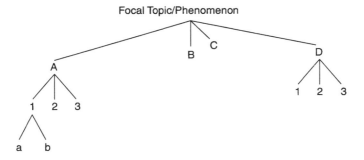

Figure 9.2 Forms of Taxonomic Diagrams.
Adapted from James P. Spradley, *Participant Observation*, 1980.

B. Matrices and Typologies

As well as diagramming the connections among the various forms or types of a focal category or topic, taxonomies provide a springboard for matrix making and typologizing by generating questions about the similarities and differences among the included items within the taxonomy or their relationship to other situationally focal topics. Matrices and typologies constitute diagrammatically expressed answers to these questions. Returning to the taxonomy of material survival strategies, for example, it is reasonable to wonder about the extent to which their use varies among the homeless. Snow and Anderson (1993) explored this question as well. Cross-classifying types of material survival strategies and types of homeless, they created a matrix that clearly illustrated what they suspected: noteworthy variation in the use of these survival strategies across different types of homeless individuals.

Matrices, in general, are based on this very kind of cross-classification of two or more dimensions, variables, or concepts of relevance to the topic or topics of interest. In their discussion of matrices, for example, Miles and Huberman define them simply and mechanically as "the 'crossing' of two lists, set up as rows and columns" (1994, p. 93) and provide a number of examples, including event/chronological, checklist, and effects matrices. A number of the figures we presented earlier further illustrate this cross-listing or classification metric that is at the genesis of matrix-making. Figure 5.1, for instance, illuminates the relationship between different kinds of data sources and different data-gathering methods, and Figure 6.1, based on the cross-classification of units of organization and aspects of situations, shows how different fieldstudies typically work at the intersection of units and aspects.

Typologies are similarly based on the cross-classification of two or more ideas, concepts, or variables, each typically with two values, such as "yes" and "no" or "present" and "absent." The prototypical typology in sociology, and perhaps in the social sciences, is the two-by-two table, which is illustrated in Figure 7.2. Because of its apparent simplicity, it often appears, at first glance, to be a relatively unsophisticated analytic device. But, as we all know well, appearances can often be deceiving, and such is the case with the two-by-two typology. Such typologies, as C. Wright Mills reminded us some time ago, are "very often genuine tools of production. They clarify the 'dimensions' of the types [you are working on], which they also help you to imagine and build" (Mills 1959, p. 213). Indeed, Mills goes on to declare that:

> I do not believe I have written more than a dozen pages first-draft without some little cross-classification [i.e., typology]—although, of course, I do not always or even usually display such diagrams. Most of them flop, in which case you have still learned something. When they work, they help you to think more clearly and to write more explicitly. They enable you to discover

the range and the full relationships of the very terms in which you are thinking and of the facts with which you are working.

For a working sociologist, cross-classification is what diagramming a sentence is for a diligent grammarian. In many ways, cross-classification is the very grammar of the sociological imagination. (Mills 1959, p. 213; see also Miles and Huberman 1994, p. 184, on "substructing" variables)

C. Concept Charts

A third display strategy useful for both developing analysis and illustrating it is to chart diagrammatically how key concepts are related to each other. Whatever the character of the concepts—be they folk-based, theoretic, or a mixture, it is not always clear how they fit together or intersect, if at all, with respect to the focal topic. Engaging in some form of concept charting can help to illuminate and understand these connections. Not surprisingly, there is no one way to explore these conceptual connections. Prior to the advent of computer databasing, fieldworkers were likely to use various confirmations of physical space—floors, walls, bulletin boards, and the like—to actually spread out their various conceptual ideas and notes. Speaking at a social science session on fieldwork in the early 1980s, for example, Carol Stack reported that when doing the fieldwork for *All Our Kin: Strategies for Survival in a Black Community* (1974), the need to keep her notes safe from her active child led her to pin notes on walls throughout her apartment. While the safety of her notes was the initial impetus for such maneuvering, she soon discovered this practice was very useful in itself as a way to display her data in various configurations and thereby enable her to order and reorder them more easily. In light of the variety of computer data input, filing, storage, and retrieval functions available today, such physical mapping and charting exercises may seem both humorous and unnecessary. However, we would caution against such a patronizing stance toward time-honored procedures since many fieldworkers find computers sometimes too confining for the task at hand. If spreading out notes on a floor or tabletop or pinning up ideas on walls, or even writing on multiple blackboards in empty classrooms (Agar 1991, p. 192), help you to work out the relationships among concepts, by all means proceed in that functional "low tech" manner.

Although it is probably reasonable to assume that most fieldworkers engage in some concept charting, it is relatively rare for these organizing charts to appear in their final reports. Sometimes, however, the substance or complexity of the materials prompts their presentation. Such was the case in Figure 7.1, where we show the relations among the eight basic questions addressed. Another example of concept charting is provided in Figure 9.3, which displays forms of work behavior and their relationships identified by Randy Hodson (1991) in his examination of ethnographies in the workplace.

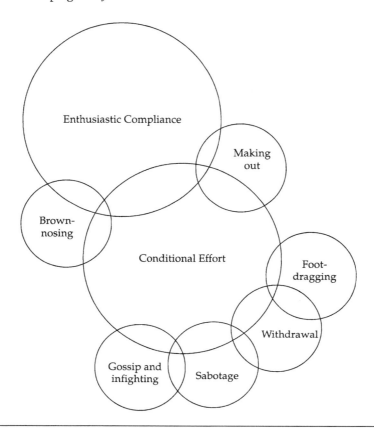

Figure 9.3 Example of a Concept Charting Diagram: Hodson on Behavioral Modes at the Workplace.
Source: Hodson, "The Active Worker: Compliance and Autonomy at the Workplace," 1991, p. 53, Figure 1, "Behavioral Modes in the Workplace." Reprinted by permission of Sage Publications, Inc. © 1991 by Sage Publications, Inc.

D. Flow Charts

Flow charts, the fourth diagramming strategy we accent, typically include some number of the key concepts or terms that may be featured in each of the above diagram forms, but are now arranged or ordered in terms of their relationships through *time* or in a *process* rather than as static entities. The three-element chart with which we began this guide (Figure I.1) is an example of a simple flow chart of the temporal relationship among the three major fieldwork tasks. As another illustration of flow charting, consider Figure 9.4, which diagrams or charts the various career paths of different types of homeless. The so-called "recently dislocated" (those who have been on the streets for less than six months), for example, sometimes quickly find their way off the streets (path 1→ 4) but also frequently evolve into "straddlers" (path 1→2), who find themselves more or less suspended

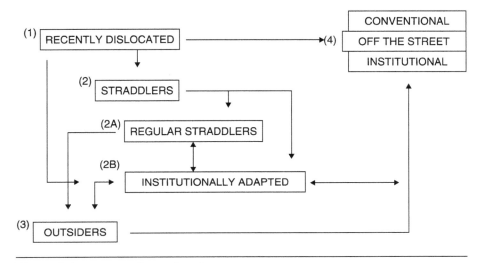

Figure 9.4 Diagram of Homeless Careers.
Adapted from David A. Snow and Leon Anderson, *Down on Their Luck*, 1993.

between the worlds of the domiciled and the more chronically street homeless typed the "outsiders."

In their detailed treatment of "data displays," Miles and Huberman (1994, p. 93) speak of flow charting as networks, which they define as "a series of 'nodes' with links between them." But we would caution here not to presume that all network diagrams are flow charts in a temporal or processual sense. Certainly network diagrams can be used to depict directional flow, but the data points represented as nodes have to be temporally dispersed in some fashion.

The graphing software packages that are now so abundantly available make the kinds of diagramming we have described (as well as yet other forms of it) relatively easy. We ought therefore to expect that diagrams will figure ever more centrally in the analytic process and in fieldwork reports.

VI. Strategy Six: Thinking Flexibly

The final analytic strategy we want to accent is best captured by the phrase "thinking flexibly." Other words or phrases that flush out what we have in mind here include mental elasticity, open-mindedness, unflinching curiosity, and even playfulness. In order to enhance the prospect of your thinking flexibly as you develop your analysis, we suggest two sets of guidelines, one proscriptive and the other prescriptive.

By proscriptive guidelines, we are suggesting, of course, a number of things you should avoid and thus guard against. The major ones include:

- Don't become too locked in or committed to a particular theoretical perspective or line of argument too early in the analysis process. Keep in mind that theoretical perspectives function much like picture frames, focusing attention only on some things to the neglect of others and articulating the relationship only between those things that are within the frame. Certainly as the analysis progresses and attention becomes more focused, some perspectives will become much more central to your analysis. But even then, don't foreclose the prospect of considering the analytic utility of other perspectives.

- Don't limit your analysis too early to a single form of theoretical development (e.g., grounded theory, theoretical extension, or theoretical refinement—see Chapter 8, Section I.B.4) or to one analytic model to the exclusion of another. While the appropriateness of one model over another is dependent on the kinds of questions asked and the kinds of data collected, there is rarely any need to make a definitive decision regarding the analytic model in the early stages of the analysis process. Far better to play with the data by coding it broadly and thinking in terms of various analytic possibilities.

- Don't allow the considerable computerized data filing and storage possibilities and the kindred qualitative data analysis programs to lull you into thinking that the hard analytic work is done once your logged notes are coded and stored. As we have noted at various points in this guide (Chapter 5 II.C and Section III.A.2 in this chapter) and as emphasized by all of the works listed earlier on computer-aided analysis, the computer and the various software programs designed for filing, storing, and retrieving qualitative data are no substitute for the hard intellectual work required to make sense of the data sociologically, anthropologically, or from the vantage point of other disciplinary interests. The computer and the associated programs can facilitate the analysis, but you still have to make the key decisions regarding appropriate conceptualizations, theoretical connections, and the "take-home" significance of your research.

Turning to the prescriptive guidelines, we refer to a number of practices that are part and parcel of thinking flexibly and that you will therefore want to pursue as you develop your analysis. These are the "do's" rather than the "don'ts."

- Rephrasing: The sheer way a question (or answer) is phrased or worded can greatly facilitate or deter your thinking. When you are blocked, try using new words and new word orders. C. Wright Mills speaks of this as an "attitude of playfulness toward the phrase and words with which various issues are defined" (1959, p. 212). For example, instead of speaking of "causes," you might use the related but different term "facilitants"; instead of the verb "functions," perhaps the word "serves" might better capture the matter at hand.

- Changing Diagrams: If you have already diagrammed an analysis in a form outlined above, but it does not quite capture what you envisioned based on your data, try a different form of representation, as in (1) a different kind of line drawing, (2) mathematical notations or their equivalents, or (3) physical objects from which you can construct three-dimensional models.

- Constantly Comparing: Constantly comparing items under analysis can stimulate ideas: How is this instance of X similar to or different from previous instances? How is X in this setting similar to or different from X in another setting? In what ways do the various members of this type or category differ? Posing and answering such questions is to engage in what has been variously termed a "constant comparative method" (Glaser and Strauss 1967, Ch. 5) and "componential analysis" (Coffey and Atkinson, 1996, 134–135; Spradley 1980, pp. 130–139).

- Talking with Fellow Analysts: As mentioned above regarding the management of anxiety, you should be in contact with others interested in your project so that you have a sounding board of sorts. (If you are engaged in team field research, then, of course, you have a built-in sounding board.) Aside from, and in addition to, the *morale boosting* function of being with friendly fellow analysts, such associates may also *stimulate your thinking*. Talking with others who are knowledgeable and supportive can help to clarify in your own mind what it is that you are trying to get at.

- Periodic Distancing: We noted in Chapter 4 that good field research is partly contingent on reaching a chronic yet healthy tension between closeness and distance or involvement and detachment (Section I.C) This tension also is of relevance to the analysis process, as it will help you zoom in and out so that you can assess things up close but also from a distance, thereby gaining perspective and thinking about the overall picture. In other words, descend into detail, to be sure, but balance that descent with self-conscious efforts to perceive a general design, overall structure, or, as phrased above, a propositional answer to a question about a topic.

In suggesting the above proscriptive and prescriptive guidelines for thinking flexibly, we do not presume that they are exhaustive. In fact, we suspect other qualitative researchers might very well add to the list. But the suggestions provided should be sufficient to help you be conscious of the importance of thinking flexibly and even, we hope, actually doing it as you develop and write your analysis.

We divide the third major task of doing a field study—that of analyzing data—into the two subtasks of developing analysis (discussed in this chapter) and writing analysis (treated in the next chapter). This division is in one sense artificial because the analyst is clearly doing an enormous amount of writing in pursuing one or more of the six strategies we describe in this chapter. But, in another sense, developing and writing analysis are different and require separate discussion. Developing has to do with articulating a general approach from and toward one's data, whereas writing is more concerned with the social psychology of writing per se and with the specific design of written reports. We now turn to these and related aspects of writing analysis.

CHAPTER 10

WRITING ANALYSIS

Take a minute to reflect on how far you have come in the research process. At this point you have negotiated access to a setting or settings and have developed and maintained field relations. You have gathered field data and organized and analyzed them. You now have an array of facts and understandings about the setting(s) and people you have studied. You have framed your analysis in terms of social science principles and concepts. All of this work has brought you to a position to prepare to share your research with a broader audience. If you have consistently followed the guidance in this manual, you should now have something—perhaps several things—that you want to communicate with others. It is time to begin writing a report—whether a research term paper, a thesis or dissertation, a journal article, or a book.

In the previous chapter we were primarily concerned with various procedures and strategies that facilitate developing an analysis of your field data. In this chapter, in contrast, we are primarily concerned with procedures for writing itself and with ways to organize that activity so that you are able to produce clear and coherent written reports.

Your fieldwork has prepared you for this. You already have a significant amount of writing in your transcripts, fieldnotes, codings, and memos. But once again, as in many stages of the fieldwork process, you are likely to experience some trepidation and uncertainty about how to proceed. As we noted in the preceding chapter, you should not be surprised to feel anxious in the face of open-ended and complex research tasks—and the report writing stage is certainly no exception. Virtually all writers experience such angst at one point or another. However, as we will explain in the following pages, writing need not be a mysterious activity that eludes your grasp. Thanks to the work of composition scholars and to the reflective observations of some notable sociologists, it is possible to understand the writing process and to organize one's time and activities in a manner that facilitates competent writing. This is not to say that writing can become easy. Most often it is hard work. But the encouraging fact is that there are strategies that can both reduce the arduousness of your labor and enhance its productivity.

Learning to write, like learning to participate in other undertakings, requires (1) knowledge of the basic rules and (2) practice in its procedures and routines. We assume that you already possess working knowledge of the basic rules regarding vocabulary, spelling, grammar, syntax, stylistic conventions, and the like—the sorts of things dealt with in handbooks of grammar and manuals of style (see, e.g., Lunsford 2003; Turabian 1996). Here we focus on selected processes and procedures associated with writing.

I. Preliminary Considerations

While writing talent, like all talents, varies considerably from one individual to another, the key to basic writing competence lies in understanding the writing process and making it work for you. This process involves two intertwined general orders of things. The first is a basic understanding of the cognitive and social processes involved and how to use them effectively. The second entails the use and structuring of time.

A. Understanding the Social Psychological Dimensions of the Writing Process

While earlier models of writing instruction viewed writing as simply a medium of communication, today composition scholars approach writing as a social psychological process in which ideas are formulated as well as communicated. As Howard Becker notes, "The best research on writing [today] . . . analyzes the process of writing and concludes that writing is a form of thinking" (1986, p. ix). Similarly, in an excellent guide to effective time management for writers, *The Clockwork Muse*, Eviatar Zerubavel (1999, p. 48) observes,

> One of the most common misconceptions inexperienced writers have of writing is that it is simply a mechanical process of reproducing already-formed ideas on paper. Nothing could be further from the truth. In reality, writing is virtually inseparable from the process of developing our ideas. In other words, much of our thinking actually takes place while we are writing!

Current paradigms of writing instruction further emphasize that the writing/thinking process is not confined to subjective cognitive activities, but is thoroughly social in nature. This social or collaborative model of the writing process parallels the pragmatist understanding of communication developed by George Herbert Mead, in which thinking and communication emerge in the context of group life. For Mead, human communication is closely linked to the social psychological development of the "social self." This "social self" involves the dynamic interplay between two aspects of the self—what Mead (1934) termed the "I" and the "me." The "I" is the relatively spontaneous or impulsive driving force of the self, while the "me" represents an awareness of and responsiveness to social expectations. For Mead, the development of the self involves both the generative force of the "I" and the "me's" ability to "take the role of the other" in interaction. The ability of a child to do this entails growth through two phases, from a more rudimentary "play" stage to a more sophisticated "game stage" in which the child becomes able to see actions and communications in a more complex social organizational frame that Mead terms the "generalized other." From this perspective, human cognition and interpersonal communication are inextricably intertwined, together comprising an ability to manage a dialectical interplay between the spontaneous and creative "I" and the socially responsive "me." In recent years "social compositionists" like Kenneth Bruffee and Peter Elbow, have effectively adapted this model of communication to writing instruction. Without devolving into an extended discussion of "composition theory," we can say that social compositionists have developed a variety of writing techniques that tap the synergistic interplay of the "I" and the "me" in the pursuit of effective written communication. The power of this approach lies in its understanding of writing as a recursive social process that enables writers to develop and clarify ideas and improve their communication through successive stages of idea formulation, feedback, and revision.

In contrast to the long-standing frequent advice to writers to first develop clear ideas and only then begin writing, social compositionists argue that beginning to write can be a way to start developing your ideas. Indeed, they advise against censoring yourself or pushing too hard to get clear writing at the early "pre-writing" or "free-writing" stages (Elbow 1998, pp. 13–19). By beginning to get words onto the page, they argue, you can provide yourself with proto-ideas and structure that you can revise and improve over time. Further, they have developed advice and techniques for soliciting feedback from others as well as for editing your own writing. The key to effective writing, they conclude, is moving back and forth between what Elbow (1998) has termed "messy writing" and "incisive editing."

In the pages ahead we suggest ways for proceeding with your writing that tap the creative social psychological synergy that is promoted by social compositionist theory. But first we turn our attention to the seldom discussed but fundamental issue of planning time for your writing.

When writing is viewed as a recursive social process, it becomes clear that the temporal aspects of writing must be synchronized with the social psychological activities involved in writing. Not only must time be apportioned to the various activities, but the sequencing of activities must be temporally coordinated to optimize progress. The following discussion is organized to lead you through that task sequence. You should recognize, however, that this process involves a spiral rather than linear process. You may find yourself looping back through activities discussed in the chapter several times rather than accomplishing them in a one-time linear sequence. Holding that awareness in the background then, we can turn to the loose sequence of activities.

B. Plan Your Writing Time and Place

The first time-related task is simply to set a clear and realistic schedule for your writing. Perhaps the single most obvious fact about writing is that it requires time. Yet many people fail in writing simply because they never plan to make the necessary time available or fail to follow through with their plans. Few people find writing (especially academic writing!) a "default activity," the natural way they use their time when not constrained by other demands. This, along with the often very real press of external demands, means that you must schedule writing time *and* hold to your schedule. To effectively do so, you must realistically examine the time availability in your life. Do not schedule your writing for times you are likely going to have to break. Not only is this ineffective (you find you are not getting writing done as you planned it on paper), but it also sets a bad habit of letting go of writing time. If you are not willing to make writing a regular priority, you are unlikely to develop your writing skills and achieve any sustained scholarship.

The adage "writing is 1 percent inspiration and 99 percent perspiration" captures the importance of routinely "showing up at the page." But there are also things you can do to make your time at the page more effective. Perhaps most importantly, you must have a comfortable and non-distracting place to write. Distractions in one's physical vicinity while writing are among the most pernicious enemies of writing. Sudden noises, irregular passersby, harsh and contrasting lighting, ringing phones, and myriad other matters disrupt the required concentration. Therefore, seek a secluded and pleasant place to write.

Such a place does more than protect you from random distractions. Entering a place that you identify as "the place to write" also serves to put you into a proper frame of mind. In contrast, to write in places largely identified with other kinds of activities is to be prompted to think about those other activities—and prompted to engage in them! Ideally, then, your writing place should be outfitted so that there is little else you can do when you are there than write.

We fully realize that not everyone has the luxury of a separate room or a part of a room devoted solely to writing. We also realize that even a desk or table one can call exclusively one's own is unattainable for some. Nonetheless, we urge you to strive to come as close to the ideal arrangement as your circumstances allow. If you have to bribe or cajole children, spouses, roommates, or parents to secure a little space, do it. If you have to demand, beg, or wheedle these same folks to secure a little peace, do it. On the assumption that successful completion of your project matters to you, laying claim to some peaceful time and space is probably the single most important thing you can do to achieve that goal.

II. Writing Practices

Having placed the writing process in perspective social psychologically and having emphasized the importance of finding the right time and place, we now turn to various practices that should help you do it—that is, putting words to the page.

A. Start Writing

The research you have done, complete with fieldnotes and interview transcripts, coded data, memos, diagrams, and reflexive observations should have brought several topics to the foreground. One sign of insufficient data and/or insufficient engagement with the data is that you still have nothing you want to say about the topic(s) of your study. Should this be the case, you may need to return to the field or engage in a more thorough analysis of your data. However, you should be cautious in this regard, lest you let your writing anxiety turn into an all-too-easy rationale for procrastination. If you have followed the strategies suggested in this guide, you already are likely to have several propositions or theses in some stage of development. One helpful strategy in beginning to write a report is to engage in what Howard Becker calls "free-writing:"

> [W]rite whatever comes into your head, as fast as you can type, without reference to outlines, notes, data, books or any other aids. The object is to find out what you would like to say, what all your earlier work on the topic or project has already led you to believe. (1986, p. 54)

Becker continues:

> If you can bring yourself to do this, you will make some interesting discoveries. If you follow the directions and write whatever comes into your head, you will find that you do not have the bewildering variety of choices you feared. You can see, once you have your work on paper, that most of it consists of slight variations on a very few themes. You do know what you want to say and, once you have the different versions before you, you can easily see how trivial the differences are. Or if there are real differences (though there seldom are), you now know what your choices are.
>
> If you write this way, you usually find out, by the time you get to the end of your draft, what you have in mind. (1986, pp. 54–55)

In the early stages of writing it is important to do all you can to help the writing flow. Be playful and feel free to experiment with different focusing strategies. One useful technique is to adopt a reportorial rather than analytic frame of mind. Viewing the substance of your writing as simply "something you want to say about something," you should begin to feel that writing is not so fearsome. It is merely a reporting task, a routine and mundane activity—as print journalists know very well and practice day in and day out.

At the specific and quite practical level, a reportorial frame of mind may be especially encouraged by having developed (or developing) diagrams of the sorts we described in Section V of the last chapter. Such viewing-all-at-once displays provide literal objects that have to be explained. As Miles and Huberman counsel, "Looking at the display helps you summarize and begin to see themes, patterns, and clusters. You write analytic text that clarifies and formalizes . . . [and] helps make sense of the display, and may suggest additional . . . [lines of analysis]" (1994, p. 101).

As you begin your writing you may well have many different strands of thought in mind at one time, leading to a hesitance to commit any particular strand to the page. Two different options can facilitate your breaking this writing barrier. First, you can decide to just arbitrarily pick one of the strands of thought and begin to write (a strategy we discuss more in the following section). Alternatively, you can begin writing in an ambiguous and noncommittal fashion. While this would hardly be an appropriate way to begin a final draft of a paper, it can be quite useful in getting started. Again we quote from Becker:

> Evasive vacuous sentences . . . are actually good ways to begin early drafts. They give you some leeway at a time when you don't want or need to be committed, and most important, they let you start. Write one down and you can go ahead without worrying that you have put your foot on a wrong path, because you haven't really taken a step yet. You just have to remember, when you have written the rest of what you have to say, to go back and replace these placeholders with real sentences that say what you mean. (1986, p. 54)

In short, begin by getting something on the page. Do not fret too much about getting it right (more on this later). If you are committed to the writing process, you will have plenty of time for revision ahead.

B. Write on Any Project Aspect, But Write

In the early stages of writing you can be a victim of your own success. Your research may offer so many different topics and directions that it is hard to organize and focus your thoughts on the page. One way to organize, of course, is to tentatively outline your ideas. While this is often useful, it is important to think of your outline as simply a heuristic device—as an aid to help you write. The process of thinking and (therefore) discovering while writing means that abstractly conceived outlines are not likely to be the same as the outlines of completed texts. This is as it should be. An analyst is never truly inside a topic—or on top of it—until he or she has written it up. There are, of course, degrees to which the writing process actually modifies your intentions and your outlines. You may need to modify thoroughly thought-out and already quasi-written plans and outlines only slightly. Sloppy outlines (even if well-intended) are likely to look very little like the accomplished report.

When your focus does not coincide with your outline, you are well advised to write on the aspect of your report that is foremost in your mind, whether that topic is the next one on (or even part of) your outline or not. Put more sweepingly, start (or forge ahead) with *any* part of the project that meets the key requirement of your *having something to say about it*. In turning to other writing, the topic about which you had nothing to say will be churning in your mind, both in and out of consciousness. The likelihood is that something you want to say will soon occur to you and that you will be well supplied the next time you try the topic. In making this same point, Barzun and Graff helpfully set it in the broader context of being attentive to what they term the "natural cohesion" of a project:

> Do not hesitate to write up in any order those sections of your total work that seem to have grown ripe in your mind. There is a moment in any stretch of research when all the details come together in a natural cohesion, despite small gaps and doubts. Learn to recognize that moment and seize it by composing in harmony with your inward feeling of unity. Never mind whether the portions that come out are consecutive. (1992, p. 387)

Conversely, you may have something to say about something in the context of your project but may not yet see how it fits into the larger frame you are currently using. This uncertainty of pertinence may make you hesitant to sit down and work it out in writing. Overcome that hesitation. It is better to have the piece written up and not know what to do with it than to continue to carry it around in your head or leave it at the level of only coded and memoed items. While we have emphasized the need to organize what you write—to think of propositions, to compose sorting and integrating memos—it is also the case that you can become a prisoner of organization. If in doubt about pertinence, *write* anyway. Once something is written, you may find in later days or weeks that, whether it is an elemental or a larger memo, it has a perfectly logical context. The important point is that you now already have it written out and ready to place in its newly discovered context. So, don't worry about where something goes, just *write it up*. It is much easier to rearrange the written material later than to stew endlessly over how something should fit prior to actually committing it to paper.

Being flexible about what parts of the project to write about may lead to your actual report developing very unevenly. This is quite common and need be of no concern. As you continue to write parts here and there, the corpus is growing, and the fact that an increasing portion of it *is physically out there* provides *new subjects* to have something to say about! That is, your new written texts for your report are themselves new objects about which you will have something you want to say.

C. Admit Aversion and Write Regularly Anyway

It is not difficult to understand why so many people find writing so hard and so easy to avoid. The act of writing commits thought to the page, and often our early written thoughts feel inadequate for capturing what we would like to say. Rather than experience the attendant disappointment, we hesitate to write. At other times we may begin writing only to find that we reach an impasse or that the discovery we are hoping for does not arrive. For these and other reasons, writing is difficult in the sense of being uncertain in both plan and outcome. And on top of this uncertainty, because it requires a great deal of mental concentration and sustained effort, writing is simply tiring work.

In their appendix on "a discipline for work" in *The Modern Researcher*, Barzun and Graff are even more radical and sweeping regarding problems of writing:

> Faced with the need to write, most people (including practiced writers) experience a strong and strange impulse to put off beginning. They would do anything rather than confront that blank sheet of paper. They start inventing pretexts for doing something else. . . . Let it be said once and for all: *there is no cure for this desire to escape.* It will recur as long as you live. (1992, p. 386; emphasis in the original)

But in recognizing writing as difficult and an object of avoidance, it is important to realize that many of the obstacles to writing also attend to other serious and skilled pursuits. Writing is like high-level athletics and risky work in the sense that it requires *regimens of self-discipline*. In exercising such discipline, you recognize your "desire to escape" but counter it with what Barzun and Graff term "palliatives," some of which will hopefully be "good enough to turn the struggle virtually into a game" (1992, p. 386). Two palliatives warrant mention here, with the discussion that follows proposing a variety of others.

First, to write well, one must write *regularly*. Commonly, this means writing as a routine and daily event for some minimum and rigidly adhered to length of time. No excuses. As put by Barzun and Graff, "the palliative principle is that a regular force must be used to overcome recurrent inertia: if you can arrange to write regularly, never missing your date with yourself, no matter whether you are in the mood or not, you have won half the battle. . . . The writer's problem is the inverse of the reformed drunkard's. The latter must *never* touch a drop; the former must *always* do his stint." (1992, p. 386)

Second, this self-disciplined regularity means, as Barzun and Graff indicate, that one sits down and actually writes whether one "feels like it" or not. Novice and student writers are especially prone not to "feel like" writing. (For a perspective on this, imagine athletic teams or professional performers practicing only when they "feel like it.") Some persons want even more than simply to "feel like it." They want to be inspired. We would advise such persons to pay attention to the words of prolific social science writer Rodney Stark.

> Perhaps the most disabling myth about intellectual activity is that writing is an art that is prompted by inspiration. Some writing can be classified as art, no doubt, but the act of writing is a trade in the same sense that plumbing

or automotive repair are trades. Just as plumbers and mechanics would rarely accomplish anything if they waited for inspiration to impel them to action, so writers would rarely write if they relied on inspiration. Approach the job of writing as you would approach household chores, as something you do regularly and routinely. I never have to ask myself if I feel like writing any more than I have to ask whether I feel like brushing my teeth or not. It's just what I do. (1994, p. 644)

Stark goes on to warn in particular against the student propensity to put "on a huge last-minute sprint to get a term paper completed. That's a bad way to write. It mixes writing with anxiety. When you write, you should be able to give your undivided attention to what you are saying, not to impending deadlines" (1994, p. 644).

Writing in the absence of inspiration and the motivation associated with it thus requires considerable discipline. But don't lose sight of the multiple benefits that can arise during the course of writing itself and help perpetuate the process. We have mentioned some of these in the foregoing and will note others in later sections, but it is useful to summarize them here. First, although you may find it difficult to get started, once you have started, the sense of "not feeling like it" often passes. You find yourself, instead, becoming intellectually engaged with the writing—sometimes because you've launched yourself into a process of discovery. Second, writing despite your mood increases the sheer amount of writing you produce. Having and using that growing corpus is rewarding. Third, since practice makes perfect, the more you write and the more regularly you write, the better you will write. Fourth, the more you write, the more the speed with which you write is likely to increase. Fifth and finally, for a variety of reasons, including an increasing skill level, the more you write, the less anxiety about writing you will feel.

D. Trust in Discovery and Surprise in Writing

As we have suggested earlier, the purpose of all the elaborate prior work involved in note taking, transcribing, coding, memoing, diagramming, and the like is to provide the data that your mind can process and otherwise mysteriously interact with in the activity of writing. In so mysteriously interacting, *new* ideas, connections, framings, or whatever, are created (see also Richardson 1990, 2000).

The exact words that you will use and the precise, detailed framing of whatever you want to say may yet remain unknown. Prototypically, an analytic writer looks through the materials yet one more time. Several similar but slightly different terms may present themselves for possible prominent use. The exact number and appropriate order of presenting components of the materials may seem unclear. Several different ways of wording and order of presentation may seem equally plausible. So sorting and stewing in the materials, many analysts simply begin to write despite the fact that there is still a lot of ambiguity about how exactly to say what it is they want to say. In beginning nonetheless to write, the analyst lunges into the unknown.

This is an anxious but also often exhilarating moment because, frequently, you are surprised by what you write! Certainly, you are saying what you have to say about something, but how you say it, how you approach it, the words and concepts you use, and other new matters that appear as text can all come as news to you. In other words, the *physical activity of writing* itself can bring into sharp focus and crystallize what you are trying to say or even produce new insights that layer or elaborate what you have to say about something in ways that you didn't anticipate.

When such a flow of discovery begins, it is important not to disrupt it with concerns over little gaps. In particular, "resist the temptation to get up and verify a fact. Leave it blank. The same holds true for the word or phrase that refuses to come to mind. It will arise much more easily on revision, and the economy in time *and momentum* are incalculable" (Barzun and Graff 1992, pp. 387–88; emphasis in the original).

Therefore, when you start writing, be prepared for, and open to, novelty, excitement, exhilarating new lines of thought, and (perhaps) some dismay. But don't be frightened by unexpected turns of events. The discoveries that occur while writing can only make your final written report more interesting.

E. Do Not Seek Perfection or the One Right Way

It is not uncommon for analysts to be dissatisfied with the quality of at least a portion of their work. For some, this leads to extended periods of more data collection, more coding, memo writing, revising, and the like. In the desire to make them perfect, or almost perfect, analysts often let projects drag on and on.

Although high standards of craft in fieldstudies are to be expected, there is no such thing as the perfect study. Once you have exercised due diligence, methodical care, analytic zeal, and careful writing, a proper sense of proportion counsels that projects must be concluded, even when they are clearly not perfect. Every reasonable person recognizes and accepts the fact that no study is without flaws. Indeed, any study claiming to be perfect is suspect for that reason! It is even part of the formal process of reporting one's inquiry to state the specific ways in which a study does or does not do particular things.

One particularly noteworthy form of the self-destructive quest for perfection is what Howard Becker (1986) has described as the error of the One Right Way. Using the language of seeking a propositional answer to a question posed about a topic (Chapters 6–9), some fieldworkers embrace the idea that there must be One Right Way to do analysis in the sense that there must be one correct proposition with which to organize one's work. Uncertainty over having found it paralyzes the analyst. Or, having successfully formulated a proposition with which to organize the data, the analyst believes that there must be One Right Way to represent that organizational format.

Becker argues that there is *no One Right Way*, and we very much agree with him. There is no single, unique, obviously correct way to analyze one's data or to set forth the prose of one's report, and it is fruitless to seek one (see also Fine 1988). Becker illustrates one form of the error of One Right Way thinking with the organizational choice he faced in presenting data from his study of Chicago schoolteachers. He studied (1) relations teachers had with (a) students, (b) parents, (c) principals, and (d) other teachers in (2) (a) slum, (b) working-class, and (c) upper-middle-class schools. As these form a two-dimensional typology with twelve cells, should he organize his report in terms of relations within which he discusses schools or in terms of schools within which he discusses relations? Becker's answer is that there is no One Right Way. Each way has its merits and demerits. And, either way, Becker says, "I would report the same results (although in a different order) and arrive at the same conclusions (although the terms they were put in and their emphases would differ)" (1986, p. 58). Such a logic extends to other forms of seeking the One Right Way.

Lest there be misunderstanding, we need also to say that this point relates to the central propositions developed and the organization of elements in reports and not to empirical "trueness," as discussed in Chapter 8, Section I.A. A set of reports on the same topic can all be true to their empirical base, but still focus on different propositions and be organized very differently. It is in these senses that there is no One Right Way.

F. Divide and Conquer

One of the greatest difficulties of writing a report of any substantial length is that there is so much to be addressed that it cannot possibly be done all at once. The writing for even an article-length report—let alone a thesis or book—extends over a significant amount of time. Consistent with our earlier comments, Zerubavel (1999) likens the writer's task to that of endurance athletes. "Like long-distance runners, cross-country bikers, and mountain climbers," he notes, "writers traverse a long road paved with serious doubts, wondering whether they will ever be able to reach their final goal" (p. 37). To effectively deal with this problem, Zerubavel suggests a strategy similar to that used by many such athletes:

> The solution lies in learning to think about your manuscript not only as one single piece, but also as a collection of a number of smaller, and therefore more manageable, pieces.
>
> In other words, you can quite easily manage the most formidable tasks if you only learn to break them down in your head into a number of less ambitious and thus also less intimidating mini-tasks, the completion of each

of which is well within your reach. You must therefore stop regarding the completion of the entire thesis, book, or dissertation you are writing as your only goal and concentrate instead on completing each of the various segments into which you have broken it down, *one at a time.* (pp. 37–38)

Smaller tasks or sections fit more easily within discrete work sessions than do whole manuscripts. When you break down your report into smaller sections and subsections, you can more easily plan your work goals day by day and revel in their accomplishment. An outline is an invaluable aid in this, providing a sequence of tasks needed to complete your manuscript. However, once again, be careful not to reify your outline—it should be a provisional structure that can be revised as you proceed. (For a useful discussion of outlining, see Zerubavel 1999, pp. 39–46.)

G. Draw on Standard Literary Organizing Devices

One set of aids for dividing and conquering your field materials, as well as organizing your report and focusing attention on aspects of your analysis, includes various literary devices and strategies that have been used in literature across the ages. With the virtual explosion over the past twenty years in "writing about writing" in social science, and particularly in relation to ethnographic fieldwork (e.g., Agar 1990; Atkinson 1990, 1992; Becker 1986; Behar and Gordon 1995; Bochner and Ellis 2001; Brown 1992; Clifford and Marcus 1986; Ellis and Bochner 1996; Fine 1988; Geertz 1988; Krieger 1991; Reed-Danahay 1997, 2001; Richardson 1990, 1992, 2000; Van Maanen 1988; Wolcott 1990, 2001; M. Wolf 1992), fieldworkers have become increasingly sensitized not only to the ways in which their writings have employed these very techniques, albeit often unwittingly, but to the literary utility of doing so consciously. In Chapter 8, we introduced and briefly discussed two of the more pervasive literary techniques: metaphor (Section I.C.3.c) and irony (Section I.C.3.d). Here we identify a number of additional literary devices in order to increase your awareness of them and in hopes of getting you to think about their use as you organize and finalize your written reports.

- *Entitlement as a Framing Device:* Effective titles establish frameworks that focus attention, set expectations, and suggest what to look for, and thus direct and facilitate reader interpretation (Atkinson 1990, pp. 75–81). Most fieldwork titles take one of three forms: straightforward statements of the focal topic, as with Kevin Henson's *Just a Temp* (1996) and Mitchell Duneier's *Sidewalk* (1999); a topical/generic pairing, as with Mary Pattillo-McCoy's *Black Picket Fences: Privilege and Peril Among the Black Middle Class* (1999); Sudhir Venkatesh's *American Project: The Rise and Fall of a Modern Ghetto* (2000); or a generic/topical pairing, as with Leslie Salzinger's *Genders in Production: Making Workers in Mexico's Global Factories* (2003) and

Pierrette Hondagneu-Sotelo's *Gendered Transitions: Mexican Experiences of Immigrants* (1994).

- *Hypotyposis*: This term denotes the use of highly graphic and vivid descriptions of a scene or line of action in a fashion that is gripping and compelling (Atkinson 1990, pp. 71–75). Such passages, often referred to as descriptive vignettes, help to develop the setting and its actors so as to make it appear that the author was in fact there and even to make the reader seem like an eyewitness. Such vignettes typically introduce a book, chapters, or papers and articles.

- *Synecdoche*: A synecdoche is a rhetorical device in which a part is presumed to stand for the whole, such as the gavel for law, DNA for life, the test tube for an experiment, and so on (Richardson, 1990, pp. 17–18). It says something about the whole via examination of just a part. Although not always explicit, it is nonetheless often a strategic device in much fieldwork, as illustrated by Evans-Pritchard's (1937) focus on Azande witchcraft and magic as the keys to understanding the Azande, Whyte's study (1993) of the Norton gang as an avenue for getting at the organized character of slum life, and Geertz's (1973) characterization of cockfighting among the Balinese as the portal through which Balinese society can be understood.

- *Narrative*: Simply conceptualized, narratives are stories about events and/or lives—individual or collective—that are organized sequentially either chronologically, consequentially, or thematically (Riessman 1993, p. 17). Narratives can access and elaborate the human experience from different vantage points—for example, the everyday, the autobiographical, the biographical, the cultural, or the collective (Richardson 1990, pp. 22–26), but whatever the subject or point of reference, they are stories we tell that situate events or lives in a temporal, causal, or thematic sequence, thus rendering the events or lives meaningful in terms of the sequence in which they are embedded. Research reports may incorporate narrative in a variety of ways. They may include methods stories that describe the dilemmas, deliberations, and actions that guided the data-collection process. Anecdotal mini-narratives are frequently used to illustrate abstract analytic concepts. And reports themselves are narratives of sorts that seek to tell a broader story. Knowing something about the different ways in which narratives can be constructed, as well as other features of narratives (see Cortazzi 2001, Richardson 1990, and Riessman 1993, among many other works on the topic), is very important because it means that you may have some alternatives to consider when organizing and writing your report. Further, since research reports are narratives, it is probably a good idea for you to think a bit about not only the kind of story you want to tell, but also about the kind of story that is most resonant with the data you have accumulated. But while we urge you to attend to the narrative aspects of your writing, we would also caution you to keep cognizant throughout the writing process of your analytic goals. The point is not just to tell a good story or stories, but to do so in service of your over-arching analytic goals consistent with the social science framing discussed in the last chapter.

H. Find Your Own Working Style

The various writing practices we have accented and elaborated represent our attempt to help you jump-start your writing and stick with it. Nonetheless, these practices can sometimes be unhelpful and possibly even counterproductive, at least for some writers. This is because each of the suggested practices works well for some writers but not for others. It is inevitable that one or more of our suggestions will not be helpful to someone. That being the case, we must emphasize that the preeminent writing practice is to *find and use your own style of working*. Be aware of the kinds of things we report above as commonly productive writing practices, certainly, but do not assume that each must work for you.

We are mindful that the underlying image of the writer embodied in the above set of practices is that of the *steady plodder*—someone who writes a little each day, methodically and laboriously building up their reports. They grind them out slowly, writing and analyzing in detail as they go along.

While we believe this image accurately captures the largest portion of writers, we also know that it does not fit everyone. There are also those we might call *grand sweepers*, persons who write very little actual text at first, but, instead, work out an analysis very carefully and in detail in the form of outlines and organized notes. After completing this organizing process, they then write the entire report in sequence from beginning to end in one fell swoop. Writing becomes the overriding and single governing principle of their lives for whatever period it takes to put their report into text. Bear in mind that this grand sweeper working style must not be confused with the *student goof-off* pattern. This pattern refers to the practice of "goofing off" all term and then writing a thirty-page paper by staying up all night before it is due. In fundamental contrast to the student goof-off pattern, the grand sweeper has performed extremely detailed and hard analytic labor before beginning to write. The analytic effort is no different from that of the steady plodder, who is analyzing and writing at the same time. The grand sweeper has simply segregated the tasks of analytic thought and detailed writing.

In our treatment throughout this guide, it is clear that we prefer the steady plodder over the grand sweeper. But we must nonetheless acknowledge that grand sweeping works for some people and can produce true, new, and important fieldstudies. Beyond our preferences, we describe this contrast in order to make the larger point that, irrespective of all the good advice you can get, you must in the end develop your own working style, and it may not be either of these.

I. Reread and Revise

Using the practices described above, over time you will amass a significant amount of writing. You are likely to find some portions of what you have written clear and satisfying in the ways they capture issues you are interested in addressing. Other parts of your writing may feel considerably less adequate to you. Most likely, significant portions of what you have written will not yet be well-articulated and/or will be poorly connected to the writing that surrounds them. And overall your writing is likely to lack a tight and compelling structure. It is important to recognize this state of affairs for what it is: an appropriate level of writing for the stage you have reached. While at first you may be frustrated with the lack of clarity and focus in your early writings, it is important to understand that most early writing tends to be this way, and that it is not only acceptable, but actually appropriate writing for this stage.

But the writing process should not stop here. At this point you need to turn your energy and focus away from writing and direct it toward editing the written draft you have produced. You have nothing to edit, of course, until you have been a productive writer. But, as we have noted, the very knowledge that your early writing is not final writing—that you will edit it later—should free you to "let your creative juices flow." Indeed, good writing must achieve a synergistic balance between the creative energies of the Meadian "I" and the editorial acumen of the Meadian "me."

Novice writers seldom understand the value of revision, but it is a staple practice of experienced writers. With confidence in the power of revision, writers can anticipate dramatic improvement in their work as they take it through successive stages of writing and editing. Seasoned writers come to depend on revision. Indeed it is a critical activity in the scholarly publication process; most articles published in academic journals only reach publication after going through an official "revise and resubmit" stage of development. Of course, as with other activities, the power of editing and revising depend on your ability to do them effectively. And while we do not wish to be overly prescriptive, we can offer some observations and advice from our collective experience and the observations of other scholarly writers.

In practice, editing and revision emerge in two different contexts. First, there is the editing that you as a writer do in response to your personal reading of your materials. Second, there is editing that is based on the feedback you may receive from other readers of your written drafts. In this section we focus on the first kind of editing and in the next section we will discuss effective use of external feedback.

One of the most useful outcomes of having written something is that the ideas are now *externalized* and therefore physically available to you as something you can scrutinize. Written analyses become objects that you can literally see. With such objects before you, you can begin to take the same actively analytic stance toward your writing as you have heretofore taken toward whatever you have been studying. You should do this at two levels: the sentence and the analytic unit.

Revision at the sentence level entails just what it implies: rereading and revising, as deemed appropriate, one sentence after another. Revision at the level of the "analytic unit" refers to revisions of paragraph or longer pieces of text, up to and including the entire report. Whatever the length of the analytic unit, you should scrutinize and revise it in any number of terms, including points overlooked, assertions undocumented, logical inconsistencies, gaps or leaps, possible criticisms unanswered, transition sections unwritten, and so on.

Before the advent of the personal computer, revision of either type was a laboriously mechanical task of marking up text on paper and retyping. It was so laborious, in fact, that people spoke of "first," "second," and additional numbered drafts, which referred to occasions of complete retyping so as to incorporate accumulated and often scrawled changes.

With the computer, revision is a whiz and a continuous process, and the concept of discrete drafts no longer describes the reality. Of course, not all successful writers espouse such continuous editing. Some, like Zerubavel (see esp. 1999, pp. 46–55 and 82–85), strongly prefer to look back very little as they write a draft, then upon completion of the draft turn to revision of their corpus of writing as a whole. But whether revision occurs on a somewhat ongoing basis or in periodic waves, keep in mind two key considerations: first, whatever you write is not written in stone and therefore can be revised; and second, revision, at both the sentence and analytic levels, almost always improves the quality of the final report. Thus, there is really no good reason for not devoting some time to revision of what you have written. You may encounter a formidable obstacle, however: your ego and associated attachments to what you have already written. Our advice, as we will elaborate shortly, is to check it at the door of the room or space in which you write.

J. Seek Feedback

In keeping with the view of writing as a social process, social compositionists emphasize the potential value of feedback. Getting feedback helps you see how accessible and meaningful your writing is to others and can enable you to see where and how it can be improved. Seeking feedback allows you to broaden your editorial circle to include new perspectives and fresh insights. As Peter Elbow (1998, p. 237) notes, "No matter how productively you managed to get words down on paper or how carefully you have revised, no matter how shrewdly you figured your audience and purpose and suited your words to them, there comes the time when you need feedback." Just any feedback at any time, however, will not do. You need appropriate feedback at appropriate times. Avoid soliciting feedback too early in the writing process, "when you are still somewhat insecure about your project and unable to respond to criticism" (Zerubavel 1999, p. 78), lest it inhibit your ability to write. You need time to get your ideas out on the page and to grapple with them yourself. Once you have a relatively complete draft—a full but by no means perfect piece of writing—then you are in a position to benefit from feedback.

On the other hand, you should also avoid holding off on feedback until you have what you feel is your best possible draft. While it can be tempting to wait until you have given the piece your best—thus avoiding unnecessary criticism of your writing—such a strategy has serious pitfalls. Most significantly, you are less likely to be able to assimilate and productively use the reactions that you receive if you are highly invested in viewing the draft as your best work. For this reason, Zerubavel counsels, "It is important to seek feedback between early drafts, when you are still open to suggestions and are willing to incorporate them into your manuscript" (1999, p. 78).

In seeking productive feedback you need to attend to two issues: who to seek feedback from and what form it should take. In relation to the first issue, Becker has noted, "[N]ot everyone is a good audience for early drafts. . . . Some people, finding it difficult to treat early drafts as early, insist on criticizing them with standards appropriate to finished products. Some readers have better editorial judgment than others and you need a circle of people you can trust to respond appropriately to the stage your work is in" (1986, p. 18). While Becker's point is certainly valid, it is often the case that readers give trite and inappropriate feedback simply because they have not received sufficient guidance as to what they are being asked to do. You can easily reduce this problem by familiarizing yourself with the feedback techniques that have been developed by composition scholars (some of whose textbooks you quite likely have used in college writing courses)—such as Peter Elbow's (1998, pp. 240–277) discussion of "criterion-based" and "reader-based" feedback and writing support groups. Well-focused reaction to your writing can be an invaluable asset in the revision process. (For further excellent guidance on soliciting, giving, and receiving editorial feedback, see Elbow and Belanoff 2002 and Bruffee 1997.)

K. Constrain Your Ego and Related Attachments

We suggested above that your ego and attachments to what you have already written may function as serious obstacles to fine-tuning your analysis and writing your final reports. If these potential obstacles loom as likely impediments to your analysis and writing, then clearly it is important to consider ways in which their influence might be constrained or muted. Here we suggest two such strategic considerations.

The first concerns the fact that it is very unlikely that all the materials you have worked hard to gather and analyze will logically or neatly resonate with the way in which you have framed your analysis and organized your report. Whether you become aware of this in your own editing or through the responses of others to your draft, you must simply face the hard truth that no matter how well conceived your final report, it is very unlikely that it can accommodate everything you have worked on and even worked up as fairly polished writing. You must, then, live with the "agony of omission."

But take heart because there are several mechanisms of ancillary accommodation that you can sometimes use. First, you can tack on a related piece of analysis as an appendix. Second, you can insert it at some point (such as at the end of a section or chapter) as a digression and frankly label it as such. Third, you can treat it briefly in a footnote. Fourth, if it is very general, it can appear in a preface, epilogue, or afterword. And there is always the possibility of an altogether separate report.

The second consideration to keep in mind is the psychological utility of providing yourself with some temporal distance from your report before it is time to present or submit it. The best way to do this, of course, is to complete the report well in advance of when it is scheduled for presentation and then put it away for a reasonable period of time. Then, just prior to presentation, give it another full rereading and revision. By not looking at it for a period of time, the ego you have invested in it has an opportunity to "drain out" and the fixed view of it you had developed can be loosened or forgotten. We all tend to develop a "locked in" view of a project on which we have been working. This view might be a very good and insightful one. Then again, it might not be. By backing off from a piece of writing for a while, getting your mind off of it, and losing your commitment to what you had in mind, you can later come back with a fresh perspective. You will then be in a better frame of mind to decide whether or not your draft was really "so hot." Even if on rereading you decide it really is quite fine and that only some prose needs revision, it will at least be improved in that regard.

The phrase "well in advance" is obviously ambiguous, and its exact meaning will vary by circumstance. One such variation is the length of the report and therefore the amount of work involved in a final revision. Even with short reports, though, such as fifteen-page student papers, an interval of at least several days between completion and revision seems to us a minimum.

A similar process of letting the ego drain out and letting fixed approaches dissipate also applies to bothersome sections of a report—sections that you have trouble organizing or writing. Difficulties may mean that something is basically wrong with the section. But they may also simply mean that you have not yet discovered the most cogent thing to say about the topic or the best way to organize it. Rather than engage in prolonged stewing, turn to some other section and temporarily forget about the troublesome one. When you return to it, a fresh start may resolve the previous difficulties.

L. Let It Go

Finally, the day comes to conclude your revisions and let go of your manuscript. While rewriting could ostensibly be endless, at some point the deadline for a manuscript arrives or the marginal utility of yet another revision is too minimal to warrant doing it. Even if you believe you could keep improving the piece, that is not always the case. As Becker notes, "Painting teachers encourage students not to overpaint a picture, continuing to put paint on the canvas until an initially good idea is buried in a muddy mess. Writers [too] can worry a piece to death" (1986, p. 131).

While you may feel insecure in your decision to let a manuscript go, the alternative of revising indefinitely is counterproductive. One obvious strategy for reaching closure is to set a target date for completion. Such a self-imposed deadline can provide motivation for sticking to your writing regimen and can be "the most effective way to put a necessary stop to what may otherwise become an endless Sisyphean ordeal" (Zerubavel 1999, p. 89). If you have conscientiously adhered to the practices delineated above, the manuscript you have produced is likely to approximate the best you can write at this time. It is time to share it with a broader audience. If you are sending it out for review for publication, you will almost certainly receive suggestions for yet further revisions. But having been through the revision process before, you should be able to respond to the editorial advice productively when that time comes.

III. Concluding Observations

In this guide, we have called attention to a number of both positive and negative experiences you might have in conducting and writing up a fieldstudy. Among negative experiences, we noted, for example, anxiety and fear. Among positive experiences, there can be exhilaration, playful fun, and a sense of adventure. We want now to add to these sometime accompaniments the possibility of a profound creative experience. We mean by this that you may experience the formulation or discovery of a proposition as a thrilling revelation, as a moment when the "blinders" fall from your eyes and you behold a new order in your materials and, hopefully, in social reality.

It will take further and careful checking to determine whether your discovery is original as well as creative, but your accomplishment is in no way diminished by having had predecessors. On the other hand, further checking may determine that you actually have done something new and important that deserves a very wide audience. In that case, you can add an achievement of consequence to your experience of creativity.

As noted above, one oft-quoted maxim about creativity—as about writing—is that it is "99 percent perspiration and 1 percent inspiration." People experience creative insight as something that happens to them. But, so goes the wisdom, creative moments seem to happen more often to people who are otherwise working very hard on their projects. The moral is that the best way to ensure creativity is to exercise a great deal of enterprising diligence.

But even in the absence of creative flashes, one can aim for the more common but no less impressive achievement of work that is elegant, thorough, clear, and carefully organized. Such an achievement requires neither exceptional creativity nor an especially sharp intelligence. Rather, what it requires is the sustained application of methodical effort, activity, and *enterprise*. The methodical, active, enterprising researcher-analyst searches out data that less diligent colleagues overlook and carries out analysis beyond the point where less diligent colleagues stop. Such persons stand in stark contrast to those who assume a stance of passive dependence. The latter expects others to guide them each step of the way; in the face of a situation calling for get-up-and-go, they offer only stone-like immobility. Unsurprisingly, they usually fail to accomplish much of anything at all.

We conclude the journey we have made in this guide with observations on the fieldstudy perspective, scholarship more generally, and the hazards embodied in methodological advice.

A. The Fieldstudies Approach as a System of Parts

The ten aspects of the fieldstudies or naturalistic perspective we have expounded in this guide tend, in our assessment, toward a more or less coherent system in which any selected subset of these parts seems logically to imply the others. Most broadly, the elements of the "gathering" phase seem to cohere, in a reasonably logical fashion, with the elements of the "focusing" and "analyzing" phases. But as we have mentioned at several points in previous chapters, not all social scientists embrace the idea that there is (or should be) a logically consistent relation among these ten parts. There are at least two major patterns or "schools" of disagreement. The first, the purely descriptive ethnographers, assert that one needs only the first phase, that of gathering. Focusing and analyzing are not required, and reporting is accomplished in an ordinary narrative manner. The second, the extreme grounded theorists, take the opposite view: They regard matters of focus and analysis as especially relevant but believe that the data can be gathered from almost anywhere in almost any fashion. These and other patterns suggest, perhaps, that the ten aspects of the naturalistic approach we have presented may not, indeed, have any inherent logical interrelation. At least that interrelation is not sufficiently obvious to produce unanimity. But even if the interrelation is not inherent, there are important reasons for considering these elements a systemic package. Together they form a constraining discipline and a creative experience that begins with an experiential or intellectual relation to a situation or setting and proceeds by steps to articulate that connection in ways that are understandable and useful to wider audiences. To omit or skimp on any part is to weaken the product—to diminish the depth of the data, the precision of the focus, or the incisiveness of the analysis.

B. The Similarity of All Scholarship

It is important to conclude by recognizing that despite some distinctive features, qualitative fieldwork research and analysis are, in the respects that count most, the same as all other research and analysis. The particulars of the source materials may differ, as may difficulties in gathering material and the substance of analysis, but the essential process is identical to other kinds of intellectual endeavor. The elements of this essential similarity include tenacious commitment to systematic observation, willingness to consider alternative explanations, careful and thoughtful analysis, and clarity of expression. Happily, all these qualities can be learned. But, like all learning, they are acquired through practice, which means getting out and doing it—that is, fieldwork and its constituent elements of data gathering, focusing, and analyzing.

REFERENCES

Abbott, Andrew. 1995. "Sequence Analysis: New Methods for Old Ideas." *Annual Review of Sociology* 21: 93–113.

———. 2001. *Time Matters: On Theory and Method*. Chicago, IL: University of Chicago Press.

Abolafia, Mitchel. 1996. *Making Markets: Opportunism and Restraint on Wall Street*. Cambridge, MA: Harvard University Press.

Adams, Jacqueline. 1998. "The Wrongs of Reciprocity: Fieldwork among Chilean Working-Class Women." *Journal of Contemporary Ethnography* 27: 219–241.

Adler, Patricia A. 1993. *Wheeling and Dealing: An Ethnography of an Upper-Level Drug Dealing and Smuggling Community* (2nd ed.). New York: Columbia University Press.

Adler, Patricia A., and Peter Adler. 1987. *Membership Roles in Field Research*. Newbury Park, CA: Sage.

———. 1991. *Backboards & Blackboards: College Athletes and Role Engulfment*. New York: Columbia University Press.

———. 1998. *Peer Power: Preadolescent Culture and Identity*. New Brunswick, NJ: Rutgers University Press.

———. 2002. "Do University Lawyers and the Police Define Research Values?" Pp. 34–42 in *Walking the Tightrope: Ethical Issues for Qualitative Researchers*, edited by Will C. van den Hoonaard. Toronto: University of Toronto Press.

Adler, Patricia, Peter Adler, and John M. Johnson (eds.). 1992. *Street Corner Society Revisited*. Newbury Park, CA: Sage. (A special issue of the *Journal of Contemporary Ethnography* 21 [no. 1])

Agar, Michael. 1973. *Ripping and Running*. New York: Seminar.

———. 1990. "Text and Fieldwork: Exploring the Excluded Middle." *Journal of Contemporary Ethnography* 19: 73–88.

———. 1991. "The Right Brain Strikes Back." Pp. 181–194 in *Using Computers in Qualitative Research*, edited by N. G. Fielding and R. M. Lee. Newbury Park, CA: Sage.

Åkerström, Malin. 2002. "Slaps, Pinches—But Not Violence: Boundary Work in Nursing Homes for the Elderly." *Symbolic Interaction* 25: 515–536.

Albas, Daniel, and Cheryl Albas. 1988. "Aces and Bombers: The Post-Exam Impression Management Strategies of Students" *Symbolic Interaction* 11: 289–302.

Allayhari, Rebecca A. 2000. *Visions of Charity: Volunteer Workers and Moral Community*. Berkeley: University of California Press.

Allen, Charlotte. 1997. "Spies Like Us: When Sociologists Deceive Their Subjects." *Lingua Franca* (November): 31–39.

Allon, Natalie. 1979. *Urban Life Styles*. Dubuque, IA: William C. Brown.

Altheide, David L., and John M. Johnson. 1994. "Criteria for Assessing Interpretative Validity in Qualitative Research." Pp. 485–499 in *Handbook of Qualitative Research*, edited by N. K. Denzin and Y. S. Lincoln. Thousand Oaks, CA: Sage.

American Sociological Association. 1997. *Code of Ethics*. Washington, DC: American Sociological Association.

Anderson, Elijah. 1976. *A Place on the Corner*. Chicago: University of Chicago Press.

———. 1990. *Streetwise: Race, Class, and Change in an Urban Community*. Chicago: University of Chicago Press.

———. 1999. *Code of the Street: Decency, Violence, and the Moral Life of the Inner City*. New York: W. W. Norton.

Anderson, Leon. 2003. "'SOS' and 'Pieces of Eight': Edgework among the Elderly and the Maimed." Society for the Study of Symbolic Interaction Meetings, Atlanta, GA.

Anderson, Leon, and Thomas C. Calhoun. 1992. "Facilitative Aspects of Field Research with Deviant Street Populations." *Sociological Inquiry* 62: 490–498.

Anderson, Leon, David Snow, and Daniel Cress. 1994. "Negotiating the Public Realm: Stigma Management and Collective Action among the Homeless." Pp. 121–143 in *The Community of the Streets*, edited by Spencer E. Cahill and Lyn Lofland. Greenwich, CT: JAI Press.

Anspach, Renee R. 1993. *Deciding Who Lives: Fateful Choices in the Intensive-Care Nursery*. Berkeley, CA: University of California Press.

Arditti, Rita. 1999. *Searching for Life: The Grandmothers of the Plaza de Mayo and the Disappeared Children of Argentina*. Berkeley, CA: University of California Press.

Atkinson, Paul. 1990. *The Ethnographic Imagination: Textual Constructions of Reality*. New York: Routledge.

———. 1992. *Understanding Ethnographic Texts*. Newbury Park, CA: Sage.

———. 1995. *Medical Talk and Medical Work*. Thousand Oaks, CA: Sage.

Atkinson, Paul, Amanda Coffey, Sara Delamont, John Lofland, and Lyn Lofland (eds.). 2001. *Handbook of Ethnography*. Thousand Oaks, CA: Sage.

Babbie, Earl R. 2003. *The Practice of Social Research*. (8th ed.). Belmont, CA: Wadsworth.

Baca Zinn, Maxine. 2001. "Insider Field Research in Minority Communities." Pp. 159–166 in *Contemporary Field Research: A Collection of Readings*, edited by R. M. Emerson. (2nd ed.). Prospect Heights, IL: Waveland Press.

Banks, Anna, and Stephen P. Banks (eds.). 1998. *Fiction and Social Research*. Walnut Creek, CA: Altamira.

Banks, Marcus. 2001. *Visual Methods in Social Research*. Thousand Oaks, CA: Sage.

Barzun, Jacques, and Henry E. Graff. 1992. *The Modern Researcher*. (5th ed.). New York: Harcourt Brace Jovanovich.

Baumgartner, M. P. 1988. *The Moral Order of a Suburb*. New York: Oxford University Press.

Becker, Howard S. 1953. "Becoming a Marijuana User." *American Journal of Sociology* 59: 235–242.

———. 1986. *Writing for Social Scientists: How to Start and Finish Your Thesis, Book, or Article.* Chicago: University of Chicago Press.

———. 1998. *Tricks Of The Trade: How To Think About Your Research While You're Doing It.* Chicago: University of Chicago Press.

Beckford, James. 1983. "Talking of Apostasy: Telling Tales and 'Telling' Tales." Pp. 281–298 in *Accounting for Action*, edited by M. Muklay and N. Gilbert. London: Greenwood Press.

Behar, Ruth. 1993. *Translated Woman: Crossing the Border with Esperanza's Story.* Boston: Beacon.

———. 1996. *The Vulnerable Observer: Anthropology That Breaks Your Heart.* Boston: Beacon Press.

Behar, Ruth, and Deborah A. Gordon (eds.). 1995. *Women Writing Culture.* Berkeley: University of California Press.

Bell, Michael Mayerfeld. 1994. *Childerly: Nature and Morality in a Country Village.* Chicago: University of Chicago Press.

Benford, Robert D. 1987. *Framing Activity, Meaning, and Social Movement Participation: The Nuclear Disarmament Movement.* Ph.D. Thesis. University of Texas, Austin.

Berg, Bruce L. 2004. *Qualitative Research Methods for the Social Sciences.* (5th ed.). Boston: Allyn and Bacon.

Berger, Bennett M. 1981. *The Survival of the Counterculture: Ideological Work and Everyday Life among Rural Communards.* Berkeley: University of California Press.

Berger, Peter L. 1963. *Invitation to Sociology.* Garden City, NY: Doubleday.

———. 1979. "Sociology as a Form of Consciousness." Pp. 2–18 in *Social Interaction*, edited by H. Robboy, S. Greenblatt, and C. Clark. New York: St. Martin's Press.

Berger, Peter L., and Thomas Luckmann. 1967. *The Social Construction of Reality.* Garden City, NY: Doubleday.

Bernard, H. Russell. 1994. *Research Methods for Anthropology: Qualitative and Quantitative Approaches.* Thousand Oaks, CA: Sage.

Bernstein, Stan. 1978. "Getting It Done: Notes on Student Fritters." Pp. 17–23 in *Interaction in Everyday Life*, edited by J. Lofland. Beverly Hills, CA: Sage.

Best, Joel. 1994. "Lost in the Ozone Again: The Postmodernist Fad and Interactionist Foibles." In *Studies in Symbolic Interaction* (Vol. 17), edited by N. K. Denzin. Greenwich, CT: JAI Press.

Biernacki, Patrick, and Dan Waldorf. 1981. "Snowball Sampling: Problems and Techniques of Chain Referral Sampling." *Sociological Methods and Research* 10: 141–163.

Biggart, Nicole W. 1989. *Charismatic Capitalism: Direct Selling Organizations in America.* Chicago: University of Chicago Press.

Blalock, Herbert. 1979. *Social Statistics.* (2nd ed.). New York: McGraw-Hill.

Blee, Kathleen M. 2002. *Inside Organized Racism: Women in the Hate Movement.* Berkeley: University of California Press.

Bloor, Michael, Jane Frankland, Michelle Thomas, and Kate Robson. 2001. *Focus Groups in Social Research.* Thousand Oaks, CA: Sage.

Blumer, Herbert. 1969. *Symbolic Interactionism: Perspective and Method.* Upper Saddle River, NJ: Prentice Hall.

Bochner, Arthur P., and Carolyn Ellis (eds.). 2001. *Ethnographically Speaking: Autoethnography, Literature, and Aesthetics*. Walnut Creek, CA: AltaMira Press.

Boelin, W. A. Marianne. 1992. "Street Corner Society Revisited." *Journal of Contemporary Ethnography* 21: 11–51.

Bogard, Cynthia J. 2003. *Seasons Such as These: How Homelessness Took Shape in America*. Hawthorne, NY: Aldine de Gruyter.

Bok, Sissela. 1983. *Secrets: On The Ethics of Concealment and Revelation*. New York: Vintage Books.

Bosk, Charles L. 1979. *Forgive and Remember: Managing Medical Failure*. Chicago: University of Chicago Press.

———. 1985. "The Fieldworker as Watcher and Witness." *Hastings Center Report* 15 (no. 3): 10–14.

———. 1996. "The Fieldworker and the Surgeon." Pp. 119–138 in *In the Field: Readings on the Field Research Experience*, edited by Carolyn D. Smith and William Kornblum. New York: Praeger.

Bourgois, Philippe. 1995. *In Search of Respect: Selling Crack in El Barrio*. New York: Cambridge University Press.

Brajuha, Mario, and Lyle Hallowell. 1986. "Legal Intrusion and the Politics of Fieldwork." *Urban Life* 14: 454–478.

Bronfenbrenner, Urie. 1952. "Principles of Professional Ethics." *American Psychologist* 7: 452–455.

Brown, Richard Harvey. 1977. *A Poetic for Sociology: Toward a Logic of Discovery for the Human Sciences*. New York: Cambridge University Press.

——— (ed.). 1992. *Writing the Social Text: Poetics and Politics in Social Science Discourse*. Hawthorne, NY: Aldine de Gruyter.

Bruffee, Kenneth. 1997. *A Short Course in Writing: Composition, Collaborative Writing, and Constructive Reading*. (4th ed.). Boston, MA: Addison-Wesley Press.

Bulmer, Martin (ed.). 1982. *Social Research Ethics: An Examination of the Merits of Covert Participant Observation*. New York: Holmes and Meier.

Bunis, William J., Angela Yancik, and David A. Snow. 1996. "The Cultural Patterning of Sympathy Toward the Homeless and Other Victims of Misfortune." *Social Problems* 43: 301–317.

Buroway, Michael. 1972. *The Colour of Class: From African Advancement to Zambianization*. Manchester: Manchester University Press.

———. 1979. *Manufacturing Consent*. Chicago: University of Chicago Press.

———. 1998. "The Extended Case Method." *Sociological Theory* 16: 4–33.

———. 2003. "Revisits: An Outline of A Theory of Reflexive Ethnography." *American Sociological Review* 68: 645–679.

Burawoy, Michael, Joseph A. Blum, Sheba George, Zsuzsa Gille, Teresa Gowan, Lynne Hancy, Maren Klawiter, Steve H. Lopez, Sean O. Riain, and Millie Thayer. 2000. *Global Ethnography: Forces, Connections, and Imaginations in a Postmodern World*. Berkeley: University of California Press.

Burawoy, Michael, Alice Burton, Ann Arnett Ferguson, Kathryn J. Fox, Joshua Gamson, Nadine Gartrell, Leslie Hurst, Charles Kurzman, Leslie Salzinger, Josepha Schiffman, and Shiori Ui. 1991. *Ethnography Unbound: Power and Resistance in the Modern Metropolis*. Berkeley: University of California Press.

Cahill, Spencer E. (with William Distler, Cynthia Lachowetz, Andrea Meaney, Robyn Tarallo, and Tenna Willard). 1985. "Meanwhile Backstage: Public Bathrooms and the Interaction Order." *Urban Life* 14: 33–58.

Cahill, Spencer E. 1986. "Language Practices and Self Definition: The Case of Gender Identity Acquisition." *Sociological Quarterly* 27: 295–311.

———. 1989. "Fashioning Males and Females: Appearance Management and the Social Reproduction of Gender." *Symbolic Interaction* 12: 281–298.

———. 1990. "Childhood and Public Life: Reaffirming Biographical Divisions." *Social Problems* 37: 390–402.

———. 1999. "Emotional Capital and Professional Socialization: The Case of Mortuary Science Students (and Me)." *Social Psychology Quarterly* 62: 101–116.

———. 2002. Personal e-mail communication.

Campbell, Donald. T., and Julian C. Stanley. 1963. *Experimental and Quasi-Experimental Designs for Research*. Chicago: Rand McNally.

Cancian, Francesca M. 1992. "Feminist Science: Methodologies that Challenge Inequality." *Gender and Society* 6: 623–642.

———. 1993. "Conflicts Between Activist Research and Academic Success: Participatory Research and Alternative Strategies." *American Sociologist* 24: 92–106.

Caplow, Theodore, Howard M. Bahr, Bruce Chadwick, and Margaret Holmes Williamson. 1982. *Middletown Families: Fifty Years of Change and Continuity*. Minneapolis: University of Minnesota Press.

Carpenter, Cheryl, Barry Glassner, Bruce Johnson, and Julia Loughlin. 1988. *Kids, Drugs, and Crime*. Lexington, MA: Lexington Books.

Cassell, Joan (ed.). 1987. *Children in the Field: Anthropological Experiences*. Philadelphia: Temple University Press.

Cassell, Joan. 1988. "The Relationship of Observer to Observed When Studying Up." Pp. 89–108 in *Studies in Qualitative Methodology* (Vol. 1), edited by R. G. Burgess. Greenwich, CT: JAI Press.

Cassell, Joan, and Sue-Ellen Jacobs. 1987. *Handbook on Ethical Issues in Anthropology*. Washington, DC: American Anthropological Association.

Cavan, Sherry. 1966. *Liquor License: An Ethnography of Bar Behaviors*. Chicago: Aldine.

Chagnon, Napoleon A. 1983. *Yanomamo: The Fierce People*. (3rd ed.). New York: CBS College Publishing.

Charmaz, Kathy. 1991. *Good Days, Bad Days: The Self in Chronic Illness and Time*. New Brunswick, NJ: Rutgers University Press.

———. 1994. "Between Postmodernism and Positivism: Implications for Methods." In *Studies in Symbolic Interaction* (Vol. 17), edited by N. K. Denzin. Greenwich, CT: JAI Press.

———. 2001. "Grounded Theory." Pp. 335–252 in *Contemporary Field Research: Perspectives and Formulations*. (2nd ed.). Edited by Robert M. Emerson. Prospect Heights, IL: Waveland Press.

———. 2002. "Qualitative Interviewing and Grounded Theory Analysis." Pp. 675–694 in *Handbook of Interview Research: Context and Methods*, edited by J. F. Gubrium and J. A. Holstein. Thousand Oaks, CA: Sage.

Charmaz, Kathy, and Richard G. Mitchell. 2001. "Grounded Theory in Ethnography." Pp. 160–74 in *Handbook of Ethnography*, edited by Paul Atkinson, Amanda Coffey, Sara Delamont, John Lofland, and Lyn Lofland. Thousand Oaks, CA: Sage.

Chin, Tiffani. 2000. "'Sixth Grade Madness': Parental Emotion Work in the Private High School Application Process." *Journal of Contemporary Ethnography* 29: 124–163.

Clark, Candace. 1987. "Sympathy Biography and Sympathy Margin." *American Journal of Sociology* 93: 290–321.

Clark-Miller, Jason, and Jennifer Murdock. 2005. "Order on the Edge: Remedial Work in a Right-Wing Political Discussion Group." Pp. 201–224 in *Together Alone: Personal Relationships in Public Places*, edited by Calvin Morrill, David A. Snow, and Cindy H. White. Berkeley: University of California Press.

Clifford, James, and George E. Marcus (eds.). 1986. *Writing Culture: The Poetics and Politics of Ethnography*. Berkeley: University of California Press.

Clough, Patricia Ticineto. 1992. *The End(s) of Ethnography: From Realism to Social Criticism*. Newbury Park, CA: Sage.

Coffey, Amanda, and Paul Atkinson. 1996. *Making Sense of Qualitative Data: Complementary Research Strategies*. Thousand Oaks, CA: Sage.

Cohn, Carol. 1987. "Sex and Death in the Rational World of Defense Intellectuals." *Signs: Journal of Women in Culture and Society* 12: 687–718.

Comaroff, John, and Jean Comaroff. 1992. *Ethnography and the Historical Imagination*. Boulder, CO: Westview Press.

Cooley, Charles Horton. 1926. "The Roots of Social Knowledge." *American Journal of Sociology* 32: 59–79.

Copes, Heith, and Andy Hochstetler. 2003. "Situational Construction of Masculinity Among Male Street Thieves." *Journal of Contemporary Ethnography* 32: 279–304.

Correll, Shirley. 1995. "The Ethnography of an Electronic Bar: The Lesbian Café." *Journal of Contemporary Ethnography* 24: 270–298.

Corrigall-Brown, Catherine, and Sharon Oselin. 2003. "Contested Patriotism: The Interactive Dynamics of War Protest Gatherings." Unpublished paper, University of California, Irvine.

Corsaro, William A. 1985. *Friendship and Peer Culture in the Early Years*. Norwood, NJ: Ablex.

Cortazzi, Martin. 2001. "Narrative Analysis in Ethnography." Pp. 384–394 in *Handbook of Ethnography*, edited by Paul Atkinson, Amanda Coffey, Sara Delamont, John Lofland, and Lyn Lofland. Thousand Oaks, CA: Sage.

Coy, Patrick G. 2001. "Shared Risks and Research Dilemmas on a Peace Brigades International Team in Sri Lanka." *Journal of Contemporary Ethnography* 30: 575–606.

Cress, Daniel and David A. Snow. 1996. "Resources, Benefactors, and the Viability of Homeless SMOs." *American Sociological Review* 61: 1089–1109.

Cress, Daniel and David A. Snow. 2000. "The Outcomes of Homeless Mobilization: The Influence of Organization, Disruption, Political Mediation, and Framing." *American Journal of Sociology* 105: 1063–1104.

Cressey, Donald R. 1953. *Other People's Money: A Study in the Social Psychology of Embezzlement*. Glencoe, IL: Free Press.

Crist, John T. (ed.). 2001. "Ethnography Under the Gun: Fieldwork in Zones of Conflict, War, and Peace. Special Issue of *Journal of Contemporary Ethnography* 30: 516–648.

Cuba, Lee J. 1988. *A Short Guide to Writing About Social Science*. Dallas, TX: HarperCollins.

Dalton, Melville. 1959. *Men Who Manage: Fusions of Feeling and Theory in Administration*. New York: Wiley.

Davis, Fred. 1960. Interview Guide for Problems of the Handicapped in Everyday Social Situations. Unpublished.

———. 1961. "Comment on 'Initial Interaction of Newcomers in Alcoholics Anonymous.'" *Social Problems* 8: 35.

———. 1973. "The Martian and the Convert: Ontological Polarities in Social Research." *Urban Life* 2: 333–343.

Davis, Murray S. 1971. "That's Interesting! Toward a Phenomenology of Sociology and a Sociology of Phenomenology." *Philosophy of Social Science* I: 309–344.

Davis, Phillip W., and Jacqueline Boles. 2003. "Pilgrim Apparition Work: Symbolization and Crowd Interaction When the Virgin Mary Appeared in Georgia." *Journal of Contemporary Ethnography* 32: 371–402.

Dawson, Lorne, and Robert Prus. 1993a. "Interactionist Ethnography and Postmodernist Discourse: Affinities and Disjunctures in Approaching Human Lived Experience." Pp. 283–297 in *Studies in Symbolic Interaction* (Vol. 15), edited by N. K. Denzin. Greenwich, CT: JAI Press.

———. 1993b. "Human Enterprise, Intersubjectivity, and the Ethnographic Other." Pp. 129–139 in *Studies in Symbolic Interaction* (Vol. 15), edited by N. K. Denzin. Greenwich, CT: JAI Press.

———. 1994. "Postmodernism and Linguistic Reality Versus Symbolic Interactionism and Obdurate Reality." In *Studies in Symbolic Interaction* (Vol. 17), edited by N. K. Denzin. Greenwich, CT: JAI Press.

Denzin, Norman K. 1984. "Toward a Phenomenology of Domestic, Family Violence." *American Journal of Sociology* 90: 483–513.

———. 1987a. *The Alcoholic Self*. Newbury Park, CA: Sage.

———. 1987b. *The Recovering Alcoholic*. Newbury Park, CA: Sage.

———. 1989a. *The Research Act*. (3rd ed.). Englewood Cliffs, NJ: Prentice-Hall.

———. 1989b. *Interpretive Interactionism*. Newbury Park, CA: Sage.

———. 1992a. *Symbolic Interactionism and Cultural Studies: The Politics of Interpretation*. Oxford, UK: Blackwell.

———. 1992b. "Whose Cornerville Is It, Anyway?" *Journal of Contemporary Ethnography* 21: 120–132.

———. 2002. "Confronting Ethnography's Crisis of Representation" (Symposium on Crisis in Representation). *Journal of Contemporary Ethnography* 31: 482–490.

Denzin, Norman K., and Yvonna S. Lincoln (eds.). 2000. *Handbook of Qualitative Research*. (2nd ed.). Thousand Oaks, CA: Sage.

Deutscher, Irwin. 1966. "Words and Deeds: Social Science and Social Policy." *Social Problems* 13: 235–254.

Deutscher, Irwin, Fred P. Pestello, and H. Frances Pestello. 1993. *Sentiments and Acts*. New York: Aldine de Gruyter.

Devereux, Stephen, and John Hoddinott (eds.). 1993. *Fieldwork in Developing Countries*. Boulder, CO: Lynne Rienner Publishers.

DeWelde, Kristine. 2003. "Getting Physical: Subverting Gender through Self-Defense." *Journal of Contemporary Ethnography* 32: 247–278.

Diamond, Timothy. 1992. *Making Gray Gold*. Chicago: University of Chicago Press.

DilOrio, Judith A., and Michael R. Nusbaumer. 1993. "Securing Our Sanity: Anger Management Among Abortion Escorts." *Journal of Contemporary Ethnography* 21: 411–438.

Dohan, Daniel, and Martin Sanchez-Jankowski. 1998. "Using Computers to Analyze Ethnographic Field Data: Theoretical and Practical Considerations. *Annual Review of Sociology* 24: 477–498.

Dordick, Gwendolyn A. 1997. *Something Left to Lose: Personal Relations and Survival Among New York's Homeless.* Philadelphia: Temple University Press.

Douglas, Jack D. 1976. *Investigative Social Research: Individual and Team Field Research.* Newbury Park, CA: Sage.

Douglas, Jack, and Paul K. Rasmussen (with Carol Ann Glanagan). 1977. *The Nude Beach.* Beverly Hills, CA: Sage.

Dowd, James J. 2000. "Hard Work and Good Ambition: U.S. Army Generals and the Rhetoric of Modesty." *Symbolic Interaction* 23: 183–206.

Drew, Robert S. 2001. *Karaoke Nights: An Ethnographic Rhapsody.* Walnut, CA: AltaMira.

Duneier, Mitchell. 1992. *Slim's Table: Race, Respectability, and Masculinity.* Chicago: University of Chicago Press.

———. 1999. *Sidewalk.* New York: Farrar, Strauss and Giroux.

Duneier, Mitchell, and Harvey Molotch. 1999. "Interactional Vandalism, Social Inequality, and the 'Urban Interaction Problem'." *American Journal of Sociology* 104: 1263–1295.

Dunn, Linda. 1991. "Research Alert! Qualitative Research May Be Hazardous to Your Health!" *Qualitative Health Research* 1: 388–92.

Duster, Troy, David Matza, and David Wellman. 1979. "Field Work and the Protection of Human Subjects." *American Sociologist* 14: 136–142.

Dynes, Russell R., and Kathleen Tierney (eds.). 1994. *Disasters, Collective Behavior, and Social Organization.* Cranbury, NJ: Associated University Presses.

Ebaugh, Helen R. F. 1988. *Becoming an Ex: The Process of Role Exit.* Chicago: University of Chicago Press.

Eder, Donna, Catherine Colleen Evans, and Stephen Parker. 1995. *School Talk: Gender and Adolescent Culture.* New Brunswick, NJ: Rutgers University Press.

Edin, Kathryn, and Laura Lein. 1997. *Making Ends Meet: How Single Mothers Survive Welfare and Low-Wage Work.* New York: Russell Sage Foundation.

Elbow, Peter. 1973. *Writing without Teachers.* New York: Oxford University Press.

———. 1998. *Writing with Power.* New York: Oxford University Press.

Elbow, Peter, and Pat Belanoff. 2002. *Being a Writer.* New York: McGraw-Hill.

Eliasoph, Nina. 1998. *Avoiding Politics: How Americans Produce Apathy in Everyday Life.* New York: Cambridge University Press.

Ellis, Carolyn. 1986. *Fisher Folk: Two Communities on Chesapeake Bay.* Lexington: University of Kentucky Press.

———. 1995. *Final Negotiations: A Story of Love, Loss, and Chronic Illness.* Philadelphia: Temple University Press.

———. 1997. "Evocative Autoethnography: Writing Emotionally about Our Lives." Pp. 115–142 in *Representation and the Text: Re-framing the Narrative Voice.* W. G. Tierney and Yvonna S. Lincoln (eds.). Albany: State University of New York Press.

Ellis, Carolyn, and Arthur P. Bochner. 1992. "Telling and Performing Personal Stories: The Constraints of Choice in Abortion." Pp. 79–101 in *Investigating Subjectivity: Research on Lived Experience*, edited by C. Ellis and M. G. Flaherty. Newbury Park, CA: Sage.

———. (eds.). 1996. *Composing Ethnography: Alternative Forms of Qualitative Writing*. Walnut Creek, CA: Altamira.

———. 2000. "Autoethnography, Personal Narrative, Reflexivity: Researcher as Subject." Pp. 733–768 in *Handbook of Qualitative Research* (2nd ed.). Edited by Norman K. Denzin and Yvonna S. Lincoln. Thousand Oaks, CA: Sage.

Ellis, Carolyn, and Michael G. Flaherty (eds.). 1992. *Investigating Subjectivity: Research on Lived Experience*. Newbury Park, CA: Sage.

Ellis, Carolyn, and Eugene Weinstein. 1986. "Jealousy and the Social Psychology of Emotional Experience." *Journal of Social and Personal Relationships* 3: 337–357.

Emerson, Robert M. (ed.). 2001. *Contemporary Field Research: A Collection of Readings*. (2nd ed.). Prospect Heights, IL: Waveland Press.

Emerson, Robert M., and Melvin Pollner. 2001. "Constructing Participant/Observation Relations." Pp. 239–259 in *Contemporary Field Research: A Collection of Readings*. (2nd ed.). Edited by R. M. Emerson. Prospect Heights, IL: Waveland Press.

Emerson, Robert M., Rachel I. Fretz, and Linda L. Shaw. 1995. *Writing Ethnographic Fieldnotes*. Chicago: University of Chicago Press.

———. 2001. "Participant Observation and Fieldnotes." Pp. 352–368 in *Handbook of Ethnography*, edited by Paul Atkinson, Amanda Coffey, Sara Delamont, John Lofland, and Lyn H. Lofland. Thousand Oaks, CA: Sage.

Epstein, Barbara L. 1991. *Political Culture and Cultural Revolution: Nonviolent Direct Action in the 1970's and 1980's*. Berkeley: University of California Press.

Erikson, Kai T. 1967. "A Comment on Disguised Observation in Sociology." *Social Problems* 14: 366–373.

Erlandson, David A., Edward L. Harris, Barbara L. Skipper, and Steve D. Allen. 1993. *Doing Naturalistic Inquiry: A Guide to Methods*. Newbury Park, CA: Sage.

Evans-Pritchard, Edward E. 1937. *Witchcraft, Oracles, and Magic Among the Azande*. Oxford: Clarendon Press.

Fantasia, Rick. 1988. *Cultures of Solidarity: Consciousness, Action and Contemporary American Workers*. Berkeley: University of California Press.

Feagin, Joe R., Anthony M. Orum, and Gideon Sjoberg (eds.). 1991. *A Case for the Case Study*. Chapel Hill: University of North Carolina Press.

Feldman, Martha S., Jeannine Bell, and Michele Tracy Berger. 2003. *Gaining Access: A Practical and Theoretical Guide for Qualitative Researchers*. Walnut Creek, CA: AltaMira Press.

Fetterman, David M. 1998. *Ethnography Step by Step*. (2nd ed.). Newbury Park, CA: Sage.

Fielding, Nigel G. 1993. "Mediating the Message: Affinity and Hostility in Research on Sensitive Topics." Pp. 146–180 in *Researching Sensitive Topics*, edited by Claire M. Renzetti and Raymond M. Lee. Newbury Park, CA: Sage.

———. 2001. "Computer Applications in Qualitative Research." Pp. 453–467 in *Handbook of Ethnography*, edited by Paul Atkinson, Amanda Coffey, Sara Delamont, John Lofland, and Lyn Lofland (eds.). Thousand Oaks, CA: Sage.

Fielding, Nigel G., and Raymond M. Lee (eds.). 1998. *Computer Assisted Qualitative Research*. Newbury Park: Sage.

Fine, Gary Alan. 1980. "Cracking Diamonds: The Observer Role in Little League Baseball Settings and the Acquisition of Social Competence." Pp. 117–132 in *Fieldwork Experience: Qualitative Approaches to Social Research*, edited by W. B. Shaffir, R. Stebbins, and A. Turowetz. New York: St. Martin's Press.

———. 1983. *Shared Fantasy*. Chicago: University of Chicago Press.

———. 1987. *With the Boys: Little League Baseball and Preadolescent Culture*. Chicago: University of Chicago Press.

———. 1988. "The Ten Commandments of Writing." *American Sociologist* 19: 152–157.

———. 1993. "Ten Lies of Ethnography: Moral Dilemmas In Field Research." *Journal of Contemporary Ethnography* 22: 267–294.

———. 1996. *Kitchens: The Culture of Restaurant Work*. Berkeley: University of California Press.

———. 2001. *Gifted Tongues: High School Debate and Adolescent Culture*. Princeton: Princeton University Press.

Fine, Gary Alan, and Barry Glassner. 1979. "Participant Observation with Children: Promise and Problems." *Urban Life* 8: 153–174.

Fine, Gary Alan, and Sherryl Kleinman. 1979. "Rethinking Subcultures: An Interactionist Analysis." *American Journal of Sociology* 85: 1–20.

Fine, Gary Alan, and Kent L. Sandstrom. 1988. *Knowing Children: Participant Observation with Minors*. Newbury Park, CA: Sage.

Fineman, Stephen (ed.). 1993. *Emotion in Organizations*. Newbury Park, CA: Sage.

Fisher, Bradley J. 1987. "Illness Career Descent in Institutions for the Elderly." *Qualitative Sociology* 10: 132–145.

Flaherty, Michael. 1999. *A Watched Pot: How We Experience Time*. New York: New York University Press.

———. 2002. "The 'Crisis' in Representation: Reflections and Assessments" (Review Symposium on Crisis in Representation). *Journal of Contemporary Ethnography* 31: 508–516.

Forgas, Joseph P. (ed.). 2000. *Feeling and Thinking: The Role of Affect in Social Cognition*. Cambridge, UK: Cambridge University Press.

Freeman, Derek. 1983. *Margaret Mead and Samoa: The Making and Unmaking of an Anthropological Myth*. Cambridge, MA: Harvard University Press.

Friedman, Norman L. 1990. "Autobiographical Sociology." *American Sociologist* 21: 60–66.

Fuller, Linda. 1988. "Fieldwork in Forbidden Terrain: The U.S. State and the Case of Cuba." *American Sociologist* 19: 99–120.

Gage, John T. 1987. *The Shape of Reason*. New York: Macmillan.

Gallagher, Patrick. 1967. "Games Malinowski Played." *New Republic* 17: 24–26.

Galliher, John F. 1980. "Social Scientists' Ethical Responsibilities to Superordinates: Looking Up Meekly." *Social Problems* 27: 298–308. (Special issue on *Ethical Problems of Fieldwork*, edited by Joan Cassell and Murray Wax.)

Gallmeier, Charles. 1991. "Leaving, Revisiting, and Staying in Touch: Neglected Issues in Field Research." Pp. 224–231 in *Experiencing Fieldwork: An Inside View of Qualitative Research*, edited by William B. Shaffir and Robert A. Stebbins. Thousand Oaks: Sage.

Gamson, Joshua. 1994. *Claiming Fame*. Berkeley: University of California Press.

———. 1995. "Stopping the Spin and Becoming a Prop: Fieldwork on Hollywood Ethics." Pp. 83–93 in *Studying Elites Using Qualitative Methods*, edited by Rosanna Hertz and Jonathon B. Imber. Thousand Oaks, CA: Sage.

Gamson, William A. 1992. *Talking Politics*. New York: Cambridge University Press.

Gans, Herbert. 1962. *The Urban Villagers: Group and Class in the Life of Italian-Americans*. New York: Free Press.

———. 1967. *The Levittowners: Ways of Life and Politics in a New Suburban Community*. New York: Pantheon.

———. 1972. "The Positive Functions of Poverty." *American Journal of Sociology* 78: 275–289.

Gardner, Carol Brooks. 1986. "Public Aid." *Urban Life* 15: 37–69.

———. 1995. *Passing By: Gender and Public Harassment*. Berkeley: University of California Press.

Garfinkel, Harold. 1967. *Studies in Ethnomethodology*. Upper Saddle River, NJ: Prentice Hall.

Gearing, Frederick O. 1970. *Face of the Fox*. Hawthorne, NY: Aldine Publishing Company.

Geertz, Clifford. 1973. *The Interpretation of Cultures*. New York: Basic Books.

———. 1988. *Works and Lives: The Anthropologist as Author*. Stanford, CA: Stanford University Press.

Georges, Robert A., and Michael O. Jones. 1980. *People Studying People: The Human Element in Fieldwork*. Berkeley: University of California Press.

Gilbert, Nigel. 2001. *Researching Social Life*. Newbury Park, CA: Sage.

Glaser, Barney. 1978. *Theoretical Sensitivity*. Mill Valley, CA: Sociology Press.

Glaser, Barney, and Anselm Strauss. 1965. *Awareness of Dying*. Chicago: Aldine.

———. 1967. *The Discovery of Grounded Theory: Strategies for Qualitative Research*. Chicago: Aldine.

———. 1968. *Time for Dying*. Chicago: Aldine.

Goffman, Erving. 1959. *The Presentation of Self in Everyday Life*. Garden City, NY: Doubleday.

———. 1961a. *Asylums: Essays on the Social Situation of Mental Patients and Other Inmates*. Garden City, NY: Doubleday.

———. 1961b. "Role Distance." Pp. 85–152 in *Encounters: Two Studies in the Sociology of Interaction*. Indianapolis: Bobbs–Merrill.

———. 1962. "On Cooling the Mark Out: Some Aspects of Adaptation to Failure." Pp. 482–505 in *Human Behavior and Social Processes*, edited by A. Rose. Boston: Houghton Mifflin.

———. 1963. *Stigma: Notes on the Management of Spoiled Identity*. Englewood Cliffs, NJ: Prentice Hall.

———. 1983. "The Interaction Order." *American Sociological Review* 48: 1–17.

———. 1989. "On Fieldwork." (Transcribed and edited by Lyn H. Lofland.) *Journal of Contemporary Ethnography* 18: 123–132.

Gold, Raymond. 1958. "Roles in Sociological Field Observation." *Social Forces* 36: 217–223.

Gold, Steven J. 1989. "Differential Adjustment Among New Immigrant Family Members." *Journal of Contemporary Ethnography* 17: 408–434.

Golde, Peggy (ed.). 1986. *Women in the Field: Anthropological Experiences* (2nd ed., expanded and updated). Berkeley: University of California Press.

Goodwin, Jeff. 2001. *No Other Way Out: States and Revolutionary Movements, 1945–1991*. New York: Cambridge University Press.

Goodwin, Jeff, James M. Jasper, and Francesca Polletta (eds.). 2001. *Passionate Politics: Emotions and Social Movements*. Chicago: University of Chicago Press.

Gordon, David E. 1987. "Getting Close by Staying Distant: Fieldwork with Proselytizing Groups." *Qualitative Sociology* 10: 267–287.

Gotlib, Ian, and Blair Wheaton (eds.). 1997. *Stress and Adversity Over the Life Course: Trajectories and Turning Points*. Cambridge, UK: Cambridge University Press.

Gould, Leroy C., Andrew L. Walker, Lansing E. Crane, and Charles W. Lidz. 1974. *Connections: Notes from the Heroin World*. New Haven, CT: University Press.

Gravel, Pierre Bettez, and Robert B. Marks Ridinger. 1988. *Anthropological Fieldwork*. New York: Garland.

Greenbaum, Thomas L. 1998. *The Handbook for Focus Group Research* (revised and expanded ed.). New York: Lexington Books.

Grønbjerg, Kirsten A. 1993. *Understanding Nonprofit Funding: Managing Revenues in Social Services and Community Development Organizations*. San Francisco: Jossey-Bass.

Gubrium, Jaber F. 1975. *Living and Dying in Murray Manor*. Charlottesville: University Press of Virginia.

———. 1986. *Oldtimers and Alzheimers: The Descriptive Organization of Senility*. Greenwich, CT: JAI Press.

Gubrium, Jaber F., and James A. Holstein. 1997. *The New Language of Qualitative Method*. New York: Oxford University Press.

———. 2002. *Handbook of Interview Research: Context and Methods*. Thousand Oaks, CA: Sage.

Gurney, Joan Neff. 1985. "Not One of the Guys: The Female Researcher in a Male-Dominated Setting." *Qualitative Sociology* 8: 42–62.

Gusfield, Joseph. 1981. *The Culture of Public Problems: Drinking-Driving and the Symbolic Order*. Chicago: University of Chicago Press.

Gusterson, Hugh. 1996. *Nuclear Rites: A Weapons Laboratory at the End of the Cold War*. Berkeley: University of California Press.

Hammersley, Martyn. 1992. *What's Wrong with Ethnography*. London: Routledge.

Hammersley, Martyn, and Paul Atkinson. 1995. *Ethnography: Principles in Practice* (2nd ed.). London: Routledge.

Harper, Douglas. 1982. *Good Company*. Chicago: University of Chicago Press.

———. 1987. *Working Knowledge: Skill and Community in a Small Shop*. Chicago: University of Chicago Press.

———. 2000. "Re-Imagining Visual Methods." Pp. 717–732 in *Handbook of Qualitative Research*, edited by Norman K. Denzin and Yvonna S. Lincoln. Thousand Oaks, CA: Sage.

———. 2001. *Changing Works: Visions of a Lost Agriculture*. Chicago: University of Chicago Press.

———. 2003. "Framing Photographic Ethnography: A Case Study." *Ethnography* 4: 241–266.

Harrison, Tyler, and Susan Morgan. 2005. "'Hanging Out' Among Teenagers: Resistance, Gender, and Personal Relationships." Pp. 93–110 in *Together Alone: Personal Relationships in Public Places*, edited by Calvin Morrill, David A. Snow, and Cindy H. White. Berkeley: University of California Press.

Heilman, Samuel C. 1980. "Jewish Sociologist: Native-as-Stranger." *American Sociologist* 15: 100–108.

Heirich, Max. 1971. *The Spiral of Conflict: Demonstrations at Berkeley 1964–1965*. New York: Columbia University Press.

Henson, Kevin D. 1996. *Just a Temp*. Philadelphia, PA: Temple University Press.

Herman, Nancy J. 1993. "Return to Sender: Reintegrative Stigma-management Strategies of Ex-psychiatric Patients." *Journal of Contemporary Ethnography* 22: 295–330.

Heyl, Barbara. 2001. "Ethnographic Interviewing." Pp. 369–383 in *Handbook of Ethnography*, edited by Paul Atkinson, Amanda Coffey, Sara Delamont, John Lofland, and Lyn Lofland. Thousand Oaks, CA: Sage.

Hilbert, Richard A. 1980. "Covert Participant Observation: On Its Nature and Practice." *Urban Life* 9: 51–78.

Hochschild, Arlie R. 1973. *The Unexpected Community: Portrait of An Old Age Subculture*. Berkeley: University of California Press.

———. 1983. *The Managed Heart: Commercialization of Human Feeling*. Berkeley: University of California Press.

Hodson, Randy. 1991. "The Active Worker: Compliance and Autonomy at the Workplace." *Journal of Contemporary Ethnography* 20: 47–78.

Hoffman, Joan Eakin. 1980. "Problems of Access in the Study of Social Elites and Boards of Directors." Pp. 45–56 in *Fieldwork Experience: Qualitative Approaches to Social Research*, edited by W. B. Shaffir, R. A. Stebbins, and A. Turowetz. New York: St. Martin's Press.

Hollingshead, August B. 1975. *Elmtown's Youth and Elmtown Revisited*. New York: John Wiley & Sons.

Holmes, Lowell. 1987. *Quest for the Real Samoa: The Mead/Freeman Controversy and Beyond*. South Hadley, MA: Bergin & Garvey.

Holyfield, Lori. 1999. "Manufacturing Adventure: The Buying and Selling of Emotions." *Journal of Contemporary Ethnography* 28: 3–32.

Holyfield, Lori, and Gary Alan Fine. 1997. "Adventure as Character Work: The Collective Taming of Fear." *Symbolic Interaction* 20: 343–363.

Holyfield, Lori and Lilian M. Jonas. 2003. "From River God to Research Grunt: Identity, Emotions, and the River Guide." *Symbolic Interaction* 26: 285–306.

Hondagneu-Sotelo, Pierrette. 1994. *Gendered Transitions: Mexican Experiences of Immigration*. Berkeley: University of California Press.

———. 2001. *Domestica: Immigrant Workers Cleaning and Caring in the Shadows of Affluence*. Berkeley: University of California Press.

Horne, Christine, Mary Kris McIlwaine, and Kristie A. Taylor. 2005. "Civility and Order: Adult Social Control of Children in Public Places." Pp. 181–200 in *Together Alone: Personal Relationships in Public Places*, edited by Calvin Morrill, David A. Snow, and Cindy White. Berkeley: University of California Press.

Horowitz, Irving Louis. 1965. "The Life and Death of Project Camelot." *Transaction* 3 (November-December): 3–7, 44–47.

Horowitz, Ruth. 1983. *Honor and the American Dream: Culture and Identity in a Chicano Community.* New Brunswick, NJ: Rutgers University Press.

———. 1986. "Remaining an Outsider: Membership as a Threat to Research Rapport." *Urban Life* 14: 409–430.

———. 1995. *Teen Mothers: Citizens or Dependents.* Chicago: University of Chicago Press.

———. 1996. "Getting In." Pp. 41–50 in *In the Field: Readings in the Field Research Experience*, edited by C. D. Smith and W. Kornblum. New York: Praeger.

Howell, Nancy (ed.). 1990. *Surviving Fieldwork: A Report of the Advisory Panel on Health and Safety in Fieldwork.* Washington, DC: American Anthropological Association.

Hughes, Everett C. 1971 (1950). "Cycles, Turning Points, and Careers." Pp. 124–131 in *The Sociological Eye*, edited by E. C. Hughes. Chicago, IL: Aldine.

Hume, David. 1978 (1739). *A Treatise of Human Nature.* Cambridge, UK: Oxford University Press.

Humphreys, Laud. 1975. *Tearoom Trade: Impersonal Sex in Public Places* (enlarged ed.). Chicago: Aldine.

Hunt, Scott A., and Robert D. Benford. 1994. "Identity Talk in the Peace and Justice Movement." *Journal of Contemporary Ethnography* 22: 488–517.

Irwin, John. 1970. *The Felon.* Englewood Cliffs, NJ: Prentice-Hall.

———. 1980. *Prisons in Turmoil.* Boston: Little, Brown.

———. 1985. *The Jail: Managing the Underclass in American Society.* Berkeley: University of California Press.

Jackson, Jean E. 1990. "'Deja Entendu': The Liminal Qualities of Anthropological Fieldnotes." *Journal of Contemporary Ethnography* 19: 8–43.

James, William. 1932. *The Meaning of Truth.* New York: Longman.

Jimerson, Jason B. 1996. "Good Times and Good Games: How Pickup Basketball Players Use Wealth-Maximizing Norms." *Journal of Contemporary Ethnography* 25: 353–371.

———. 1999. "'Who Has the Next?' The Symbolic, Rational, and Methodical Use of Norms in Pickup Basketball." *Social Psychology Quarterly* 62: 136–156.

Johnson, John M. 1975. *Doing Field Research.* New York: Free Press.

Johnson, John M., and David L. Altheide. 1993. "The Ethnographic Ethic." Pp. 95–107 in *Studies in Symbolic Interaction* (Vol. 14), edited by N. K. Denzin. Greenwich, CT: JAI Press.

Johnson, Norris R. 1988. "Fire in a Crowded Theater: A Descriptive Investigation of the Emergence of Panic." *International Journal of Mass Emergencies and Disasters* 6: 7–26.

Johnston, Drue M. and Norris R. Johnson. 1988. "Role Extension in Disaster: Employee Behavior at the Beverly Hills Supper Club Fire." *Sociological Focus* 22: 39–51.

Jonas, Lilian M. 1999. "Making and Facing Danger: Constructing Strong Character on the River." *Symbolic Interaction* 22: 247–268.

Junker, Buford H. 1960. *Field Work: An Introduction to the Social Sciences*. Chicago: University of Chicago Press.

Kalab, Kathleen. 1987. "Student Vocabularies of Motive: Accounts for Absence." *Symbolic Interaction* 10: 71–83.

Kanter, Rosabeth Moss. 1977. *Men and Women of the Corporation*. New York: Basic Books.

Kaplan, Danny, and Eyal Ben-Ari. 2000. "Brothers and Others in Arms: Managing Gay Identity in Combat Units of the Israeli Army." *Journal of Contemporary Ethnography* 29: 396–432.

Kaplan, Ilene M. 1991. "Gone Fishing, Be Back Later: Ending and Resuming Research Among Fisherman." Pp. 232–237 in *Experiencing Fieldwork: An Inside View of Qualitative Research*, edited by William B. Shaffir and Robert A. Stebbins. Thousand Oaks: Sage.

Karp, David A. 1973. "Hiding in Pornographic Bookstores: A Reconsideration of the Nature of Urban Anonymity." *Urban Life* 1: 427–452.

———. 1996. *Speaking of Sadness*. New York: Oxford University Press.

———. 2001. *The Burden of Sympathy: How Families Cope with Mental Illness*. New York: Oxford University Press.

Katovich, Michael A., and William A. Reese II. 1987. "The Regular: Full-Time Identities and Memberships in an Urban Bar." *Journal of Contemporary Ethnography* 16: 308–343.

Katz, Jack. 1982. *Poor People's Lawyers in Transition*. New Brunswick, NJ: Rutgers University Press.

———. 1997. "Ethnography's Warrants." *Sociological Methods and Research* 25: 391–423.

———. 1999. *How Emotions Work*. Chicago: University of Chicago Press.

———. 2001. "Analytic Induction Revisited." Pp. 331–334 in *Contemporary Field Research: Perspectives and Formulations*, (2nd ed.), edited by Robert M. Emerson. Prospect Heights, IL: Waveland Press.

Kelle, Udo (ed.). 1995. *Computer-aided Qualitative Data Analysis: Theory, Methods and Practice*. Thousand Oaks, CA: Sage.

Kemmis, Stephen, and Robin McTaggart. 2000. "Participatory Action Research." Pp. 567–606 in *Handbook of Qualitative Research* (2nd ed.), edited by Norman K. Denzin and Yvonna S. Lincoln. Thousand Oaks, CA: Sage.

Kendall, Diane. 2002. *The Power of Good Deeds: Privileged Women and the Social Reproduction of the Upper Class*. Lanham, MD: Rowman and Littlefield Publishers.

Kendall, Lori. 1998. "Meaning and Identity in 'Cyberspace': The Performance of Gender, Class, and Race Online." *Symbolic Interaction* 21: 129–153.

———. 2002. *Hanging Out in the Virtual Pub: Masculinities and Relationships Online*. Berkeley: University of California Press.

Klapp, Orrin. 1958. "Social Types." *American Sociological Review* 23: 673–681.

Klatch, Rebecca E. 1987. *Women of the New Right*. Philadelphia: Temple University Press.

———. 1999. *A Generation Divided: The New Left, The New Right, and the 1960s*. Berkeley: University of California Press.

Kleinman, Sherryl. 1984. *Equals Before God: Seminarians as Humanistic Professionals*. Chicago: University of Chicago Press.

———. 1996. *Opposing Ambitions: Gender and Identity in an Alternative Organization*. Chicago: University of Chicago Press.

Kleinman, Sherryl, and Martha A. Copp. 1993. *Emotions and Fieldwork*. Newbury Park, CA: Sage.

Kleinman, Sherryl, Barbara Stenross, and Martha McMahon. 1994. "Privileging Fieldwork over Interviewing: Consequences for Identity and Practice." *Symbolic Interaction* 17: 37–50.

Kornblum, William. 1974. *Blue Collar Community*. Chicago: University of Chicago Press.

Kotarba, Joseph A. 1980. "Discovering Amorphous Social Experience: The Case of Chronic Pain." Pp. 57–67 in *Fieldwork Experience: Qualitative Approaches to Social Research*, edited by W. B. Shaffir, R. A. Stebbins, and A. Turowetz. New York: St. Martin's Press.

———. 1983. *Chronic Pain: Its Social Dimensions*. Beverly Hills, CA: Sage.

Krieger, Susan. 1983. *The Mirror Dance: Identity in a Woman's Community*. Philadelphia: Temple University Press.

———. 1991. *Social Science and the Self: Personal Essays on an Art Form*. New Brunswick, NJ: Rutgers University Press.

Krueger, Richard A., and Mary Anne Casey. 2000. *Focus Groups: A Practical Guide for Applied Research*. (3rd ed.). Thousand Oaks, CA: Sage.

Kuklick, Henrika. 1991. *The Savage Within: The Social History of British Anthropology, 1885–1945*. Cambridge, UK: Cambridge University Press.

Kunda, Gideon. 1992. *Engineering Culture: Control and Commitment in a High-Tech Corporation*. Philadelphia: Temple University Press.

Lal, Jayati. 1996. "Situating Locations: The Politics of Self, Identity, and 'Other' in Living and Writing the Text." Pp. 185–214 in *Feminist Dilemmas in Fieldwork*, edited by Diane L. Wolf. Boulder, CO: Westview.

Lamont, Michele. 1992. *Money, Morals, and Manners: The Culture of the French and American Upper-Middle Class*. Chicago: University of Chicago Press.

———. 2000. *The Dignity of Working Men: Morality and the Boundaries of Race, Class, and Immigration*. Cambridge, MA: Harvard University Press.

Lankenau, Stephen E. 1999. "Stronger than Dirt: Public Humiliation and Status Enhancement among Panhandlers." *Journal of Contemporary Ethnography* 28: 288–318.

Lareau, Annette, and Jeffrey Shultz (eds.). 1996. *Journeys Through Ethnography: Realistic Accounts of Fieldwork*. Boulder, CO: Westview Press.

LeCompte, Margaret D., and Jean J. Schensul. 1999. *Analyzing & Interpreting Ethnographic Data*. Walnut Creek, CA: AltaMira Press.

Lee, Jennifer. 2002. *Civility in the City: Blacks, Jews, and Koreans in Urban America*. Cambridge: Harvard University Press.

Leidner, Robin. 1993. *Fast Food, Fast Talk: Service Work and the Routinization of Everyday Life*. Berkeley: University of California Press.

Lemert, Edwin M. 1962. "Paranoia and the Dynamics of Exclusion." *Sociometry* 25: 2–20.

Leo, Richard A. 1995. "Trial and Tribulations: Courts, Ethnography, and the Need for an Evidentiary Privilege for Academic Researchers." *The American Sociologist* 26: 113–134.

Levine, Felice J. 1993. "ASA Files Amicus Brief Protecting Confidential Research Information." *Footnotes* 21 (no. 5): 2.

Leyser, Ophra. 2003. "Doing Masculinity in a Mental Hospital." *Journal of Contemporary Ethnography* 32: 336–359.

Lichterman, Paul. 1996. *The Search for Political Community: American Activists Reinventing Commitment*. Cambridge, UK: Cambridge University Press.

Liebow, Elliot. 1967. *Tally's Corner: A Study of Negro Streetcorner Men*. Boston: Little, Brown.

———. 1993. *Tell Them Who I Am: The Lives of Homeless Women*. New York: Free Press.

Lincoln, Yvonne S., and Egon G. Guba. 1985. *Naturalistic Inquiry*. Beverly Hills, CA: Sage.

Lindesmith, Alfred R. 1947. *Opiate Addiction*. Bloomington, IN: Principia Press.

Lockford, Lesa. 2004. *Performing Femininity: Rewriting Gender Identity*. Walnut Creek, CA: AltaMira Press.

Lofland, John. 1970. "Interactionist Imagery and Analytic Interruptus." Pp. 35–45 in *Human Nature and Collective Behavior: Papers in Honor of Herbert Blumer*, edited by Tamotsu Shibutani. New Brunswick, NJ: Transaction Books.

———. 1971. *Analyzing Social Settings: A Guide to Qualitative Observation and Analysis*. Belmont, CA: Wadsworth Publishing Company.

———. 1977. *Doomsday Cult: A Study of Conversion, Proselytization, and Maintenance of Faith* (enlarged ed.). New York: Irvington.

———. 1978. "Becoming a World-Saver Revisited." Pp. 10–23 in *Conversion Careers*, edited by J. Richardson. Beverly Hills, CA: Sage.

———. 1985. *Protest: Studies of Collective Behavior and Social Movements*. New Brunswick, NJ: Transaction Books.

———. 1993. *Polite Protesters: The American Peace Movement of the 1980s*. Syracuse, NY: Syracuse University Press.

———. 1995. "Analytic Ethnography: Features, Failures, Futures." *Journal of Contemporary Ethnography* 24: 25–40.

Lofland, John, and Michael Fink. 1985. "Symbolic Sit-Ins." Pp. 299–319 in *Protest: Studies of Collective Behavior and Social Movements*. New Brunswick, NJ: Transaction Books.

Lofland, John, and Lyn H. Lofland. 1984. *Analyzing Social Settings: A Guide to Qualitative Observation and Analysis*. (2nd ed.). Belmont, CA: Wadsworth Publishing Company.

———. 1995. *Analyzing Social Settings: A Guide to Qualitative Observation and Analysis*. (3rd ed.). Belmont, CA: Wadsworth Publishing Company.

Lofland, John, and Rodney Stark. 1965. "Becoming a World-Saver: A Theory of Conversion." *American Sociological Review* 30: 862–874.

Lofland, Lyn H. (ed.). 1980. "Reminiscences of Classic Chicago: The Blumer-Hughes Talk." *Urban Life* 9: 251–281.

———. 1982. "Loss and Human Connection: An Exploration into the Nature of the Social Bond." Pp. 219–242 in *Personality, Roles and Social Behavior*, edited by W. Ickes and E. Knowles. New York: Springer-Verlag.

———. 1985a. "The Social Shaping of Emotion: The Case of Grief." *Symbolic Interaction* 8: 171–190.

———. 1985b. *A World of Strangers: Order and Action in Urban Public Space.* Prospect Heights, IL: Waveland Press. (Originally published by Basic Books in 1973).

———. 1998. *The Public Realm: Exploring the City's Quintessential Social Territory.* Hawthorne, NY: Aldine De Gruyter.

Lois, Jennifer. 2003. *Heroic Efforts: The Emotional Culture of Search and Rescue Volunteers.* New York: New York University Press.

Lopata, Helena Z. 1980. "Interviewing American Women." Pp. 68–81 in *Fieldwork Experience: Qualitative Approaches to Social Research*, edited by W. B. Shaffir, R. A. Stebbins, and A. Turowetz. New York: St. Martin's Press.

Loseke, Donileen R. 1992. *The Battered Woman and Shelters: The Construction of Wife Abuse.* Albany: State University of New York Press.

Lowney, Kathleen S. 1995. "Teenage Satanism as Oppositional Youth Culture." *Journal of Contemporary Ethnography* 23: 453–484.

Lunsford, Andrea. 2003. *The St. Martin's Handbook.* (5th ed.). Boston: Bedford/St. Martin's Press.

Lynd, Robert S., and Helen Merrell Lynd. 1929. *Middletown: A Study in Contemporary American Culture.* New York: Harcourt Brace and Co.

Lyng, Stephen. 1998. "Dangerous Methods: Risk Taking and the Research Process." Pp. 221–251 in *Ethnography at the Edge: Crime, Deviance, and Field Research*, edited by Jeff Ferrell and Mark S. Hamm. Boston: Northeastern University Press.

Lyng, Stephen, and David A. Snow. 1986. "Vocabularies of Motive and High-Risk Behavior: The Case of Skydiving." Pp. 157–179 in *Advances in Group Processes*, Vol. 3, edited by Edward J. Lawler. Greenwich, CT: JAI Press.

Mahmood, Cynthia. 1996. *Fighting for Faith and Nation: Dialogues with Sikh Militants.* Philadelphia: University of Pennsylvania Press.

Maines, David R., William Shaffir, and Allan Turowetz. 1980. "Leaving the Field in Ethnographic Research: Reflections on the Entrance-Exit Hypothesis." Pp. 261–281 in *Fieldwork Experiences: Qualitative Approaches to Social Research*, edited by W. Shaffir, R. A. Stebbins, and A. Turowetz. New York: St. Martin's Press.

Malinowski, Bronislaw. 1967. *A Diary in the Strict Sense of the Term.* New York: Harcourt Brace & World.

Mandell, Nancy. 1986. "Peer Interaction in Day Care Settings: Implications for Social Cognition." Pp. 55–79 in *Sociological Studies of Child Development* (Vol. 1), edited by P. A. Adler and P. Adler. Greenwich, CT: JAI Press.

———. 1988. "The Least-Adult Role in Studying Children." *Journal of Contemporary Ethnography* 16: 433–467.

Mann, Chris, and Fiona Stewart. 2001. *Internet Communication and Qualitative Research: A Handbook for Researching Online.* Thousand Oaks, CA: Sage.

Manning, Peter K. 1977. *Police Work.* Cambridge, MA: MIT Press.

———. 2002. "The Sky Is Not Falling" (Symposium on Crisis in Representation). *Journal of Contemporary Ethnography* 31: 490–498.

Marcus, George E., and Michael M. J. Fisher. 1986. *Anthropology as Cultural Critique: An Experimental Moment in the Human Sciences.* Chicago: University of Chicago Press.

Margolis, Eric. 1990. "Visual Ethnography: Tools for Mapping the AIDS Epidemic." *Journal of Contemporary Ethnography* 19: 370–391.

Massey, Joseph E., and Trina Hope. 2005. "A Personal Dance: Emotional Labor, Fleeting Relationships, Local Social Power and Exchange in a Strip Bar." Pp. 66–90 in *Together Alone: Personal Relationships in Public Places*, edited by Calvin Morrill, David A. Snow, and Cindy H. White. Berkeley: University of California Press.

McCabe, Donald L. 1992. "The Influence of Situational Ethics on Cheating Among College Students." *Sociological Inquiry* 62: 365–373.

McCall, George J., and J. L. Simmons (eds.). 1969. *Issues in Participant Observation: A Text and Reader*. Reading, MA: Addison-Wesley.

McPhail, Clark. 1969. "Student Walkout: An Examination of Elementary Collective Behavior." *Social Problems* 16: 441–455.

———. 1991. *The Myth of the Madding Crowd*. Hawthorne, NY: Aldine de Gruyter.

———. 1994. "The Dark Side of Purpose: Individual and Collective Violence in Riots." *The Sociological Quarterly* 35: 1–32.

McRoberts, Omar M. 2003. *Streets of Glory: Church and Community in a Black Urban Neighborhood*. Chicago: University of Chicago Press.

Mead, George Herbert. 1934. *Mind, Self, and Society*. Chicago: University of Chicago Press.

———. 1938. *The Philosophy of the Act*. Chicago: University of Chicago Press.

Mead, Margaret. 1928. *Coming of Age in Samoa*. New York: William Morrow.

Melbin, Murray. 1987. *Night As Frontier: Colonizing the World After Dark*. New York: Free Press.

Merton, Robert K. 1968. *Social Theory and Social Structure* (enlarged ed.). New York: Free Press.

———. 1972. "Insiders and Outsiders: A Chapter in the Sociology of Knowledge." *American Journal of Sociology* 78: 9–47.

Meyer, J. R., and A. H. Conrad. 1957. "Economic Theory, Statistical Inferences, and Economic History." *Journal of Economic History* 17: 532.

Miles, Matthew B., and A. Michael Huberman. 1994. *Qualitative Data Analysis: An Expanded Sourcebook* (2nd ed.). Thousand Oaks, CA: Sage.

Miller, S. M. 1952. "The Participant Observer and 'Over-rapport'." *American Sociological Review* 17: 97–99.

Milligan, Melinda J., and April Brayfield. 2004. "Museums and Childhood: Negotiating Organizational Lessons." *Childhood: A Global Journal of Child Research* 11: 45–71.

Mills, C. Wright. 1959. *The Sociological Imagination*. New York: Oxford University Press.

Mitchell, Richard G., Jr. 1983. *Mountain Experience: The Psychology and Sociology of Adventure*. Chicago: University of Chicago Press.

———. 1993. *Secrecy and Fieldwork*. Newbury Park, CA: Sage.

———. 2002. *Dancing at Armageddon*. Chicago: University of Chicago Press.

Moffatt, Michael. 1989. *Coming of Age in New Jersey: College and American Culture*. New Brunswick, NJ: Rutgers University Press.

Monaghan, Peter. 1993a. "Sociologist Jailed Because He 'Wouldn't Snitch' Ponders the Way Research Ought to Be Done." *The Chronicle of Higher Education*, September 1, pp. A8–A9.

———. 1993b. "Free After 6 Months: Sociologist Who Refused To Testify is Released." *The Chronicle of Higher Education*, November 3, p. A14.

———. 1994. "Bitter Warfare in Anthropology." *The Chronicle of Higher Education*, October 26, pp. A10, A18–19.

Monti, Daniel J. 1992. "On the Risks and Rewards of Going Native." *Qualitative Sociology* 15: 325–332.

Morales, Edmundo. 1989. *Cocaine: White Gold Rush in Peru*. Tucson: University of Arizona Press.

Morgan, David L. 1997. *Focus Groups as Qualitative Research*. (2nd ed.). Thousand Oaks, CA: Sage.

Morrill, Calvin. 1995. *The Executive Way: Conflict Management in Corporations*. Chicago: University of Chicago Press.

Morrill, Calvin, David B. Buller, Mary Klein Buller, and Linda L. Larkey. 1999. "Toward an Organizational Perspective on Identifying and Managing Formal Gatekeepers." *Qualitative Sociology* 22: 51–72.

Morrill, Calvin, and Gary Alan Fine. 1997. "Ethnographic Contributions to Organizational Sociology." *Sociological Methods and Research* 25: 424–451.

Morrill, Calvin, David A. Snow, and Cindy White (eds.). 2005. *Together Alone: Personal Relationships in Public Places*. Berkeley: University of California Press.

Morse, Janice M. (ed.). 1994. *Critical Issues in Qualitative Research Methods*. Thousand Oaks, CA: Sage.

Moyser, George. 1988. "Non-Standardized Interviewing in Elite Research." Pp. 109–136 in *Research in Qualitative Methodology* (Vol. 1), edited by R. G. Burgess. Greenwich, CT: JAI Press.

Munch, Allison. 2005. "'Everyone Gets to Participate': Floating Community in an Amateur Softball League." Pp. 111–133 in *Together Alone: Personal Relationships in Public Places*, edited by Calvin Morrill, David A. Snow, and Cindy White. Berkeley: University of California Press.

Murphy, Alexandra G. 2003. "The Dialectical Gaze: Exploring the Subject-Object Tension in the Performances of Women Who Strip." *Journal of Contemporary Ethnography* 32: 305–335.

Murphy, Elizabeth. 2004. "Anticipatory Accounts." *Symbolic Interaction* 27: 129–154.

Murphy, Elizabeth, and Robert Dingwall. 2001. "The Ethics of Ethnography." Pp. 339–351 in *Handbook of Ethnography*, edited by Paul Atkinson, Amanda Coffey, Sara Delamont, John Lofland, and Lyn Lofland. Thousand Oaks, CA: Sage.

———. 2003. *Qualitative Methods and Health Policy Research*. Hawthorne, NY: Aldine de Gruyter.

Myers, Dowell. 1992. *Analysis with Local Census Data: Portraits of Change*. Boston: Academic Press.

Naples, Nancy A., with Emily Clark. 1996. "Feminist Participatory Research and Empowerment: Going Public as Survivors of Childhood Sexual Abuse." Pp. 160–183 in *Feminism and Social Change: Bridging Theory and Practice*, edited by Heidi Gottfried. Urbana: University of Illinois Press.

Nash, Jeffrey, and Anedith J. Nash. 1994. "The Skyway System and Urban Space: Vitality in Enclosed Public Places." Pp. 167–181 in *The Community of the Streets*, edited by S. E. Cahill and L. H. Lofland. Greenwich, CT: JAI Press.

Newman, Katherine. 1999. *No Shame in My Game: The Working Poor in the Inner City*. New York: Russell Sage Foundation and Knopf.

Nippert-Eng, Christena. 1996. *Home and Work: Negotiating Boundaries through Everyday Life*. Chicago: University of Chicago Press.

Nordstrom, Carolyn, and Antonius C. G. Robben (eds.). 1995. *Fieldwork Under Fire: Contemporary Studies of Violence and Survival*. Berkeley: University of California Press.

Oakley, Ann. 1981. "Interviewing Women: A Contradiction in Terms." Pp. 243–261 in *Doing Feminist Research*, edited by H. Roberts. London: Routledge and Kegan Paul.

Olesen, Virginia. 2000. "Feminisms and Qualitative Research at and into the Millenium." Pp. 215–55 in *Handbook of Qualitative Research*, (2nd ed.), edited by N. K. Denzin and Y. Lincoln. Thousand Oaks, CA: Sage.

Ortiz, Steve. 1994. "Shopping for Sociability in the Mall." Pp. 183–199 in *The Community of the Streets*, edited by Spencer E. Cahill and Lyn H. Lofland. Greenwich, CT: JAI Press.

Oselin, Sharon S. 2004. "Leaving the Streets: Transformation of Prostitute Identity Through Rehabilitation." Paper presented at the Annual Meeting of the Society for the Study of Symbolic Interaction.

Ostrander, Susan A. 1984. *Women of the Upper Class*. Philadelphia: Temple University Press.

———. 1993. "'Surely You're Not in This Just to Be Helpful': Access, Rapport, and Interviews in Three Studies of Elites." *Journal of Contemporary Ethnography* 22: 1–27.

———. 1995. *Money For Change: Social Movement Philanthropy at Haymarket People's Fund*. Philadelphia: Temple University Press.

Ouellet, Lawrence J. 1996. *Pedal to the Metal: The Work Lives of Truckers*. Philadelphia: Temple University Press.

Paterniti, Deborah A. 2000. "The Micropolitics of Identity in Adverse Circumstance: A Study of Identity Making in a Total Institution." *Journal of Contemporary Ethnography* 29: 93–119.

Pattillo-McCoy, Mary. 1999. *Black Picket Fences: Privilege and Peril Among the Black Middle Class*. Chicago: University of Chicago Press.

Patton, Michael Q. 1990. *Qualitative Evaluation and Research Methods*. Newbury Park, CA: Sage.

Paules, Greta F. 1991. *Dishing It Out: Power and Resistance Among Waitresses in a New Jersey Restaurant*. Philadelphia: Temple University Press.

Perrow, Charles. 2002. *Organizing America: Wealth, Power, and the Origins of Corporate Capitalism*. Princeton, NJ: Princeton University Press.

Pestello, Fred E. 1991. "Discounting." *Journal of Contemporary Ethnography* 20: 26–46.

Pieke, Frank N. 1996. *The Ordinary and the Extraordinary: An Anthropological Study of Chinese Reform and the 1989 People's Movement in Beijing*. London: Kegan Paul.

Pierce, Jennifer L. 1995a. *Gender Trials: Emotional Lives in Contemporary Law Firms*. Berkeley: University of California Press.

———. 1995b. "Reflections on Fieldwork in a Complex Organization: Lawyers, Ethnographic Authority, and Lethal Weapons." Pp. 94–110 in *Studying Elites Using Qualitative Methods*, edited by Rosanna Hertz and Jonathon B. Imber. Thousand Oaks, CA: Sage.

Pink, Sarah. 2001. *Doing Visual Ethnography*. Thousand Oaks, CA: Sage.

Platt, Jennifer. 1988. "What Can Case Studies Do?" Pp. 1–23 in *Studies in Qualitative Methodology* (Vol. 1), edited by R. G. Burgess. Greenwich, CT: JAI Press.

Plummer, Ken. 2001. *Documents of Life 2: An Invitation to Critical Humanism.* Thousand Oaks, CA: Sage.

Poland, Blake D. 2002. "Transcription Quality." Pp. 629–650 in *Handbook of Interview Research: Context and Methods,* edited by J. F. Gubrium and J. A. Holstein. Thousand Oaks, CA: Sage.

Pollner, Melvin, and Robert M. Emerson. 1983. "The Dynamics of Inclusion and Distance in Fieldwork Relations." Pp. 235–252 in *Contemporary Field Research: A Collection of Readings,* edited by R. M. Emerson. Boston: Little, Brown.

Ponticelli, Christy M. 1999. "Crafting Stories of Sexual Identity Reconstruction." *Social Psychology Quarterly* 62: 157–172.

Powdermaker, Hortense. 1966. *Stranger and Friend: The Way of an Anthropologist.* New York: W. W. Norton.

Prus, Robert. 1987. "Generic Social Processes: Maximizing Conceptual Development in Ethnographic Research." *Journal of Contemporary Ethnography* 16: 250–293.

———. 1989. *Making Sales: Influences as Interpersonal Accomplishment.* Newbury Park, CA: Sage.

———. 1994. "Generic Social Processes and the Study of Human Lived Experiences: Achieving Transcontextuality in Ethnographic Research." Pp. 436–458 in *Symbolic Interaction: An Introduction to Social Psychology,* edited by N. J. Herman and L. T. Reynolds. Dix Hills, NY: General Hall.

———. 1996. *Symbolic Interaction and Ethnographic Research: Intersubjectivity and the Study of Human Lived Experience.* Albany, NY: SUNY Press.

Punch, Maurice. 1986. *The Politics and Ethics of Fieldwork.* Newbury Park, CA: Sage.

Rabinow, Paul. 1977. *Reflections on Fieldwork in Morocco.* Berkeley: University of California Press.

Ragin, Charles C. 1987. *The Comparative Method: Moving Beyond Qualitative and Quantitative Strategies.* Berkeley: University of California Press.

———. 2000. *Fuzzy-Set Social Science.* Chicago: University of Chicago Press.

Ragin, Charles C., and Howard S. Becker (eds.). 1992. *What is a Case? Exploring the Foundations of Social Inquiry.* New York: Cambridge University Press.

Rainwater, Lee, and D. J. Pittman. 1967. "Ethical Problems in Studying a Politically Sensitive and Deviant Community." *Social Problems* 14: 357–366.

Rauch, Jonathan. 1993. *Kindly Inquisitors: The New Attacks on Free Thought.* Chicago: University of Chicago Press.

Ray, Melvin C., and Ronald L. Simons. 1987. "Convicted Murderers' Accounts of Their Crimes: A Study of Homicide in Small Communities." *Symbolic Interaction* 10: 57–70.

Reed-Danahay, Deborah E. (ed.). 1997. *Auto/Ethnography: Rewriting the Self and the Social.* New York: Oxford University Press.

———. 2001. "Autobiography, Intimacy, and Ethnography." Pp. 407–425 in *Handbook of Ethnography,* edited by Paul Atkinson, Amanda Coffey, Sara Delamont, John Lofland, and Lyn Lofland. Thousand Oaks, CA: Sage.

Reinharz, Shulamit. 1992. *Feminist Methods in Social Research.* New York: Oxford University Press.

———. 1993. "Neglected Voices and Excessive Demands in Feminist Research." *Qualitative Sociology* 16: 69–76.

Richards, Thomas J., and Lyn Richards. 1994. "Using Computers in Qualitative Research." Pp. 445–462 in *Handbook of Qualitative Research*, edited by N. K. Denzin and Y. S. Lincoln. Thousand Oaks, CA: Sage.

Richardson, Laurel. 1985. *The New Other Woman: Contemporary Single Women in Affairs with Married Men.* New York: Free Press.

———. 1990. *Writing Strategies: Reaching Diverse Audiences.* Newbury Park, CA: Sage.

———. 1992. "The Consequences of Poetic Representation: Writing the Other, Rewriting the Self." In *Investigating Subjectivity: Research on Lived Experience*, edited by C. Ellis and M. G. Flaherty. Newbury Park, CA: Sage.

———. 2000. "Writing: A Method of Inquiry." Pp. 923–949 in *Handbook of Qualitative Methodology*, (2nd ed.), edited by N. K. Denzin and Y. S. Lincoln. Thousand Oaks, CA: Sage.

Reid, Lori L., Carolyn J. Karlin, and Michael D. Bonham-Crecilius. 2005. "Inclusion and Intrusion: Gender and Sexuality in Gay, Lesbian, and Straight Bars." Pp. 134–158 *Together Alone: Personal Relationships in Public Places*, edited by Calvin Morrill, David A. Snow, and Cindy H. White. Berkeley: University of California Press.

Riecken, Henry W. 1969. "The Unidentified Interviewer." Pp. 39–44 in *Issues in Participant Observation: A Text and Reader*, edited by G. McCall and J. L. Simmons. Reading, MA: Addison-Wesley.

Rieder, Jonathan. 1985. *Canarsie: The Jews and Italians of Brooklyn Against Liberalism.* Cambridge, MA: Harvard University Press.

Riemer, Jeffrey W. 1977. "Varieties of Opportunistic Research." *Urban Life* 5: 467–477.

Riessman, Catherine Kohler. 1993. *Narrative Analysis.* Newbury Park, CA: Sage.

Robins, Douglas M., Clinton R. Sanders, and Spencer E. Cahill. 1991. "Dogs and Their People: Pet-Facilitated Interaction in a Public Setting." *Journal of Contemporary Ethnography* 20: 3–25.

Rochford, E. Burke, Jr. 1985. *Hare Krishna in America.* New Brunswick, NJ: Rutgers University Press.

———. 1994. "Field Work in Membership in the Hare Krishna." Pp. 56–67 in *Constructions of Deviance: Social Power, Context and Interaction*, edited by Patricia A. Adler and Peter Adler. Belmont, CA: Wadsworth.

———. 1992. "On the Politics of Member Validations: Taking the Findings back to Hare Krishna." *Perspectives on Social Problems* 3: 99–116.

Rodriguez, Noelie M., and Alan L. Ryave. 2002. *Systematic Self-Observation: A Method for Researching the Hidden and Elusive Features of Everyday Social Life.* Thousand Oaks, CA: Sage.

Romero, Mary. 1992. *Maid in the U.S.A.* New York: Routledge.

Ronai, Carol Rambo. 1992. "The Reflexive Self Through Narrative: A Night in the Life of an Erotic Dancer/Researcher." Pp. 102–124 in *Investigating Subjectivity*, edited by Carolyn Ellis and Michael G. Flaherty. Newbury Park, CA: Sage.

Ronai, Carol, and Carolyn Ellis. 1989. "Turn-Ons for Money: Interactional Strategies of the Table Dancer." *Journal of Contemporary Ethnography* 18: 271–298.

Rosaldo, Renato. 1989. *Culture and Truth: The Remaking of Social Analysis.* Boston: Beacon Press.

Rosenthal, Rob. 1994. *Homeless in Paradise: A Map of the Terrain*. Philadelphia: Temple University Press.

Roth, Julius. 1966. "Hired Hand Research." *American Sociologist* 1: 190–196.

———. 1970. "Comments on 'Secret Observation.'" Pp. 278–280 in *Qualitative Methodology: Firsthand Involvement with the Social World*, edited by W. J. Filstead. Chicago: Markham.

Roy, Donald E. 1959/60. "'Banana Time': Job Satisfaction and Informal Interaction." *Human Organization* 18: 158–168.

Rubenstein, Steven. 2002. *Alejandro Tsakimp: A Shuar Healer in the Margins of History*. Lincoln: University of Nebraska Press.

Rupp, Leila J., and Verta Taylor. 2003. *Drag Queens at the 801 Cabaret*. Chicago: University of Chicago Press.

Salzinger, Leslie. 2003. *Genders in Production: Making Workers in Mexico's Global Factories*. Berkeley: University of California Press.

———. 2004. "Revealing the Unmarked: Finding Masculinity in a Global Factory." *Ethnography* 5: 5–27.

Sampson, Robert J., and John H. Laub. 1993. *Crime in the Making: Pathways and Turning Points Through Life*. Cambridge, MA: Harvard University Press.

Sanchez-Jankowski, Martin. 1991. *Islands in the Street: Gangs in American Urban Society*. Berkeley: University of California Press.

Sanders, Clinton R. 1989. *Customizing the Body: The Art and Culture of Tattooing*. Philadelphia: Temple University Press.

———. 1994. "Stranger Than Fiction: Insights in Pitfalls in Post-Modern Ethnography." In *Studies in Symbolic Interaction* (Vol. 17), edited by N. K. Denzin. Greenwich, CT: JAI Press.

———. 1999. *Understanding Dogs: Living and Working with Canine Companions*. Philadelphia: Temple University Press.

Sandstrom, Kent. 1990. "Confronting Deadly Disease: The Drama of Identity Construction Among Gay Men with Aids." *Journal of Contemporary Ethnography* 19: 271–294.

Sanjek, Roger (ed.). 1990. *Fieldnotes: The Makings of Anthropology*. Ithaca, NY: Cornell University Press.

———. 1990a. "On Ethnographic Validity." Pp. 385–418 in *Fieldnotes: The Makings of Anthropology*, edited by R. Sanjek. Ithaca, NY: Cornell University Press.

———. 1990b. "A Vocabulary for Fieldnotes." Pp. 92–121 in *Fieldnotes: The Makings of Anthropology*, edited by R. Sanjek. Ithaca, NY: Cornell University Press.

Scarce, Rik. 1990. *Ecowarriors: Understanding the Radical Environmental Movement*. Chicago: Noble Press.

———. 1994. "(No) Trial (But) Tribulations: When Courts and Ethnography Conflict." *Journal of Contemporary Ethnography* 23: 123–149.

Schatzman, Leonard, and Anselm Strauss. 1973. *Field Research: Strategies for a Natural Sociology*. Englewood Cliffs, NJ: Prentice-Hall.

Schensul, Jean J., Margaret D. LeCompte, Robert T. Trotter II, Ellen K. Cromley, and Merrill Singer. 1999. *Mapping Social Networks, Spatial Data, and Hidden Populations*. Walnut Creek, CA: AltaMira.

Scheper-Hughes, Nancy. 1992. *Death Without Weeping: The Violence of Everyday Life in Brazil*. Berkeley: University of California Press.

———. 2000. "Global Trafficking in Organs." *Cultural Anthropology* 41: 191–224.

———. 2004. "Parts Unknown: Undercover Ethnography of the Organ-Trafficking World." *Ethnography* 5: 29–73.

Schneider, Louis. 1975. *The Sociological Way of Looking at the World*. New York: McGraw-Hill.

Schutt, Russell. 2004. *Investigating the Social World: The Process and Practice of Social Research*. (4th ed.). Thousand Oaks, CA: Pine Forge Press.

Schutz, Alfred. 1962. "Common-Sense and Scientific Interpretation of Human Action." Pp. 3–47 in *Collected Papers of Alfred Schutz*, (Vol. 1). The Hague, Netherlands: Martinus Nijhoff.

———. 1967. *The Phenomenology of the Social World*. Evanston, IL: Northwestern University Press. (Originally published in 1932)

Schwalbe, Michael. 1996a. *Unlocking the Iron Cage: The Men's Movement, Gender Politics, and American Culture*. New York: Oxford University Press.

———. 1996b. "The Mirror in Men's Faces." *Journal of Contemporary Ethnography* 25: 58–82.

Schwartz, Dona. 1989. "Visual Ethnography: Using Photography in Qualitative Research." *Qualitative Sociology* 12: 119–154.

Schwartz, M. S., and C. G. Schwartz. 1955. "Problems in Participant Observation." *American Journal of Sociology* 60: 343–353.

Scott, Marvin B., and Stanford M. Lyman. 1968. "Accounts." *American Sociological Review* 33: 46–62.

Seale, Clive. 1999. *The Quality of Qualitative Research*. Thousand Oaks, CA: Sage.

Seidman, Irving E. 1998. *Interviewing as Qualitative Research: A Guide for Researchers in Education and the Social Sciences*. (2nd ed.). New York: Teachers College Press.

Shaffir, William B., and Robert A. Stebbins (eds.). 1991. *Experiencing Fieldwork: An Inside View of Qualitative Research*. Newbury Park, CA: Sage.

Shaw, Clifford. 1930. *The Jack-Roller: A Delinquent Boy's Own Story*. Chicago: University of Chicago Press.

Shils, Edward. 1961. "The Calling of Sociology." Pp. 1405–1448 in *Theories of Society: Foundations of Modern Sociological Theory* (Vol. 2), edited by T. Parsons, E. Shils, K. D. Naegele, and J. R. Pitts. New York: Free Press.

Silverman, David. 2001. *Interpreting Qualitative Data: Methods for Analyzing Talk, Text, and Interaction*. Newbury Park, CA: Sage.

Simpson, George G. 1961. *Principles of Animal Taxonomy*. New York: Columbia University Press.

Singleton, Jr., Royce A., and Bruce C. Straits. 1999. *Approaches to Social Research*. (3rd ed.). New York: Oxford University Press.

Sjoberg, Gideon (ed.). 1967a. *Ethics, Politics and Social Research*. Cambridge, MA: Schenkman.

———. 1967b. "Project Camelot: Selected Reactions and Personal Reflections." Pp. 141–162 in *Ethics, Politics, and Social Research*, edited by Gideon Sjoberg. Cambridge, MA: Schenken.

Sjoberg, Gideon, and Roger Nett. 1997 [1968]. *A Methodology for Social Research*. Prospect Heights, IL: Waveland Press.

Skeggs, Beverly. 2001. "Feminist Ethnography." Pp. 426–442 in *Handbook of Ethnography*, edited by Paul Atkinson, Amanda Coffey, Sara Delamont, John Lofland, and Lyn Lofland. Thousand Oaks, CA: Sage.

Skocpol, Theda (ed.). 1984. *Vision and Method in Historical Sociology*. New York: Cambridge University Press.

Smelser, Neil. 1962. *Theory of Collective Behavior*. New York: Free Press.

Smith, Allen C., and Sherryl Kleinman. 1989. "Managing Emotions in Medical School: Students' Contacts with the Living and the Dead." *Social Psychology Quarterly* 52: 56–69.

Smith, Carolyn D., and William Kornblum (eds.). 1996. *In the Field: Readings on the Field Research Experience*. New York: Praeger.

Smith, Vicki. 1990. *Managing in the Corporate Interest: Control and Resistance in an American Bank*. Berkeley: University of California Press.

———. 2001. *Crossing the Great Divide: Worker, Risk, and Opportunity in the New Economy*. Ithaca, NY: ILR Press.

Snow, David A. 1980. "The Disengagement Process: A Neglected Problem in Participant Observation Research." *Qualitative Sociology* 3: 100–122.

———. 1993. *Shakabuku: A Study of the Nichiren Shoshu Buddhist Movement in America, 1960–1975*. New York: Garland Publishing Co.

———. 2002. "On the Presumed Crisis in Ethnographic Representation: Observations from a Sociological and Interactionist Standpoint." *Journal of Contemporary Ethnography* 31: 498–507.

Snow, David A., and Leon Anderson. 1987. "Identity Work Among the Homeless: The Verbal Construction and Avowal of Personal Identities." *American Journal of Sociology* 92: 1336–1371.

———. 1993. *Down on Their Luck: A Study of Homeless Street People*. Berkeley: University of California Press.

Snow, David A., Leon Anderson, and Susan Baker. 1989. "Criminality and Homeless Men: An Empirical Assessment. *Social Problems* 36: 532–549.

Snow, David A., Susan Baker, Michael Martin, and Leon Anderson. 1986. "The Myth of Pervasive Mental Illness Among the Homeless." *Social Problems* 33: 407–423.

Snow, David A., and Robert D. Benford. 1988. "Ideology, Frame Resonance, and Participant Mobilization." Pp. 197–217 in *International Social Movement Research: A Research Annual*, edited by B. Klandermans, H. Kriesi, and S. Tarrow. Greenwich, CT: JAI Press.

Snow, David A., Robert D. Benford, and Leon Anderson. 1986. "Fieldwork Roles and Informational Yield: A Comparison of Alternative Settings and Roles." *Urban Life* 14: 377–408.

Snow, David A., and Richard Machalek. 1983. "The Convert as a Social Type." Pp. 229–289 in *Sociological Theory*, edited by Randall Collins. San Francisco: Jossey-Boss.

Snow, David A., and Calvin Morrill. 1993. "Reflections on Anthropology's Ethnographic Crisis of Faith." *Contemporary Sociology* 22: 8–11.

Snow, David A., Calvin Morrill, and Leon Anderson. 2003. "Linking Ethnography and Theoretical Development." *Ethnography* 2:181–200.

Snow, David A., and Cynthia L. Phillips. 1980. "The Lofland-Stark Conversion Model: A Critical Reassessment." *Social Problems* 27: 430–447.

Snow, David A., Cherylon Robinson, and Patricia McCall. 1991. "Cooling Out Men in Singles Bars and Nightclubs: Observations on Survival Strategies of Women in Public Places." *Journal of Contemporary Ethnography* 19: 423–449.

Snow, David A., and Danny Trom. 2002. "The Case Study and the Study of Social Movements." Pp. 146–172 in *Methods in Social Movement Research*, edited by S. Staggenborg and B. Klandermans. Minneapolis: University of Minnesota Press.

Snow, David A., Louis A. Zurcher, and Robert Peters. 1981. "Victory Celebrations as Theater: A Dramaturgical Approach to Crowd Behavior." *Symbolic Interaction* 4: 21–41.

Snow, David A., Louis A. Zurcher, and Gideon Sjoberg. 1982. "Interviewing by Comment: An Adjunct to the Direct Question." *Qualitative Sociology* 5: 285–311.

Sobel, Michael E. 1993. "Causal Inferences in the Social Sciences." Pp. 1–38 in *A Handbook for Statistical Modelling in the Social and Behavioral Sciences*, edited by G. Arminger, C. C. Clogg, and M. E. Sobel. New York: Plenum Press.

Spector, Malcolm. 1980. "Learning to Study Public Figures." Pp. 98–110 in *Field Work Experience: Qualitative Approaches to Social Research*, edited by W. B. Shaffir, R. A. Stebbins, and A. Turowetz. New York: St. Martin's Press.

Spencer, Jonathan. 2001. "Ethnography After Postmodernism." Pp. 443–452 in *Handbook of Ethnography*. Paul Atkinson, Amanda Coffey, Sara Delamont, John Lofland, and Lyn Lofland (eds.). Thousand Oaks, CA: Sage.

Spradley, James P. 1980. *Participant Observation*. New York: Holt, Rinehart and Winston.

Spradley, James P., and Brenda J. Mann. 1975. *The Cocktail Waitress: Women's Work in a Man's World*. New York: Wiley.

Stacey, Judith. 1988. "Can There Be a Feminist Ethnography?" *Women's Studies International Forum* 11 (no. 1): 21–27.

Stack, Carol B. 1974. *All Our Kin: Strategies for Survival in a Black Community*. New York: Harper and Row.

Staggenborg, Suzanne. 1988. "'Hired Hand Research' Revisited." *American Sociologist* 19: 260–269.

Stark, Rodney. 1994. *Sociology*. (5th ed.). Belmont, CA: Wadsworth.

Stebbins, Robert A. 1991. "Do We Ever Leave the Field? Notes on Secondary Fieldwork Involvements." Pp. 248–255 in *Experiencing Fieldwork: An Inside View of Qualitative Research*, edited by William B. Shaffir and Robert A. Stebbins. Thousand Oaks: Sage.

Stein, Maurice. 1964. *The Eclipse of Community*. New York: Harper Torchbooks.

Stets, Jan E. 2003. "Emotions and Sentiments." Pp. 309–335 in *Handbook of Social Psychology*, edited by Jon Delamater. New York: Kluwer Academic/Plenum Publishers.

Stevens, Mitchell L. 2001. *Kingdom of Children: Culture and Controversy in the Homeschooling Movement*. Princeton, NJ: Princeton University Press.

Stevenson, Christopher L. 1999. "The Influence of Nonverbal Symbols on the Meaning of Motive Talk: A Case Study from Masters Swimming." *Journal of Contemporary Ethnography* 28: 364–388.

Stinchcombe, Arthur L. 1975. "Merton's Theory of Social Structure." Pp. 11–33 in *The Idea of Social Structure*, edited by L. Coser. New York: Harcourt Brace Jovanovich.

Stocking, George Jr. (ed.). 1989. *Romantic Motives: Essays on Anthropological Sensibility*. Madison: University of Wisconsin Press.

Stoecker, Randy, and Edna Bonacich (eds.). 1992. Participatory Research, Part 1. New Brunswick, NJ: Transaction Publishers. (Special issue of *American Sociologist* 23 [no. 4].)

———. (eds.). 1993. Participatory Research, Part II. New Brunswick, NJ: Transaction Publishers. (Special issue of *American Sociologist* 24 [no. 1].)

Stokes, Randall, and John O. Hewitt. 1976. "Aligning Actions." *American Sociological Review* 41: 839–849.

Strauss, Anselm L. 1962. "Transformations of Identity." Pp. 63–85 in *Human Behavior and Social Processes: An Interactionist Approach*, edited by Arnold M. Rose. London: Routledge & Kegan Paul.

———. 1987. *Qualitative Analysis for Social Scientists*. New York: Cambridge University Press.

Strauss, Anselm, and Juliet Corbin. 1990. *Basics of Qualitative Research: Grounded Theory Procedures and Techniques*. Newbury Park, CA: Sage.

Strauss, Anselm, Leonard Schatzman, Rue Bucher, Danuta Erlich, and Melvin Sabshin. 1964. *Psychiatric Ideologies and Institutions*. New York: Free Press.

Stryker, Sheldon. 1980. *Symbolic Interaction: A Social Structural Version*. Menlo Park, CA: Benjamin/Cummings.

Sullivan, Mercer L. 1989. *"Getting Paid" Youth Crime and Work in the Inner City*. Ithaca, NY: Cornell University Press.

Suttles, Gerald D. 1968. *The Social Order of the Slum: Ethnicity and Territory in the Inner City*. Chicago: University of Chicago Press.

Sykes, Gresham M., and David Matza. 1957. "Techniques of Neutralization: A Theory of Delinquency." *American Sociological Review* 22: 664–670.

Tarrow, Sidney. 1998. *Power in Movement: Social Movements, Collective Action and Politics*, (2nd ed.). New York: Cambridge University Press.

Tashakkori, Abbas, and Charles Teddlie. 2003. *Handbook of Mixed Methods in Social and Behavioral Research*. Thousand Oaks, CA: Sage.

Taylor, Steven J. 1987. "Observing Abuse: Professional Ethics and Personal Morality in Field Research." *Qualitative Sociology* 10: 288–302.

———. 1991. "Leaving the Field: Research, Relationships, and Responsibilities." Pp. 238–247 in *Experiencing Fieldwork: An Inside View of Qualitative Research*, edited by William B. Shaffir and Robert A. Stebbins. Thousand Oaks, CA: Sage.

Taylor, Verta. 1996. *Rock-a-by Baby: Feminism, Self-Help, and Postpartum Depression*. New York: Routledge.

———. 1998. "Feminist Methodology in Social Movements Research." *Qualitative Sociology* 21: 357–379.

Taylor, Verta, and Leil J. Rupp. 2005. "Participatory Action Research in the Study of Social Movements: Drag Queens and the Performance of Protest." Forthcoming in *Rhyming Hope and History: Activism and Social Movement Scholarship*, edited by David Croteau, William Hoynes, and Charlotte Ryan. Minneapolis: University of Minnesota Press.

Thomas, Robert J. 1994. *What Machines Can't Do: Politics and Technology in the Industrial Enterprise*. Berkeley: University of California Press.

———. 1995. "Interviewing Important People in Big Companies." Pp. 1–17 in *Studying Elites Using Qualitative Methods*, edited by Rosanna Hertz and Jonathon B. Imber. Thousand Oaks, CA: Sage Publications.

Thomas, W. I., and Florian Znaniecki. 1927. *The Polish Peasant in Europe and America*. New York: Knopf.

Thorne, Barrie. 1979. "Political Activist as Participant Observer: Conflicts of Commitment in a Study of the Draft Resistance Movement of the 1960s." *Symbolic Interaction* 2: 73–88.

———. 1993. *Gender Play: Girls and Boys in School*. New Brunswick, NJ: Rutgers University Press.

———. 2001. "Learning from Kids." Pp. 224–238 in *Contemporary Field Research: A Collection of Readings*, (2nd ed.), edited by R. M. Emerson. Prospect Heights, IL: Waveland Press.

Timmermans, Stefan. 1999. *Sudden Death and the Myth of CPR*. Philadelphia: Temple University Press.

Titscher, Stefan, Michael Meyer, Ruth Wodak, and Eva Vetter. 2000. *Methods of Text and Discourse Analysis: In Search of Meaning*. Thousand Oaks, CA: Sage.

Traugott, Mark (ed.). 1995. *Repertoires & Cycles of Collective Action*. Durham, NC: Duke University Press.

Tunnell, Kenneth D. 1998. "Honesty, Secrecy, and Deception in the Sociology of Crime: Confessions and Reflections from the Backstage." Pp. 206–220 in *Ethnography at the Edge: Crime, Deviance and Field Research*, edited by J. Ferrell and M. S. Hamm. Boston, MA: Northeastern University Press.

Turabian, Kate L. (revised by John Grossman and Alice Bennett). 1996. *A Manual for Writers of Term Papers, Theses, and Dissertations* (6th ed.). Chicago: University of Chicago Press.

Turner, Ralph H. 1947. "The Navy Disbursing Officer as a Bureaucrat." *American Sociological Review* 12: 342–348.

———. 1953. "The Quest for Universals in Sociological Research." *American Sociological Review* 24: 605–611.

Turner, Ralph, and Lewis Killian. 1987. *Collective Behavior*. Englewood Cliffs, NJ: Prentice-Hall.

Vail, D. Angus. 2001. "Researching From Afar: Distance, Ethnography, and Testing the Edge. "*Journal of Contemporary Ethnography* 30: 704–725.

van den Hoonard, Will C. (ed.). 2002. *Walking the Tightrope: Ethical Issues for Qualitative Researchers*. Toronto: University of Toronto Press.

Van Maanen, John. 1988. *Tales of the Field: On Writing Ethnography*. Chicago: University of Chicago Press.

Van Maanen, John, and John G. Kunda. 1989. "'Real Feelings': Emotional Expression and Organizational Culture." *Research in Organizational Behavior* 11: 43–103.

Van Zandt, David E. 1991. *Living in the Children of God*. Princeton: Princeton University Press.

Vaughan, Diane. 1990. *Uncoupling: Turning Points in Intimate Relationships*. New York: Vintage Books. (Originally published by Oxford University Press in 1986)

———. 1996. *The Challenger Launch Decision: Risky Technology, Culture, and Deviance at NASA*. Chicago: University of Chicago Press.

———. 2003. "History as Cause: Columbia and Challenger." Pp. 195–20 in *Report Volume 1*. Columbia Accident Investigation Board. Washington, DC: Government Printing Office.

Venkatesh, Sudhir Alladi. 2000. *American Project: The Rise and Fall of a Modern Ghetto*. Cambridge, MA: Harvard University Press.

Vidich, Arthur J. 1955. "Participant Observation and the Collection and Interpretation of Data." *American Journal of Sociology* 60: 354–360.

Vidich, Arthur J., and Joseph Bensman. 1968. *Small Town in Mass Society: Class, Power and Religion in a Rural Community* (2nd ed.). Princeton, NJ: Princeton University Press.

Vidich, Arthur J., and Stanford M. Lyman. 2000. "Qualitative Methods: Their History in Sociology and Anthropology." Pp. 23–59 in *Handbook of Qualitative Research* (2nd ed.), edited by N. K. Denzin and Y. S. Lincoln. Thousand Oaks, CA: Sage.

Vigil, James D. 2002. *A Rainbow of Gangs: Street Cultures in the Mega-City*. Austin: University of Texas Press.

Wacquant, Löic. 1998a. "Inside the Zone: The Social Art of the Hustler in the Black American Ghetto." *Theory, Culture, and Society* 15: 1–36.

———. 1998b. "The Prizefighter's Three Bodies." *Ethnos* 63: 325–352.

Wagner, David. 1993. *Checkerboard Square: Culture and Resistance in a Homeless Community*. Boulder, CO: Westview.

Walker, Andrew, and Rosalind Kimball Moulton. 1989. "Photo Albums: Images of Time and Reflections of Self." *Qualitative Sociology* 12: 183–214.

Warren, Carol A. B. 1977. "Fieldwork in the Gay World: Issues in Phenomenological Research." *Journal of Social Issues* 33: 93–107.

———. 2001. "Gender and Fieldwork Relations." Pp. 203–223 in *Contemporary Field Research: A Collection of Readings*, (2nd ed.), edited by Robert M. Emerson. Prospect Heights, IL: Waveland Press.

Warren, Carol A. B., and Jennifer K. Hackney. 2000. *Gender Issues in Ethnography*. (2nd ed.). Thousand Oaks, CA: Sage.

Warren, Carol A. B., and William G. Staples. 1989. "Fieldwork in Forbidden Terrain: The State, Privatization and Human Subjects Regulations." *American Sociologist* 20: 263–277.

Warwick, D. E. 1975. "Social Scientists Ought to Stop Lying." *Psychology Today*, February: 38, 40, 105–106.

———. 1982. "Tearoom Trade: Means and Ends in Social Research." Pp. 35–58 in *Social Research Ethics*, edited by M. Bulmer. London: Macmillan.

Wax, Murray, and Joan Cassell. 1981. "From Regulation to Reflection: Ethics in Social Research." *American Sociologist* 16: 224–229.

Wax, Rosalie H. 1971. *Doing Fieldwork: Warnings and Advice*. Chicago: University of Chicago Press.

———. 1979. "Gender and Age in Fieldwork and Fieldwork Education: No Good Thing Is Done by Any Man Alone." *Social Problems* 26: 509–522.

Webb, Eugene, Donald T. Campbell, Richard D. Schwartz, Lee Sechrest, and Janet B. Grove. 1981. *Nonreactive Measures in the Social Sciences* (2nd ed.). Boston: Houghton Mifflin.

Weick, Karl. 1985. "Systematic Observational Methods." Pp. 567–634 in *Handbook of Social Psychology*, (Vol. 2, 3rd ed.), edited by Gardner Lindzey and Elliot Aronson. New York: Random House.

Weitzman, Eben A. 2000. "Software and Qualitative Research." Pp. 803–820 in *Handbook of Qualitative Research*, (2nd ed.), edited by N. K. Denzin and Y. Lincoln. Thousand Oaks, CA: Sage.

Wesely, Jennifer K. 2003. "Exotic Dancing and the Negotiation of Identity: The Multiple Uses of Body Technology." *Journal of Contemporary Ethnography* 32: 643–669.

Whyte, William F. 1993. *Street Corner Society: The Social Structure of an Italian Slum*. (4th ed.). Chicago: University of Chicago Press. (Fiftieth anniversary edition; originally published in 1943)

Williams, Christine L. 1995. *Still a Man's World: Men Who Do Women's Work*. Berkeley: University of California Press.

Williams, Terry. 1989. *The Cocaine Kids: The Inside Story of a Teenage Drug Ring*. New York: Addison-Wesley.

Williams, Terry, Eloise Dunlap, Bruce Johnson, and Ansley Hamid. 1992. "Personal Safety in Dangerous Places." *Journal of Contemporary Ethnography* 21: 343–374.

Willis, Paul. 1977. *Learning to Labor: How Working Class Kids Get Working Class Jobs*. New York: Columbia University Press.

Wolcott, Harry E. 1990. "Making a Study 'More Ethnographic.'" *Journal of Contemporary Ethnography* 19: 44–72.

———. 1994. *Transforming Qualitative Data: Description, Analysis, and Interpretation*. Thousand Oaks, CA: Sage.

———. 2001. *Writing Up Qualitative Research*. Second edition. Thousand Oaks, CA: Sage.

Wolf, Margaret. 1992. *A Thrice-Told Tale: Feminism, Postmodernism, and Ethnographic Responsibility*. Stanford, CA: Stanford University Press.

Wolf, Diane L. 1992. *Factory Daughters: Gender, Household Dynamics, and Rural Industrialization in Java*. Berkeley: University of California Press.

———. 1996. "Situating Feminist Dilemmas in Fieldwork." Pp. 1–55 in *Feminist Dilemmas in Fieldwork*, edited by D. L. Wolf. Boulder, CO: Westview Press.

Wolkomir, Michelle. 2001. "Emotion Work, Commitment, and the Authentication of the Self.: The Case of Gay and Ex-Gay Christian Support Groups." *Journal of Contemporary Ethnography* 30: 305–334.

Workman, John E. Jr. 1992. "Use of Electronic Media in a Participant Observation Study." *Qualitative Sociology* 15: 419–425.

Wright, Sam. 1978. *Crowds and Riots: A Study in Social Organization*. Beverly Hills, CA: Sage.

Wright, Talmadge. 1997. *Out of Place: Homeless Mobilizations, Subcities, and Contested Landscapes*. Albany, NY: State University of New York Press.

Yanay, Niza and Golan Shahar. 1998. "Professional Feelings as Emotional Labor." *Journal of Contemporary Ethnography* 27: 346–373.

Yin, Robert K. 2003. *Case Study Research: Design and Methods*. Thousand Oaks, CA: Sage.

Yoels, William C., and J. M. Clair. 1994. "Never Enough Time: How Medical Students Manage a Scarce Resource." *Journal of Contemporary Ethnography* 23: 185–213.

Zablocki, Benjamin, and Rosabeth Moss Kanter. 1976. "The Differentiation of Lifestyles." *Annual Review of Sociology* 2: 269–298.

Zavella, Patricia. 1996. "Feminist Insider Dilemmas: Constructing Ethnic Identity with Chicana Informants." Pp. 138–159 in *Feminist Dilemmas in Fieldwork*, edited by D. L. Wolf. Boulder, CO: Westview Press.

Zelditch, Morris, Jr. 1962. "Some Methodological Problems of Field Studies." *American Journal of Sociology* 67: 566–576.

Zerubavel, Evitar. 1980. "If Simmel Were a Fieldworker: On Formal Sociological Theory and Analytical Field Research." *Symbolic Interaction* 3: 25–33.

———. 1991. *The Fine Line: Making Distinctions in Everyday Life*. Chicago: University of Chicago Press.

———. 1999. *The Clockwork Muse: A Practical Guide to Writing Theses, Dissertation, and Books*. Cambridge, MA: Harvard University Press.

Zimmerman, Don H., and D. Lawrence Wieder. 1977. "The Diary-Interview Method." *Urban Life* 5: 479–498.

Znaniecki, Florian. 1934. *The Method of Sociology*. New York: Farrar and Rinehart.

Zurcher, Louis A. 1983. *Social Roles: Conformity, Conflict, and Creativity*. Beverly Hills, CA: Sage.

INDEX

Abolafia, Mitchel, 172
Absolutism, 174
Abstract truth, 169
Abstracted typologies, 149
Academic interests, 12
Acceptable incompetence, 69–70
Access to data sites, 21–27, 33–53. *See also* Social settings
Accounts, explanation of proposed research to participants, 43–46
Activist social research, 65, 189–190
Adler, Patricia, 24, 33, 41, 50, 64, 75, 135, 141, 151
Adler, Peter, 24, 33, 41, 50, 135, 141
Age, 23, 61, 122
Agency, human, 165–167
Alienation, 14, 60, 61
Allahyari, Rebecca, 73, 135
American Anthropological Association, 78
American Sociological Association, 29, 31, 52, 78, 98
"Amorphous social experiences," 19
Analytic excess, 183–184
Analytic files, 206–208
Analytic ideas and hunches in fieldnotes, 113–114
Analytic induction, 161–162
"Analytic interruptus," 211
Analyzing data in fieldstudies, 1, 4–5, 187, 195–196. *See also* Fieldstudies
Anderson, Elijah, 36, 126, 130, 134, 139
Anderson, Leon, 66, 74, 111, 147, 154, 172, 182, 183, 217
Anxiety normalization and management in fieldstudy analysis, 198–200
Applied sociology, 190
Appropriateness of data site, 18–21
Archival materials, 89, 95
Arditti, Rita, 53
Arousing interest in audiences for fieldstudies, 168–169. *See also* Framing
Artifacts, socially embedded, 94
Ascriptive categories of researcher and researched, 23–25, 61

Aspects of topics. *See also* Topics
  cognitive aspects or meanings, 132–136
  ideologies (and kindred concepts) as meanings, 133–134
  rules as meanings, 134–135
  self-concepts and identities as meanings, 135–136
  emotional aspects or feelings, 136–139
  and organizations, 138–139
  in practices, episodes, and encounters, 136–137
  and roles, 137–138
  hierarchical aspects or inequalities, 139–141
  in encounters, 139–140
  in groups, 141
  in roles and relationships, 140
  two or more units or aspects as topics, 141–142
  units and aspects defined, 121–122
  units, aspects, and topics form mind-set for coding, 143
Assessment of data sites, 18–33, 121
  access, 21–27, 33–53
  appropriateness, 18–21
  ethics, 28–30
  personal consequences, 30–32
  physical and emotional risks, 27–28
Atkinson, Paul, 196
Audiences for fieldstudies, 5, 238. *See also* Framing
  arousing interest in, 168–169, 189
Audiotapes, 85, 89
  of interviews, 106–107
  of researcher's observations, 112
  transcriptions of, 107, 112
Autobiographical sociology, 12
Autoethnography, 12, 191

Becker, Howard, 221, 224, 225, 229–230, 236
Bell, Michael, 130
Benford, Robert, 61, 173
Bensman, Joseph, 51, 131
Berg, Bruce, 68
Berger, Bennett, 133
Berger, Peter, 188

273

Biases, 16, 58, 61. See also Error and bias problems
Biggart, Nicole, 129, 139, 180
Biography of researchers, 9–12
Blee, Kathleen, 58, 62, 63, 69, 71, 135
Blumer, Herbert, 84, 165–166
Boelen, Marianne, 171
Bogard, Cynthia, 89
Bosk, Charles, 72
Brayfield, April, 87
Bronfenbrenner, Urie, 79
Bruffee, Kenneth, 222
Burawoy, Michael, 171, 173
Bureaucratic barriers to data sites, 47–50

Cahill, Spencer, 12–13, 36, 138, 173
Calhoun, Thomas, 70
Case comparative models of causality, 158, 160–161
Case studies, 21, 81, 88
Casual interviewing, 88
Causal explanation conditions, 157
Causal explanation of topics, 156–162
Census data, 21, 81, 88
Center for Disaster Research, 26
Central tendency measures, 149–150
Chagnon, Napoleon, 27, 48, 130
Challenges in fieldstudies, 54–66
  dealing with, 65–66
  emotional challenges, 54–63
    deception and the fear of disclosure, 56–57
    distance and surrender, 57–63
    information overload, 55
    physical dangers, 63–65
Charmaz, Kathy, 71, 106, 173, 201, 202
Chin, Tiffani, 138
Chronological records, 209
Clair, Jeffrey, 140
Clark, Candace, 136–137
Clark, Emily, 53
Clinical sociology, 190
Cliques as unit of social settings, 127–128
Closed questions, 106
Code memos, 210
Coding, 107, 200–209
  chronological records, 209
  physical methods of, 203–204
    computer databasing, 203–204
    filing, 203
  types of coding files, 204–209
    analytic files, 206–208
    folk/setting-specific files, 205–206
    methodological/fieldwork files, 208–209
  units, aspects, and topics form mind-set for coding, 143
Cognitive aspects or meanings, 132–136
Coleman, James, 12
Collective actions and behavior, 124. See also Episodes
Communication, interpersonal, 221–222

Competence, selective, 70
Computer-assisted qualitative data analysis (CAQDAS), 204
Computers
  in data logging, 95–98
  databasing in coding, 203–204
  in writing, 235
Concept charts, 215–216
Concreteness in fieldnotes, 112–113
Condemnation from colleagues, 31–32
Confidentiality, 30, 31, 50, 51–53
  and data logging, 98, 116
  disguising identities and localities, 98. See also Ethics
Conflict zones, 63. See also Physical dangers in fieldstudies
Conjoint variations, 148. See also Typologizing
Connections of researcher, 41–43
Consequences of topics, 162–165
Content analyses, 2
Contents of fieldnotes, 112–115
Contextual models of causality, 158, 160
Conversations, guided, 105
Conversion model, 161
"Convert" stance, 22
Converting, 62, 73, 75
Copp, Martha, 28, 63
Corsaro, William, 24
Courtesy, 47, 68
Covariation between independent and dependent variables, 157
Covert research, 29, 35–40, 56. See also Ethics
Creativity, 238
Credentialed expert role, 70
Cress, Daniel, 147, 161, 164, 183
Crime, 63, 124. See also Episodes
Criminal justice system, giving information to, 31
Critical sociology, 190
Crowd behavior, 25, 124. See also Episodes
Cultural practices as units of social settings, 123–124
Cultural products of social interaction, 16–17
Cycles as processes, 152–153

Dalton, Melville, 127
Dangerous settings, 26, 63–64
Darwin, Charles, 181
Data
  analyzing, 1, 4–5
  census, 21
  focusing, 1, 4
  gathering data, 1, 3, 7
  quantitative, 20–21, 89, 149–151
Data logging, 81–117
  fact or fiction, 82–84, 90–95
  fieldnotes, 108–117
  intensive interviewing, 99–108
    doing the interview, 104–107
    interview guide, 99–104

task of, 84–98
  confidentiality, 98, 116
  data sources, 85–90
  error and bias problems, 90–95
  mechanics of logging, 95–98
Data sites, 33, 121
  barriers to, 47–50
  getting in, 34
  participant observation and intensive interviewing, 16, 17–18
  richest possible data as overall goal, 15–17
Data sources, 85–90
"Data-theory boot-strapping," 211
Data triangulation, 21
Davis, Fred, 22, 104, 184
Davis, Kingsley, 180
Davis, Murray, 172
Deception and the fear of disclosure, 56–57
Declining and withdrawing in field relations, 75
Deduction, 195
Democratizing representation of informants, 52, 53
Demographic data, 89
Demystification of social arrangements, 187–188
Denzin, Norman, 83, 135, 155
Dependent variables in causal explanation, 157
Descriptive excess, 184
Descriptive vignettes, 232
Diagramming, 212–217
  concept charts, 215–216
  flow charts, 216–217
  matrices, 214
  taxonomies, 212–213
  typologies, 214–215
  in writing, 224–225
Diamond, Tim, 191
Diary/diary-interview method of research, 19
"Dilemma of distance," 22. See also Distance/surrender continuum
Direct experience as data source, 85
Direct observation, 1, 15–16
Disciplines using fieldstudies, 5
Disengagement process, 30–31, 75–78
Distance/surrender continuum, 57–63
Distancing, periodic, 219
Distrust within settings, 26
Document collection, 81, 88, 89
Documentation, 81. See also Data logging
Dordick, Gwen, 73–74
Douglas, Jack, 169
Dress and grooming, 69
Drug dealing and use, 26, 64, 74–75
Duneier, Mitchell, 24, 53, 90, 126, 130
Dunn, Linda, 28

Ecological mapping, 47
Economic imperialism, 48
Economically dominated lifestyles, 132

Elbow, Peter, 222, 236
Ellickson, Robert, 12
Ellis, Carolyn, 62
Emerson, Robert, 24–25, 73, 75, 195
Emotional aspects or feelings, 136–139
Emotional challenges in fieldstudies, 54–63
Emotional risks for researchers, 27–28
Empirical accuracy of trueness, 169
Empirical adequacy of data, 82–84, 90–95. See also Data logging
Encounters as unit of social settings, 124–125
Entitlement, 231–232
Ephemeral activities, 26
Episodes as unit of social settings, 124
Equality between researcher and researched, 29. See also Feminist ethics
Error and bias problems, 90–95, 169
  control measures, 91, 93–95, 175
"Ethical hangover," 30, 76
Ethics, 65
  and confidentiality, 51–53
  and covert research, 35–40
  evaluating research project for, 28–30
  feminist, 29
  in field relations, 78–79
  human subjects, 29–30
  in logging data, 98. See also Ethics
Ethnicity, 11, 23, 61, 122
Ethnographer's path, 170
Ethnographic studies, 1, 5, 6, 11, 192
Evaluating data sites. See Assessment of data sites
Evaluation research, 190
Evans-Pritchard, Edward, 130
Evidentiary privilege, 52
Exchange strategies in field relations, 71–72
Experimental models of causality, 157–158
Expert role of social researchers, 46, 70
Expressive voicing, 191–192
"Extended case method," 173

Face-to-face interaction, 15, 16, 20
Facesheets for fieldnotes, 103–104
Federal regulations, 49
Federal statutes relative to privacy, 53
Feedback on written reports, 222, 234, 235–236
Feelings. See Emotional aspects or feelings
Feminist ethics and ethnography, 29, 32, 62, 65
Feminist participant action fieldstudies, 53
Field relations, 66–75. See also Social researchers
Fielding, Nigel, 58
Fieldnote evidence, 170–171
Fieldnotes, 108–117. See also Participant observation
  as compulsion, 116–117
  contents of, 112–115

276   Index

jotted notes, 109–110
mechanics, 110–112
mental notes, 109
style, 115–116
Fieldstudies. *See also* Challenges in fieldstudies; Framing; Naturalistic approach to social research; Social researchers; Topics; Writing
  analysis in, 195–219
    anxiety normalization and management, 198–200
    coding, 200–209
    diagramming, 212–217
    flexible thinking, 211–219
    memoing, 209–211
    social science framing, 197–198
  arousing interest in, 168–169
  audiences for and disciplines using, 5
  features of, 2
  "getting in" the data site, 34
  importance of, 168, 174–187
  labels for, 1, 5–6
  newness in, 168, 171–174
  questions about topics, 144–145, 167–168, 176
  similarity of all scholarship, 239–240
  social science guidance in, 4
  "starting where you are," 9–14, 41
  tasks in, 1–5
    analyzing data, 1, 4–5, 193, 195–196
    focusing data, 1, 4, 119
    gathering data initial task for, 1, 3, 7
  trueness in, 168, 169–171
Fieldwork approach to social research, 6, 9, 239
Fine, Gary Alan, 11, 24, 37, 44, 74, 129, 151
Finessing in field relations, 74–75
Fink, Michael, 26
Fisher, Bradley J., 155
Flaherty, Michael, 162, 205
Flexible format for intensive interviewing, 105
Flexible thinking in fieldstudy analysis, 211–219
Flow charts, 216–217
Focus group interviews, 20
Focused coding, 201
"Focused revisit," 171
Focusing data in fieldstudies, 1, 4
Folk/setting-specific files, 205–206
Folk typologies, 149
"Forbidden terrain," 26, 49
Formal organizations, 25–26, 128–129
Framing, 168–187, 189–192. *See also* Fieldstudies
  importance, 168, 174–187
    developed treatment, 180–185
    generic concepts, 177–180
    propositional framing, 175–177
    questioning mind-set, 174–175

newness, 168, 171–174
  first report, 172
  new analytic focus and perspective, 173–174
  relating to existing work, 171–172
other types of framing, 189–192
  expressive voicing, 191–192
  liberation frame, 190
  muckraking frame, 191
  technocratic/social engineering frame, 190
trueness, 168, 169–171
  ethnographer's path, 170
  fieldnote and interview evidence, 170–171
  theoretical candor, 170
Freeman, Derek, 171
Frequencies of topics in relation to counting, 149–150

Gallagher, Patrick, 59
Gamson, William, 20
Gans, Herbert, 130, 180
Gatekeepers, 26, 40, 42, 43, 45, 46, 70
Gathering data for fieldstudies, 1, 3, 7
Gearing, Frederick O., 58
Geertz, Clifford, 15, 130, 170
Gender, 11, 23–24, 61, 122, 139
Gender harassment, 73–74
"Generalized other," 222
Generic concepts and understanding, 177, 187
Glaser, Barney, 173, 196, 210, 211
Global sorting and ordering for intensive interviewing, 100–101
Goffman, Erving, 129, 135, 136, 137, 146, 159, 164, 178
Gould, Leroy, 88
Grønbjerg, Kirsten, 148
Grounded theory, 5, 173, 195–196, 210, 218
Groups and cliques as units of social settings, 127–128
Gubrium, Jaber, 24
Guided conversations, 105

Habitats as unit of social settings, 130–131
Hammersly, Martyn, 169
Harper, Douglas, 90
Heirich, Max, 154
Herman, Nancy, 182, 184, 185
Heyl, Barbara Sherman, 68
Hierarchical aspects or inequalities, 139–141
Hilbert, Richard, 38
Hochschild, Arlie, 24, 138, 140
Hodson, Randy, 215, 216
Holistic dispassionate understanding, 188–189
Hollingshead, August, 128
Hondagneu-Sotelo, Pierette, 71

Horne, Christine, 36
Horowitz, Ruth, 70, 71, 73, 75, 165
Hughes, Everett, 155
Human agency, 165–167
Human perception and human conception, 83
Human subjects
  ethics in research on, 29–30, 49
  protection regulations, 51
Hume, David, 156
Humphreys, Laud, 31, 173
Hunt, Scott, 173
Hypotyposis, 232

"I" and "me" of the self, 222, 234
Identification with informants, 62–63
Identities as meanings, 135–136
Ideologies (and kindred concepts) as meanings, 133–134
Incompetence, acceptable, 69–70
Independent variables in causal explanation, 157
Indirect observation, 15–16
Induction, 195, 198
Inequality, 122, 139–141
Informal interviewing, 88
Informants
  ascriptive categories of researcher and researched, 23–25
  boundaries with, 73
  confidentially, 51–53
  converting researchers, 56, 73, 75
  democratizing representation, 52, 53
  disengagement process, 30–31, 75–78
  distance and surrender from, 57–63
  field relations with, 66–75
  informed consent of, 30, 49, 50
  member checking, 94–95
  strategic selection of, 93–94
Information overload, 55
Informed consent, 30, 45, 49, 50, 103–104. See also Ethics and IRB
Insider/outsider dilemma, 24–25
"Insider" participant researcher role, 41
Institutional Review Boards (IRBs), 29–30, 78, 98
  and confidentiality, 51, 53
  initial screening by, 49–50
  local, 39
  signed informed consent forms, 45, 103–104
  use of pseudonyms, 98. See also Ethics
Institutions, 122, 146
Intellectual curiosity, 9, 11, 12–13
Intensive interviewing, 1, 16, 17–18, 68, 99–108. See also Interviews
  in covert research, 35
  doing the interview, 104–107
  introduction, 104–105
  interview guide, 99–104
    facesheets and fieldnotes, 103–104
    section sorting and ordering, 101–102
  talk in, 87–88
  writing up the interview, 107–108, 116–117
Intentional consequences, 163–164
Interest in audiences for fieldstudies, 168–169. See also Framing
Internal conflicts in groups, 25
Internet, 20, 88, 96
Interpenetration, 184–185
Intervening variables in causal explanation, 157
Interview evidence, 170–171
Interviews, 68
  guide for intensive interviewing, 99–104
  informal, 88
  reinterviewing, 107, 108
  structured, 17
  taping, 106–107
  writing up, 107–108, 116–117
Intimate familiarity with the setting, 15, 16
Investigative reporters, 52
Investigators. See Social researchers
Irony, 180, 231
Irwin, John, 11

James, William, 85
Jimerson, Jason, 12, 70
Johnson, Norris, 140
Johnston, Drue, 140
Junker, Buford, 33

Kanter, Rosabeth, 132
Katz, Jack, 137, 162, 172
Kendall, Lori, 172
Kleinman, Sherryl, 17, 24, 28, 63, 137–138
Knowledge about setting and participants, 46–47
Known social researchers, 40–47
Kotarba, Joseph, 19
Kunda, Gideon, 128–129

Labels for fieldstudies, 1, 5–6
Leading questions, 105–106
"Learner" or "incompetent" role of researchers, 46
LeCompte, Margaret, 196
Lee, Jennifer, 87
Legal barriers to data sites, 47–50
Leidner, Robin, 140
Lemert, Edwin, 154
Leo, Richard, 52
Libel suits, 49
Liberation frame, 190
Liberation sociology, 190
Liebow, Elliot, 24
Lifestyles, economically dominated, 132
Lifestyles as units of social settings, 131–132
Literary organizing devices, 231–232
Loathing of informants, 58–59

Lofland, John, 26, 55, 76, 133–134, 136, 142, 153, 155, 156, 161, 180, 198, 211
Lofland, Lyn, 25, 36, 100, 101, 102, 127, 134–135, 142
Lois, Jennifer, 39, 64, 70, 137, 141, 155
Lynd, Helen, 131
Lynd, Robert, 131

Macro systems of inequality, 139
Magnitudes of topics, 151
Malinowski, Bronislaw, 59, 61, 66
Mandell, Nancy, 24
Mapping, 47, 81, 88
Marginal and vulnerable groups, 48
Marginalization of informants, 59–61
"Martian" stance, 22
Matrices, 214
Maximum variation sampling, 93
McIlwaine, Mary Kris, 36
Mead, George Herbert, 221, 222
Mead, Margaret, 130, 171
Meanings defined, 132
Means (averages), 149
Mechanics of fieldnotes, 110–112
Medians, 149
Melbin, Murray, 179
Member checking, 94–95
Memoing, 107, 209–211
Merton, Robert, 164, 180
Metaphors, 179–180, 231
Methodological/fieldwork files, 208–209
Milligan, Melinda, 87
Mills, C. Wright, 214, 218
Mitchell, Richard, 26, 38, 173
Models of causal explanation of topics, 157–158
Modes, 150
Moffat, Michael, 128
Morrill, Calvin, 42, 43, 46, 86, 92, 100–101, 102, 129, 153, 173, 180
Muckraking, 52, 191
Multiple types and taxonomies of topics, 146–147
Munch, Allison, 36, 37
Mundane assistance, 71
Murphy, Elizabeth, 123

Naples, Nancy, 53
Narrative, 232
Naturalistic approach to social research, 1, 6, 9, 18. *See also* Fieldstudies
control in, 33
emergent nature of, 32
flexibility of, 32
Naturalistic tradition, 13
Negative case models of causality, 158, 161
Networking, 43. *See also* Connections of researcher
Newman, Katherine, 130
Newspaper articles, 89
Nonthreatening demeanor, 68–69

Notational system for member comments in fieldnotes, 113
Note taking in intensive interviewing, 106–107
NUD*IST, 211

Objectivation, 167
Objectivity, 16, 83. *See also* Data logging
Observing talk in action, 87, 88
One Right Way in writing, 229–230
Open-mindedness, 217
Open public settings, 25
Operational/procedural memos, 210
Opinion polling, 17, 99
Opportunistic research, 10
Oppressed and less powerful groups, 28–29
Organization scale, units of, 121–122
Organizations as unit of social settings, 128–129
Ostrander, Susan, 42, 43
Outline diagrams, 213
"Outsider" participant researcher role, 41–47
knowledge of researcher, 46–47

Park, Robert, 13
Participant observation, 1, 16, 17–18, 35. *See also* Fieldnotes
"Participating-to-write style," 108–109
Participatory action research, 65, 190
"Passing" situations, 57
Passivist versus agentic conceptions, 165–166
Pattillo-McCoy, Mary, 130
Paules, Greta, 140
Peirce, Charles Sanders, 175
Perceptual and interpretive distortions, 91
Perfection or the One Right Way in writing, 229–230
Periods defined, 152
Perrow, Charles, 128
Personal accounts of the field experience, 79–80
Personal consequences for researcher, 30–32
Personal experience and biography of researcher, 9–12
Personal impressions and feelings in fieldnotes, 114–115
Personal relationships as units of social settings, 126–127
Personal stories, 12, 191
Phases defined, 152
Photographic data, 85, 90
Physical dangers in fieldstudies, 63–65
Physical risks for researchers, 27–28
Physical traces as data source, 85, 89–90
Pierce, Jennifer, 28, 139
Policy research, 190
Political barriers to data sites, 47–50
Postmodernism, 83, 191

Power imbalances, 65. *See also* Challenges in fieldstudies
Preempting in field relations, 73–74
Prescriptive guidelines, 218–219
Presentational strategies in field relations, 68–70
Private and quasi-private settings, 35, 37–40
Private documents, 89
Probes for intensive interviewing, 102–103
Processes defined, 152
Processes of topics, 152–156
Professional credentials, 70
"Project Camelot," 48
Propositional framing, 175–177
Propositions in fieldstudies, 197–198
Proscriptive guidelines, 217–218
Protest gatherings, 26. *See also* Episodes
Prus, Robert, 125
Pseudonyms in fieldstudies, 52, 98
Public and commercial documents, 89
Public and quasi-public settings, 34, 36–37
Public figures, 52
Public/private continuum, 34, 41
Puzzlements and jottings for intensive interviewing, 99

Qualitative comparative analysis (QCA), 160–161
Qualitative field research and causal explanation, 158–162
Qualitative methodology, 1, 5, 17, 21
Quantitative data, 20–21, 88, 149–151
Quasi-private settings, 35, 37–40
Quasi-public settings, 25, 34, 36–37
Questioning mind-set, 187
Questions, 99. *See also* Topics
  closed, 106
  ineffective, 105–106
  leading, 105–106
  in topics, 144–145, 167–168, 176

Race, 23, 61, 122
Ragin, Charles, 154
Rapport, 59, 67
Rauch, Jonathan, 175, 176
Reactive effects in error and bias, 91
"Reader-based" feedback, 236
Recalled information in fieldnotes, 113
Relational closeness in field relations, 72–75
Reminders in fieldnotes, 115
Rereading and revising written reports, 233–235
Research
  activist social, 65
  collaborative, 53
  covert, 29, 35–40, 56
  future agendas, 78
  interests in, 6
  laboratory animal, 33
  medical, 33, 49
  motivation for, 13
  online, 20
  on oppressed and less powerful groups, 28–29
  participatory action, 65, 190
  policy and evaluation, 190
Research subjects. *See* Informants
Researchers. *See* Social researchers
Resonating content, 185–187
Revising written reports, 229, 233–235, 237–238
Richards, Lyn, 211
Richards, Thomas J., 211
Richest possible data as overall goal, 15–17
Rieder, Jonathan, 130
Riemer, Jeffrey, 11
Rochford, Burke, 25, 133
Roles as unit of social settings, 125–126
Romero, Mary, 11
Rosaldo, Renato, 12
Roth, Julius, 36, 37, 40
Roy, Donald, 129, 171
Rule of exhaustiveness, 149
Rule of mutual exclusiveness, 149
Rules as meanings, 134–135
Rules of typologizing, 149
Rupp, Leila, 131

Sampling, 43, 91, 93
Sanders, Clinton, 192
Sanjek, Roger, 109, 169–171
Scale, organizational units of, 121–122
Scarce, Rik, 31, 52
Schensul, Jean, 196
Scheper-Hughes, Nancy, 130, 191
Schneider, Louis, 164
Schultz, Alfred, 174
Schwalbe, Michael, 13
"Scope conditions," 175
Secrecy in groups, 27. *See also* Social settings
Secret observers, 37. *See also* Covert research
Section sorting and ordering for intensive interviewing, 101–102
Selective competence, 70
Self-concepts and identities as meanings, 135–136
Self-critical ethos, 175
Self-discipline regularity in writing, 227
Self-fulfilling answers to questions, 105
Sequences as processes, 154–156
Settings. *See* Social settings
Settlements as unit of social settings, 129–130
Shaffir, William and Robert Stebbins, 54–55
Shaw, Clifford, 164
Single types of topics, 146
Sjoberg, Gideon, 88
Skepticism, 174
Smith, Allen, 137–138

Smith, Vicki, 129
Snow, David A., 62, 66, 74, 77, 86, 88, 92, 111, 147, 154, 161, 164, 182, 183, 217
"Snowball" sampling, 43
Sobel, Michael E., 157
Social action as data source, 85, 87
Social and personal relationships as units of social settings, 126–127
Social compositionists, 222. See also Writing
Social engineering frame, 190
Social groups, 127–128
Social movement organizations (SMOs), 161
Social movements, 124
Social or cultural practices as units of social settings, 123–124
Social psychological dimensions of the writing process, 221–223
Social realism, 83. See also "Subtle realist" tradition
Social researchers, 3. See also Fieldstudies; Informants
  ascriptive categories of researcher and researched, 23–25, 61
  as central agents in analysis process, 195–196
  dealing with challenges, 65–66
  emotional challenges, 54–63
    deception and fear of disclosure, 56–57
    distance and surrender, 57–63
    information overload, 55
  examples of starting where you are, 10, 11
  expert role of, 46, 70
  field relations, 66–75
    disengagement, 75–78
    ethical concerns, 78–79
    exchange strategies, 71–72
    personal accounts of the field experience, 79–80
    presentational strategies, 68–70
    relational closeness, 72–75
  intellectual curiosity, 9, 11, 12–13
  known, 40–47
  "learner" or "incompetent" role, 46
  personal consequences for, 30–32
  personal experience and biography, 9–12
  personal standards, 78, 79
  physical and emotional dangers for, 27–28, 63–65
  relationship to setting, 22–23
  roles of, 33–34
  student role of, 69
  tradition and justification, 13–14
  unknown, 35–40, 56–57
  as witness and instrument, 3
Social science guidance in fieldstudies, 4. See also Fieldstudies

Social science value commitments, 187–189
  demystification of social arrangements, 187–188
  generic understanding, 187
  holistic dispassionate understanding, 188–189
  questioning mind-set, 187
"Social-self," 221–223
Social settings, 33, 121. See also Topics; Units
  access to, 9, 11
  difficult, 25–27
  historical, 16
  private and quasi-private settings, 37–40
  public and quasi-public settings, 36–37
  types of, 34–35
  units of, 122–132
    encounters, 124–125
    episodes, 124
    groups and cliques, 127–128
    habitats, 130–131
    organizations, 128–129
    roles, 125–126
    settlements, 129–130
    social and personal relationships, 126–127
    social or cultural practices, 123–124
    social types, 126
    subcultures and lifestyles, 131–132
Social ties, 42. See also Connections of researcher
Social types as unit of social settings, 126
Socially embedded artifacts, 94
Software programs, 96, 98, 204
Sound recording, 81. See also Audiotapes
Sources and rules of topic types, 149
Spirals as process, 153–154
Spradley, James P., 213
Spuriousness in causal explanation, 157
Stacey, Judith, 65–66
Stack, Carol, 215
Stages defined, 152
Stark, Rodney, 155, 156, 161, 227–229
Statistical analysis, 149–151
Statistical models of causality, 158
Stebbins, Robert, 54–55
Step/process models of causality, 158, 161
Steps defined, 152
Stratification in social life, 122, 139–141
Strauss, Anselm, 113, 173, 196
Structured interviewing, 17
Structures of topics, 151–152
Subcultures and lifestyles as units of social settings, 131–132
Subjects of research. See Informants
"Subtle realist" tradition, 169
Sullivan, Mercer, 130
Supplementary data, 88–90
Survey research, 2, 14, 99, 150
Suspension of belief, 174, 192
Suspension of doubt, 174

Suttles, Gerald, 130, 151
Sympathy for informants, 61–62
Synecdoche, 232

Talk as data source, 87–88
Talk in action, observing, 87, 88
Taping. *See* Audiotapes
Tarrow, Sidney, 153
Taxonomic diagrams, 212–213
Taxonomies of topics, 146–147
Taylor, Kristie, 36
Taylor, Verta, 131
Team research, 66, 93, 219
Technocratic/social engineering frame, 190
Temporal ordering of variables in causal explanation, 157
Term papers, 197–198, 228
Theoretical candor, 170
"Theoretical extension," 173
Theoretical memos, 210
Theoretical sampling, 93
Theoretical typologies, 149
Thomas, W. I., 89, 162
Thorne, Barrie, 24, 28, 60
Thrill-seeking recreational activities, 64
Timmerman, Stefan, 164
Titles as framing devices, 231
Topics, 121–167. *See also* Aspects
　aspects and, 132–141
　causes, 156–162
　　models of causal explanation, 157–158
　　qualitative field research and causal explanation, 158–162
　　requirements of causal explanation, 157
　consequences of, 162–165
　frequencies of, 149–150
　human agency, 165–167
　magnitudes of, 151
　matrix of studies based on the intersection of units and aspects, 142
　processes of, 152–156
　　cycles, 152–153
　　sequences, 154–156
　　spirals, 153–154
　questions about, 144–145, 167–168, 176
　structures of, 151–152
　two or more units or aspects as topics, 141–142
　types, 145–149
　　multiple types and taxonomies, 146–147
　　single types, 146
　　sources and rules of, 149
　　typologizing, 148–149
　units and aspects combine into topics, 121–122
　units, aspects, and topics form mind-set for coding, 143
　units (social settings), 122–132
Total institutions, 146, 178

Tracing back sequences in topics, 154–155
Tracing forward sequences in topics, 155
Tradition and justification of social researchers, 13–14
Transcriptions of audiotapes, 107
Tree/network diagrams, 213
Triangulation of data, 21
Trust, 59, 67
Truth in research, 90, 168–171
Turning points in topics, 155–156
Tuskegee case of black syphilis victims, 49
Typologies, 214–215
Typologizing topics, 148–149

Uniform Crime Reports, 89
Unintentional consequences, 163–164
United States Census Reports, 89
Units, 121–122. *See also* Social settings; Topics
　and aspects and topics form a mind-set for coding, 143
　of organizational scale, 121–122
　two or more units or aspects as topics, 141–142
Unknown social researchers, 35–40
"Unobtrusive measures" in data collection, 89–90

Validity, 82, 90, 169
Value commitments. *See* Social science value commitments
Van Zandt, David, 75
Variables in causal explanation, 157
Vaughan, Diane, 160
Video conferences, 20
Videotapes, 85, 89
Vidich, Arthur, 51, 131
Violence, 63, 74. *See also* Physical dangers in fieldstudies
Virtual research sites, 20

Wacquant, Loic, 24
Wallace, Alfred Russell, 181
Warner, W. Lloyd, 131
Warren, Carol, 98
Wax, Rosalie, 23, 82
Whyte, William F., 31–32, 43, 72, 126, 130, 141, 151, 171
Williams, Terry, 75
Willis, Paul, 131
Withdrawing in field relations, 75. *See also* Disengagement process
Wolcott, Harry, 195
Wolf, Diane, 29
Word-processing programs, 96, 98
Workman, John, Jr., 20
Wright, Talmadge, 131
Writing, 220–240
　"agony of omission," 236
　barriers to, 225, 227–228
　basic rules, 221

diagramming in, 224–225
editing, 222, 234
inspiration in, 227–228
instruction in, 221–223
the interview, 107–108, 116–117
preliminary considerations, 221–223
propositional, 197–198
rephrasing, 218
reportorial, 224
self-discipline regularity in, 227
subject and idea, 176, 197
writing practices, 224–238
  admit aversion and write regularly, 226–228
  discovery and surprise, 228–229
  divide and conquer, 230–231
  ego and attachments, 235, 236–237
  feedback from others, 222, 234, 235–236
  literary organizing devices, 321–332
  perfection or the One Right Way, 229–230
  personal working style, 233
  reaching closure—let it go, 237–238
  rereading and revising, 229, 233–235
  start writing, 224–225, 227
  write on any aspect, 225–226
Writing support groups, 236

"Yankee City" study, 131
Yoels, William, 140

Zablocki, Benjamin, 132
Zavella, Patricia, 23–24
Zelditch, Morris, 93
Zerubavel, Eviatar, 221, 231, 236, 238
Znaniecki, Florian, 89, 162
Zurcher, Louis, 88